D1104576

USEFUL ADVERSARIES

PRINCETON STUDIES IN INTERNATIONAL HISTORY
AND POLITICS

Series Editors
Jack L. Snyder
Richard H. Ullman

———————

History and Strategy by Marc Trachtenberg (1991)

George F. Kennan and the Making of American Foreign Policy, 1947–1950
by Wilson D. Miscamble, c.s.c (1992)

*Economic Discrimination and Political Exchange: World Political Economy in the
1930s and 1980s* by Kenneth A. Oye (1992)

Whirlpool: U.S. Foreign Policy toward Latin America and the Caribbean
by Robert A. Pastor (1992)

Germany Divided: From the Wall to Reunification by A. James McAdams (1992)

A Certain Idea of France: French Security Policy and the Gaullist Legacy
by Philip H. Gordon (1993)

The Limits of Safety: Organizations, Accidents, and Nuclear Weapons
by Scott D. Sagan (1993)

*Mercenaries, Pirates, and Sovereigns: State-Building and Extraterritorial Violence
in Early Modern Europe* by Janice E. Thomson (1994)

We All Lost the Cold War by Richard Ned Lebow and Janice Gross Stein (1994)

Who Adjusts? Domestic Sources of Foreign Economic Policy during the Interwar Years
by Beth A. Simmons (1994)

*America's Mission: The United States and the Worldwide Struggle for Democracy in the
Twentieth Century* by Tony Smith (1994)

The Sovereign State and Its Competitors: An Analysis of Systems Change
by Hendrik Spruyt (1994)

Cooperation among Democracies: The European Influence on U.S. Foreign Policy
by Thomas Risse-Kappen (1995)

The Korean War: An International History by William Stueck (1995)

Cultural Realism: Strategic Culture and Grand Strategy in Chinese History
by Alastair Iain Johnston (1995)

Does Conquest Pay? The Exploitation of Occupied Industrial Societies
by Peter Liberman (1996)

Satellites and Commissars: Strategy and Conflict in the Politics of Soviet-Bloc Trade
by Randall W. Stone (1996)

*Useful Adversaries: Grand Strategy, Domestic Mobilization, and Sino-American
Conflict, 1947–1958* by Thomas J. Christensen (1996)

USEFUL ADVERSARIES

GRAND STRATEGY,
DOMESTIC MOBILIZATION,
AND SINO-AMERICAN
CONFLICT, 1947–1958

Thomas J. Christensen

PRINCETON UNIVERSITY PRESS   PRINCETON, NEW JERSEY

Library of Congress Cataloging-in-Publication Data

Christensen, Thomas J., 1962–
    Useful adversaries : grand strategy, domestic mobilization, and
Sino-American conflict, 1947–1958 / Thomas J. Christensen.
      p.   cm. — (Princeton studies in international history and
politics)
    Includes bibliographical references (p.   ) and index.
    ISBN 0-691-02638-6 (acid-free paper). — ISBN 0-691-02637-8 (pbk.
acid-free paper)
    1. United States—Foreign relations—China.   2. China—Foreign relations—United
States.   3. United States—Foreign relations—1945–1953.   4. United States—
Foreign relations—1953–1961.   I. Title.   II. Series.
E183.8.C5C558   1997   96-8082
327.51073—dc20   CIP

This book has been composed in Sabon

TO THE MEMORY OF MY PARENTS

———————— Henry N. and Elvira F. Christensen ————————

Contents

List of Figures and Tables   ix

Preface   xi

Note on Translation and Romanization   xv

Chapter 1
Introduction   3

Chapter 2
Grand Strategy, National Political Power, and Two-Level
Foreign Policy Analysis   11

Chapter 3
Moderate Strategies and Crusading Rhetoric: Truman
Mobilizes for a Bipolar World   32

Chapter 4
Absent at the Creation: Acheson's Decision to Forgo Relations
with the Chinese Communists   77

Chapter 5
The Real Lost Chance in China: Nonrecognition, Taiwan,
and the Disaster at the Yalu   138

Chapter 6
Continuing Conflict over Taiwan: Mao, the Great Leap
Forward, and the 1958 Quemoy Crisis   194

Chapter 7
Conclusion   242

Appendix A
American Public Opinion Polls, 1947–1950   263

Appendix B
Mao's Korean War Telegrams   271

Bibliography   277

Index   305

Figures and Tables

FIGURES

2.1.	The Mobilization Model	13
3.1.	Political Cartoon about the Truman Doctrine	51
3.2.	Political Cartoon about Congressional Efforts to Cut Interim Aid for Europe and the Implications for the Marshall Plan	55
3.3.	Political Cartoon about Congressional Efforts to Trim the Federal Budget and the Marshall Plan in Particular	56
4.1.	Political Cartoon about Truman and the 81st Congress	81
4.2.	Political Cartoon about NATO and the Military Assistance Program	94
5.1.	Map of Korea	150
6.1.	A Militarized Work Brigade in a People's Commune in Rural Hebei Province in the Summer of 1958	218
6.2.	Political Cartoon Depicting Steel Worker Repelling an American Imperialist and Chiang Kai-shek	220
6.3.	Political Cartoon Depicting Grain and Steel Production as Forces for National Defense	222
7.1.	Almond's Salience Measure: Percentage Who Regarded Foreign Policy Issues as the Most Important Problems Facing the American People	257

TABLES

2.1.	Three Measures for Directness of Threat	28
3.1.	A Comparison of Military Spending in the Truman Years and in Previous Periods of Peace	45
3.2.	A Comparison of Federal Spending in the Truman Years and in Previous Periods of Peace	46
6.1.	Reported Increases in Chinese Light and Heavy Industry, 1957–1959	215
6.2.	Number of Shells Fired Daily at the Offshore Islands, August 23–30, 1958	228

Preface

I BEGAN THINKING about the theoretical problems at the heart of this book when I studied with Professors Chong-Sik Lee and Avery Goldstein at the University of Pennsylvania. They taught that there was no necessary separation between theoretical argumentation and area studies expertise. They also convinced me that, to understand the international relations of East Asia, one needs to study the relations of the great powers in Europe.

The most important years in my education were spent at Columbia University, where I wrote the doctoral dissertation from which the book is derived. I developed the theoretical sections under the tutelage of Professors Robert Jervis and Jack Snyder. Their intelligence, generosity, and open-minded approach to teaching have provided the yardstick by which I will measure my own career in academia. I am particularly grateful to Professor Snyder, who cheerfully responded to countless requests for help despite his busy schedule. I was also fortunate to have studied at Columbia under two of the world's leading specialists in Chinese politics: Professors Thomas Bernstein and Andrew Nathan. Their expert guidance was crucial to my development as a student of Chinese politics and foreign policy. They not only provided useful critiques of my written work but also went the extra mile to help me in ways that China specialists especially appreciate: writing letters of introduction, assisting in obtaining travel grants, and offering sound, realistic advice on how to carry out field research in the People's Republic of China.

For general guidance during my graduate school years, I also thank Professors David Baldwin, Francine Frankel, Frederick Frey, Joanne Gowa, Eugene Liu, Irene Liu, Helen Milner, Alexander Motyl, Carl Riskin, Robert Shapiro, and Peter Swenson. The fellow graduate students at Columbia who have helped me are too numerous to name. I particularly thank two, Randall Schweller and Jonathan Mercer, both of whom have been true friends and available colleagues in all phases of my professional life. Throughout college and graduate school, my sister, Nancy Hall, provided encouragement and a place to stay in New York. Along with Jennifer Camille Smith, she patiently critiqued my writing. If the reader is able to grasp the basic arguments of the book, they deserve much of the credit.

In addition to my advisers, the following people read entire drafts of the dissertation or book manuscript and offered invaluable comments: Robert Art, Chen Jian, Peter Katzenstein, Jonathan Kirshner, Walter

LaFeber, Robert Ross, Anders Stephanson, Allen Whiting, and Donald Zagoria. I consider it a great privilege that a group as accomplished as this paid such careful attention to my work.

For generous financial and institutional support I thank the Social Science Research Council/MacArthur Fellowship Program in International Peace and Security. For guidance during the fellowship I am grateful to Professors Judith Reppy and Michel Oksenberg. From 1991 to 1993 I also had the great fortune to be a National Security Fellow at the Olin Institute for Strategic Studies at Harvard University's Center for International Affairs. For their guidance and generosity I particularly thank Professors Samuel Huntington and Stephen Rosen.

For helpful critiques, comments, and advice I also thank Richard Bensel, Thomas Berger, Andrew Cortell, Bruce Elleman, John Gaddis, John Garafano, Merle Goldman, Roger Hilsman, Hu Weixing, Ethan Kapstein, Robert Keohane, Yuen Foong Khong, Elizabeth Kier, Alastair Iain Johnston, Li Hong, Peter Liberman, Sean Lynn-Jones, Roderick Mac-Farquhar, James McAllister, Alexandre Mansourov, Walter Mebane, Andrew Moravcsik, Timothy Naftali, Niu Jun, Joseph Nye, Sally Paine, Bruce Porter, Gideon Rose, Alan Rousso, David Rowe, Michael Schoenhals, Benjamin Schwartz, Karel Sedlacek, Vivienne Shue, Charles Sorrels, William Stokes, Shibley Telhami, Xu Yan, and Fareed Zakaria. Dennis Bilger of the Truman Library and Nancy Hearst of the Fairbank Center Library at Harvard were also of great assistance. Malcolm DeBevoise, Beth Gianfagna, Malcolm Litchfield, and Janet Mowery offered expert editorial advice. John Park and Li Hong provided invaluable assistance in the copyediting phase. Matthew Rudolph assisted in compiling the index.

For scholarly and friendly assistance during my field research in China I am grateful to the following organizations and people: Beijing University's Department of International Politics, particularly Professors Xue Mouhong, Zhao Baoxu, and Xu Xin; Fudan University's Department of International Politics, particularly Professor Ni Shixiong; Shanghai Institute of International Studies, particularly Dr. Ding Xinghao; the Chinese Academy of Social Sciences, particularly Professors Wang Jisi and He Di; Xiamen University's Taiwan Research Institute, particularly Professor Fan Xizhou; the University Services Center at Hong Kong's Chinese University, particularly Jean Hong; the International Relations Research Center at National Cheng-Chi University, especially Drs. Lin Bih-jaw, Su Chi, and Yu Yu-lin; and Taipei's Academia Sinica, particularly Professor Lin Ch'eng-yi. Various interviewees in China, who must remain anonymous, generously offered their time and expertise. I also thank Heidi Schumacher for her friendship and help in China over the years, and Josh Klenbort for many discussions about my research at the "Coffee Shop" of Beijing University's Shaoyuan Dormitories.

Two sections of Chapter 5 are derived from earlier articles and are published here with the permission of the journals in which they originally appeared, *International Security* and the *Journal of American–East Asian Relations*. I am indebted to the following people for expert advice on those sections of the book: Anthony Cheung, Michael Hunt, Teresa Lawson, Lucian Pye, Barry Strauss, William Stueck, Ren Yue, Stephen Van Evera, and Kathryn Weathersby.

Special gratitude goes to my wife, Barbara Edwards, who provided support and patience throughout the often trying times of research trips, job searches, and multiple moves. Despite her own professional responsibilities, she has always understood what this project means to me. My other family members have also been very supportive.

I dedicate the book to the memory of my parents, Henry N. and Elvira F. Christensen, who taught by example. Thank you for everything.

Ithaca, New York

Note on Translation and Romanization

UNLESS OTHERWISE noted, all translations from the Chinese are by the author. In general I use the "pinyin" romanization for Chinese words and translate Chinese characters into the Mandarin pronunciation. Both methods are favored in contemporary China. There are, however, exceptional circumstances in which I use alternative romanizations and non-Mandarin dialects for places and names. I do this in cases such as Chiang Kai-shek, Hong Kong, Quemoy, and Kuomintang (KMT), where non-Mandarin names and/or non-pinyin spellings are best known in the West. I offer the Mandarin translation and pinyin romanization in either parentheses or footnotes the first time a non-Mandarin or non-pinyin spelling is used in the text.

USEFUL ADVERSARIES

CHAPTER 1

Introduction

IF POLITICS makes strange bedfellows, then international politics makes the strangest. In fact, scholars of international relations are so accustomed to balance-of-power politics that they rarely seem surprised when ideologically different countries cooperate against common foes or when ideologically similar nations fight over differences of national interest. For example, few scholars puzzle over the Soviet-American alliance of World War II or the Sino-Vietnamese border war of 1979. Certain axiomatic statements of realpolitik have become widely accepted: e.g., "the enemy of my enemy is my friend" and "nations have no permanent friends, only permanent interests."[1] From the realist perspective, state leaders are expected to counter potential threats by mobilizing available domestic resources, devoting those resources to vital security interests, and seeking alliances with whatever foreign partners present themselves, regardless of ideology. When leaders fail to meet these expectations, analysts suspect either that they suffer from ideological or psychological biases or that they favor their domestic political interests over the security of the nation as a whole.

In this book I argue that scholars are sometimes too quick to assume distorted thinking or ulterior motives when analyzing foreign policies that appear overly aggressive, ideological, or otherwise wasteful of resources and alliance opportunities. At times leaders might rationally adopt such policies in order to guarantee public support for core strategies that they consider essential to national security. For example, when mobilizing the public behind long-term grand strategy, leaders may manipulate or prolong short-term conflicts that, on their own merits, do not warrant the costs or risks involved. If the domestic price of selling grand strategy includes making some foreign policy compromises, we should not treat leaders making those compromises as either irrational or self-serving.

Below I present a bridge between theories of foreign policy that emphasize the impact of international pressures and those that focus on domestic politics. I argue that, when international changes suggest the

---

[1] The latter is a paraphrase of Lord Palmerston's famous quotation about Great Britain's lack of permanent friends. For the original, see Walt, *The Origins of Alliances*, p. 33.

need for new, controversial, and expensive national security policies, leaders will often have difficulty implementing those policies. In order to secure public support for their most basic strategy, they may, in certain cases, decide to adopt a more hostile or more ideological foreign policy than they otherwise would prefer. In these cases, we cannot understand such hostility or crusading by studying international factors or domestic politics in isolation. Domestic politics matter, but they do so precisely because leaders respond to changes in the international environment by adopting strategies that are controversial in the domestic arena.

Scholarly treatment of Sino-American relations during the Cold War provides a good demonstration of the analytical problem outlined above. The Nixon administration's rapprochement with the Chinese leader, Mao Zedong, is often cited as a classic case of balance-of-power politics. In order to extract American forces from Vietnam and still counter the growth of Soviet influence in Asia, the president put his anticommunist past aside and established a working relationship with Communist China. A similar ideological journey was made by Mao, who had long vilified the United States but then decided that Washington was a useful partner in countering Soviet power in the region. Marriages of convenience are the stock in trade of balance-of-power politics, and in diplomatic history it is difficult to find a less likely couple than Richard Nixon and Mao Zedong.

But while realists wear post-1972 Sino-American cooperation as a feather in their cap, they quickly concede that something other than national security concerns drove bilateral relations before the rapprochement. This is not because relations in the earlier period were trivial. On the contrary, China and the United States were each other's most active enemy in the years 1949–1972, fighting wars in Korea and Vietnam that claimed the vast majority of each country's Cold War casualties. The problem is, rather, a theoretical one. Particularly from a balance-of-power perspective, the Cold War world was strikingly similar before and after 1972. If bipolarity and the common Soviet threat prescribed cooperation in 1972, why did they not push leaders in similar directions in the 1950s?

It seems then that Washington or Beijing, or both, squandered chances for improved bilateral relations in the decades preceding the Nixon visit. Robert Keohane writes: "[The] theory of the balance of power . . . could have alerted American policy makers in the 1950s (who were excessively imbued with an ideological view of world politics) to the likelihood of an eventual Sino-Soviet split. Realist maxims would have counseled the United States to be in a position to make an alliance, or at least an accommodation, when feasible, with the weaker Chinese to counterbalance the Soviet Union—as Henry Kissinger and Richard Nixon eventually did."[2] A working relationship with Beijing could have been a major American security asset, as it generally was after Nixon's initial trip.[3] As a regional power, a weak but independent China should have sought American assistance in countering its powerful Soviet neighbor, as it did after 1972. At a minimum, China should have sought good relations with both superpowers, allowing them to compete for China's allegiance.[4] This is not just post hoc analysis created after the advantages of Sino-American alignment had become clear. Before rapprochement, realists such as Hans Morgenthau and Kenneth Waltz were openly critical of American policy toward China precisely because it was driven by moralism rather than a hardheaded analysis of the commonalities and differences in the two countries' security interests.[5]

Since bilateral relations in the pre-1972 period seem at odds with realist predictions and prescriptions, many analysts fully abandon realist approaches, instead emphasizing the impact of ideological differences, domestic political pressures, and leadership psychology on both nations' policies. For example, arguments that stress the importance of Beijing's anti-Western ideology and Washington's anticommunism abound in the current literature.[6] Other approaches place central emphasis on party politics, factional struggle, and political logrolling in determining each country's policy toward the other.[7] As Robert Keohane suggests, 1971–72 is viewed as a watershed not simply because former enemies became collaborators, but because there seemed to be a shift in the fundamental motivations driving each leadership's policy toward the other.

My analysis of archival documentation, interview data, memoirs, media sources, and scholarly works from both China and the United States suggests that this periodization is too stark. In two key chapters of the

---

[2] Keohane, "Neorealism and World Politics," pp. 2–3.

[3] In fact, from the early 1970s through the rise of Gorbachev, the military tensions on the long Sino-Soviet border pinned down a larger number of Soviet troops than the Central European theater. See Garthoff, *Detente and Confrontation*, p. 208.

[4] Robert Ross argues that this middle role was China's natural posture in a bipolar world. See Ross, "International Bargaining and Domestic Politics."

[5] Morgenthau, *Politics among Nations*, p. 12; and Waltz, "The Politics of Peace."

[6] For discussions of the effect of ideology on PRC foreign relations, see Goldstein, "Chinese Communist Policy toward the United States"; and Treadgold, "Alternative Western Views of the Sino-Soviet Conflict," p. 328. For a discussion of McCarthyism in American foreign policy, see Kolko, *The Politics of War*; and Freeland, *The Truman Doctrine and the Origins of McCarthyism*.

[7] For a discussion of congressional logrolling, see Snyder, *Myths of Empire*, chaps. 1 and 7. Also see Koen, *The China Lobby in American Politics*. On the importance of factions in Chinese foreign policy, see Lieberthal, "Domestic Politics and Foreign Policy," pp. 43–70.

earlier conflict—American policy toward China from 1947 to 1950 and Chinese policy toward the United States during the 1958 Taiwan Straits crisis—leaders' policies were driven by concerns with shifts in the international balance of power. This is not to say that all previous analyses of Chinese-American relations in the 1950s are essentially wrong. I agree that ideology and domestic politics were more important in bilateral relations before 1972 than after. The two cases discussed here are no exception to that general rule. But in those cases the domestic political problems leaders faced and the ideological campaigns launched to solve them flowed directly from the need to mobilize public support for new security strategies. Viewing basic changes in the international balance of power, Truman in 1947 and Mao in 1958 decided to mobilize their nations around long-term strategies designed to respond to those shifts. In both cases, the strategies adopted required significant public sacrifice in peacetime, so the leaders faced difficulties in selling those strategies to their respective publics. The manipulation or extension of short-term conflict with the other nation, while not desirable on straightforward international or domestic grounds, became useful in gaining and maintaining public support for the core grand strategy. In short, balance-of-power politics, domestic political mobilization, and the manipulation of ideology and foreign policy conflict were integrally related.

THE THEORETICAL APPROACH AND ITS IMPLICATIONS FOR REALISM

The overly stark periodization of Sino-American relations in the Cold War is not coincidental: it relates to shortcomings in the general field of international relations, shortcomings that are echoed strongly in the literature on China's relations with the outside world. Although there is widespread acceptance in theoretical circles that more work needs to be done on the interaction of international and domestic variables, the development of actual two-level models or "bridging theories" is still in its nascent stages.[8] The field of Chinese foreign policy has made even less progress on this count.[9] Without solid bridging theories, analysts often find themselves choosing an international, domestic, or cognitive explanation as the major focus of their studies or listing multiple factors in comprehensive but analytically less interesting ways.

The theoretical approach offered in Chapter 2 provides a causal explanation of how international and domestic factors can interact to cause

[8] Putnam, "Diplomacy and Domestic Politics."

[9] For this critique, see Kim, *China and the World*, 3d ed. pp. 21–32; and Zhao, "Micro-Macro Linkages in the Study of Chinese Foreign Policy."

more hostile foreign policies than simpler versions of realism would predict. A causal link is drawn between shifts in the international balance of power, leaders' creation of long-term grand strategies to address those shifts, the domestic political difficulties in mobilizing the public behind those strategies, and the manipulation of ideological crusades and short-term conflicts in order to gain popular support for long-term grand strategies. I define grand strategy as the full package of domestic and international policies designed to increase national power and security. Grand strategy can therefore include policies varying from military expenditures and security alliances, to less frequently discussed policies, such as long-term investment in domestic industrialization and foreign aid to nations with common security concerns.[10] By understanding the relationship between the international and domestic pressures leaders face in designing and implementing these sets of policies, we can sometimes expose a deeper rationale behind leaders' decisions to create or prolong conflicts that might otherwise appear irrational or counterproductive.

THE MAJOR CASES

Truman's China Policy and the Early Stages of U.S.-PRC Confrontation

Chapters 3 and 4 address the relationship between America's early Cold War mobilization and the policy of President Harry Truman toward China in the years 1947–50. After the disappointing collapse of British power and the widespread realization that the international system had become bipolar, the Truman administration launched a peacetime drive to increase American influence around the world. The administration viewed the Soviet Union as a threat and recognized the inability of Western Europe to counter that threat alone. Therefore, Truman broke the American tradition of peacetime isolationism by concluding collective security treaties in Europe, and what is more important, by spending unprecedentedly large amounts on wide-ranging security programs, including defense, nuclear research, and economic and military assistance to Europe.

The Truman administration's international plan was extremely pragmatic. It was guided by George Kennan's strongpoint defense strategy, the prototype of limited containment policies lauded by contemporary

---

[10] For a similar conception of grand strategy, see Rosecrance and Stein, eds., *The Domestic Bases of Grand Strategy*, introduction.

realists.[11] Despite its pragmatic and moderate nature, the grand strategy was revolutionary and expensive, thus requiring a great deal of salesmanship. The American population and its congressional representatives were principled America-firsters, but above all they were fiscal conservatives. Most Americans were opposed to their country's involvement in "entangling alliances" and were extremely reluctant to help pay for the resurgence of Western European power.

The propaganda line taken in the Truman Doctrine speech in March 1947 and maintained throughout the Korean War was that America was not just containing the Soviet Union but was opposing the spread of communist tyranny. At each phase of the American effort to strengthen Western Europe, American leaders feared that a conciliatory posture toward the Chinese Communists, no matter how practical on its own merits, would contradict and weaken Truman's call for mobilization. In order to guarantee consensus on grand strategy under the banner of anticommunism, Truman, George Marshall, and Dean Acheson first delayed and ultimately rejected outright their preferred policy of ending U.S. involvement in the Chinese Civil War and establishing working relations with the Chinese Communists.

While Truman consciously chose conflict over accommodation in his China policy, he never intentionally provoked open warfare with the Chinese Communists. War with China was seen as a dangerous waste of resources better employed in opposing Soviet expansion. It was also seen as a sure-fire way to strengthen Beijing's relations with Moscow. However, as is discussed in Chapter 5, even the lower level of hostility that Truman maintained toward the PRC contributed greatly to the unintended outcome of military conflict between Chinese and American forces in autumn 1950. To support this line of reasoning, this chapter analyzes Chinese documents to see how various American policies affected Mao's calculations during the Korean War.

Continuing Conflict over Taiwan: The 1958 Straits Crisis

After Eisenhower took office and the Korean War wound to a close, the biggest remaining point of controversy between the two sides was continued American support for Chiang Kai-shek's Kuomintang (KMT) on Taiwan.[12] Never accepted by Beijing, the bilateral relationship between

---

[11] For an excellent example of the application of Kennanesque analysis, see Van Evera, "Why Europe Matters." Many look back with nostalgia on the year 1947. See Ignatius, "They Don't Make Them Like George Marshall Anymore," *Washington Post*, June 8, 1987, national edition.

[12] The pinyin romanization for the Mandarin pronunciation of Chiang's name is Jiang Jieshi. The Kuomintang in pinyin is Guomindang, sometimes abbreviated as GMD.

Taipei and Washington became the recognized status quo in American Asia policy. In 1954–55 a crisis ensued when Mao tested America's commitment to the KMT. The People's Liberation Army (PLA) attacked the KMT-held offshore islands because Mao wanted to dissuade Washington from signing a defense pact with Chiang. The effort backfired when Eisenhower responded by backing the KMT and signing just such a treaty.

In 1958 another major crisis erupted in the Taiwan Straits. In Chapter 6, I argue that this crisis was fundamentally different from the earlier straits crisis. The Americans had already made a firm commitment to defending Chiang, so Mao could not have been trying to prevent such an outcome. I argue that, by attacking in the straits, Mao was primarily attempting to stir up international tensions short of war. He wanted to use these tensions to replicate the spirit of public sacrifice found in the CCP base areas during the anti-Japanese and civil war periods. This popular fervor would help Mao implement his new grand strategy: the radical drive for self-sufficient industrial growth and nuclear weapons development launched under the banner of the Great Leap Forward.

Chapter 6 argues that the Great Leap Forward was, in large part, a response to a fundamental shift in the balance of power, in particular the fast-paced growth of the Soviet Union in the 1950s, capped by the launching of Sputnik in 1957. Mao worried that China was falling dangerously behind its communist "big brother." He associated the growth in Soviet power with Communist Party Secretary Nikita Khrushchev's increasingly conciliatory posture toward the United States and Moscow's growing demands on Beijing. Fearing both abandonment and exploitation by the Soviets, Mao decided to increase China's international bargaining power with both the West and the Soviets by accelerating China's own industrial and military modernization.

Although some of the general notions of labor mobilization and rural capital accumulation were not irrational, the ill-conceived agricultural and industrial policies actually associated with the Great Leap proved a disaster. They failed, however, because of utopian assumptions about organizational politics, economics, and human nature, not because Mao had failed to mobilize sufficient public enthusiasm for the policies. One of the only true successes of the Great Leap Forward was Mao's ability to convince the society to follow his radical plans and make the enormous sacrifices called for by the party. The concurrent tensions in the Taiwan Straits were important in creating the siege mentality necessary to achieve such public support.

The American and Chinese cases are clearly very different in many ways, but in the interest of theoretical generalizability, this is good. If nations with such different domestic structures and ideologies follow comparable patterns of mobilization and conflict manipulation, this suggests a broad applicability for the theoretical approach offered here. The concluding chapter offers some suggestions for research on additional cases using the theoretical tools presented in Chapter 2. It also draws theoretical and policy-relevant lessons from the earlier chapters of the book.

Grand Strategy, National Political Power, and Two-Level Foreign Policy Analysis

DOMESTIC POLITICAL support behind national security policy constitutes a power resource as essential to national survival as others commonly weighed by realists (e.g., financial capital, industrial production, weapons, and conscripts). Simply, without a healthy degree of consensus behind security strategies, no state can harness its population and project national power abroad. A low degree of political support may cause even the most rational and resolute national leadership to shelve prudent policies. Also, as in the quest for other power resources, certain trade-offs may be necessary in establishing popular support for risky and expensive security programs. Realist scholars have often discussed the trade-offs between economic and military power but have not addressed sufficiently how a degree of one or both may be sacrificed to maintain public support behind grand strategy.[1] In order to develop a model that takes such trade-offs into account, here I develop the concept of national political power, defined as *the ability of state leaders to mobilize their nation's human and material resources behind security policy initiatives.*

NATIONAL POLITICAL POWER AND REALISM

Much of the contemporary realist work on security policy finds its intellectual foundation in Waltz's structural theory of stability and instability in the international system.[2] But as Waltz himself recognizes, his balance-of-power theory is not designed to explain individual countries' foreign

---

[1] Realists, like mercantilists, generally view the long-term relationship between economic wealth and military power as mutually supporting. See, for example, Carr, *The Twenty Years' Crisis*, pp. 117–120. But both mercantilists and realists recognize short-term trade-offs between allocations for military might and sustained economic growth. See, for example, Jacob Viner, "Power versus Plenty," esp. p. 10; and Knorr, *The War Potential of Nations*, esp. chap. 12.

[2] Waltz, *Theory of International Politics*. For examples of neorealist foreign policy analysis, see Posen, *The Sources of Military Doctrine*; Walt, *The Origins of Alliances*; Walt, "The Case for Finite Containment"; Van Evera, "Why Europe Matters"; and Schweller, "Tripolarity and the Second World War."

policies.[3] Given the insufficient determinacy of Waltz's original approach for analyzing foreign policy, realists have added elements to give it additional predictive accuracy.[4] At the very least, additional assumptions about actors' rationality in responding to the international system are necessary if we are to argue from the international distribution of capabilities to the security strategies of particular nation-states.[5]

Although the tendency among contemporary realist foreign policy analysts is to augment purely structural theories in the most parsimonious manner possible, in one important way they have pared the structural theories down. Analysts often measure nations' power using only material indicators, such as soldiers, weapons, and gross national product (GNP).[6] Waltz himself claims that national power is constituted by a web of military, economic, *and* political capabilities, asserting that a "state's political competence and stability" constitute an inseparable element of national power.[7] Though a bit vague, this notion makes sense. Without political power, national economic and military potential would never be actualized.[8] Since leaders' quest to maintain or improve their nations' position within the international distribution of capabilities drives realist foreign policy analysis, it is essential to understand what capabilities are of concern to leaders.[9] The overemphasis on national economic and military power has handicapped realism's ability to address a number of interesting policy outcomes that may be related to domestic mobilization, or the creation or maintenance of national political power.[10]

[3] Waltz, *Theory of International Politics*, p. 175. Here Waltz explicitly states that his is not a theory of foreign policy.

[4] For a more complete critique of the indeterminacy of Waltz's theory in predicting foreign policy, see Christensen and Snyder, "Chain Gangs and Passed Bucks."

[5] Waltz himself advocates the addition of a rationality assumption to structural realism in order to derive certain policy predictions. See Waltz, "A Response to My Critics," pp. 330–331.

[6] For example, see Walt, "The Case for Finite Containment," esp. p. 11, where he states: "National power is usually seen as a function of material assets like size of territory, population, military power, industrial capacity, and resource endowments." Ted Hopf trims power measurement further, considering only military capabilities. See Hopf, "Polarity, the Offense-Defense Balance, and War," p. 493.

[7] Waltz, *Theory of International Politics*, p. 131.

[8] For a critique of contemporary realism's failure to consider this aspect of national security, see Barnett, "High Politics Is Low Politics."

[9] For a discussion of this, see Gilpin, *War and Change in International Politics*, pp. 85–96.

[10] Some works already factor domestic political consensus into their calculations of national power; but unlike this book they do not focus on political power as a key factor in the policy outcomes that they study, and they are not interested in consensus creation and maintenance as a *goal* that may alter leaders' military and economic policy preferences. See Kugler and Domke, "Comparing the Strengths of Nations"; Organski and Kugler, *The War Ledger*, pp. 71–84; and Cline, *World Power Assessment*.

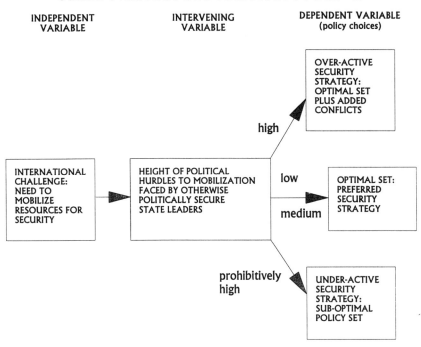

| INDEPENDENT VARIABLE | INTERVENING VARIABLE | DEPENDENT VARIABLE (policy choices) |

2.1. The Mobilization Model

THE DOMESTIC MOBILIZATION MODEL: A TWO-LEVEL APPROACH

A major limitation of the realist analyses discussed above is that they assume that states can simply mobilize their material and human resources in responding to international challenges and opportunities. The nation-state is treated as a "black box." Public willingness to sacrifice lives and wealth for national security is treated as given. As an alternative, the model below treats the state's ability to mobilize the public as a key intervening variable between the international challenges facing the nation and the strategies eventually adopted by the state to meet those challenges.

In the mobilization model, the policy that elites choose depends on the value of the intervening variable. If the political hurdles to mobilization are relatively low, then we should expect policies that are consistent with the expectations of black-box realists. If the hurdles are high or prohibitively high, we should expect policies that would be considered by realists to be either overreactions or underreactions to the international environment facing the nation.

Realists often disagree among themselves about precisely what policies fall within the expectations of their theories, but there is more agreement among them that certain types of policies are inconsistent with realist tenets. Underactive policies entail the failure to mobilize domestic power resources or to form effective balancing alliances in the face of a rising international threat (e.g., interwar American and British strategies). Overactive policies include those that waste valuable resources on areas of peripheral value to national security (e.g., American intervention in Vietnam and the Soviet invasion of Afghanistan) and those that need-lessly either increase the number and power of one's enemies or decrease the number and strength of one's allies (e.g., Chinese foreign policy dur-ing the Cultural Revolution). No single theory explains all cases of over-reaction and underreaction that black-box realism misses. The approach here is designed to explain only cases relating to state leaders' problems in mobilizing their public for grand strategy. It does not explain the flag-ship examples of overreaction and underreaction mentioned above, which are offered only for the purpose of illustrating policies that diverge from the expectations of realism.

This study concentrates on cases of apparent overreactions to the inter-national environment that are rooted in state leaders' need to overcome high, but surmountable, hurdles to mobilization. It is important to note that, in such cases, leaders try to limit the costs of the added conflicts used to mobilize the public around the core strategy. If large-scale war results from conflict manipulation, then the added costs of that conflict manipulation might easily outweigh the added security benefits of mobil-ization. So leaders generally try to maintain tensions short of war so as to both mobilize resources and avoid squandering them on unnecessary conflicts. But, as we will see, conflict manipulation is dangerous and can lead to escalation and warfare despite the more limited intentions of leaders in the mobilizing state.

The Concept of the State

Here I adopt the concept of the state employed by Stephen Krasner and David Lake. The state consists of the elite foreign policy leaders within the government. (In the case of the United States, the state is the foreign policy leadership of the executive branch.)[11] For the purposes of interna-tional relations theory, a useful distinction exists between those actors who directly represent the nation abroad and "the government." In many

---

[11] See Krasner, *Defending the National Interest*, p. 12. Also see Lake, "The State and American Trade Strategy." Lake actually has a more encompassing view of the state but makes clean conceptual distinctions between legislative or representative elements of gov-ernment and the foreign policy executive.

cases, broad sections of the government may be so dependent on and representative of societal groups that they might be categorized as transmission belts between society and foreign policy elites. Arguably, the American Congress plays the role of the public's representative in determining the federal budget and constraining the foreign policy options of the executive branch. In such cases, it seems theoretically useful to distinguish between the representative branches of government and the foreign policy elites on whom they have a restraining effect.[12] In other cases, governmental subgroups may be able to hijack the foreign policy process to further their own professional interests or the goals of narrow societal actors they represent. For these cases, straightforward domestic explanations are more useful than two-level theories.

For reasons of theoretical parsimony, the mobilization model shares key assumptions with realist foreign policy analyses. It posits a unified state as the central decision maker and assumes that state actors are primarily committed to furthering the security or power interests of the nation-state as a whole. It assumes the state is rational (at least in Herbert Simon's restricted sense of "bounded rationality").[13] In addition it assumes that leaders are not threatened by revolution or coup before the mobilization drive. Of course, these three simplifying assumptions will not be useful in analyzing every case. Leaders, like all people, may behave irrationally or demagogically. But in order to understand the pressures facing any state in mobilizing support for grand strategy, we should first understand the pressures facing even rational, politically secure, and patriotic leaderships.

Unlike states in straightforward domestic politics approaches, in the approach I offer here the state does not act internationally merely to further its own interests within the domestic political arena.[14] For this reason the mobilization model should not be confused with "diversionary conflict" or "scapegoating" theories, which argue that leaders sometimes exploit foreign conflict for the purposes of averting revolution and solidifying their own hold over their nations.[15] In the scapegoating thesis,

---

[12] Borrowing from Pareto, Lake claims that representative elements of the state act in the interest "of society" whereas the executive acts "for society." See Lake, "The State and American Trade Strategy," pp. 36–38.

[13] Simon, *Models of Bounded Rationality.*

[14] In the current literature perhaps the closest approximation to the model presented here is offered by Alan C. Lamborn. See Lamborn, *The Price of Power,* pp. 58 and 69. The major difference is that for Lamborn's leaders, as for leaders in scapegoating theories, the main incentive in manipulating conflict is to stay in power (reduce "domestic risk"), not to mobilize support for security policy.

[15] These theories of diversionary war and scapegoating find their roots in the conflict and cohesion theories of George Simmel and Lewis Coser. See Simmel, *Conflict;* and Coser, *The Functions of Social Conflict.* For reviews of the international relations literature, see

conflict is designed to prop up the state, not to create consensus around preferred national security programs.[16] In the approach I present here, it is the mobilization effort itself that potentially stirs controversy and that must, therefore, be legitimized. The state-society problems to be rectified cannot be understood without reference to the security programs leaders have already designed as responses to the international environment. The mobilization model therefore is a true two-level approach: both international and domestic factors matter and they affect policy outcomes in concert.[17]

THE SOCIETAL PROBLEM FACING THE STATE IN MOBILIZING RESOURCES

Even if we accept the theoretical distinction between the state and society in analyzing two-level games, it is not immediately clear why state leaders who design policies with the national interest in mind should have trouble selling those policies to the general public. After all, as Rousseau argued long ago, the long-term interests of the public will generally equate with the long-term interests of the nation-state as a whole.[18] Moreover, realpolitik strategies are generally cheaper and less risky than the overactive strategies explained here. Below I offer three interrelated reasons why leaders might have difficulty convincing the public to make significant sacrifices for international security efforts, even if those efforts are in the public's own long-term interest. Because of these difficulties with the public, leaders may attempt to find a moral or ideological foundation for grand strategy and alter foreign policies in order to maintain

---

Blainey, *The Causes of War*, chap. 5; Levy, "The Diversionary Theory of War"; Stein, "Conflict and Cohesion"; and Stein, *The Nation at War*. For applications to empirical cases, see Mayer, "Domestic Causes of the First World War," pp. 286–300; Berghahn, "Naval Armaments and Social Crisis," pp. 61–88.

[16] In this way, the approach advocated here is closer than the diversionary war models to Coser's original formulations. Scapegoating and diversionary war theories assume that a leadership's legitimacy is extremely low before the scapegoating conflict is launched. But Coser points out that out-group conflict assists in in-group cohesion only when the group enjoys a minimum level of cohesion before the conflict starts. Otherwise, conflict could strain relations and divide an already fragile group. Coser writes: "The relation between outer conflict and inner cohesion does not hold true when internal cohesion before the outbreak of the conflict is so low that the group members have ceased to regard preservation of the group as worthwhile." Coser, *The Functions of Social Conflict*, p. 93.

[17] For examples of the two-level theorizing and "state as pivot" arguments, see Putnam, "Diplomacy and Domestic Politics"; Evans, Jacobson, and Putnam, eds., *Double-Edged Diplomacy;* and Ikenberry, Lake, and Mastanudo, eds., *The State and American Foreign Economic Policy.*

[18] Rousseau, *The Social Contract*, chap. 4.

the appearance of consistency between rhetoric and practice. Leaders may also create or prolong small international crises in order to exaggerate the immediacy of the international threats facing the nation.

Limited Information/Limited Rationality

The public simply does not have the time or expertise to understand the subtleties of balance-of-power politics. State leaders spend their entire careers grappling with the intricacies of the international system, yet they are unable to make exhaustive searches of all options and choose maximally rational policies. Like all decision makers, state leaders enjoy only bounded rationality. They satisfy rather than maximize utility and they simplify the world by adopting interpretive categories and standard operating procedures.[19]

If such simplifications and cognitive shortcuts are necessary for full-time foreign policy experts, they should prove more prevalent in the thinking of average citizens, who are less educated about and less occupied with international affairs. Even in nations like the United States, with a highly educated population and extensive media networks, the average citizen spends little time each day thinking about world affairs. Moreover, because much of the information that is relevant to policy is classified, state leaders are generally better informed about world affairs than even the most diligent news buffs. Because of this information gap and competing claims on the public's attention, citizens are more likely than state elites to adopt highly stylized and ideological views of international conditions and proper policy responses to them.[20] Therefore, leaders need to sell expensive policies by stating them in easily digestible ways, shunning complicated logic about abstract or long-term threats.

When employing ideological rhetoric or manipulating international tensions to mobilize their society, leaders may run the risk of undercutting their support if they adopt apparently accommodative policies to-

[19] For the classic analysis of bounded rationality and cognitive shortcuts, see Simon, *Models of Bounded Rationality.* For an analysis of the practical advantage of employing cognitive shortcuts over undergoing exhaustive searches of all options and data, see Lindblom, "Science of Muddling Through." For an international relations work that employs these concepts, see Keohane, *After Hegemony,* chap. 7.

[20] There will still be a theoretically important information gap in cases where the classified information available to leaders is wrong and misleading. In such cases, leaders and average citizens will still view the world differently, and leaders may therefore design policies that seem unjustified to those citizens. I am grateful to Jonathan Mercer for help on this point. The constraint on public attention was first stressed by Almond in *The American People and Foreign Policy.* Almond's thesis has been widely critiqued. In Chapter 7, I review that critical literature and explain why, particularly in periods of peacetime mobilization, Almond's approach remains useful for our purposes here.

ward states that are ideologically similar to those ostracized in the mobilization campaign. This may hold true even if, according to realist logic, these states warrant different treatment because of differing resource endowments or geostrategic locations. Even when ideological consistency or belligerent posturing seems counterproductive, leaders may opt for simplicity and consistency in security policies in order to maintain necessary public support for the core grand strategy. In more normal budgetary times or in periods of planned demobilization, the dangers of appearing inconsistent or ideologically insincere are not as great.[21]

Discounting the Future and the Need for a Tangible, Immediate Threat

Particularly in the politically stable environments we are assuming, state leaders are more likely than average citizens to be concerned with the long-term security of the nation. Because they understand the long-term challenges facing the nation better than the average citizen, they are more likely to accept short-term national sacrifices necessary to meet those challenges. In economists' terms, foreign policy elites often have a lower discount rate for the future than average citizens.[22] For the general public, long-term international concerns will appear vague at best and may easily be overshadowed by immediate domestic political concerns and the desire to bring home a larger paycheck.

This problem is greatest in countries with a poor and uneducated population. Poorer and less educated citizens are less likely to be informed about international affairs and, moreover, will naturally have a higher discount rate for the future if new taxes for long-term security cut deeply into the marginal value of an already small income.[23] An analogy from the insurance market may prove helpful. Those most able to afford to hedge for future catastrophes are both most likely to appreciate the long-term value of insurance and most willing to pay the short-term costs of

[21] This is one major reason why Richard Nixon had an easier time reaching out to the Chinese Communists than Harry Truman.

[22] One might argue that in democracies or unstable authoritarian regimes leaders will be unlikely to take a long-term view if it could lead to electoral defeat or popular rebellion. This, of course, merely demonstrates that long-term strategies are generally unpopular and difficult to sell to the public. As Margaret Levi has argued, rulers threatened by overthrow and execution may discount the future highly. But in a relatively unthreatening domestic environment for the state, high levels of discounting would be less likely. See Levi, *Of Rule and Revenue*, esp. pp. 32–33 and 178–179.

[23] States can employ various institutional means to reduce this problem. For example, if education and wealth correlate, as they so often do, a graduated tax structure may place the burden of future security most heavily on those who both best understand long-term security problems and who can most afford to pay for current policies designed to counter them.

insurance policies. The less fortunate citizen is both less likely to understand the benefits of insurance and more likely to discount the future and spend his or her resources on current economic concerns. Ironically and tragically, for reasons simply stated in terms of marginal value, it is the less fortunate citizen who would benefit most from an insurance policy if catastrophe were to strike and would be least likely to own one.[24]

Similarly, in international politics the average citizen will likely suffer most in the long run if the nation's relative position declines dramatically or if the nation becomes embroiled in war. But at the same time, the average citizen is least likely to agree to pay for long-term security policies if those policies cut into personal short-term income or funding for other government programs—such as entitlements, hiring of police, and improvement of public works—that make the immediate environment more secure.

Collective Action and Ideology

Since national security is a classic collective good and society is made up of diverse individuals and groups, it may be difficult for states to extract the necessary sacrifices from society, even if an intellectual consensus is reached about the justifiable expense of security policy. Tax evasion and draft dodging, for example, may be rational individual strategies even if everyone agrees in principle about the need for higher taxes and a draft.[25] Similarly, group actors in society may all attempt to pass the buck of increased sacrifices on to other groups, thus leading to suboptimal national outcomes.[26]

Although selective rewards and punishments facilitate collective action, for it to flourish in most cases there still must be some degree of ideological or moral glue in a polity, or at least in the subgroups that police compliance.[27] This is true even in the most repressive and hierarchical regimes. As David Hume wrote: "The Soldan of Egypt or the

---

[24] In the case of a devastating house fire, for example, a rich uninsured person stands to lose more than a poor person in absolute terms, but in marginal terms the reverse is likely the case since a much larger percentage of the poorer person's overall wealth is likely to be tied up in the house.

[25] For the original formulation of the collective goods problem, see Olson, *The Logic of Collective Action;* for a related work, see Kahn, "The Tyranny of Small Decisions."

[26] For the application of collective-goods theory to diverse interest groups within industrial nations, see Olson, *The Rise and Decline of Nations.*

[27] On this point, see North, *Structure and Change in Economic History,* pp. 36–37, 57–58, 65, and passim. North argues persuasively that laws and their enforcement are themselves public goods. Enforcement problems are eased in many cases by actors' moral sense of fairness.

Emperor of Rome might drive his harmless subjects like brute beasts against their sentiments and inclinations. But he must at least have led his *mamelukes* or pretorian bands like men by their opinions."[28] This is not to say that ideology is a panacea for collective-action problems, but rather that it is often a necessary complement to favorable structural and institutional arrangements that enhance the likelihood of collective action.[29] In mobilizing resources for foreign policy, an ideological crusade not only makes citizens more willing to approve expensive state programs but also stigmatizes free-riding as evil or treasonous. The moral stigma reduces the incentives to free-ride and increases the incentive to police against free-riding.

Public distaste for expensive policies based purely on power considerations need not be painted in a negative light. Rather than emphasizing public ignorance or selfishness, one might argue that typical citizens are simply less jaded or Machiavellian than their state leaders.[30] But, whether one finds the public intellectually deficient or state leaders morally so (or both), it remains plausible to posit a divergence of opinion about the proper basis for security policy. As E. H. Carr writes: "The necessity, recognized by all politicians both in domestic and international affairs, for cloaking interests in a guise of moral principles is in itself a symptom of the inadequacy of realism."[31]

NATIONAL POLITICAL POWER AND STATE-SOCIETY DYNAMICS ACROSS REGIME TYPES

As conceived above, "national political power" is neither an attribute of the state nor an attribute of society. Rather, it is the degree of compatibility (or the nexus) of the two in tackling international challenges. If policy leaders are so dominant that they can override counterproductive societal pressures, then the nation's policy will be consistent with those

[28] David Hume, cited in Carr, *The Twenty Years' Crisis*, p. 132.

[29] Olson himself accepts that ideology is often helpful in ameliorating collective action problems. See *The Logic of Collective Action*, pp. 12–13, 87, and 160–162.

[30] This appears to be particularly true for liberal democracies faced with an opportunity to launch a preventive war against a rising challenger. See Schweller, "Domestic Structures and Preventive War." In Schweller's account it is not entirely clear why liberal democracies are more pacific in these circumstances. It could be that publics in liberal democracies are more liberal in their views of international affairs than publics in nondemocratic countries. It could simply be that publics everywhere are antirealist, particularly when the short-term costs of realpolitik policies are high, but that publics in democracies have more sway over policy.

[31] Carr, *The Twenty Years' Crisis*, p. 92.

leaders' preferred strategies. The same may hold true if the society itself is well aligned and well informed and therefore offers little resistance to those strategies. In such cases, even otherwise weak leaders will have little difficulty implementing their optimal grand strategies. So, for our purposes, a nation is politically powerful to the degree that its society forms "encompassing" coalitions that lobby for policies in the national security interest or to the degree that disaggregated societal groups surrender decision-making authority to state elites pushing such policies.[32]

This formulation of political strength is consistent with notions of strong and weak states set forth in key works in comparative politics and international political economy. Samuel Huntington's classic work on political development measures a nation's political competence by the relation of state and societal structures. For Huntington, "stability" is measured not only by the state's level of institutional complexity or by the degree of political participation, but by the ratio of the two.[33] Peter Katzenstein's analysis of nations' domestic structures also involves elements of both state and societal power, including the degree of state centralization and the degree to which influential societal actors are organized into peak-level associations. For Katzenstein, Japan's "domestic structure" is strong—able to adopt neomercantilist, competitive economic policies—because the centralized state bureaucracy and organized societal groups that influence the state, like the zaibatsu and peak banking interests, all tend in the direction of such policies.[34]

Although state-society dynamics certainly differ across democracies, communist dictatorships, and traditional monarchies, all states face certain common problems, such as the need to conscript soldiers and secure funds for weapons, research, and development. Democratic states may require legislative support for military and foreign aid packages that dictatorships do not, but even authoritarian leaders atop command economies face mobilizational problems of their own. Whereas passing laws to expropriate funds from society is relatively easy for authoritarian or totalitarian states, guaranteeing a high quantity and quality of production under higher tax rates may not be. For reforming command economies there is often a starker trade-off between economic efficiency and ease of taxation. In Dengist China, for example, large inefficient state enterprises still pay the bulk of state operating costs, but constitute an ever-shrinking section of the Chinese reform economy. Because the Com-

---

[32] For discussions of k-groups, see Snidal, "The Limits of Hegemonic Stability Theory."

[33] Huntington, *Political Order in Changing Societies*, pp. 78–82.

[34] See Katzenstein, ed., *Between Power and Plenty*, Conclusion. For another theoretical discussion of the beneficial effects of peak-level, encompassing groups on national policy, see Olson, *The Rise and Decline of Nations*, pp. 57–63.

munist Party wanted the Chinese economy to thrive, it encouraged private enterprise; but private enterprise has proven much more difficult to tax than the state factories.[35]

In his classic analysis of the modern American federal government, Theodore Lowi argues that the American president often oversells policies in a manner consistent with the mobilization model above.[36] While the unique institutional weakness of the U.S. government might call for an independent theory of how oversell plays out in the American case, there is no reason why we cannot also develop a more general approach to mobilization politics that accounts for ideological oversell and foreign policy crusading in very different political systems. Although important differences exist between regimes, more basic theorizing is still possible. At times, every state will need to implement controversial security strategies, and leaders will need to justify their costs in order to implement them. So, if leaders respond to changes in the international environment by calling for military modernization, for democratic nation-states, national political power may be operationalized by analyzing the legislative ability of elites to push through bills involving larger military budgets and higher taxes; for authoritarian states, it might be operationalized by the ability to persuade citizens to work harder, accept less remuneration, or both. The details may be different, but the state-society constraints of taxation for defense can be compared across very different types of regimes, as I compare the American and Chinese cases here. A model that can shed light on the policy dynamics of two such different political systems likely has broad applicability.

OPERATIONALIZING NATIONAL POLITICAL POWER VARIABLES

By arguing that national power must be measured by assessing the integrated economic, military, and *political* capabilities of the nation in relation to international competitors, Waltz continues in the classical realist tradition. E. H. Carr wrote: "Power over opinion is therefore not less essential for political purposes than military and economic power, and has always been closely associated with them."[37] Hans Morgenthau

---

[35] For a concise review of the contradictory forces influencing Chinese state economic planners, see Sheryl WuDunn, "As China's Economy Thrives, the Public Sector Flounders," *New York Times*, December 18, 1991, p. 1. While central government revenues have increased significantly in absolute terms over the period of reform and high GNP growth, they have shrunk dramatically as a percentage of GNP—from an estimated 14.57 percent in 1979 to 8.85 percent in 1990. See Wang, "Falling State Extractive Capacity in China and Its Results," pp. 5–14.

[36] Lowi, *The End of Liberalism*, esp. pp. 139–145.

[37] Carr, *The Twenty Years' Crisis*, p. 132.

went further, arguing that domestic political factors, such as "morale," are "the most important . . . components of national power."[38]

The problem for scholars is how to measure these nonmaterial aspects of national power. There are basically two ways in which national political power can be assimilated into balance-of-power analysis. First, it can be entered into the initial calculations of the international balance of power. In other words, we would include each nation's political stability and resolve as primary elements in its relative national power reserves. Scholars have employed this method, but designing such measures is extremely difficult at best.[39] As Hans Morgenthau argued:

> National character and, above all, national morale and the quality of government, especially in the conduct of foreign affairs, are . . . the most elusive components of national power. It is impossible for the observer of the contemporary or the explorer of future trends to assess with even approximate accuracy the relative contribution these elements may make to the power of different nations. Furthermore, the quality of these contributions is subject to incessant change.[40]

Though basically correct, Morgenthau's conclusions may be too sweeping. In some cases, political power variables can be easily worked into calculations of the international distribution of power. Since the political atrophy and then dissolution of the Soviet Union, analysts no longer consider the world bipolar.[41] The domestic political instability of the Turkish Empire, the "sick man of Europe," is also considered a factor that altered precariously the European balance of power before World War I.[42] In his classic study of Indian and Chinese conflict, Neville Maxwell argues that the shift in the Sino-Indian balance of power was confirmed by the "emergence in China of a strong central authority" in 1949. For Maxwell and Indian observers at the time, the balance of power had shifted by the mere fact that in 1949 some central government could

[38] Morgenthau, *Politics among Nations*, p. 198. Paul Kennedy and Alan Lamborn have made similar arguments. See Kennedy, *The Rise and Fall of the Great Powers*, p. 202; and Lamborn, *The Price of Power*, chap. 2.

[39] For examples of works that do attempt to figure political power variables into initial balance-of-power equations, see note 10 above.

[40] Morgenthau, *Politics among Nations*, p. 198.

[41] Domestic political aspects of national power have even affected the calculations of realist analysts most insulated from such considerations, arms reduction negotiators. Many of them had concluded that the 1991 START treaties (Strategic Arms Reduction Treaties) would be the last superpower arms accords because they assumed the Soviet Union would no longer exist by the time future accords could be reached. See Thomas L. Friedman, "Clearing the Final Hurdles to a Strategic Arms Accord," *New York Times*, July 18, 1991, p. A12.

[42] For a discussion of the divisive effects of the internal collapse of the Turkish Empire, see Lafore, *The Long Fuse*, pp. 45, 168–179.

finally harness China's extant power potential.[43] But such clear-cut cases of political strength and weakness are rare. In general, designing measures of relative national political power that are generalizable across nations, time periods, and policy issue areas is, as Morgenthau argued, much more difficult.

A second and more manageable way to use the concept of national political power is at the level of security policy making and implementation. If we first study the distribution of international economic and military power and the preferred security policies leaders design in response to it, we can then measure the political hurdles facing leaders with more accuracy. This is the method adopted in the mobilization model above. First, we must determine which policy options the leadership would prefer if it enjoyed an ideal state-society environment. Second, we must determine what adjustments leaders make in preferred policy after they consider both international and domestic arenas. Models employing national political power would determine the effects that state-society constraints might have on the implementation of a predetermined optimal policy package.

Such a two-step approach is not just theoretical sleight of hand. Policy elites often operate in just this manner. After receiving reports from advisers who are insulated from the domestic political arena, state leaders design ideal strategies and then adjust them according to the domestic political constraints on implementation. In interwar Britain, for example, strategists first devised optimal policies for addressing the projected growth of German power and then adjusted them on the basis of domestic political constraints.[44] Similarly, George Kennan would often preface his policy recommendations to Acheson and Truman with assumptions of ideal domestic political conditions. In August 1950 he wrote to Acheson about policy toward Asia: "In the light of this [the international] situation, what course of action would be dictated by considerations of pure national interest, leaving aside our domestic political inhibitions?"[45] It was left to Acheson, John Foster Dulles, and Truman to

---

[43] Maxwell, *India's China War*, p. 74. Maxwell's analysis was shared by certain Indian elites. On November 7, 1950, Sardar Patel wrote to Nehru, "Throughout history we have seldom worried about our North-east frontier. The Himalayas have been regarded as an impenetrable barrier against any threat from the north. We had a friendly Tibet which gave us no trouble. The Chinese were divided. They had their own domestic problems and never bothered us about our frontiers . . . . China is no longer divided. It is united and strong." See Appendix I in Dalvi, *Himalayan Blunder*.

[44] For Winston Churchill's two-level analysis of Britain's naval policy, see Ferris, *Men, Money and Diplomacy*, pp. 161–162. For Prime Minister Stanley Baldwin's flirtation with and then retreat from a policy of placing British defense commitments at the Rhine in 1934–35, see Schuker, "France and the Remilitarization of the Rhineland, 1936," p. 312.

[45] Kennan to Acheson, August 21, 1950, *Papers of Dean Acheson*, Box 65, File: Mem-

consider Kennan's proposals both for their internal logic and for their plausibility and implications in the existing domestic political conditions.

MEASURING THE HEIGHT OF POLITICAL HURDLES

In the mobilization model outlined above, the concept of national political power is represented by the variable "hurdles to mobilization." The degree to which state-society relations distort leaders' preferred policies depends on the height of the domestic political obstacles facing those leaders. As Morgenthau argued, these are very difficult to measure and are quite context dependent. But state-society constraints are important to policy makers, so we cannot ignore them simply because they are difficult to measure. Below I offer a method for measuring the challenges leaders face in attempting to mobilize their publics behind new grand strategies. I posit that three major factors must be considered when measuring political hurdles to resource mobilization: (1) the ability of the state to raise or maintain levels of taxation before the mobilization drive; (2) the nature and immediacy of the international challenge and the expense of the leaders' preferred policies in comparison with past responses to similar challenges; (3) the novelty and salient history of policy details within the preferred grand strategy. By integrating these factors, this method attempts to address Morgenthau's concerns about context dependence.

The Ability to Raise and Maintain Tax Levels

In order to understand the constraints leaders face when extracting a high level of taxation for security mobilization, we must understand the general political environment regarding taxation before the mobilization campaign is launched. How great has popular resistance to increased taxation been in the recent past? Has there been a push to reduce taxation? Before we determine the political marketability of any tax program we must establish the baseline expectations of the public about legitimate tax levels.

Related to popular attitudes about taxation are attitudes toward the nontax opportunity costs of security mobilization drives. These can be levied by the state through budgetary and nonbudgetary measures. Nontax costs to the public include the diversion to security programs of funds usually allocated for other, more popular, government programs. An-

---

oranda of Conversations, August 1950, p. 2, Harry S Truman Library (hereafter cited as HSTL).

other potentially controversial measure is government accumulation of budgetary deficits that spark inflation or increase borrowing costs to the public through competition in limited capital markets. Nonbudgetary measures include military conscription and stationing of soldiers abroad. These policies require public sacrifice that cannot be measured in dollar terms alone. In addition to financial expense, the maintenance of a large military presence overseas carries high nonmonetary opportunity costs for soldiers and their families.

For each nation we must derive measures of public sacrifice for grand strategy that are sensitive to that country's political and economic system. So, in the empirical chapters that follow, for the United States we look at tax rates and the percentages of GNP and of the overall state budget devoted to security. For Mao's China we look at the rate of capital accumulation by the state and the percentage of state expenditures going into long-term investment rather than consumption.

To determine public attitudes toward taxation and related sacrifices in some countries, it may be necessary to account for more than just overt popular opposition to tax legislation. Especially in nondemocratic nations, we must also determine whether increased tax rates affect public enthusiasm and productivity. A great reduction in these might offset the long-term benefits to the state of new expropriation strategies. As with taxation measures, for each nation and regime type the analyst must derive a measure for public attitudes toward taxation. In open democratic systems such as the United States and Britain we can look at voting behavior and poll results; in closed societies we need to find proxy measures such as worker productivity in periods of higher state accumulation.

Finally, in order to determine the level of public support for new grand strategies, we must do more than employ poll data demonstrating public approval of the goals of mobilization drives. For example, citizens' responses to pollsters that the United States should be "active" in international affairs or "tough" with the Soviets do not necessarily mean that citizens value those positions enough to pay higher taxes or to divert current tax funds from other federal programs that they also support. In times of mobilization, state leaders must do more than win consensus for active international strategies; they must get the public to pay for their implementation.

The Burden of Security Programs in Historical Perspective

Because a state's ability to raise resources varies with circumstances, we cannot simply analyze the increased costs of mobilization to determine how controversial a mobilization drive might prove. In different international environments, different types of policies and levels of expenditure seem legitimate to the public. It would be absurd to compare the political hurdles to mobilization facing President Franklin Roosevelt in November 1941 with those he faced in January 1942 without mentioning the sea change in public opinion toward interventionism that followed the attack at Pearl Harbor. Because of the immediacy and salience of an international threat, high levels of wartime mobilization will almost certainly be less controversial than even significantly lower levels of expenditure during peacetime.

In order to measure political hurdles to implementation of a specific set of policies, we must compare the costs of those policies with the burdens previously placed on the public in comparable historical conditions. But how do we determine the comparability of historical conditions? In light of the differences between the way elites and the public view international affairs, it would be fruitless to compare periods using some abstract realist measure of the international distribution of power resources. Since the mass public generally does not analyze the international environment in this way and its support for policy largely determines the political difficulties facing the state, we should compare historical challenges using simpler criteria.

Although changes in the distribution of abstract power indicators may influence the decision of elites to mobilize capital for heavy industrialization or military modernization, the changes themselves are unlikely to sell the new and expensive policies to the public. As argued above, mass publics concern themselves instead with more tangible, immediate threats and with ideological enemies. Given limited information and high discount rates, the public will judge the importance of international challenges by how immediately and clearly they seem to compromise national security. For comparing historical periods, we should develop a simple typology of international challenges based on how directly they might appear to the public to threaten national interests.

I propose three measures of directness in analyzing types of challenges: (1) the target of the international challenge: who faces the gravest immediate danger—the homeland, allies, or nonaligned nations? (2) the time frame of the challenge: is national security immediately compromised by changes in the international environment, or do current trends portend shifts in the international balance of power that may take several years to affect national security? (3) the type of challenge: is it initially military, political, or economic in nature? Table 2.1 lists the three measures of directness in descending order.

Such measures of international conditions are difficult if not impossible to quantify. Here I simply argue that, all other things being equal, it will be easiest for states to mobilize national resources for security policy if an international challenge takes the form of an immediate military attack on a nation's homeland (such as the attack on Pearl Harbor or the

TABLE 2.1
Three Measures for Directness of Threat

	Target of Challenge	Time Frame	Type of Challenge
High	Home Country	Immediate	Military
Medium	Allied Nation/ Friendly Power	Short Term (Crisis)	Political
Low	Third Party	Long Term	Economic

Battle of Britain); it will be most difficult to garner support for expensive policies designed to protect the long-term economic and political stability of third parties (such as the European Recovery Program).[46] Between these two extremes fall a range of challenges, including more abstract long-term threats to the homeland, such as high economic and industrial growth of potential enemies, as well as direct military challenges to important third-party actors in the international system.

When analyzing the challenges facing a mobilizing state, one should compare the level of public sacrifice necessary to implement the preferred policies with the historical precedents for sacrifices made in the face of similarly "direct" international challenges. To the degree that expenditures for security policy exceed those of a salient period in the past, the policies will be politically difficult for the state to implement.

Policy Novelty and the Lessons of History

Certain policies in the leaders' optimal policy set may be unprecedented in the nation's history. If the elements of the optimal policy set are novel, they will most likely be more controversial and the state will likely face a more difficult time justifying the expense of the policies. The same will hold true for policies that have a history but are associated with past disasters and negative lessons. For example, the public memory of British losses on land in World War I deterred Prime Minister Stanley Baldwin from carrying out his preferred strategy of committing British troops to the defense of the Rhine in 1934–35.[47]

[46] For a similar argument, stating that leaders will have relative difficulty focusing public attention on nonmilitary threats to security, see Ullman, "Redefining Security."

[47] See Schuker, "France and the Remilitarization of the Rhineland, 1936," p. 312. For a general discussion of the effects of the lessons of history on policy formation, see Jervis, *Perception and Misperception in International Politics,* chap. 6; May, *"Lessons" of the Past;* and Khong, *Analogies at War.*

HYPOTHESIS TESTING AND THE PROBLEMS OF MEASUREMENT

The measures described above provide a general set of guidelines for the analyst to use in judging the political hurdles that face leaders trying to mobilize significant new resources for security policy. Unfortunately, the measures do not lend themselves to simple quantification. Even increased taxation, which is easily measured in terms of absolute and marginal growth, cannot be easily translated to indicate the height of political obstacles. Factors that vary from nation to nation, such as national wealth and the marginal value of additional sacrifices for poorer and richer populations, complicate the equations. Still, using the broad guidelines above, we should be able to discern the general degree of political difficulty leaders will face when attempting to mobilize significant new resources for national security.

Though general, the measures still allow for hypothesis falsification. The model will be challenged if, in periods of low short-term threat, leaders are able to implement unprecedented and expensive policies designed to counter long-term challenges without first exploiting crusading rhetoric and otherwise counterproductive levels of international conflict. For example, the model would be challenged if, after the collapse of the Soviet threat, an American administration had implemented a program of the Marshall Plan's scope to help prevent the rise of fascism and encourage democracy in the former Soviet republics. Assuming such a flow of funds would have had a positive influence, such a sacrifice ($150–200 billion administered over four years, or about 15–20 percent of the defense budget for each of the four years) might have been a rational one from the standpoint of America's long-term security.[48] But, given the reduced immediate threat and America's "turning inward," such an expensive foreign aid program would have been out of the question, regardless of its merits.

The existence of formidable hurdles to mobilization will be easiest to demonstrate when leaders underestimate domestic challenges and simply fail to mobilize sufficient support for their preferred grand strategies. But the problem of determining the height of hurdles becomes more difficult in cases where leaders perceive hurdles, alter the public presentation and content of their grand strategy, and then successfully implement that

[48] The hypothetical policy is used only for demonstration purposes. The author does not possess the knowledge of the region or the technical skill to determine whether such an effort would have been effective or advisable. The estimated figure of 150–200 billion 1992 dollars is derived by calculating the percentage of annual GNP spent on the Marshall Plan. After significant trimming of the original $17 billion proposals, the European Recovery Program cost $12.5 billion over the years 1948–51. This was about 4 percent of 1948 U.S. GNP. Even a cursory application of the political power measures offered above would demonstrate the futility of attempting to sell such a bill to the public in the early 1990s.

strategy. In such cases, it is necessary to establish that the degree of mobilizational crusading adopted by the leaders was indeed necessary in
order to sell their original, preferred grand strategy. We should first establish that the leaders perceived domestic obstacles to mobilization and that
these perceptions affected their policy decisions. Although individual political leaders' conclusions might be tainted by psychological biases or the
requisites of party or factional politics, certain methods help distinguish between these phenomena and our own variables. In addition to
applying the measures developed above, we can analyze the viewpoints of
several actors within the elite, as well as the conclusions of foreign policy
experts within the political opposition and the media. For example, if
Democrats Acheson and Truman basically agreed with Republicans
Dulles and Senator Arthur Vandenberg about the international challenge
facing the nation and the domestic problems facing the state in meeting
that challenge, it is unlikely that Truman's concerns about mobilizing
support resulted from cognitive dysfunction or Democratic Party politics.
Second, in determining whether crusading in foreign policy was necessary
to sell basic security strategies, we might also find a basis of comparison
in the recent past or at various stages of mobilization, when leaders attempted and failed to sell related programs without the crusading spin.

In decision-making analysis perhaps the most difficult distinction to
make is between high and prohibitively high domestic hurdles to mobilization. In some cases leaders might simply view mobilization as hopeless,
even with the added value of threat exploitation or moral crusading. But
in others the risk that ideological campaigning and saber rattling will
anger potential adversaries or alienate potential allies might deter leaders
from using such methods, even if they would have proven effective in the
domestic arena. A decision to mobilize will be driven not only by the
height of domestic hurdles, but also by the potential costs of mobilizational crusading to the nation's security. If the costs of mobilizational
crusading offset the value of activating national power potential, then we
would expect leaders to settle for more anemic security strategies. In multipolar worlds, for example, there may be a trade-off between the goal of
increasing public support for defense programs by exploiting international tensions and that of passing the high cost of opposing aggressors
early on to others by maintaining a low international profile.[49] As with
many other political phenomena, these trade-offs and distinctions often
defy simple numerical measurement. Government documents and memoirs can help us determine the degree to which perceived trade-offs influence policy outcomes. Though we may never be certain of the accuracy of

---

[49] For analysis of buck-passing under structural conditions of multipolarity, see Waltz,
Theory of International Politics, chap. 8; Posen, *The Sources of Military Doctrine*; and
Christensen and Snyder, "Chain Gangs and Passed Bucks."

leaders' conclusions about the potential international dangers of mobilizing the public behind a crusade, we should, however, be able to make
some judgment by comparing the leaders' evaluations with the conclusions reached by well-informed analysts inside and outside the state leadership. With these limitations and caveats in mind, I now turn to the
empirical cases.

CHAPTER 3

Moderate Strategies and Crusading Rhetoric: Truman Mobilizes for a Bipolar World

[We should] refrain from offering moral and
ideological advice. We should cease to talk
about vague and—for the Far East—unreal
objectives such as human rights, the raising of
the living standards, and democratization. The
day is not far off when we are going to have to
deal in straight power concepts. The less we are
then hampered by idealistic slogans the better.
(George Kennan)

The best ideas in the world are of no benefit
unless they are carried out. In order to carry
them out, reason and persuasion must be
employed. If enthusiasm for them can be
aroused, so much the better. Some men have
the ability to arouse that enthusiasm more
than others. They are the political leaders.
(Harry S Truman)

I believe it must be the policy of the United
States to support free peoples who are resisting
subjugation by armed minorities or by
outside pressures.
(Harry S Truman, March 12, 1947)

THE NEW INTERNATIONAL challenge facing the United States in 1947 was,
quite simply, the realization that the world was bipolar. Truman fundamentally mistrusted the Soviets as early as 1946. He did not act earlier to
counter Soviet expansionism for two related reasons: first, he understood
the high degree of domestic resistance to government spending in peacetime; second, he hoped to rely on the British to assist the United States in
containing the Soviets in Europe. In early 1947, the discovery that Britain

could not do so meant that Truman had to take the bull by the horns and mobilize the American public for action.[1]

In late 1945, the Truman administration became increasingly suspicious of Soviet intentions, especially toward the Middle East, the Persian Gulf, and Greece and Turkey. These suspicions were based on captured Nazi documents that suggested the Soviets were seeking warm-water ports near the Persian Gulf. Further evidence revealed Soviet designs on the Turkish Straits, where Stalin hoped to build a new Mediterranean naval influence. In January 1946, Truman told Secretary of State James Byrnes, "I'm tired of babying the Soviets," asserting that the only language Moscow understands is "how many divisions have you?"[2]

On the ideological front, 1946 was also a formative year for Soviet-American conflict. Joseph Stalin's February "Presidential" speech painted the world as two hostile camps. Scrapping the World War II distinction between fascism and democratic capitalism, Stalin argued that there was no chance for prolonged peace with the capitalist world.[3] Kennan's famous "Long Telegram" arrived in Washington in the same month, portraying the Soviet Union as a particularly entrenched and paranoid version of the Russian Empire. Only long-term Western material strength, political resolve, and patience would allow for a change in Moscow.[4] In March 1946, the appraisal of the Soviet Union as an ideological foe as well as a rival in the global balance of power was dramatically articulated in Churchill's "Iron Curtain" speech in Fulton, Missouri.[5]

Concern about Soviet expansionist tendencies continued throughout 1946, reaching a peak in August with the Iran Crisis. The Truman administration fully understood the ideological and realpolitik nature of the

[1] This straightforward realist explanation has been lost by revisionist and corporatist histories that emphasize threats to America's international markets and by psychological arguments that portray Truman as not yet certain about the need for Cold War containment policies. For revisionist arguments, see Williams, *The Tragedy of American Diplomacy;* Purifoy, *Harry Truman's China Policy;* and Freeland, *The Truman Doctrine.* While Freeland does grant that there were strategic goals in balancing against the Soviet Union, he generally paints the American strategic problem as the need to protect American markets or to dominate European politics. For the best corporatist account, see Hogan, *The Marshall Plan.* For the psychological thesis, see Larson, *Origins of Containment.*

[2] Pollard, *Economic Security,* pp. 110–111.

[3] Donovan, *Conflict and Crisis,* pp. 187–189. For a text of the Feb. 9, 1946, speech, see Dmytryshn, *The USSR,* appendix 29.

[4] Mayers, *George Kennan,* pp. 97–101; Gaddis, *Strategies of Containment,* chap. 2.

[5] With Truman at his side, Churchill portrayed Europe as divided between the forces of evil despotism and enlightened democracy. Truman avoided endorsing Churchill's speech publicly. Larson, *Origins of Containment,* pp. 263–266. Although Truman's silence may have signified reluctance to endorse Churchill's arguments, it may have been founded in tactical prudence, not intellectual disagreement with Churchill's fundamental conclusions. Truman may simply have wanted to avoid speaking loudly while carrying a little stick.

struggle with the Soviet Union, as was demonstrated by the September 1946 Clifford-Elsey report. Two of the president's advisers, Clark Clifford and George Elsey, portrayed the world as divided into totalitarian and democratic camps. They called for American assistance to democratic forces threatened by the Soviet Union. Clifford emphasized that, although Truman ordered the report destroyed, he fundamentally agreed with its portrayal of the Soviet threat. Clifford's argument is logically consistent: Truman's intellectual transformation to cold warrior was complete in 1946, but he believed that making this known to the American public and the Kremlin was too dangerous during a time in which the Republicans would seize Capitol Hill on a platform of significant tax cuts.[6] As Joseph Jones described the administration consensus in early 1947: "The problem was not what should be done, but how to get authorizing legislation through Congress."[7]

Rather than supporting new international efforts, the American public and Congress demanded demobilization at a pace much faster than foreign policy leaders preferred, and with a fervor that no one in either the executive or legislative branch could easily reverse. In addition, there was a sense in Washington that the American role was to support British policing efforts in the Mediterranean. American leaders still viewed Britain as a potent actor in world affairs and considered the checking of Russian expansion in the Dardanelles and Bosporus to be an inherently British responsibility, dating back to the Crimean War.[8] The public desire for fiscal conservation and the faith in Britain's power worked in tandem to create a false sense of security and a strong opposition to spending on foreign policy.[9] Congressional leaders echoed the public concerns at a February 27 meeting with Marshall and Acheson about the crisis in Greece and Turkey. The two major points of controversy over the aid program were the seemingly open-ended and expensive nature of the commitment and the general sense that the United States was "pulling British chestnuts out of the fire."[10]

The administration clearly would have preferred to rely on the British as well. As Truman pondered how to gain political support for a more active American posture in the winter of 1946–47, he and his advisers assumed that Britain would continue to play its traditional balance-of-power role in the eastern Mediterranean. The Americans knew the Brit-

---

[6] For the argument that Truman's destruction of the Clifford-Elsey report demonstrated that Truman did not agree, see ibid., pp. 297–298. For the counterargument, see Clifford, *Counsel to the President*, chap. 7.

[7] Jones, *The Fifteen Weeks*, p. 138.

[8] Pollard, *Economic Security*, p. 111.

[9] Isaacson and Thomas, *The Wise Men*, pp. 393–394.

[10] Jones, *The Fifteen Weeks*, p. 139.

ish economy had been in trouble after the war—Washington had loaned the British government the substantial amount of $3.75 billion in 1945–46. But the depth and duration of British malaise was not fully appreciated. Moreover, administration officials had not yet made the critical intellectual link between Britain's economic weakness and its inability to contribute to European stability. The original strategies designed by George Kennan and by Clifford and Elsey were premised not on the notion of American containment of the Soviet Union, but on joint Anglo-American efforts.[11] Until 1947, the American foreign policy elite still viewed a British-dominated Western Europe as a groggy but potent "third force" in world politics. As Richard Gardner writes of 1946 America: "Ignorance of Britain's economic difficulties had grown to appalling proportions."[12]

This worldview became bankrupt in February 1947, as the true implications of bipolarity came crashing down on Washington.[13] In that month London informed American leaders in no uncertain terms that Britain could no longer fulfill its traditional role as balancer in the Mediterranean. This was not simply a case of the British passing the buck to the Americans, but was the result of a serious collapse of British power after World War II. The bitter winter of 1946–47 paralyzed the British economy, leaving half of British industries idle, creating a massive coal shortage, and laying waste to some 5 million jobs. As a result, Britain was forced to cut its military manpower by 20 percent (from 1.5 to 1.2 million personnel). On February 21, 1947, London sent urgent diplomatic memoranda to Washington painting a grim picture of Soviet pressure on Athens and Ankara. Most important, citing the United Kingdom's near economic collapse, the British claimed they would no longer be able to extend their traditional military and economic assistance to that geostrategically vital region.[14]

As others have pointed out, the problem of communist pressure on Greece and Turkey was not itself a shock to the administration.[15] Greece and Turkey had already been considered worthy recipients of the extended aid program that was being developed in Washington planning rooms. But the British collapse necessitated a much larger European pro-

---

[11] For the importance of the partnership with England in Kennan's initial containment strategies, see Mayers, *George Kennan*, chaps. 6 and 7. In the so-called Long Telegram of 1946 and the famous "X Article" of July 1947, Kennan referred to a struggle between the Soviet Union and an Anglo-American world.

[12] Gardner, *Sterling-Dollar Diplomacy*, p. 240.

[13] For the original academic formulation of a postwar, three-power system, see Fox, *The Super-Powers*.

[14] Pollard, *Economic Security*, p. 118; and Mayers, *George Kennan*, p. 134.

[15] LaFeber, *America, Russia and the Cold War*, p. 52; and Leffler, *Preponderance of Power*, p. 143.

gram than was originally considered. Of equal importance, British decline meant that Truman needed to begin selling such a program to the public immediately.[16]

For American leaders the shock of 1947 was related to a shift in the international structure: it was the realization that however undesirable that outcome was for the United States, the world was bipolar.[17] The British retrenchment apparently caught Acheson off guard. He stated nervously to the journalist Louis Fischer on February 24: "There are only two powers left. The British are finished. They are through. And the trouble is this hits us too soon, before we are ready for it. We are having a lot of trouble getting money from Congress. If the Near East goes Communist, I very much fear for this country and the world."[18] In the same vein, Assistant Secretary William Clayton stated: "The reins of world leadership are fast slipping from Britain's competent but now very weak hands. These reins will be picked up either by the United States or by Russia. If by Russia, there will almost certainly be war in the next decade or so, with the odds against us. If by the United States, war can almost certainly be prevented."[19] Because of British decline, for the first time in history the United States government was to ask its citizenry for substantial peacetime sacrifices for foreign policy.

THE PREFERRED GRAND STRATEGY: LIMITED CONTAINMENT

Given the new recognition of international bipolarity and the immediate risks in the eastern Mediterranean, administration officials began to upgrade their expectations about the necessary intensity and duration of American intervention in Europe and other strategic areas of the globe, including the Middle East and Japan. But as early as March 1947, their strategic plan went far past an ad hoc response to the crisis in Greece and Turkey. The administration and its congressional and media allies were fully aware that the request for aid to Greece and Turkey, later labeled the Truman Doctrine speech, was but the first step in a massive infusion of economic and military aid to Europe. According to the president himself, the Truman Doctrine and the Marshall Plan (the European Recovery Program) were "two halves of the same walnut."[20] Although the details of the Marshall Plan and related programs had not yet been hammered

[16] Pollard, *Economic Security*, p. 119; Gaddis, *Strategies of Containment*, p. 23.
[17] Jones, *The Fifteen Weeks*, pp. 94–95, 141.
[18] Isaacson and Thomas, *The Wise Men*, p. 393.
[19] Leffler, *Preponderance of Power*, p. 143.
[20] Jones, *The Fifteen Weeks*, p. 233.

out, the need for a revolutionary and expensive new strategy had been agreed upon.

Uncomfortable with the notion of "Fortress America" and its implications for the long-term survival of American liberal values, the administration's response to bipolarity was to invest in transforming the world by fostering the development of independent but friendly centers of power—"strongpoints"—in Europe and Asia. Doing so would serve four primary functions: the increase of the overall power of the Free World in relation to the Soviet camp; the prevention of additional Soviet seizure of industrialized areas; the reduction of the long-term security burden on the United States in containing the Soviet Union; and the provision of a subversive example to peoples within the Soviet camp, demonstrating that the Western system was superior economically and politically to anything offered by the communists. While it took some months to distill a clear picture of exactly what areas were and were not "strongpoints" in George Kennan's vision of limited containment, there was a consistent sense that America needed to take positive action in geostrategically important areas around the globe without getting bogged down in peripheral areas.[21]

For contemporary realists, who consider bipolarity to be a stabilizing influence, the goal of American grand strategy in 1947 should seem rather strange. In their theories, one of the key stabilizing aspects of bipolarity is that the superpowers need not rely on third parties to guarantee their security.[22] For American foreign policy elites, by 1947 bipolarity was a reality, but a dreaded one. As Kennan put it: "It should be a cardinal point of our policy to see to it that other elements of independent power are developed on the Eurasian land mass as rapidly as possible in order to take off our shoulders some of the burden of 'bi-polarity.'"[23] Kennan and others did not believe a liberal, democratic America could both maintain its national character and compete alone with the Soviet dictatorship in an extended bipolar struggle for power.[24]

While America was hoping one day to establish alliances with strong countries that might share the burden of the Cold War, the arrival of the British notes signified that such help would be a long time in coming

---

[21] The best account of the development of Kennan's limited-containment strategy is Gaddis, *Strategies of Containment*, chaps. 3 and 4. For a detailed account of the evolution of Kennan's thinking on what areas should be included within and excluded from the American defense perimeter, see Mayers, *George Kennan*, chap. 6.

[22] Waltz, *Theory of International Politics*, chaps. 6–8.

[23] Kennan to Cecil B. Lyon, Oct. 13, 1947, Policy Planning Staff Records (hereafter cited as PPS Records), Box 33, File: Chronological-1947, cited in Gaddis, *The Long Peace*, p. 58.

[24] On this point see Gaddis, *The Long Peace*, chap. 3. Also see Gaddis, "The Emerging Post-Revisionist Thesis," pp. 182–183.

under any circumstances, and might be hastened only by an infusion of American resources. In this way, American security policy fits realist thinking to a tee. As Kenneth Waltz argues, bipolar superpowers need to rely more on their own resources than great powers in a multipolar world, which by necessity rely more heavily on the contribution of allies.[25] So, even though American policy elites wanted eventually to rely more heavily on a powerful Europe, they also needed to mobilize American resources in the short term in order to help create such a Europe.

There is another sense in which American strategy was only partially consistent with realism. Ideological differences between the United States and the Soviet Union mattered to American analysts. The Soviet Union was viewed as dangerous because it was both powerful *and* ideologically hostile. George Kennan, the principal author of the Truman grand strategy of strongpoint defense, saw the global struggle as one between fundamentally opposing political systems. But, as John Gaddis argues, the American strategists were not ideological crusaders. They did not adopt a uniform response to communist movements around the globe regardless of the strategic interests at stake.[26] In a frustrated response to a friend at the National War College, Kennan most clearly summed up his long-held views on the differences between communist threats in strongpoints such as Europe and peripheral areas such as China:

> I do not know the basis of the assertion that communist advances in China are likely to lead to the defeat of whatever we are trying to do in Western Europe. I personally do not see the logic in this. In Western Europe, we are trying to keep out of Russian hands the only center of military-industrial power on the surface of the earth with which, if they controlled it, the Russians could conceivably develop military power and attain a strategic position which taken together, would constitute a serious military danger to this country. I do not see that this effort will be greatly affected by what happens in China.[27]

Although Soviet ideology made the USSR hostile, there was no reason to counter similar ideologies everywhere in order to prevent the Soviet Union from accruing global influence. Kennan viewed neither strong democratic nor weak communist nations as security threats.

The administration's initial Cold War grand strategy contained several interrelated elements that would take shape over the next three years. First, the standing American military would have to be stronger than in previous periods of peace. A stronger military would not only deter the

[25] Waltz, *Theory of International Politics*.

[26] Gaddis, *Strategies of Containment*, pp. 56–61.

[27] Kennan to Rudy Winnacker, Dec. 8, 1948, PPS Records, Box 13, File: China 1947–48, National Archives (hereafter cited as NA).

Soviets from adventurism but also reassure struggling regimes in Europe and elsewhere that America was not returning to isolationism after the war. There was also to be a significant effort to develop a larger and more sophisticated nuclear arsenal so that the United States could continue using its nuclear monopoly to deter the Soviets and minimize costs for more expensive conventional forces. Finally, over the next three years, the United States would help to rebuild the European economy through transfers of credit under the Marshall Plan, reassure friendly Western European states through the signing of mutual defense treaties, and bolster those states' own defenses by granting military aid packages.

WHY WAS THE NEW GRAND STRATEGY CONTROVERSIAL? TRUMAN'S POLITICAL HURDLES TO MOBILIZATION

Hurdle I: Public Opinion toward American Interventionism, Taxation, and Inflation

In late 1945, the American public began pushing hard for demobilization. Whenever the return of soldiers, sailors, or flyers fell behind schedule, congressional representatives were flooded with letters from young mothers, demanding action to "bring Daddy home." When logistical tie-ups were cited as reasons for the slow pace of demobilization, the cry was "no boats, no votes." In the fall of 1945, when troops were being demobilized at the astonishing rate of 15,200 a day, Truman was widely criticized for not bringing them home fast enough.[28]

After the searing experience of World War II, most Americans rejected the principled isolationist attitudes they had held before the war. Truman was able to create consistent spoken support for the idea of American internationalism, but he was not nearly as successful at gaining permanent public commitments to fund international efforts. For example, a thin majority of respondents consistently supported Marshall Plan aid, but a similar majority often rejected the programs if they meant increasing or even maintaining existing tax levels.[29] In addition, public interna-

[28] Larson, *Origins of Containment*, pp. 219, 227, 240.

[29] In a July 23, 1947, Gallup Poll, 55 percent of respondents favored $5 billion in credits to Europe, but 50 percent opposed it if it meant higher taxes (while 41 percent still supported it). In Dec. 1947–Jan. 1948, from the administration's standpoint the figures were even grimmer. A Jan. 14, 1948, Gallup Poll asked: "Some people say we should reduce income taxes now because of the high cost of living. Others say we should not reduce taxes because we must give food and other aid to Europe and reduce our national debt first. What is your opinion on this—do you think income taxes should or should not be reduced now?" Fifty-one percent responded that taxes should be cut, 36 percent that they should not, and 13 percent had no opinion. See *Gallup Poll*.

tionalism often took the form of support not for American leadership but for multilateral efforts and burden sharing under the auspices of the United Nations.[30] Americans were not yet prepared for the responsibility and burden of world leadership.

Particularly in reference to the Marshall Plan, public support for Truman's policies varied according to two factors discussed in Chapter 2: the perceived costs of the program and the education and income levels of the respondents. When the program was associated with higher taxes or higher inflation, support dropped precipitously. More-educated subgroups of the public were more likely to support the long-term aid program, while those with only a grade-school education were more likely to oppose it. These factors were duly noted by State Department opinion analysts.[31]

PUBLIC ANTITAX ATTITUDES

In November 1946, the Republicans won a majority in both houses of Congress for the first time since the beginning of the New Deal.[32] Running on a party platform of 20 percent tax reductions, Republicans had already begun to view Truman as a lame-duck president.[33] Just before Britain sent the historic notes on Greece and Turkey, the Congress passed a resolution calling for what one administration official described as a

[30] For example, while a majority of Americans supported aid to Greece and Turkey after the Truman Doctrine speech, an Apr. 13, 1947, Gallup Poll showed that 63 percent thought the problem should be turned over to the UN. See *Gallup Poll.*

[31] For example, "Monthly Survey on American Opinion on International Affairs" (hereafter cited as "Monthly Survey"), Oct. 1947 and Dec. 1947, Foster Papers, Box 11, NA. Both surveys demonstrate the devastating effects of fears about inflation or higher taxes on levels of support for the program. In October concerns about inflation reduced levels of support from 80 to 50 percent. In discussing the December poll, which included the tax issue, the analysts noted that "if adoption of ERP means postponement of tax reduction, then the margin of popular approval is relatively slight—49% for and 40% against." In this poll, support for the Marshall Plan was strongly correlated with education levels. The majority of those who finished only grade school opposed the Marshall Plan if it meant inflation, while only 25 percent of college graduates took that position. Because education and income levels are positively correlated, the variation could be explained by differences across groups in the salience of international affairs or differences in discount rates for the future. In December the analysts wrote: "The education-and-income differential remains significant: with 66% support among those who attended college, 51% among those who have been to high school, and only 37% (with 47% opposed) among those with only a grammar school education."

[32] The Democrats dropped six seats in the Senate and fifty-three in the House of Representatives.

[33] Sundquist, *The Decline and Resurgence of Congress,* p. 69. Also see Donovan, *Conflict and Crisis,* p. 237; Isaacson and Thomas, *The Wise Men,* p. 393; Robert Higgs, "The Cold War Economy"; Larson, *Origins of Containment,* p. 304.

"meat ax" cut of $6 billion in an already meager federal budget of $37.7 billion.[34] The administration struggled for bipartisan support just to halve the proposed budget cuts.[35] Moreover, economic nationalism was on the rise, threatening proposed free-trade agreements under the General Agreement on Tariffs and Trade (GATT) and casting a large shadow on the more controversial concept of outright economic aid to Europe.[36]

In calling for American retrenchment and lower budgets, the Republicans were reflecting, not leading, the general attitudes of society.[37] In November 1946, a majority of taxpayers wanted to cut taxes even if it meant that the United States would not be able to repay promptly the massive national debt accrued during the war years.[38] In March 1947, more than half of those polled believed taxes were too high, while less than 1 percent thought they were too low.[39] In that same month, 62 percent of respondents believed that the administration could cut its budget without affecting necessary programs.[40] In December 1947, approval of the European Recovery Program (ERP) dropped below 50 percent when respondents associated it with even the maintenance of current tax levels, let alone higher taxes.[41] This antitax attitude continued through the debates over funding for the Marshall Plan in early 1948.[42] Following this popular trend, in the heat of the Marshall Plan debates in 1947–48, Democrats and Republicans alike joined together to vote a tax-cutting bill that the administration strongly opposed.[43]

THE FEAR OF INFLATION

While Americans did not want to see cuts in relatively popular domestic and military programs, they also did not seem willing to pay for them.[44]

[34] Jones, *The Fifteen Weeks*, p. 97; and Donovan, *Conflict and Crisis*, p. 278.

[35] It was only the intervention of the administration's Republican savior, Senator Arthur Vandenberg, that preserved a budget of $34.7 billion for fiscal year 1948.

[36] Jones, *The Fifteen Weeks*, pp. 94–96.

[37] Pollard, *Economic Security*, p. 107.

[38] *Gallup Poll*, Nov. 29, 1946.

[39] *Gallup Poll*, Mar. 29, 1947. Fifty-four percent said their taxes were too high, 40 percent about right, and less than 1 percent too low.

[40] *Gallup Poll*, Mar. 7, 1947.

[41] "Monthly Survey," Dec. 1947, Foster Papers, Box 11, NA.

[42] *Gallup Poll*, Mar. 27, 1948. Fifty-seven percent complained that their taxes were too high, 38 percent said they were about right, and 1 percent believed they were too low. A Jan. 9, 1948, Gallup Poll showed no majority support for current tax levels among any taxpaying group, even those paying less than $50 per year.

[43] See Hartmann, *Truman and the 80th Congress*, p. 135. The tax reduction bill passed with a vote of 78 to 11 in the Senate. Thirty democrats joined the Republican majority. Truman vetoed the measure and was overridden.

[44] A general survey of Gallup Polls from 1947 to 1950 shows that public support for

Moreover, because of a widespread fear of deficits and inflation both within and outside the administration, Truman had little choice but to raise revenues for whatever programs he advocated.[45] The administration was aware of the dangerous domestic and international political implications of high levels of American inflation. In a quickly growing economy with a significant public debt remaining from World War II, Truman's room to maneuver was therefore extremely constrained.

In the typology offered in Chapter 2, inflation is a major nontax sacrifice associated with high levels of government spending. Because inflationary budget deficits are one way to pay for grand strategy, societal opposition to increased inflation plays a role similar to opposition to taxation in limiting the state's foreign policy options. In public opinion polls inflation was a leading concern throughout the late 1940s. In a December 1946 poll the task of controlling prices and the cost of living was mentioned even more commonly than tax reform among issues the public would like the new Republican Congress to tackle.[46] Although it is hard to imagine in contemporary America, in early 1947 citizens who expected prices to drop in the next six months outnumbered those expecting increases by a ratio of more than 2:1.[47] In October 1947, public opinion analysts in the State Department emphasized that support for the Marshall Plan dropped off sharply if the program was associated with continuing inflation or shortages at home.[48] In February 1948, respondents most commonly mentioned inflation and the danger of depression as issues they would raise with President Truman if given the chance.[49] The administration was acutely aware of this popular trend. One of its key tactics in selling the Marshall Plan was the release of the Harriman Committee report in November 1947, which, somewhat disingenuously, sought to allay fears that massive foreign assistance would strain the budget and cause inflation.[50]

---

housing and education policies was at least equivalent to that for foreign policies. But there was consistent resistance to paying more taxes to fund Truman's domestic or international efforts.

[45] Schilling, "The Politics of National Defense," pp. 139–140.

[46] *Gallup Poll,* Dec. 2, 1946.

[47] *Gallup Poll,* Apr. 26, 1947. The following question was asked: "Do you think that prices, in general, will be higher, lower, or about the same six months from now?" Twenty-two percent responded higher, while 46 percent responded lower.

[48] "Monthly Survey," Oct. 1947, Foster Papers, Box 11, NA. Support dropped from 80 percent to 50 percent when the possibility of continued inflation and shortages was mentioned. This fact was underlined in the survey.

[49] *Gallup Poll,* Feb. 13, 1948.

[50] Pollard, *Economic Security,* pp. 147–149. Officials, including Harriman, in fact feared that without a larger tax base Truman's grand strategy might indeed trigger inflation.

Internationally, American deficits and inflation might undercut the confidence-building measures in Europe that were considered a priority in Truman's grand strategy. The U.S. dollar was the standard international currency in postwar Western Europe. American inflation would decrease the real value of nominal dollar credits granted to Europe under the Marshall Plan. American budget deficits would also be taken as a symbol of American economic instability, which might send panic through a financially unstable Europe looking to the American economy as a life preserver. This was particularly true in areas on the front line of the Cold War, such as West Berlin in 1948.[51]

Hurdle II: Unprecedented Expense in Peacetime

The Truman administration has often been portrayed as fiscally conservative toward security policy in the years preceding the Korean War.[52] This interpretation is based on two misplaced emphases: an unwarranted fixation on defense spending alone and a tendency to compare Truman's expenditures with later Cold War budgets rather than with peacetime budgets before 1947. A true picture of the domestic implications of Truman's grand strategy should account for total spending on foreign policy, including defense spending, Marshall Plan aid, and nuclear research. Moreover it should compare the costs of that grand strategy with those of comparable periods before 1947, because those constituted the public's baseline of expectations.

In Chapter 2, I developed a rough typology for use in comparing historical periods: the "directness" of security threats. This measure helps us understand how international changes might appear to the general public. By this criterion, the United States was relatively secure in 1947. The most immediate military threat to American interests was to countries not traditionally allied with the United States: Greece, Turkey, and Iran. While American government analysts believed that America's closest future allies—Britain, France, and occupied Germany and Japan— were threatened by Soviet domination, they viewed the threat not as im-

[51] During the Soviet blockade, General Lucius Clay argued that American budget deficits caused by increased defense spending would be taken in Europe as an omen of American inflation and would trigger hysteria in West Berlin, reversing the upswing in German morale that followed monetary stabilization in the spring of 1948. Clay believed that American deficits would also compromise efforts to convince nervous West Europeans that the free-market system would prevail over the Soviet one. See Millis, ed., *Forrestal Diaries*, p. 526.

[52] See, e.g., Wells, "Sounding the Tocsin," p. 124; Wells writes: "Truman's commitment to budgetary imperatives prevailed over the Soviet threat." Also see Pollard, *Economic Security*, pp. 156, 228–229; and Donovan, "Truman's Perspective," p. 18.

mediate and military, but as long term and related to economic and political difficulties faced by their governments. The threat to the American homeland was of an even longer-term nature. Kennan, Marshall, and Acheson feared most that America could, over time, become isolated and unable to compete economically and militarily with a Soviet Empire that controlled the bulk of Eurasia.[53]

THE MILITARY BUDGET, 1947–1950

In comparison to post–Korean War peacetime military budgets, Truman's budgets at the end of the decade were small. But to judge the degree of difficulty Truman had in attaining the earlier levels of spending, we must compare Truman's spending to previous peacetime expenditures, since these alone established the public's baseline of expectation. From this perspective Truman can no longer be seen as a fiscal conservative. In fact, he was a revolutionary in the history of American military spending. Using the most conservative formula (excluding budgetary supplements and atomic energy research), Truman's military spending constituted nearly 5 percent of GNP in these years. As a percentage of GNP this was more than four times the peacetime expenditures of the 1930s (in absolute terms it was more than twelve times larger). Although American defense budgets are generally higher in the years following a war than in the years preceding it, the size of the variation before and after World War II led the budget expert Warner Schilling to describe the 1947–49 budgets as "a qualitative change."[54] In addition to this increase in military spending, the entire federal budget was higher as a percentage of GNP than it was during the heyday of the New Deal and Keynesian economics.

Finally, federal budgets continued to increase throughout the Cold War period, but in other peacetime periods the nonmilitary portions of the budget grew as fast or faster than the military portions. In those other periods, while budgets were increasing so was the federal provision of civilian goods and services. The late 1940s was a unique phase in the postwar era in that the most important increase in federal spending was in military spending. Social spending actually shrank as a percentage of GNP. In fact, because of the extremely tight budgets offered by Congress, Truman's nonmilitary domestic spending dropped to less than 8 percent of GNP, levels similar to those of the late 1920s. According to economist Michael Edelstein, the new military-centered increase in federal spending was paid for by sacrifices in private, nondurable consumption. In other

[53] Isaacson and Thomas, *The Wise Men*, p. 393; Mayers, *George Kennan*, p. 122; Gaddis, *Strategies of Containment*, p. 57.

[54] Schilling, "The Politics of National Defense," p. 30.

TABLE 3.1

A Comparison of Military Spending
in the Truman Years and in
Previous Periods of Peace

Calendar Year	% GNP
1934	1.1
1935	1.3
1936	1.3
1937	1.2
1938	1.4
1939	1.6
1947	5.3
1948	4.7
1949	4.7
1950	5.8

Source: Kendrick, *A Century and a Half of Federal Expenditures*, p. 12.

words, guns were clearly being paid for by butter sacrificed. This did not hold true in later periods of the Cold War, when military expenditures were matched or outstripped by increases in government spending on consumption.[55]

AMERICAN DEFENSE AND THE PROBLEM OF EUROPEAN MILITARY AND ECONOMIC ASSISTANCE

Another reason Truman is considered a fiscal conservative on security is that he put strict ceilings on military spending that were significantly lower than the amounts requested by the Joint Chiefs of Staff (JCS). For example, in deliberations over the fiscal year 1950 defense budget, the military trimmed its minimum estimate to $17 billion, while Truman maintained a strict ceiling of $15 billion. Scholars also note that, in 1948–49, Truman actually shelved funding offered by Congress for the Air Force.[56] But these two facts have been misunderstood because they have been viewed in isolation, without consideration of other budgetary constraints and expensive nonmilitary aspects of Truman's grand strategy.

Truman's ceilings on defense spending were not created in isolation from public and congressional opinion or from the requisites of other key

[55] Edelstein, "What Price Cold War?" pp. 429–432.

[56] See, e.g., Wells, "Sounding the Tocsin," pp. 124–125; and Pollard, *Economic Security*, pp. 228–230.

TABLE 3.2

A Comparison of Federal Spending
in the Truman Years and in
Previous Periods of Peace

Calendar Year	% GNP
1935	10.9
1936	11.0
1937	9.6
1938	10.8
1939	11.7
1947	15.6
1948	14.9
1949	16.2
1950	15.7

Source: Kendrick, *A Century and a Half of Federal Expenditures*, p. 12.

programs. His much-discussed $15 billion ceiling for fiscal year 1950, for example, was derived from a governmentwide consensus on what the political climate would bear. This consensus was reached in consultation with Senator Arthur Vandenberg, the Republican champion of bipartisan foreign policy and the administration's congressional barometer.[57] Congress had rejected or cut the administration's requests for supplementary military appropriations in 1947 and 1948, so there was strong reason to believe that higher military budgets would meet the continued resistance of fiscal conservatives.

A second and more complicated problem for Truman was that his total security budget for fiscal year 1950 was about $21.6 billion, or more than 7 percent of GNP. This figure includes programs considered absolutely essential to the strongpoint defense strategy: foreign economic aid under the Marshall Plan, military assistance for Europe, and atomic energy research (totaling $7.4 billion).[58] As a percentage of GNP, security programs under Truman in the late 1940s rivaled those of Ronald Reagan in the high-spending 1980s. Moreover, given the already emaciated budgets for domestic programs, security programs constituted nearly 50 percent of federal spending from 1948 to 1950. Secretary of Defense James Forrestal described the federal budget as "a barrel that is completely full now, and one blow of the hammer is going to burst the bungs on it."[59] The

[57] Schilling, "The Politics of National Defense," p. 72.

[58] Ibid., p. 100. Paul Hammond wrote of the foreign policy budget in 1948: "Foreign policy had never before in peacetime been tied to an operating program of such scope." See Hammond, "NSC 68," p. 278.

[59] Forrestal to Byrnes, Apr. 28, 1948, in Millis, ed., *Forrestal Diaries*, p. 429; Schilling, "The Politics of National Defense," p. 139.

lack of domestic budgetary fat, congressional pressure for cuts in federal taxation, and a persistent fear of inflation combined to leave no room for increased military spending without heavy sacrifices in other critical foreign policy programs.

The Truman administration could find few welcome allies on defense spending. Pure fiscal conservatives wanted to cut federal budgets regardless of the international threat. At the same time, those on Capitol Hill who perceived an international threat often painted that threat in the simplest terms: as an immediate military challenge to the United States and its allies. For the psychological reasons offered in Chapter 2, this portrayal of the international challenge meant easier marketability to the American public. Moreover, pushing for pure defense spending rather than a more integrated grand strategy allowed the representatives two other advantages: they could spend more money on domestic (defense-related) constituencies, and they could design quick-fix programs, such as the creation of a large Air Force, that would minimize the need for long-term foreign policy expenditures.[60] It was this "Fortress America" coalition in the House of Representatives that in 1948 pushed through an $822 million supplement for the Air Force.[61] This supplement, trimmed by the Senate, was accepted but not spent by Truman.

Truman's restraint on Air Force spending demonstrated to some that Truman was leading rather than following the trend of fiscal conservatism.[62] In fact, in general Truman was less fiscally conservative than Congress on defense issues.[63] In 1948 Congress had rejected Truman's plan for universal military training and had cut the administration's proposed appropriations for the Army and Navy, only increasing the amount allocated for the Air Force.[64] The logic of the congressional strategy was to place American defense on home-based nuclear bombers (an Air Force of seventy groups) that would deter Soviet aggression.[65] Truman eventually shelved the money for the Air Force because he felt that the Fortress America argument would gain more currency if the Air Force grew disproportionately. Truman said to Forrestal in 1948: "The very people in

[60] Referring to the difficulties of implementing a foreign aid program as part of a grand strategy, Robert Oppenheimer said: "There are plenty of advocates on that [the military spending] side. There are no advocates of Britain, France and Germany." Princeton Seminars, Oct. 11, 1953, Reel 5, Tape 2, pp. 13–14, HSTL.

[61] Schilling, "The Politics of National Defense," pp. 44–45.

[62] See, for example, Rearden, *Office of the Secretary of Defense*, Vol. 1, pp. 356–361; and Wells, "Sounding the Tocsin," pp. 124–125.

[63] The administration had particular difficulty in the House on funding for the Navy. See Millis, ed., *Forrestal Diaries*, p. 268.

[64] Hartmann, *Truman and the 80th Congress*, p. 170.

[65] Schilling, "The Politics of National Defense," p. 79. This antiadministration position was even supported by Representative Clarence Cannon, a Democrat from Truman's home state of Missouri.

Congress who would now vote for heavy air appropriations are those who a year from now would deny anything to the armed forces."[66] The arguments of the quick-fix advocates were very persuasive. For the public, American armed forces and, in particular, the Air Force, seemed to provide the most direct answer to a threat whose subtlety it could not fully grasp. When asked if they would support more defense spending even if it meant tax increases, in February 1949 the majority of respondents supported only Air Force increases.[67] Support for military spending increased during major crises in the late 1940s, but Air Force expenditures consistently enjoyed the highest level of public support.[68]

As with other programs, popular support for increases in military spending dropped when the issue of increased taxes was raised.[69] So, while some influential representatives on Capitol Hill would have spent more than Truman on all branches of the armed forces, these groups also would have tapped the extra funds from less popular long-term economic and military aid programs to Europe. Given the antitax climate in Congress, any defense increases would either cut into more efficient use of resources in assisting Europe (France in particular), or risk overheating the economy, which enjoyed fast growth and record levels of employment.[70]

Hurdle III: The Novelty and Expense of European Aid in Peacetime

Certain expensive policy elements of Truman's grand strategy were also unprecedented and therefore especially controversial. Because the United States had no history of massive foreign aid in peacetime, Marshall Plan aid alone has been described as a revolution in American foreign policy. Recalling the initial 1948 request for $17 billion over four years for European recovery, Clark Clifford wrote: "There will never be another Marshall Plan. The conditions that led up to it and made it successful cannot

[66] Millis, ed., *Forrestal Diaries*, pp, 431–432, cited in Schilling, "The Politics of National Defense," p. 153.

[67] *Gallup Poll*, Feb. 21, 1949. It is also worth noting that a majority supported an increase in all three services, but only the Air Force majority survived the crucial supplemental question about whether respondents supported increases even if they meant higher taxes. When international tensions were higher, as in early 1948, higher taxes for all three branches were supported. Still, the majorities were not high (around 55 percent) and representatives could answer the public call for more defense with less political backlash by cutting into other foreign programs to pay for military increases rather than raising taxes. See *Gallup Poll*, Mar. 19, 1948.

[68] Almond, *The American People and Foreign Policy*, pp. 103–105.

[69] Ibid.

[70] For debates on these issues between Marshall, Forrestal, and James Webb, director of the budget, see Millis, ed., *The Forrestal Diaries*, pp. 435–439 and passim; and Schilling, "The Politics of National Defense," pp. 139–150, 192–199.

be re-created, and the scope of it defies modern budgets. . . . It was six-teen percent of the federal budget, an inconceivable proportion today."[71] From 1948 to 1951 actual appropriations for ERP (Europe only) were about $12.4 billion, or about 1.2 percent of GNP. Between April 1948 and June 1949, ERP constituted 2.3 percent of GNP, or nearly half the defense budget for this period.[72] Truman tried to play down the high costs of the program by comparing it to the astronomically higher costs of World War II.[73] But the directness of international threats and, subse-quently, the attitude of the American people toward foreign policy expen-ditures, were quite different during the war. The ease of mobilization cannot be compared across such different periods.

Also controversial were the 1949 NATO (North Atlantic Treaty Orga-nization) alliance and accompanying military assistance programs for Europe. Schilling asserts that the creation of NATO itself "was a truly revolutionary act, [it was] the first time the nation had committed itself in advance of a European War to the terms and side on which it would fight since the ill-fated 'permanent' alliance with France in 1778."[74] The United States had consistently avoided "entangling alliances" and peace-time involvement in European balance-of-power politics, which were viewed as immoral and dangerous. Moreover, America's early relation-ship with the NATO alliance was an unusual one. In general, countries reduce their domestic security burden by joining an alliance and relying partially on the efforts of others. But the NATO alliance actually heaped new burdens on the American public in the form of military assistance packages for the new European allies.

SELLING THE GRAND STRATEGY

The Truman Doctrine Speech: "Scare the Hell out of the American People"

In a historic meeting with congressional leaders on February 27, 1947, Marshall and Acheson attempted to convince them of the necessity for a massive aid package for Greece and Turkey. Marshall began the discus-sion with the uninspiring and arcane language of realpolitik, citing the economic and geostrategic importance of the eastern Mediterranean, par-ticularly to Great Britain.[75] In addition, he included a plea for assistance on humanitarian grounds. The representatives were visibly unimpressed

[71] Clifford, *Counsel to the President*, p. 145.
[72] Wexler, *The Marshall Plan Revisited*, pp. 248–251.
[73] Pollard, *Economic Security*, p. 149. The initial $17 billion Marshall Plan proposals constituted only 5 percent of the expenditures for World War II.
[74] Schilling, "The Politics of National Defense," p. 33.
[75] Larson, *Origins of Containment*, pp. 306–309.

with the secretary's presentation, arguing that the aid amounted to British free-riding on American efforts. Among those unmoved was Arthur Vandenberg, chairman of the Senate Foreign Relations Committee and Truman's Republican point man on the Hill.[76]

Sensing the audience's indifference, Acheson began a long and ideologically charged presentation about how the United States must help Greece and Turkey because America was involved in a mortal global struggle with the forces of totalitarian communism. The assistant secretary of state also tried to divest the audience of notions of global multipolarity and British buck-passing. Comparing the international system to that of Rome and Carthage, Acheson stated that British power was destroyed and that only the United States could defend the Free World from Soviet incursions. The representatives were impressed, knowing that this line would legitimize the bill in the eyes of the American people.[77] Vandenberg promised his all-important support as long as Truman himself presented the case in strong ideological terms to the American people. The senator added that the goal of the administration's speech should be to "scare [the] hell out of the American people."[78]

Truman recognized the difficulty he would have launching and then sustaining a long-term assistance program for Europe. The administration knew what the international environment called for but was concerned about how to push the package through Congress. In a cabinet meeting five days before the Truman Doctrine speech, Truman said: "The decision is to ask Congress for 250 million [dollars] and say this decision is only the beginning. It means the U.S. going into European politics. It means the greatest selling job ever facing a President." Agreeing with the president, Secretary of Defense Forrestal said: "We cannot have a half-hearted approach."[79]

In *The Fifteen Weeks*, the author of the Truman Doctrine speech, Joseph Jones, chronicles the State Department campaign to educate the American public about the need for unprecedented peacetime intervention in Europe. From the initial staff meeting of February 28, the view among the State Department's domestic political analysts was unanimous. Given their understanding of public apathy and the differing responses of congressional leaders to Marshall's and Acheson's pleas for support, they decided that the "new policy of the United States should be presented to the public in terms of assistance of free governments everywhere that needed our aid to strengthen and defend themselves against

[76] Jones, *The Fifteen Weeks*, Part 4, chap. 1.

[77] Donovan, *Conflict and Crisis*, p. 281; Jones, *The Fifteen Weeks*, Part 4, chap. 1; Gaddis, *The United States and the Origins of the Cold War*, p. 349.

[78] Divine, *Foreign Policy and U.S. Presidential Elections*, p. 170.

[79] Cabinet Meeting, Mar. 7, 1947, Connelly Papers, Set 1, HSTL.

3.1. Political Cartoon about the Truman Doctrine. "The Alternative." by Frederick O. Seibel, 1947, *Richmond Times-Dispatch*. Alderman Library, University of Virginia at Charlottesville, in James N. Giglio and Greg G. Thielen, *Truman in Cartoon and Caricature* (Ames: Iowa State University Press, 1984), p. 112. Reprinted with permission of the publisher.

Communist aggression or subversion." As one official stated in the meeting, "The only way we can sell the public on our new policy is by emphasizing the necessity of holding the line: communism vs. democracy should be the major theme." While top officials and certain congressional leaders understood that assistance was based largely on the geostrategic importance of the region, Jones points out that this theme was intentionally omitted from the Truman Doctrine speech, because in 1947, "the American people were not accustomed to thinking, then, as they are now, in strategic-military terms in time of peace."[80]

The selection of anticommunism as the major theme of the public information campaign was related not only to the threat facing the Greek government but also to the peculiar tastes and hatreds of the American pub-

[80] Jones, *The Fifteen Weeks*, pp. 151, 162.

lic. Richard Freeland has argued that the Truman administration's ideological posturing during the Greek-Turkish crisis was largely responsible for the rise of domestic McCarthyism in America.[81] But this interpretation ignores the almost shocking fervor with which the American public and the Congress opposed communism before the Doctrine speech. In July 1946, when Americans were asked, "What should be done about the Communists in this country?" the most common response was, "Kill or imprison them!"[82]

The administration understood the usefulness of stressing anticommunism, having learned from important precedents in rallying support for foreign aid. In 1946 Truman had requested a $3.5 billion loan to help reconstruct England, America's closest wartime ally. The assistance was originally presented to the House in unemotional and economic terms. After six months of debate, the bill finally passed after sympathetic senators and representatives such as Arthur Vandenberg and Christian Herter argued for the loan on the grounds that the United Kingdom was the United States' biggest ally in the struggle against Russian communism.[83]

The administration adopted the ideological rhetoric of the Doctrine speech consciously but reluctantly.[84] Truman's advisers were aware of the dangers of painting practical, strongpoint policies in terms of ideological crusades against totalitarianism or communism. These dangers were driven home by foreign policy elites less sensitive to domestic politics than Acheson and Truman. The March 12 speech received quick criticism from Kennan and Marshall. Kennan bemoaned the speech's "universalistic rhetoric" and feared that its focus on communism might provoke the Soviets into an early military attack against American interests. Marshall

[81] Freeland, *The Truman Doctrine*.

[82] Thirty-six percent of the general population answered in this draconian manner (a slightly higher percentage of manual workers—37 percent—gave this response). *Gallup Poll*, July 6, 1946.

[83] Isaacson and Thomas, *The Wise Men*, pp. 364–365; Pollard, *Economic Security*, p. 71; Donovan, *Conflict and Crisis*, p. 281.

[84] As Gaddis points out, the March 12 Doctrine speech mentioned communists on only one occasion. See Gaddis, *Strategies of Containment*, pp. 65–66. But the speech was not long, and its harping on totalitarianism and the explicit link between "armed minorities" in Greece and "communists" left little doubt among media analysts and the public about the main focus of the speech. The administration records kept by Joseph Jones and others point to a conscious effort to manipulate the theme of communism in order to gain public support. They also show that Congress, the public, and the media focused on anticommunism as the main thrust of Truman's speech. For congressional and public reaction, see "Truman Doctrine: Important Relevant Facts," and File: Greece, Newspaper Clippings, Jones Papers, Box 2, HSTL. On Capitol Hill, leaders in both parties such as Senators Tom Connally and Styles Bridges cited communism as the target of the Doctrine speech.

similarly argued that the speech oversimplified the struggle America faced.[85] Even George Elsey, a domestic political adviser, argued that the Soviets had not behaved in a manner that warranted the crusading tone of the address.[86] These critics feared that the sweeping rhetoric would unnecessarily antagonize the Soviets at a time when neither Europe nor the United States was ready to counter them. Moreover, they worried that the crusading tone would create false expectations in the United States that America was committed to the impossible task of opposing communism everywhere.[87]

To these critics, administration officials in Washington responded that the rhetoric was necessary to ensure the approval of Congress.[88] As Theodore Lowi posits: "[The president] turns public because his major resources are public. . . . He oversells because that is what one must do to sway a large public. . . . And 'he who can mobilize the public can mobilize the elite.' "[89] Acheson backed the highly charged version of the speech from the outset. But he demonstrated in subsequent weeks that he did not accept at face value the doctrine's ideologically simplistic implications. For example, on March 24, Acheson attempted to disabuse the Senate Foreign Relations Committee of the notion that the Truman Doctrine compelled the administration to support democracy and oppose communism in all parts of the globe. But, as Kennan lamented about the Truman Doctrine: "The misapprehension already conveyed was, as I see it, never corrected. . . . All another country had to do, in order to qualify for American aid, was to demonstrate the existence of a communist threat."[90]

This "misapprehension" did not, however, live in the minds of top foreign policy makers in the Truman administration. In fact, the issue of communism versus democracy was consciously played down in Acheson's Delta Conference speech (in May) and Marshall's Harvard speech (in June), both of which outlined the preliminary American plan for assisting European recovery. Politically alert reporters in Washington noted the more sober tone of administration speeches in the spring but also questioned whether a more subtle approach could arouse congressional and

[85] Kennan, *Memoirs*, Vol. 1, chap. 13; Gaddis, *Strategies of Containment*, pp. 52–53; Donovan, *Conflict and Crisis*, p. 282.

[86] On March 7, 1947, Elsey said to Clark Clifford: "There has been no overt action in the immediate past by the USSR which serves as an adequate pretext for an 'All-Out' speech. The situation in Greece is relatively abstract." Quoted in Donovan, *Conflict and Crisis*, p. 282.

[87] Mayers, *George Kennan*, p. 137.

[88] Bohlen, *Witness to History*, p. 261.

[89] Lowi, *The End of Liberalism*, pp. 182–83.

[90] Kennan, *Memoirs*, Vol. 1, p. 322.

popular support for expensive policies. Significantly, such articles were studied and filed by Truman's State Department spin doctors.[91]

Presenting and Selling the Marshall Plan

It is important to note that during the spring of 1947, Acheson and Marshall were only beginning to present the outlines for the Marshall Plan; they were not yet asking Congress to appropriate funds for the programs. In private, Truman had from the outset described aid to Greece and Turkey as "only the beginning," but administration officials were careful not to create a dangerous backlash by presenting programs larger than the current crisis and barrage of anticommunist rhetoric could justify.[92] As we will see, whenever actual appropriations were sought from Congress, the administration would fall back on the mobilizational rhetoric of anticommunism and try to silence critics of Truman's record in both Eastern Europe and China. So, while Acheson and Marshall clearly did not believe the crusading rhetoric, they would return to it whenever American apathy seemed to threaten grand strategy. When interim funds were sought later in the year and when the core $17 billion package was presented to Congress in early 1948, anticommunism once again became a central theme in administration rhetoric.[93]

Although congressional representatives rarely opposed the Marshall Plan openly, they often leveled attacks on its expense that "cut to the heart of the program." Even after the Czech coup in February 1948, revised bills that would have severely cut into funds for Europe were introduced on the Hill. (For example, Taft requested a cut of over one-third for the first fifteen months of European assistance.)[94] The media also often focused on the proposed expense of the Marshall Plan as the flagship example of Truman's controversially high federal budgets. As one might expect, in the public and on Capitol Hill, cuts in foreign aid were considered

---

[91] See, for example, Thomas L. Stokes, "New Isolationism," *Washington News* (probably May 16, 1947), Jones Papers, Box 1, File: Correspondences Re: Transfer of Materials in Writing the Fifteen Weeks, HSTL.

[92] Cabinet Meeting, Mar. 7, 1947, Connelly Papers, Set 1, HSTL.

[93] Mee, *The Marshall Plan*, pp. 230–245. Even in spring 1947, Truman would sometimes return to the anticommunist theme under counsel from his advisers. See the text of Truman's Jefferson Day Dinner speech of Apr. 5, 1947, in Jones, *The Fifteen Weeks*, pp. 284–285.

[94] Westerfield, *Foreign Policy and Party Politics*, pp. 282–285. In early April the ERP bill once again ran into trouble as the fiscally tight John Taber questioned the worthiness of European recipients in the House. Pressure by Vandenberg ensured the $5.3 billion first-year appropriation. See Doenecke, *Not to the Swift*, p. 115.

3.2. Political Cartoon about Congressional Efforts to Cut Interim Aid for Europe and the Implications for the Marshall Plan. "Comes Now the Painful Operation." by Jay Norwood (Ding) Darling, 1947, *Des Moines Register*. University Libraries, University of Iowa, Iowa City, in James N. Giglio and Greg G. Thielen, *Truman in Cartoon and Caricature* (Ames: Iowa State University Press, 1984), p. 113. Reprinted with permission of the publisher.

among the least painful sacrifices in federal spending.[95] For the administration, however, these cuts were considered threats to national security.

Another problem for the administration was that world events did not

---

[95] See, for example, *Gallup Poll*, Apr. 8, 1949, in which only bureaucratic waste was listed more frequently than foreign aid as an area in which the public thought the government could cut spending. Also see Huntington, *The Common Defense*, pp. 242–243.

3.3. Political Cartoon about Congressional Efforts to Trim the Federal Budget and the Marshall Plan in Particular. "Even Santa Claus Doesn't Need All That Hair." by Jay Norwood (Ding) Darling, 1948, *Des Moines Register*. University Libraries, University of Iowa, Iowa City, in James N. Giglio and Greg G. Thielen, *Truman in Cartoon and Caricature* (Ames: Iowa State University Press, 1984), p. 34. Reprinted with permission of the publisher.

afford time to ease the American public into peacetime interventionism. In August 1947 the British economy was floundering once again, and State Department officials thought action needed to be taken lest Western Europe collapse before Congress considered the proposed $17 billion appropriation for Marshall Plan relief. Still, the State Department balked at burdening an almost hostile Congress with another request, particularly for Britain, which had received the lion's share of aid packages in 1946–47.[96] In late September, Truman broke his silence when it seemed that

[96] Pollard, *Economic Security*, pp. 146–147.

governments in France, Italy, and Austria would have great difficulty surviving another winter. Truman called for a special session of Congress in November to request $597 million in interim aid.

Congress had offered the administration clear cues for its next propaganda campaign. Christian Herter, a representative from New York, led an influential congressional fact-finding committee that toured Europe in 1947, returning in the early fall. The committee's analysis of the European situation sent an unambiguous message to Truman: the Marshall Plan should be supported, but not on either humanitarian or economic grounds. Europeans appeared well fed and the aid program seemed potentially damaging to American economic interests. The Herter committee stressed that it was the communist threat alone that justified the expense of the program.[97]

Public opinion polls also supported the strategy of selling the Marshall Plan by employing anticommunist rhetoric. In a poll conducted in September 1947, less than half the respondents knew about the Marshall Plan, and of those only half were in favor of the program. As one would expect from the analysis of salience and discounting rates in Chapter 2, support levels for the program correlated strongly with knowledge about the program. The least-informed groups were by far the least supportive of the plan. When the program was explained in nonideological terms, those previously uninformed about the program opposed it by a ratio of 2:1 (54 percent opposed, 25 percent in favor).[98] Also consistent with the analysis in Chapter 2, a November 1947 poll showed that adding ideological policy justifications for the program had a startling influence on the group for which international affairs were least salient (those who had not heard of the Marshall Plan). When this uninformed group was asked whether it supported a $20 billion program for European countries "to be spent for goods to be bought in this country," 26 percent said yes and 48 percent said no. When the last clause was changed to "to prevent these countries from going communistic" the figures reversed, with 47 percent supporting the program and 33 percent opposing it. As the fall progressed and the public was exposed to official and media discussion of interim aid for Europe, awareness of and support for ERP grew. But support for the program continued to increase and opposition to decrease when anticommunist language was included in questions about the Marshall Plan.[99]

Rejecting the advice of less domestically oriented advisers to remain

---

[97] Ibid., pp. 147–148; Hartmann, *Truman and the 80th Congress*, p. 111.

[98] *Gallup Poll*, Oct. 8, 1947.

[99] For the most dramatic change of opinion after a change in wording, see *Gallup Poll*, Nov. 2, 1947. This effect still exists but is much less dramatic in a December poll; see *Gallup Poll*, Dec. 7, 1947.

unemotional and businesslike, in late 1947 Truman returned to the Truman Doctrine theme, particularly when he stated that "the future of free nations in Europe hangs in the balance."[100] Truman's speech to Congress in November rallied enough support to guarantee interim aid, but State Department public opinion analysts still viewed as dangerously low the levels of support for the smaller interim aid package. They feared that generating support for the much more expensive ERP legislation in the new year could prove more difficult, particularly if it affected tax levels.[101] It is not surprising, then, that in January 1948, Marshall appealed to Congress for funding by stating, "The way of life we have known is literally in the balance."[102]

The February–March crisis in Czechoslovakia, the suspicious death of its pro-Western foreign minister, Jan Masaryk, and the early rumblings about restricted Western access to Berlin provided a necessary boost to the administration's efforts to push through ERP. As James Reston warned in 1948, "If it hadn't been for the activity of Communists in Europe, there would never have been a program of this magnitude, and if they were to lie down even now, the Administration would be in serious trouble."[103] In order to make sure that these crises were interpreted by Congress and the public in a way that would assist in the passage of ERP, on March 17, 1948, Truman outdid his Doctrine speech, stating that communism's deepest evil is that it "denies the very existence of God."[104] In Congress, Vandenberg was pushing a similar ideological line in order to gain support for ERP from his fellow Republicans. He stated: "Communism threatens all freedom and all security, whether in the old world or the new, when it puts free people anywhere in chains."[105]

THE EFFECT OF MOBILIZATION ON CHINA POLICY: THE CHINA AID BILL

China was clearly not on the list of the State Department's global strongpoints. Moreover, in 1947–48 there was a growing sense within the ad-

[100] Pollard, *Economic Security*, p. 147.

[101] "Monthly Survey," Foster Papers, Box 11, NA. The survey noted that: "Early reaction, particularly in Congress, to the President's message of Dec. 19, *seemed to bear out predictions of rough going for the recovery program*" (emphasis in original). It noted that most of the problems in Congress were based on the size of the program. But congressional resistance was seen as firmly rooted in domestic opinion. The report continued: "If adoption of the ERP means postponement of tax reduction, then the margin of popular support is relatively slight" (49 percent for and 40 percent against).

[102] Marshall, quoted in Pollard, *Economic Security*, p. 151.

[103] James Reston, quoted in Pollard, *Economic Security*, p. 152.

[104] Hartmann, *Truman and the 80th Congress*, p. 169.

[105] Pollard, *Economic Security*, p. 152.

ministration that the United States could not affect political outcomes in the Chinese Civil War. Before becoming secretary of state, George Marshall spent a year in China attempting to forge a compromise between the warring parties in the Chinese Civil War. At the end of 1946 he left China frustrated with the ineptness and corruption of Chiang's KMT government. Though hardly fond of the Chinese Communists, Marshall did not view them as mere dupes of Moscow. Marshall did not predict full-blown Titoism in China before it blossomed in Yugoslavia itself, but he understood the local and nationalist appeal of the Chinese Communist Party (CCP). Before Marshall left China, Zhou Enlai reportedly informed him that the degree to which the Chinese Communists would ally with Moscow would depend largely on American policy.[106] Marshall also knew that only massive reform within the KMT could help it win the hearts and minds of the Chinese people.[107]

With little hope of influencing such reform, Marshall returned to Washington advocating American disengagement from China on the grounds that further involvement in its civil war would be a waste of American resources, and might lead to increased anti-Americanism among the Chinese people.[108] He still held some hope that if the KMT could reform itself, assistance to Chiang might be a useful policy tool in the future. Still, after Marshall became secretary of state, it became increasingly clear that disengagement was the preferred strategy of the administration. In June 1947, Marshall's China adviser, John Carter Vincent, drafted a memo in which he argued that the United States could help the KMT win in China only if it granted assistance on a "very large scale [which] would lead to our direct participation in the civil war." Vincent pointed out that when various countries were considered for assistance by the standard of "urgency of need and importance to the national security of the United

[106] John F. Melby, Oral History, pp. 121–122, HSTL. Melby, Marshall's assistant in China in 1946, reports: "[In] one of the last conversations that Chou En-lai had with General Marshall, he said 'We would like to be friends with you. It is true we are Marxists; we are Communists, and of course, we are going to have an affinity of sorts with the Russians, with the Kremlin. But that doesn't mean we can't be friends with you. However, how far we lean toward the Russians is going to depend in no small measure on how hard you push us. If you push us hard enough we're not going to have any choice except to lean on the Russians. We've got to have friends some place. If you won't be friends, then who else is there?' I think that Chou En-lai meant it, and I think Marshall believed it too."

[107] *Executive Sessions of the Senate Foreign Relations Committee, 1947–48*, Vol. 1, p. 4; Mayers, *George Kennan*, p. 177.

[108] Arguing against underwriting Chiang's regime in February 1948, Marshall said, "Strong Chinese sensibilities regarding the infringement of China's sovereignty, the intense feeling of nationalism among all Chinese and the unavailability of qualified American personnel in the large numbers required argue strongly against such a solution." See "Executive Session Testimony before the Senate Foreign Relations Committee and the House Foreign Affairs Committee, Feb. 21, 1948," in documentary appendix to May, *The Truman Administration and China*, p. 82.

States," China ranked very low. He also pointed out that many Chinese were opposed to American support of the KMT.[109] By 1948 even foreign service officers in China, who were professionally less concerned with opportunity costs for European assistance, believed that further American assistance to Chiang was futile at best.[110]

George Kennan, the head of the Policy Planning Staff, came to a similar understanding of the Chinese Civil War under the tutelage of Joseph Davies, the former U.S. ambassador to the Soviet Union. If anything, Kennan resigned himself even earlier than Marshall to the fact that the Chinese Communists would win the civil war outright. In June 1947, Kennan was discussing what America could do to cause splits between nationalist and pro-Moscow elements in the CCP. Kennan stated, "In case the Communists were to succeed in taking over the great part of the country, I doubt that they would retain the ideological fibre of their movement or the present degree of dependence on Moscow." Kennan expressed "great misgivings as to the advisability of placing funds or goods at the disposal of the Chinese Government" and instead advocated fostering splits in the Chinese Communist movement between "indoctrinated communists" and "agrarian reformers."[111] In November his office showed only limited concern over the prospect of total communist victory in China. While recognizing that this would be a serious setback for the United States, a Policy Planning Staff document from that month also states that "no convincing evidence has been seen that, even should the Chinese National Government collapse, the communists could in the foreseeable future assume effective control over all of China and at the same time remain seriously susceptible to Soviet guidance or control in international affairs. Thus while a collapse of the Nationalist Government would be deplorable, it probably would not be a catastrophe for American interests in China."[112] By early 1948, Kennan went further, suggesting that a communist China might prove a drain on the Soviet empire because it would require massive economic and technological assistance just to recover from over a decade of war. Moreover, Kennan predicted a rivalry between a communist China and the Soviet Union that would embarrass Moscow.[113] Thus, months before Yugoslavian leader Josip

[109] "Memorandum for Use in Presenting to the President the Problem of Military Assistance to the Chinese National Armies," June 27, 1947, Office of Chinese Affairs, Film C0012, Reel 11, frames 37–38, NA.

[110] Blum, *Drawing the Line*, p. 8.

[111] "Memorandum for Mr. Lovett," June 23, 1947, PPS Records, Box 13, File: China 1947–48, NA.

[112] "The Situation in China and U.S. Policy," Nov. 3, 1947, PPS Records, Box 13, File: China 1947–48, NA.

[113] Mayers, *George Kennan*, pp. 172–173. In early 1948, Kennan wrote, "A united Communist China would be much more dangerous to Russia than the present sort of China and might threaten Russian security and Russian control of the Communist movement."

Broz Tito's break with Moscow, the Policy Planning Staff was anticipating a nationalist streak in Chinese communism.

Kennan continued in this vein in 1948 and 1949, warning the administration that continued military or financial assistance to the politically bankrupt KMT regime would only reduce American diplomatic flexibility after the Communist victory and would serve only to push the CCP closer to Moscow.[114] Frustrated with the implications of the Truman Doctrine, Kennan stated: "If I thought for a moment that the precedent of Greece and Turkey obliged us to try to do the same thing in China, I would throw up my hands and say we had better have a whole new approach to the affairs of the world."[115] Regardless of the implications of the Truman Doctrine speech, from a realist perspective China was not as important as Greece and Turkey, and American resources were insufficient to guide political outcomes there.[116] For its part, the JCS listed China as a very low and declining priority in its strategic assessments for 1947 and 1948.[117] Even if China did become communist, State Department officials believed that the Soviets would gain little global power by the formation of a communist government there.[118] China was vast and backward, and aside from Manchuria and the northeast, relatively weak in strategic resources.

But no matter how tight the strongpoint logic of disengagement and flexible diplomacy on the Asian mainland, China fit cleanly into the purview of the Truman Doctrine. Armed communists were thriving in an economically devastated postwar environment and the recognized government, an American ally in World War II, was threatened by overthrow. Because Congress consistently made this critical link, the administration was left with little choice but to continue to aid Chiang. This type of compromise frustrated Kennan. He reflected: "My specialty was the defense of the United States' interests against others, not against our own representatives."[119] An administration as a whole cannot be so specialized, even if its first priority is the defense of American interests abroad. It must develop the grand strategy that can best further those interests but still capture the imagination and support of the nation and

[114] Ibid., p. 175.

[115] George Kennan, as quoted in Gaddis, *Strategies of Containment*, p. 41.

[116] Acheson argued to Representative Walter Judd that China was forty-five times as large as Greece with a population eighty-five times as large. See Ferrell, *Harry S. Truman*, p. 73.

[117] China was listed as thirteenth and seventeenth among nations of strategic significance to American security in the 1947 and 1948 global assessments. Gaddis, *The Long Peace*, p. 78. It should be noted that when the Joint Chiefs of Staff treated the China case in isolation they generally viewed it as more important to American security and often advocated increased American military assistance to the KMT.

[118] Kennan, *Memoirs*, Vol. 1, pp. 374–375; Mayers, *George Kennan*, p. 173.

[119] Kennan, as quoted in Gaddis, *Strategies of Containment*, p. 52.

Congress. Aware of this, Acheson claimed that 80 percent of the job of policy work is "management of your domestic ability to have a policy." Truman had similar feelings about his post, claiming that the president is "a glorified public relations man who spends his time flattering, kissing, and kicking people to get them to do what they are supposed to do anyway."[120]

As early as March 1947, the administration had a fledgling understanding that the rhetoric of the Truman Doctrine contradicted the policy of disengagement from the Chinese Civil War. At the final Cabinet meeting before the Truman Doctrine speech, Secretary of the Interior Julius Krug agreed with Secretary of Defense Forrestal that the administration could not have "a half-hearted approach" and still ensure support for aid to Greece and Turkey. But, Krug added, "Our decision in pulling out of China is in conflict with this approach." Acheson responded: "[The] fundamentals of [the] problems [are] the same. The incidences are different."[121] Truman then exclaimed that "Chiang Kai-shek will not fight it out. Communists will fight it out—they are fanatical. It [parallel assistance to China] would be pouring money down a rat hole under [the] present situation." Admiral William Leahy added, "Marshall has hopes for China at [some] later date when we may assist China with a degree of success but not now."[122]

Despite his recognition that the policy of disengagement in China conflicted with the ideological tone of the Doctrine speech, Truman decided to stick with the simple emotional appeal, stating: "The job is to get the facts to the country to get the support necessary. We can't afford to revive the isolationists. . . . The people of the U.S. should be brought in and told—it is communism and free enterprise."[123] A conscious decision was made: overselling, replete with the risk of glaring contradictions between rhetoric and policy, was preferable to mobilizing the people insufficiently.

Before the Truman Doctrine speech, there was some public criticism of the administration's hands-off policy, but these statements were few and mild.[124] The real rise in criticism of Truman's China policy followed the Doctrine speech. In light of the speech, in mid-March there was negative congressional reaction to Truman's China policy. Representative Alvin E.

---

[120] Acheson and Truman as quoted by Tucker, *Patterns in the Dust*, p. 159.

[121] Cabinet Meeting, Mar. 7, 1947, Connelly Papers, Set 1, HSTL.

[122] Cabinet Meeting, Mar. 7, 1947, Connelly Papers, pp. 4–5, HSTL.

[123] Ibid.

[124] In January, Senator Vandenberg agreed with the policy of bringing home American marines but warned, "There will never be a minute when China's destiny is not of acute concern to the United States." Westerfield, *Foreign Policy and Party Politics*, p. 256. In early March the State Department noted magazine articles that criticized Marshall's efforts to "wash his hands of China." "Outstanding Magazine Articles Relating to International Affairs," Mar. 7, 1947, Jones Papers, Box 1, HSTL.

O'Konski claimed he was "befuddled" by the contradiction between Truman's anticommunism in Greece and Turkey and the "State Department['s] support of communism in China." Senator Owen Brewster said he was interested "in having the Administration define the subtle difference between Chinese Communists and Greek Communists." Perhaps most ominous for the administration was the promise made by Joseph McCarthy, the senator from Wisconsin. The record reads: "If President Truman applies the same policy all over the world, he [McCarthy] will back it. He wondered whether China was being forgotten." Truman's foreign policy spin doctor, Joseph Jones, underlined this statement by McCarthy in his copy of the State Department's congressional report.[125]

Jones seemed surprised by congressional harping on China policy. In his copy of a March 20 State Department media analysis, Jones flagged the following section, writing the single-word question "China?" in the margin:

> Rep. [Walter] Judd charges "contradictions" in Truman program and declares he will ask Acheson and every other witness "if we have one policy in Greece and another in China." Same question was asked prominently in Senate questionnaire he is preparing. . . . Meanwhile, Sen. Brewster, who has advocated more support for Chiang Kai-shek, predicts there will be a change in U.S. policy in China "within two or three weeks" and firmer support will be given to Chiang Kai-shek. However, State Department disclaims knowledge of any impending change in our China policy.[126]

This new manifestation of pro-China sentiment was not accidental. If congressional representatives had failed to make the connection between Greek and Chinese communists, the KMT government in Nanking (Nanjing) would have made it for them. The response to the Truman Doctrine speech in the Chinese capital was prompt and extremely positive. The Chinese government made three requests for aid in the few months after the Doctrine speech.[127]

The debate about the question "if Greece, why not China?" had an early effect on Truman's policy of withdrawal from the Chinese Civil War. In May 1947 the administration sent limited military stocks to Chiang, having lifted an earlier arms embargo on China. The JCS ap-

[125] "Truman Doctrine: Important Relevant Facts," Congressional Statements on President Truman's Address Seeking Aid for Greece and Turkey, Mar. 18, 1947, Jones Papers, Box 2, HSTL.

[126] "News Digest," Dept. of State, Mar. 20, 1947 (compilation of *Washington Times*, Associated Press, *Herald-Tribune*, and *Washington Post* reports), Jones Papers, p. 3, HSTL.

[127] See Tillman Durdin, "Nanking Sees Help in Truman Speech," *New York Times*, Mar. 14, 1947, in Newspaper Clippings, Jones Papers, HSTL; Tsou, *America's Failure in China*, p. 452; and Tucker, *Patterns in the Dust*, pp. 9–13.

proved of American military assistance to Chiang in mid-1947, but the Far East desk of the State Department was clearly against it.[128] The decision to lift the embargo was designed largely to appease pro-China groups in Congress and the public before the introduction of the Marshall Plan.[129] This policy reversal presaged a number of future compromises that would delay the American distancing from the China quagmire.

In fall 1947, as Truman called a special session of Congress to gain approval for interim aid for Europe, congressional representatives insisted on some China aid as part of the program. Marshall resisted, viewing it as a bad omen for the upcoming legislation for Europe. Senator Vandenberg tried to mediate between the two sides, arriving at a compromise of a smallish China aid bill ($20 million) in late 1947. But Vandenberg also extracted a firm promise from Marshall that when the full $17 billion Marshall Plan aid package was presented to Congress in early 1948 a significant China aid bill ($570 million) would also be presented. This China bill would eventually be attached in the House to continuing aid to Greece and Turkey, thus ensuring that the link between China and the Truman Doctrine would remain clear.[130]

Some scholars argue that domestic pressure alone was insufficient to compel the administration to stay involved in the Chinese Civil War. They point out that Marshall himself brought the China Aid Bill to Capitol Hill in early 1948. They also argue that public opinion on China was not strong enough to compel Truman to adopt policies that he otherwise would want to avoid, and that the China Lobby, while vocal, was too small to force the administration's hand.[131] I agree that if all things had been equal, Truman could have fought off the pro-Chiang forces in the public and in Congress. If I did not agree, I would be advocating a straightforward domestic explanation for China policy. But all things were not equal. *In the context of the mobilization drive for Europe*, domestic politics played a decisive role in the creation of the China Aid Bill.

While it is true that Marshall himself brought the China Aid Bill to Congress, it is important to note that Marshall's commitment to such a

---

[128] Vincent to Marshall, June 20, 1947, Office of Chinese Affairs, Film C0012, Reel 11, frame 42, NA.

[129] Pollard, *Economic Security*, pp. 187–188; Tsou, *America's Failure in China*, p. 453. In June, Marshall specifically mentioned the "reaction of Congress and the public" as an important determinant of any decision on military assistance. See Minutes of the Meeting of the Secretaries of State, War, and Navy, June 26, 1947, Office of Chinese Affairs, Film C0012, Reel 11, frame 40, NA.

[130] See "A Legislative History of the China Aid Bill" (originally included in an Apr. 19, 1948, letter from Walton Butterworth to Mr. Moore), Sumner Papers, Box 3, China Files, HSTL. Also see Westerfield, *Foreign Policy and Party Politics*, p. 264.

[131] Feaver, "The China Aid Bill of 1948"; Leffler, *Preponderance of Power*, pp. 247–251; and Kusnitz, *Public Opinion and Foreign Policy*, pp. 24–25.

bill had been secured in advance by Vandenberg in order to help ensure congressional support for European aid. As Marshall's director for Far Eastern affairs, Walton Butterworth, reported on the development of the China Aid Bill: "The aid program arose out of the fact [that] Senator Vandenberg let it be known that the chances of getting through the Marshall Plan would be vastly improved if there was a China Aid program."[132] Marshall had been badgered in Congress about the administration's inaction in China during his November 1947 testimony on interim aid for Europe. On November 14, Marshall made the following report to Truman about his experience on the Hill: "Senate was friendly but House Committee took him down a lot of side streets with reference to China, Communism, etc. Opposition does not take stand on what we are trying to do but *how* we are going to do it."[133]

Sympathetic to Truman's strongpoint strategy, Vandenberg was initially worried that the House's emphasis on China would cut into available funds for Europe in the coming year. But Vandenberg came to support a China aid bill after speaking to Representative John Vorys, who argued persuasively that China aid would actually increase House support for ERP because it would allow representatives to approve foreign aid without seeming merely to follow the administration's lead in fighting communism abroad.[134] Demonstrating the importance of such Republican input, Marshall's proposed aid package, $570 million, was very similar to that requested by the prominent Republican William Bullitt in an influential article printed in *Life* magazine in October 1947, something Bullitt himself pointed out in congressional testimony.[135]

Although Marshall sent the tough anticommunist General Albert Wedemeyer on a mission to China in July 1947, this did not mean that Marshall still had great hopes of saving Chiang. In fact, according to one participant in American China policy, Marshall used Wedemeyer to send secret instructions to the American consulate in Mukden (Shenyang) to begin building cooperative bridges with the communists in Manchuria.[136] The Wedemeyer[136] report did call for further assistance to Chiang, but

[132] W. Walton Butterworth, July 6, 1971, Oral History, p. 41, HSTL.

[133] Cabinet Meeting, Nov. 14, 1947, Connelly Papers, HSTL.

[134] Westerfield, *Foreign Policy and Party Politics*, pp. 262–263. For this general trend in Congress, see Pollard, *Economic Security*, p. 151.

[135] Westerfield, *Foreign Policy and Party Politics*, pp. 262–265. Bullitt wanted $600 million for China over two years. Hearing on the China aid bill, House Committee on Foreign Affairs, Mar. 2, 1948, Office of Chinese Affairs, Film C0012, Reel 13, frame 96, NA.

[136] These orders were carried out by the consular staff, who would later be held by the Communists in 1948–49. The early contacts between the Americans and the Chinese Communists reportedly infuriated Soviet officials stationed in the northeast. Personal discussion with retired American foreign service officer. For a published statement that by 1948 Mar-

the entire mission was approved by Marshall because it would prove useful to the administration as it approached Congress for European aid in early 1948.[137]

According to one of Marshall's key advisers on Chinese affairs, by 1948 Marshall was completely convinced that the KMT's future was hopeless.[138] Demonstrating a fundamental lack of faith in Chiang's future, a 1947 Policy Planning Staff document reads:

> While it is highly doubtful that any foreign intervention in China can produce the results desired, there exist strong traditional ties of sentiment between the U.S. and China and a highly vocal body of opinion in this country advocating U.S. aid to the National Government in the current Chinese Civil conflict. *For practical reasons these voices cannot be ignored.* Furthermore, a certain amount of aid to China at this time is justified as moral support to the Central Government, the rapid collapse of which would be contrary to our interests. *It follows, therefore, that the United States should extend the minimum aid necessary to satisfy American public opinion* and, if possible, to prevent any sudden and total collapse of the Chinese Government. On the other hand, it would be futile to attempt to bring about a complete Government victory in the civil war, including the recovery of all of Manchuria. Firstly, that objective is not within the realm of feasibility. Secondly, such an attempt would be regarded by the U.S.S.R. as a repudiation of American commitments and might well lead to a U.S.-Soviet conflict in an area of dubious strategic advantage to the U.S.[139]

This document makes it clear that domestic political constraints were the most important factor behind the aid program. Given the implicit granting of control of Manchuria to the Soviet Union at Yalta and the minimal strategic value of the rest of China, for reasons of straightforward realpolitik the administration would have preferred withdrawal from the Chinese Civil War over additional aid.[140]

---

shall had secret plans to build bridges to the Communists, see Stokes, "War and the Threat of War," p. 9.

[137] Tsou, *America's Failure in China*, p. 453–454. Tsou posits that the original idea for the Wedemeyer Mission was Representative Judd's; also see Stueck, *The Wedemeyer Mission*, pp. 8–10. For a summation of the Wedemeyer report's recommendations, see "Implementation of the Recommendations of the Wedemeyer Report," Feb. 18, 1948, Office of Chinese Affairs, Film C0012, Reel 11, frame 617, NA.

[138] Melby, Oral History, p. 155, HSTL.

[139] "The Situation in China and U.S. Policy," Nov. 3, 1947, PPS Records, Box 13, File: China 1947–48, NA (emphasis added).

[140] In June 1947 Kennan stated about Manchuria: "The loss of Manchuria and Dairen were implicit in the Yalta arrangements concerning the Far East, and I have since regarded these events as a fore-gone conclusion." "Memorandum for Mr. Lovett," June 23, 1947, PPS Records, Box 13, File: China 1947–48, NA. Kennan would repeat this in September

In February 1948 staffers were busy preparing Marshall's testimony on ERP to joint congressional committees. Their mission had two important elements. The first was to justify expenditures on ERP. The second was to convince critics of Truman's China policies that the threat of communism to China was strategically much less significant than the threat to Europe. The original PPS draft memorandum on China policy took the standard strongpoint line:

> It is not believed that the national security of this country would be seriously prejudiced by a continuation of the present trend toward lessened resistance to the Chinese Communist forces. . . . But even assuming that the Chinese Communists were able, and encouraged by Moscow, to take over all of China, it is difficult to see how they could seriously threaten the U.S. in a military sense. . . . There is no prospect that China could develop strong sea and air power even under Communist domination, in the foreseeable future; nor could China make any serious contribution to the development of Russian power in the Far East, except from the areas which are already for the most part in Chinese Communist hands.[141]

Scribbling in the margins on a copy he sent back to Kennan, Marshall objected to this draft on two grounds. First, he pointed out that it was "inconsistent with previous official statements by our officials." Second, and more important, he stated that "all of this is virtually an invitation to the opponents of ERP to assail us, to justify the accusation that we deliberately delayed the introduction of the China Program, etc."[142]

Marshall's objections were upheld. An internal State Department analysis of the final draft pointed out the problem that would hound the administration for the next two years: "The revised draft, as it now stands, . . . does not make clear the lesser importance to the U.S. in terms of our national security, of China as against Western Europe and thus opens the way to the charges that are being made that we are unrealistic in failing to meet the Communist threat in the Far East while concentrating on Western Europe although each is equally vital to our national security."[143]

1949, pointing out that the United States agreed at Yalta to the "restoration to the Soviet Union of the *physical* and *legal* advantages which the Czars' governments enjoyed in Manchuria prior to the Russian-Japanese War. . . . What has occurred there is substantially what the Russians had a right to think that we expected to occur." Kennan to Jessup, Sept. 8, 1949, PPS Records, Box 13, File: China 1949, NA.

[141] Kennan to Carter, Feb. 10, 1948, PPS Records, Box 13, File: China 1947–48, NA.

[142] Ibid. Attached to the letter is a copy of the original draft with Marshall's marginal, handwritten comments.

[143] Executive Session Statement Regarding China Aid Program, Feb. 18, 1948, Office of Chinese Affairs, Film C0012, Reel 13, frames 103–103, NA.

Marshall's need to sell the strongpoint grand strategy precluded the possibility of explaining that strategy. Kennan grudgingly accepted his boss's orders and called for the omission of the China discussion. In the directive, Kennan focused on Marshall's own concerns about the "opponents to ERP" and the difficulties in spelling out that "further communist successes [in China] would not be dangerous to the security of this country." He called this the "crux of the whole problem" in China policy.[144]

This line of reasoning was not limited to the State Department. In March 1948 the National Security Council (NSC) did a full study of the options open to the United States regarding short-term assistance to China. The first option was total withdrawal, the second was massive economic and military assistance to Chiang, and the third was limited military and financial assistance. Limited resources and the relative strategic insignificance of China made massive assistance undesirable. The third option—limited assistance—was seen as ineffective in stopping communist advances. The NSC felt that limited aid would, at best, be useful only in "buying time" for Chiang. Although limiting aid would reduce the drain on U.S. resources, the policy was still seen as dangerous since America might be slowly dragged into the China quagmire. The report reads: "As it became evident that such aid was inadequate to check the communists, the limited military aid given could be represented as an obligation necessitating further military, as well as economic, commitments to China."[145] Despite the strong reservations about the other two options, the only solid reason offered against total withdrawal was that "refusal of further aid would be a reversal of past US policy and contrary to the sentiment in the United States in favor of 'helping China.'" Given this domestic stumbling block, all NSC officials viewed limited aid as the best of all options.[146]

Compromises on China policy had become a political expedient used to guarantee the approval of the administration's broader grand strategy. As consul general to China, O. Edmund Clubb reflected on the China Aid Bill: "President Truman felt it necessary to mollify the opposition to some extent by adopting a Cold War stand, thus to enable him to put across the Marshall Plan for Europe."[147] As 1948 progressed, domestic political concerns continued to dominate China policy. Kennan moaned in August

---

[144] Kennan to Carter, Feb. 10, 1948, PPS Records, Box 13, File: China 1947–48, NA.

[145] Draft Report of the National Security Council on the Position of the United States Regarding Short-term Assistance to China, Mar. 24, 1948, in *Foreign Relations of the United States: 1948*, Vol. 8, pp. 44–50.

[146] Ibid.

[147] O. Edmund Clubb, June 26, 1974, Oral History, HSTL. Clubb argues that this process was similar to the administration's adopting of the "Loyalty Program" in early 1947.

1948, "Aid to China has been made a domestic political issue," divorced from strategic prudence.[148]

By the end of the year the Policy Planning Staff all but pronounced the death of Chiang Kai-shek's regime.[149] Recognizing that "of major importance at present in our relations with China are the confusion and bewilderment in the public mind regarding our China policy," Kennan continued to push Marshall and the president to "regain the understanding [and] confidence of the American public, without which we cannot effectively implement China policy." In this regard, he suggested a speech by Truman. Marshall rejected the proposal by direct order of the president, stating, "We must not be responsible for [an] announcement that would, in effect, destroy the influence of Chiang Kai-shek."[150]

Why the China Lobby Was So Powerful: The Role of Public Opinion in Congressional "Asialationism"

Congressional opposition to a leaner, strongpoint grand strategy that included Europe but excluded China was also largely based in concerns about public opinion. Public opinion analysts have argued that congressional, not public, pressure forced the administration to alter its preferred policies in China.[151] But the debate on Capitol Hill shows that leaders there were acutely sensitive to public opinion. Domestic opinion about how to fight communism, not the inherent strategic importance of China or the belief that a limited program might be effective, led senators to approve the China aid measures. In the March 1948 meetings, Vandenberg conceded: "I think it is perfectly obvious that this [the China Aid

[148] "From the Secretary for Ambassador Stuart," Aug. 9–11, 1948, PPS Records, Box 13, NA.

[149] A PPS paper reads: "The disappearance of the Chinese Nationalist Government, as now constituted, is only a matter of time and nothing we can realistically hope to do will save it." PPS 45, Nov. 26, 1948, "U.S. Policy toward China in Light of the Current Situation," PPS Records, Box 13, File: China 1947–48, NA. U.S. military officials in Nanjing instructed Washington on Nov. 16, 1948: "Communist forces will eventually overwhelm the government wherever it locates itself. This will occur before the government, even with United States assistance, can train, equip, and put into the field sufficient forces to stem the tide." JUSMAGCHINA to Dept. of Army, Personal to Wedemeyer, Nov. 16, 1948, Office of Chinese Affairs, Film C0012, Reel 11, frames 555–556, NA.

[150] PPS 45, Nov. 26, 1948, "U.S. Policy toward China in Light of the Current Situation," PPS Records, Box 13, File: China 1947–48, NA. For proof that it was Truman himself who pushed for the continuation of policy, see the handwritten note from Marshall to Kennan on the same date in Office of Chinese Affairs, State Department, Film C0012, Reel 11, frame 918, NA.

[151] Kusnitz, *Public Opinion and Foreign Policy*, p. 153.

Bill] is essentially three cheers for the Nationalist government in the hope that it can get somewhere in the face of communist opposition." Senator Bourke Hickenlooper questioned whether the $570 million would not be useless in light of the problems facing the Nationalists. To this, Vandenberg argued that at least the Chinese collapse would not be placed on the shoulders of the American government. He said: "There is one other factor . . . that I do not think can be overlooked because it crops out in all of the thinking of the country, and in most of the newspaper comment, and it is *this basic abstraction that we are undertaking to resist Communist aggression, and we are ignoring one area completely and letting it completely disintegrate without even a gesture of assistance.*"[152] In the same discussions links were made between the delaying of the fall of Chiang and success in passing ERP legislation. Vandenberg added: "I think the American people generally are deeply sympathetic with China . . . and her resistance against communism even more than Europe's against communism." Senator Walter George grudgingly agreed with Vandenberg's analysis of public opinion. The senators saw aid to Chiang as a temporary measure at best and probably no more than "a complete waste of money," but they also saw it as essential to maintain public support for the government's general foreign aid program.[153] As State Department opinion analysts noted, support for ERP was not very hardy in late 1947 and diminished significantly when the public associated the program with "postponements of tax reduction."[154] If anticommunism were to be used to overcome that resistance, a degree of consistency between policies toward Europe and Asia needed to be maintained, even if this meant somewhat more foreign policy expense than strongpoint containment alone.

Jack Snyder views America's overactive grand strategy in 1950 as the result of compromises between the governmental representatives of regional economic coalitions.[155] Snyder argues that the Truman administration's global anticommunist posturing, eventually codified in NSC 68, was not the result of simple, anticommunist hysteria, but of a logroll between "Europe-first internationalists" and "Asia-first nationalists." The resulting overactive grand strategy and the ideological "myths" underpinning it involved more interventionism than each group alone would have preferred.

I agree with Snyder that coalitional politics were important in shaping congressional pressure on the White House. But the coalitions were not

---

[152] Foreign Relief Assistance Act of 1948, U.S. Senate, Executive Session of the Committee on Foreign Relations, 80th Cong., 2d sess., Mar. 19–20, 1948, pp. 448–449 (emphasis added).

[153] Ibid., pp. 422, 447–455.

[154] "Monthly Survey," Dec. 1947, Foster Papers, Box 11, NA.

[155] Snyder, *Myths of Empire*, chap. 7.

created by competing regional economic interests, but by the basic politics of mobilization and ideological oversell, which were rooted in state-society relations. Therefore the coalitional logroll that Snyder accurately describes occurred mainly for reasons other than those offered in his core theory.[156] In American politics there was no natural economic or political coalition of "Asia-first nationalists," because there was no Asia-oriented equivalent of the northeastern banking and manufacturing coalitions that favored European reconstruction.[157] Rather, there was a broad-based, fiscally conservative coalition that fed off traditional American isolationism and the public's desire to reduce both taxation and inflation in the postwar years. In order to badger the administration on the count of ideological insincerity, this group borrowed the China Lobby's attack on Truman's contradictory policies toward Asian and European communism. The goal of these "Asialationists" was not so much to expand American commitments in Asia, but to embarrass the administration and undercut expensive policies toward Europe. If the administration did expand its grand strategy, the Asialationists could at least take credit for being more anticommunist than the administration. Asialationism, fraught with internal contradictions, grew not out of tensions among socioeconomic groups in America, but out of the contradictions between Truman's limited, yet expensive, containment strategy and the universalistic rhetoric designed to gain public and congressional support for that strategy.

Congressional Asialationism was rooted most firmly in nationwide public opinion about government spending and foreign aid in particular. Areas like the South and Midwest had stronger traditions of isolationism and fiscal conservatism than others, but these differences are often exaggerated. Polls showed relatively uniform cross-regional levels of support for pro-Europe policies such as the Marshall Plan.[158] The distribution of re-

[156] At times, Snyder recognizes that fiscally conservative, neoisolationist Republicans insincerely exploited Truman's record in Asia only as a popular electoral tactic. This was not driven by a desire to expand American commitments to Asia. See ibid., pp. 267–268.

[157] In fact, administration officials reflecting on the late 1940s pointed out that one major problem they faced was that there was no natural coalition in Congress for European aid, let alone aid for Asia. In a 1953 roundtable discussion, Paul Nitze and Robert Oppenheimer complained that congressional coalitions formed around domestic and military programs because domestic constituents benefited directly from these programs, but that committees dealing with foreign assistance, such as the House Foreign Affairs Committee, lacked prestige because they enjoyed no domestic coalitional support. Nitze said: "This Committee is dealing with foreign affairs; it has no constituents. . . . The department of agriculture has got constituents, and it can log roll. How can the House Foreign Affairs Committee log roll?" Princeton Seminars, Oct. 11, 1953, Reel 5, Tape 2, pp. 13–14, HSTL (emphasis added).

[158] For example, see Poll 1 in Appendix A in this volume.

gional support was similarly uniform for additional military assistance to Chiang Kai-shek.[159] A public consensus on fiscal and foreign policy questions can also be demonstrated across party lines.[160] Although the Republicans were more solidly behind budget cutting than the Democrats, in 1947 a majority in both parties believed federal budgets could be cut without sacrificing programs they viewed as necessary.[161] The significant victories of the Republicans in the 1946 interim elections clarified public dissatisfaction with taxes and inflation. Learning this lesson, both Democrats and Republicans on the Hill voted to cut taxes and balked at the expense of various new security strategies from the Marshall Plan to Universal Military Training (UMT).[162] Acheson recalled that, even after the 1948 electoral victories, Democratic members of Congress who backed the administration's international efforts on intellectual grounds would still join the Republicans in trying to cut any foreign aid bill that the administration sent to the Hill.[163]

The key electoral strategy for congressional representatives immediately after World War II was to appear more fiscally conservative than the administration on most foreign policy issues, including China, so as to pass the blame of high costs on to the administration. Before the March 1947 anticommunist rallying cry, the best political strategy for congressional representatives was to push for less, not more, foreign intervention, whether the area in question was Europe or Asia.[164] This calculation became complicated after the Truman Doctrine speech, because representatives wanted to appear in the lead both on cost cutting and on international anticommunism. Representatives found an answer to public

[159] See, for example, Poll 2 in Appendix A in this volume.

[160] See Poll 3 in Appendix A in this volume.

[161] *Gallup Poll*, Mar. 7, 1947. Sixty-two percent of the general public (52 percent of Democrats, and 72 percent of Republicans) believed that "government spending could be cut without doing away with programs that they thought were necessary."

[162] For discussion of tax-cutting measures in 1948, see Hartmann, *Truman and the 80th Congress;* For discussion of bipartisan reluctance on both of these programs in particular, see Hammond, "NSC 68," pp. 274–279. For discussion of Democratic Party representatives who balked at the cost of the UMT program in 1948, see Millis, ed., *Forrestal Diaries*, p. 446.

[163] Princeton Seminars, Oct. 11, 1953, Reel 5, Tape 2, pp. 12–13, HSTL.

[164] As one administration analyst put the mood on China policy in the media before 1947: "[In 1946] you find a great deal more comment among American publicists on the degree to which we were intervening in China, than you would complaint about the shortage of intervention." Unidentified voice in the July 22, 1953, Princeton Seminars, a roundtable discussion by former administration officials. Princeton Seminars, July 22, 1953, Reel 5, p. 0000727, HSTL. At the time, Secretary of State James Byrnes and Acheson worried that such opinion might actually block America's limited military efforts in China, including the ferrying of Chiang's troops to North China after World War II. May, *The Truman Administration and China*, p. 25.

demands for both economy and anticommunism by forcing Truman to assume relatively inexpensive and symbolic anticommunist policies toward China whenever major legislation was raised for Europe.

Asialationism constituted a no-lose strategy for representatives. Administration compliance with demands on China would not significantly increase the cost of foreign aid packages and would allow representatives to argue that they were in the lead on issues of global anticommunism. Administration noncompliance would open Truman up to the charge that he was insincere in his anticommunist justifications for European policies, thus justifying deep cuts in ERP funding. So, by pushing China aid, representatives could portray themselves as leaders either in anticommunism or in cutting wasteful and unprincipled programs, or both. Dean Acheson summed up the strategy of the "China bloc" as "an attempt to embarrass provision of funds for the non-partisan policy in Europe."[165] The administration was not compelled to spend "massive" resources to answer this attack on their Europe policy, but it needed to demonstrate some level of opposition to communism in China so as to prevent nominally pro-China representatives from attacking budgets for Europe. The end result of this strategy was a legislative process lamented by realist analysts removed from domestic politics.[166]

It is instructive to note that the most fiscally conservative groups in Congress often demanded a tougher anticommunist foreign policy and that China aid be tacked on to administration bills for Europe in 1947 and 1948. For example, the chairman of the House Appropriations Committee, John Taber, consistently supported bills to reduce international appropriations. But during the initial wave of criticism over Truman's China policy he also fervently called for an "end to appeasement in the State Department."[167] A task force from the tight-belted House Appropriations and Armed Services Committees returned from China in fall 1947 insisting on additional aid to Chiang, arguing, "It is a tragic error for our country in its efforts to stem the spread of communism in the world to concentrate its programs exclusively in the European theater."[168] Similarly, it was the fiscally conservative House Foreign Affairs Committee that tacked China aid on to Truman's emergency relief bill for Europe in late 1947.[169] Under Vandenberg's tutelage, the administration

[165] Acheson, *Present at the Creation*, p. 304.

[166] As George Kennan complained, Congress began to approve aid not to individual nations of geostrategic importance but to categories of nations and to "compel the executive to act in a uniform way in relation to all of them." *Memoirs*, Vol. 1, p. 323.

[167] "Truman Doctrine: Important Relevant Facts," Congressional Statements on President Truman's Address Seeking Aid for Greece and Turkey, Jones Papers, Box 2, HSTL.

[168] Hartmann, *Truman and the 80th Congress*, p. 117.

[169] Westerfield, *Foreign Policy and Party Politics*, pp. 261–263.

allowed these groups to take credit both for cost cutting in the general ERP package *and* the addition of China aid. In so doing Truman guaranteed bipartisan support for ERP from 1948 to 1951.[170]

China was often an emotional issue for large percentages of the American public, but analysts are correct to point out that it was rarely, if ever, an issue of such salience that the public could have forced the administration to alter its China policy.[171] Sincere pro-Chiang elements in Congress and the public were too small in number to secure aid to Chiang if they lacked the alliance with isolationists and fiscal conservatives.[172] Truman's own tapping of isolationism would have stripped the China Lobby of its powerful allies.[173]

Despite the accuracy of this analysis, a key question remains: how could Truman have fostered fiscal conservatism and isolationism toward China *at the same time that he was asking for expensive and interventionist programs for Europe?* The problem for the administration was that support for Chiang seemed to follow in lockstep with support for aid to Europe. This is because during crises both were functions of the increased salience for the American people of international relations generally and communism in particular. Acheson and others had apparently succeeded only in convincing the public that the biggest difference between Greece and China was "the immediate situation" in both areas.[174] In August 1947 most observers believed that China was of "vital strategic importance" to the United States.[175] The public was evenly divided about assistance to Chiang in the first half of 1947 (43 percent both for and against) and seemed to accept Marshall's June suggestion that the United States reject a proposal for $500 million in export-import credits to Chiang.[176] But it should also be noted that, as early as April 1947, those opposing military aid to Greece also outnumbered those supporting it. In fact, in the two months immediately after the Truman Doctrine speech, popular support for loans to Chiang was quite similar to that for economic assistance to "governments attacked by armed Communists" (43 percent for Chiang, 44 percent for the general category).[177]

[170] Doenecke, *Not to the Swift*, p. 114; Westerfield, *Foreign Policy and Party Politics*, pp. 266–268; and Pollard, *Economic Security*, p. 151.

[171] Kusnitz, *Public Opinion and Foreign Policy*, chap. 3.

[172] As Nancy Tucker points out, "the China bloc itself did not control a large number of votes, [but] in alliance with economy-minded isolationists and legislators . . . it could present a formidable barrier to approval of administration plans." Tucker, *Patterns in the Dust*, pp. 165–166.

[173] Feaver, "The China Aid Act," p. 118, n.22.

[174] See "Monthly Survey," Mar. and May 1947, Foster Papers, Box 11, NA.

[175] Ibid., Aug. 1947.

[176] Ibid., Mar. and June 1947.

[177] Ibid., June 1947. However, opposition to support for Chiang was higher than that

As the approach offered here would predict, the biggest change in public attitudes toward China policy occurred during the biggest administration appeals for European assistance. After Truman's push to gain congressional support for the interim aid program for Europe, public support for aid to China increased markedly. In late December 1947, for the first time a majority of the American public (55 percent) supported loans to Chiang, while disapproval dropped sharply (to 27 percent).[178] State Department analysts noted that Chiang's approval rating in the American public rose "appreciably" in late 1947 and that the majority of media observers also began advocating long-term assistance to the KMT.[179] The combination of the Czech coup, increased tensions over Berlin, and administration lobbying gained the necessary approval for the larger European program in March 1948. But, consistent with the approach offered here, in the process of general mobilization the public came to support a more active pro-Chiang policy as well. While support for loans increased in December, the public remained wary about the more controversial measure of increasing military assistance to Chiang. But with the crisis in Europe and the administration's anticommunist rhetoric relating to ERP, popular approval for military aid to Chiang skyrocketed from 32 percent in February to 55 percent in April.[180] As Walter LaFeber argues, in the early spring of 1948, it was evident that "the public had taken the Truman Doctrine at its word and now wanted . . . [it] extended to Asia."[181]

To return to the mobilization model offered in Chapter 2, if the Truman administration had held withdrawal from China as a higher priority than increased intervention in Europe, it might have decided to withdraw from

---

for aid to the more general category of states threatened by armed Communists (43 percent disapproved of loans to Chiang, 29 percent opposed aid to the general category). This difference may have derived from underestimation of the likelihood of KMT collapse and Communist victory in 1947 or from the belief that the KMT most needed reform.

[178] Ibid., Dec. 1947. Public support for assistance to Chiang was not as great as that for interim aid to Europe (71 percent). It is interesting and contrary to the thesis here that another document in Foster's files suggests that the public in January 1948 was more interested in Chinese "recovery" (55 percent) than in "U.S. financial aid against the Chinese Communists" (34 percent). The questions involving communism, however, are worded very unclearly. They ask whether the United States should "take sides in China" by "helping the Chinese government against the Communists," which may have implied to many respondents that the United States might become directly involved in the Chinese Civil War. Given this, the 34 percent approval rate may be seen as impressive indeed. See "Public Attitudes on U.S. Policy toward China," Report 13, Jan. 28, 1948, Foster Papers, Box 33, NA.

[179] "Monthly Survey," Dec. 1947, Foster Papers, Box 11, NA.

[180] Stueck, *The Road to Confrontation*, p. 60. Also see "Monthly Survey," May 1948, Foster Papers, Box 11, NA; Kusnitz, *Public Opinion and Foreign Policy*, p. 153; and *Gallup Poll*, Apr. 28, 1948.

[181] LaFeber, "American Policy Makers," p. 56.

the Chinese Civil War at the expense of undercutting the domestic legitimacy for peacetime expenditures in Europe. In this case, the costs of mobilization would have been considered prohibitively high, and there would have been an underactive American grand strategy. But the administration believed that support for Europe was essential and that the costs of altering the preferred China policy were tolerably low. Therefore, officials decided that, within limits, too much foreign policy activity—opposing communism in both Europe and China—was necessary to avoid too little foreign policy activity—insufficient funding for European reconstruction and defense. As they would in the following two years, in 1948 the administration settled for continued support to Chiang but still worked to minimize the fiscal and political costs of continued American involvement in the Chinese Civil War.

CHAPTER 4

Absent at the Creation: Acheson's Decision to Forgo Relations with the Chinese Communists

In 1949 various factors reinforced the Truman administration's desire to remove itself from the Chinese Civil War and establish a working relationship with the Chinese Communists: the recent example of Titoism in Yugoslavia; the continued military onslaught of the Chinese Communists; and the appointment of the European-oriented Dean Acheson as secretary of state. But in 1949–50 Mao adopted policies that complicated the adoption of this strategy. These included the detention of American consul Angus Ward and his staff in Mukden from late 1948 to late 1949 on trumped-up accusations of espionage, the decision to "lean toward" and then ally with the Soviet Union, and the seizure of American consular property in China in January 1950. Although those policies were important in the evolution of American policy toward China, below I argue that their importance is often overstated. The main stumbling block to the adoption of a Tito strategy toward the CCP was the domestic need to maintain a degree of anticommunism in China policy while Truman mobilized support for containment in Europe.

LETTING THE DUST SETTLE: ACHESON'S FIRST MONTHS

Within the administration, disagreements about the direction of American foreign policy, and in particular China policy, persisted throughout Truman's second term. But it was clear that one man, Dean Acheson, had the ear of the president on all important decisions. Acheson succeeded George Marshall in January 1949. For the next four years he would closely approximate the "unified rational actor" in American foreign policy. Truman was inconsistent and sometimes emotional about China, as he was about other issues, advocating imprudent military or political action in response to CCP affronts to American prestige. But Truman nearly always submitted to the more experienced reasoning of Acheson, who advocated calm and patience in the hope of more constructive relations with the ascendant Communists.

Unlike other realist analysts in the American foreign policy elite, such as George Kennan, Dean Acheson was the consummate two-level player:

he understood both why the United States should take certain actions abroad and why certain advantageous policies were difficult to sell to the public and Congress. Acheson, therefore, crafted a grand strategy that walked the line between securing sufficient money for Europe from fiscal conservatives and placating pro-KMT critics.[1] Whenever a tough choice had to be made, Acheson opted to delay progress on China in order to sell European packages to Congress. This pattern lasted until the outbreak of the Korean War.

By February 1949, Acheson declared to the National Security Council (NSC) that for all intents and purposes the Chinese Civil War was finished. Acheson's report reads:

> As anticipated, the Communists have shattered . . . the power of the National Government. . . . It is sufficient here to recognize that a) preponderant power has now clearly passed to the Communists, b) although a remnant of the National Government may survive in South China or in Formosa [Taiwan] for months or years to come, it will at best be a local regime with its claims to international recognition based on insubstantial legalisms and c) eventually most or all of China will come under Communist rule.[2]

Typically, Acheson predicted that "the full force of nationalism remains to be released in Communist China." He declared that any further military aid to the KMT would be worse than ineffectual, because it would "solidify the Chinese people in support of the Chinese Communists and perpetuate the delusion that China's interests lie with the USSR."

Given the recent hopeful example of Titoism in Yugoslavia, the administration became increasingly concerned about the effects of America's continuing support of the KMT on the Chinese public and on nationalists within the Chinese Communist Party. In October 1948, Ambassador John Leighton Stuart in Nanking (Nanjing) cabled Marshall stating that "any direct aid to resistance group on theory that we are fighting communism all over the world would . . . only delay their ultimate liquidation and would meanwhile arouse increased anti-American sentiment."[3] By

---

[1] Tsou, *America's Failure in China*, pp. 452–453.

[2] "U.S. Policy toward China," A Report to the National Security Council by the Secretary of State, NSC 34/2, Feb. 28, 1949, in *Foreign Relations of the United States: 1949* (hereafter cited as *FRUS: 1949*), Vol. 9, pp. 491–495.

[3] Telegram, Nanking to Marshall, Oct. 27, 1948, Clifford Papers, Box 2, File: China 1948–50, Harry S Truman Library (hereafter cited as HSTL). Another telegram argued: "Bulk people and virtually all officials except Gimo [Chiang] and immediate entourage . . . are resigned to early communist victory and believe immediate cessation of fighting would be in best interests of all concerned. . . . It is difficult to see how US Govt. or Anti-Comm. forces could benefit at this stage by US official statement that we consider communism in China and Far East equally as important as in Europe." Outgoing telegram, Dept. of State

the end of the year, many American officials in China had reversed their earlier position of supporting additional aid for Chiang. Under the advice of his experts in both China and Washington, in late 1948 Truman rejected requests from the KMT for additional military assistance.[4]

In Washington, however, differences of opinion still existed. The American military was more likely than the State Department to advocate an active anticommunist role in China.[5] The NSC was, however, able to reach consensus on the general policy prescription backed by the State Department: the United States should prepare to use economic relations to "lure a Communist China away from too-close relations with the Soviet Union."[6] The strategy was codified in late February 1949 in NSC 41. The document states that "economic relations with China" constitute America's "most effective weapons vis-a-vis a Chinese Communist regime," and that these weapons should be used to "prevent China from becoming an adjunct of Soviet power."[7] In early March, Truman agreed with NSC 41's basic conclusions. He argued to Senator Vandenberg that if America played its cards correctly "the Russians will turn out to be the foreign devils in China and that the situation will establish a Chinese government that we can recognize and support."[8]

The Decision against Providing Assistance to CCP-Controlled Areas

Despite the growing intellectual consensus about the most realistic China policy, officials in the State Department itself remained cautious for fear of domestic backlash. Since the Communists had taken over large sections of northern China, a decision had to be made regarding the continuation of Economic Cooperation Administration (ECA) assistance to those areas. Some officials in the ECA and other branches of the State Department advocated continued aid, lest the Chinese people draw the conclusion that assistance was only designed to prop up Chiang. Acting Secretary Robert Lovett and his assistant, Walton Butterworth, rejected aid to Communist-held areas because they better understood the domestic political climate in America. Truman and the Cabinet sided firmly with the domestic political argument. On January 19, 1949, Truman

---

for the Secretary from Lovett, Nov. 11, 1948, p. 3, "Recent Telegram from Nanking," Clifford Papers, File: China 1948–1950, Box 3, HSTL.

[4] See, for example, outgoing telegram, Nov. 18, 1948, Dept. of State for the Secretary from Lovett, Clifford Papers, Box 3, File: China 1948–50, HSTL.

[5] Blum, *Drawing the Line*, chap. 2.

[6] Kusnitz, *Public Opinion and Foreign Policy*, p. 26.

[7] *FRUS: 1949*, Vol. 9, pp. 826–834.

[8] Truman to Vandenberg, quoted in Tucker, *Patterns in the Dust*, p. 175.

ended the debate, stating plainly, "We can't be in the position of making any deals with a communist regime."[9]

The administration had reason to fear a domestic backlash if it abandoned Chiang or reached out to the Chinese Communists. At the beginning of 1949 the American public was confused about China. There was little enthusiasm for expensive American involvement on the mainland, and Chiang Kai-shek was increasingly unpopular. Still the American public was strongly anticommunist and hostile to any accommodation with the CCP. There was a popular belief that the Chinese Communists were puppets of Moscow, and those opposing trade with communist areas easily outnumbered those supporting it.[10] As noted in State Department analyses, the American media continued to portray Communist domination of China as a "major defeat for U.S. Far Eastern policy."[11] For Truman's opponents, the biggest lesson of the shocking 1948 presidential election was that foreign policy could no longer be considered out of bounds in partisan politics. The easiest point of attack was Truman's China policy, particularly since Truman himself continued to use anticommunist rhetoric to support his international program, as he did in his fiery inaugural address in January.[12]

ERP Renewal and the Continuation of Aid to Chiang

One of the compromises that Truman reached with Congress in 1948 was that ERP allocations would be subject to congressional review every year. In April 1949 the second installment of European aid was to be considered by the newly seated 81st Congress. At this time, the term of the China Aid Bill of 1948 was also due to expire before all of the assistance had been delivered. This outcome suited the administration's plans perfectly. The State Department's logic was clearly laid out in a February memorandum, stating: "Further U.S. military aid to the Nationalists will probably be ineffectual and would eventually contribute to the Communist military strength and solidify the Chinese people in support of the Communists. Our political support of the remaining and largely impotent anti-Communist public figures in China may be equally unprofita-

[9] Truman, quoted by Blum, *Drawing the Line*, pp. 24–28. Also see *FRUS: 1949*, Vol. 9, pp. 610–615; and Cabinet Meeting, Jan. 19, 1949, Connelly Papers, HSTL.

[10] Blum, *Drawing the Line*, p. 23.

[11] "Monthly Survey of American Opinion on International Affairs" (hereafter "Monthly Survey"), Jan. 1949, Foster Papers, Office of Public Opinion Studies, Box 12, National Archives (hereafter cited as NA).

[12] Tucker, *Patterns in the Dust*, pp. 162–164; for a discussion of the Truman inaugural speech and its coverage in the media, see "American Press and Radio Reaction to the President's Inaugural Address," Feb. 4, 1949, Foster Papers, Box 46, NA.

4.1. Political Cartoon about Truman and the 81st Congress. "The Honeymoon Is Over." by Fred L. Packer, c. 1949, *Daily Mirror*. Harry S Truman Library, in James N. Giglio and Greg G. Thielen, *Truman in Cartoon and Caricature* (Ames: Iowa State University Press, 1984), p. 77. Reprinted with permission of the publisher.

ble."[13] Congress's reaction to the planned withdrawal was abrupt. On February 5, 1949, Vandenberg visited the White House to warn against a cessation of aid. Vandenberg realized that further aid to the KMT was at

[13] Under Secretary's Meeting, Feb. 28, 1949, Policy Planning Staff Records (hereafter cited as PPS Records), Box 13, File: China 1949, NA.

best a useless gesture on the part of the United States. But he argued that the administration and its bipartisan supporters in Congress should avoid "the charge that we are the ones who gave poor China the final push into disaster."[14] Vandenberg believed that the American people's ignorance of China would play against the administration—that they would not understand the difficulties for American policy on the mainland, but would focus on the abandonment of a World War II ally to the forces of communism. Given the high profile of the China Lobby and its media allies, Vandenberg was almost certainly correct that explicit abandonment of Chiang could be worked into a highly salient and dangerous political issue for the administration's continuing efforts abroad.

A few days after Truman's initial meeting with Vandenberg, fifty-one members of Congress sent a letter to Truman demanding a review of China policy. Increasingly aware of Acheson's desire for disengagement and sensing a hot political issue, these representatives demanded an independent review board for China policy.[15] In response, on February 24 Acheson called leaders from Capitol Hill to his office for a closed meeting during which he specified the difficulties and dangers of continuing to provide aid to Chiang. Acheson described his preferred strategy as one in which America would stand back and allow the "dust to settle" in the Chinese Civil War before adopting a more positive policy.[16]

Acheson's appeal to Congress did not work, and he walked out of their meeting in frustration.[17] On February 25, Senator Pat McCarran introduced a $1.5 billion China aid bill in the Senate. The real danger to the administration was not the McCarran bill per se, the expense of which would easily strip the China Lobby of its neoisolationist allies, but the effect of a new China debate on the upcoming legislation for European recovery. Vandenberg predicted that the publicity over the McCarran bill would ensure that there would be China amendments to the upcoming ERP legislation.[18] Public opinion trends provided reason for Vandenberg and Acheson to be concerned about gaining support for full ERP funding. In March 1949 majority support for current levels of spending was dangerously slim (51 percent).[19]

In order to find a compromise between total withdrawal from China

[14] Kepley, *Collapse of the Middle Way,* pp. 40–41.

[15] Blum, *Drawing the line,* p. 39.

[16] Westerfield, *Foreign Policy and Party Politics,* p. 347; Tucker, *Patterns in the Dust.*

[17] Blum, *Drawing the Line,* pp. 40–44.

[18] Kepley, *Collapse of the Middle Way,* p. 43; Westerfield, *Foreign Policy and Party Politics,* pp. 347–48. Fifty senators, half of them Democrats, signed the March 10 letter to Senator Tom Connally demanding a wider hearing for the McCarran bill.

[19] "Monthly Survey," Mar. 1949, Foster Papers, Box 12, NA. Consistent with the discussion in Chapter 2, support for ERP correlated strongly and positively with level of education.

and expensive intervention in a peripheral area, Vandenberg suggested extending the terms of the 1948 China Aid Bill to allow the United States to spend the unused portions of the initial aid package. Vandenberg argued that the "the only case for it [extension of aid] is not to put ourselves in the position where they can prove that we ran out on the Nationalist Government at the last minute before it had disintegrated."[20] Apparently accepting Vandenberg's argument, Acheson met in March with congressional representatives and reiterated Marshall's closed-door testimony of 1948, arguing that the government should aid China only so as not to appear to be abandoning Chiang. Although there was little the administration could do in China, it needed to keep up the appearance of helping Chiang.

NATO AND THE SCRAPPING OF PLANS FOR DETENTE

If in spring 1949 the administration had been finished with proposals relating to its grand strategy in Europe, then Acheson could have followed through on his preferred China policy. However, the push for Senate approval of NATO and MAP (the Military Assistance Program) would follow soon after ERP renewal, and Acheson would once again counsel the administration to delay any apparent appeasement of the Chinese Communists. The administration could not take for granted public and congressional support for NATO and MAP, particularly the latter, more expensive program. Americans liked the idea of helping Europe, but not the real costs and risks involved. For example, if the rather realistic term "promise to go to war" was included in questions about American commitment to the NATO pact, popular support for the treaty dropped to dangerously low levels (40 percent for and 48 percent against).[21] Similarly, when taxes were associated with military assistance, support dropped off significantly. Once again, support levels for costly policies were strongly correlated with levels of education.[22] To gain and maintain majority support, Truman would have to appeal to

---

[20] Vandenberg, quoted in Kepley, *Collapse of the Middle Way*, p. 43.

[21] "Popular Opinion on U.S. Relations with Brussels Powers," no date, but clearly from May 1949. This document was apparently misfiled as a 1948 document in Foster Papers, Nov. 15, 1948, Box 46, NA. The college-educated respondents were most likely to approve of the commitment.

[22] Ibid. Support dropped from 54 percent to 39 percent when increasing costs were associated with the program. Fifty percent of college graduates, 39 percent of high school graduates, and 33 percent of grade school graduates still approved of the program when increasing taxes were associated with them. This general trend held true in early 1950. See "Public Opinion on Military Aid to the Atlantic Treaty Countries," Feb. 27, 1950, Foster Papers, Box 46, File: European Security, 1950, NA.

those least likely to understand a subtle, strongpoint strategy and those least willing to make economic sacrifices for its implementation.

As tensions relating to the Berlin blockade lessened in spring 1949, the American public, feeling safer in the short term, once again turned inward. In April the number of people arguing that America had gone "too far" in international affairs increased to a two-year high (41 percent), with excessive spending being the most common complaint.[23] General support for military aid to Europe (not linked to taxes) dropped significantly from March through May 1949, with more respondents opposing aid than supporting it. Moreover, the opponents felt more strongly about their position than the supporters.[24] Consistent with this general trend, in April and May, State Department analysts also noted an increased popular and bipartisan push to cut ERP appropriations. As the immediate threat in Berlin receded, concerns about taxes, the domestic economy, and "spending too much abroad" rose to the fore.[25]

Moreover, after the lifting of the Berlin blockade in early May, the majority of the public grew confused about the general direction of American foreign policy. The State Department determined in July that only one-third of those expressing interest in foreign affairs believed they understood Truman's foreign policy program.[26] The public was particularly confused about U.S. China policy. In May the State Department noted that Congress and the public were calling for the secretary of state to clarify the nation's China policy.[27] Given flagging support for core European programs and the need to rally congressional and public support for ratification of NATO and approval of MAP, abandonment of

[23] "Popular Attitudes toward Foreign Policy," June 20, 1949, Foster Papers, Box 46, NA. Once again the least educated were most likely to argue that America had gone too far, a fact highlighted in the State Department report.

[24] According to one poll, support dropped from 60 percent to 48 percent. See Page and Shapiro, *The Rational Public*, p. 201. Another series of polls shows a drop from 55 percent in March to 43 percent (with 46 percent opposed) by May. See "Monthly Survey," May 1949, Foster Papers, Box 12, NA. For the relative strength of attitudes, see "Popular Opinion on NAP and MAP," May 11, 1949, Foster Papers, Box 46, NA. There was a slight recovery in May, but the country remained fairly evenly divided. See "Popular Attitudes toward Foreign Policy," June 20, 1949, Foster Papers, Box 46, NA.

[25] "Monthly Survey," April and May 1949, Foster Papers, Box 12, NA. Also see "Popular Opinion on NAP and MAP—April Survey Results," May 11, 1949, Foster Papers, Box 46, NA.

[26] As we would expect, those who confessed to confusion about the direction of American foreign policy were more strongly opposed to spending on international affairs. See "Popular Attitudes toward Foreign Policy," Aug. 11, 1949, Foster Papers, Box 46, NA. Compounding the problem was that only half of the respondents showed basic interest in foreign affairs

[27] Russell to Rusk, May 11, 1949, China: Internal Affairs, LM69, Reel 19, frame 945, NA.

Chiang and detente with the CCP would only have blurred the administration's message about grand strategy.

Despite public opinion setbacks in early 1949, in private the administration continued to explore options related to establishing economic and political contacts with the Chinese Communists. The general thrust of the administration's strategy was to hold out the possibility of trade and recognition as leverage with the CCP. On March 28, Washington received a communique from Ambassador Stuart in Nanjing advocating that he remain in that city after the advancing Communist forces seized it. On April 11, Acheson agreed that Stuart should stay. Under Secretary Butterworth also agreed with this policy but on April 22 recommended that Stuart return to America before deciding to stay in either Nanjing or Canton (Guangzhou) after Communist seizure. As Dean Rusk saw it, "The primary purpose in making this recommendation is to help meet the domestic political situation in this country."[28] Eventually it was decided that Stuart would not return to Washington because "to bring him home at this stage would make impossible his return to Communist-occupied Nanjing unless the U.S. Government was prepared to extend *de jure* recognition to a new government."[29] Given the domestic political situation referred to by Rusk, this option was obviously out of the question.

The Communists pushed south in April, crossing the Yangtze (Yangzi) and sealing the KMT's fate on the mainland. In that month, a leading Chinese Communist, Yao Yilin, contacted the U.S. consul general, O. Edmund Clubb, to advocate barter trade between northern China and American-occupied Japan. The CCP also responded positively to a request by the American ambassador, John Leighton Stuart, to set up a meeting between Stuart and party leaders. To send out these feelers, Stuart dispatched his personal secretary, Philip Fugh, and apparently also contacted Chen Mingshu, a fellow traveler of the Communists from the KMT Revolutionary Committee.[30] Zhou Enlai sent his assistant, Huang Hua, to approach Ambassador Stuart's office in May.[31] On May 13, Stuart and Huang met. Huang accommodated Stuart somewhat by apologizing for an incident in April in which Communist soldiers had entered

[28] *FRUS: 1949*, Vol. 8, pp. 676, 682–683; Blum, *Drawing the Line*, pp. 52–53.

[29] Status of Our Ambassador at Nanking, Apr. 14, 1949, Office of Chinese Affairs, Film C0012, Reel 13, frame 466, NA.

[30] Chen, "The Myth of America's Lost Chance."

[31] Huang, "My Contacts with John Leighton Stuart," pp. 47–56. According to American documents, Huang was "careful to avoid use of [Stuart's] official title [because] he did not recognize me as Ambassador nor any other Ambassadors in Nanking because we were accredited to the KMT Government." Nanking to Secretary of State, May 11, 1949, China: Internal Affairs, LM69, Reel 19, frame 936, NA.

Stuart's residence while the ambassador was sleeping. But Huang complained bitterly about continuing U.S. assistance to the KMT. As is discussed in more detail in the next chapter, it is clear that, from the CCP perspective, America's continuing relationship with and support for the KMT was the main hindrance to CCP-U.S. detente. But despite America's history of support for CCP enemies, Huang held out the possibility of improved contacts, arguing that the CCP wanted relations with the outside world. According to American documents, Huang "expressed much interest in recognition of Communist China by USA on terms of equality and mutual benefit." Stuart, in turn, said that U.S. recognition of a Communist regime would depend on its behavior.[32]

In June, John Cabot in Shanghai reported that the mayor of Shanghai and China's future foreign minister, Chen Yi, had stated that the CCP might have to turn to the United States and Britain for economic assistance.[33] The relatively cautious Clubb advocated a response in line with NSC 41: the United States and the West should trade with China but hold off on direct aid until the Communists showed a more pro-Western stand.[34] Clubb's advice was consistent with the American experience in Yugoslavia. Carrots (such as Marshall Plan aid) were held out to Tito as an incentive to comply with Western norms. Aid was not simply given to him unconditionally to buy his friendship. Truman apparently approved this course of action, counseling that American representatives should not "indicate any softening toward the Communists" but judge them by their actions.[35]

Also in June, Huang renewed his appeal to Ambassador Stuart in Nanjing for improved relations. He insisted that "as soon as normal diplomatic relations [were] established" various bilateral sore points could be "easily cleared up," including the continuing captivity of Consul Angus Ward and his staff in Mukden.[36] He also proposed a meeting between Stuart, Mao, and Zhou Enlai in Beiping (renamed Beijing when the CCP founded the PRC on October 1, 1949). On June 28, Huang Hua visited Stuart in Nanjing again in order to finalize a date and meeting place for Stuart's trip to Beiping. The next day, Stuart cabled Washington for instructions, suggesting that he could travel to Beiping ostensibly to

[32] Nanking to Secretary of State, May 14, 1949, China: Internal Affairs, LM69, Reel 19, frames 992–994, NA.

[33] Blum, *Drawing the Line*, p. 58; Tucker, *Patterns in the Dust*, p. 48.

[34] See Telegram from Clubb to Acheson, June 2, 1949, President's Secretary's Files, File: Foreign Affairs, China 1949, Box 173, HSTL.

[35] "Meeting with the President," June 16, 1949, PPS Records, Box 13, File: China 1949, NA.

[36] Nanking to Secretary of State, June 9, 1949, China: Internal Affairs, LM69, Reel 19, NA.

visit Yenching (Yanjing) University (now Beijing University), where previously he had been president. Stuart's cable took a solidly positive tone toward the option of visiting Mao and Zhou, though he also expressed some reservations:

> [The trip] would enable me to carry to Washington most authoritative information regarding CCP intentions. Such trip would be step toward better mutual understanding and should strengthen more liberal anti-Soviet elements in the CCP. It would prove unique opportunity for American official to talk to top Chinese Communists in informal manner which might not again present itself. It would be imaginative, adventurous indication of US open-minded attitude toward changing political trends in China and would probably have beneficial effect on future Sino-American relations. . . . On negative side, trip to Peiping [Beiping] before my return to US on consultation would undoubtedly start rumors and speculations in China and might conceivably embarrass Department because of American criticism.[37]

Stuart continued that this negative effect on American domestic politics might be ameliorated by his traveling to the temporary KMT capital in Canton as well. But he pointed out that this would likely confuse the CCP and destroy the purpose of his Beiping trip.[38]

Officials in Washington had every reason to believe that Huang Hua's overtures were genuine. In May and early June 1949 a flurry of telegrams arrived in Acheson's office from American officials in China speculating that: Zhou Enlai was powerful in the CCP and that he was pushing Mao in a nationalist and potentially Titoist direction; "Virulent anti-Americanism" in CCP propaganda was a "natural" reaction to U.S. support for KMT; and tensions between the CCP and Soviet Union were already present.[39] As Stuart put it on June 15, while the CCP was making every effort to impress the Soviets that it was a genuine communist movement, "Communist activities in China are far from [a] Soviet Punch and Judy show."[40]

---

[37] Stuart to Acheson, received June 30, 1949, in *FRUS: 1949*, Vol. 8, pp. 766–767. After discussing his concerns about domestic politics, Stuart listed other concerns, including the added prestige his trip might lend the CCP. As is shown below, officials in Washington focused on the domestic politics issue.

[38] Ibid.

[39] See, for example, Nanking to Secretary of State, May 21, 1949, and Shanghai to Secretary of State, June 1, 1949, 89300B, China: Internal Affairs, LM69, Reel 19. As the next chapter points out, some of the premises of these analyses were false, particularly the one about Huang Hua working for an independently powerful pro-American faction in the CCP under the leadership of Zhou Enlai. Still, the important issue is that Washington saw a real opportunity to improve relations with the CCP in mid-1949.

[40] Nanking to Secretary of State, June 15, 1949, China: Internal Affairs, LM69, Reel 19, frame 1134, NA.

Judging from Acheson's earlier stated position on contacts with the Communists, approval of the Stuart trip to Beiping seemed assured. After all, Stuart's offices had reached out to the CCP in the first place by dispatching Fugh and contacting Chen Mingshu. Moreover, in April, Acheson seemed to bemoan the fact that the CCP had provided little opportunity to contact high-level Chinese Communist officials.[41] But domestic factors would eventually argue against accepting detente with the Chinese Communists. In Washington, Far Eastern Affairs and PPS officials Butterworth and Davies considered Stuart's telegram carefully. Their primary concern was with the domestic political reaction in the United States. Davies cabled Kennan:

> What worries Walt [Butterworth] most is the domestic reaction in this country to such a move. And that reaction could be violent. . . . Walt's position is that *the ultimate decision turns on an estimate of American domestic reaction* and that is a factor which he is not competent to judge. It must be weighed by the Secretary and a decision made by him.[42]

On July 1, Acheson cabled Nanjing and ordered Stuart not to visit Beiping. The short telegram merely cited Stuart's own negative reasons in his original telegram; in other words, domestic political support for the State Department was too important to sacrifice for the goal of detente with the Chinese Communists.[43]

Why were Truman, Stuart, Acheson, Butterworth, and Davies all so worried about the domestic political implications of Stuart's visit to Beiping? One month after the initial Stuart-Huang meetings, rumors were circulating in China and in the Japanese and European press that Stuart was preparing to recognize the Chinese Communists and that a trip to Washington was planned to convince leaders there of the prudence of such a strategy.[44] In the Congress and the American media, the China issue was heating up, especially following the administration's signing on to the NATO treaty in April.[45]

In June the Republicans stepped up their harping on the issue of appeasement of Chinese Communism. Late in the month, twenty-one senators sent a letter to Acheson demanding that the United States not recog-

---

[41] "Memorandum for Mr. Sidney W. Souers," Apr. 4, 1949, in *Documents of the National Security Council*, Film A 438.1, Supplement 1.

[42] Davies to Kennan, June 30, 1949, *FRUS: 1949*, Vol. 8, pp. 768–769 (emphasis added).

[43] Ibid., p. 769.

[44] Telegram from Ambassador Bruce in Paris to Acheson, June 16, 1949, President's Secretary's Files, File: Foreign Affairs, China 1949, Box 173, HSTL.

[45] For the rise of congressional and media attacks, see "Recent Opinion regarding the Effect of the 'Loss' of China on U.S. Foreign Policy," Apr. 22, 1949, Foster Papers, Box 33, File: China 1949–52, NA.

nize the Chinese Communists. Even Arthur Vandenberg could not resist attacking the administration on its China policy.[46] As a June 28 memo from Kennan to Acheson pointed out:

> The magnitude and strength of the Congressional offensive against the Executive's Far Eastern policy requires from us more than defensive expedients. The Staff feels that the Executive should aggressively assume the offensive in what is rapidly developing into a major issue between it and the Legislature. . . . In November 1948, the Staff strongly recommended (PPS 45) to Secretary Marshall that we place our cards on the table because the need to clear up the confusion in the mind of the American public was greater than the need to protect a moribund and vestigial foreign government. . . . [The Cabinet and the President] did not approve our proposal.[47]

Once again, the less politically insulated Acheson rejected this approach, choosing instead in mid-July to meet quietly with Republican and Democratic congressional leaders to search for a bipartisan agreement on American policy toward Asia.[48]

The administration had received clear warning that rapprochement in China would endanger other programs. Hours before Acheson sent the telegram to Stuart rejecting direct contacts with the CCP, he was hounded on Capitol Hill for requesting a smallish $150 million aid package for South Korea. The *New York Times* summed up the controversy as follows: "Heavy Republican opposition [to Korean aid] was gathering in the House, mainly on the contention that the administration had declined to take a strong hand against the Communists in China and should not now seek aid for Korea alone."[49] The message to the administration was clear. If communism were not actively opposed in China, the administration could not be sure of congressional support for fighting it elsewhere.[50]

While congressional and party politics were important, they reflected deeper trends in public opinion. Consul John Cabot recalled that American public opinion had been the primary reason for scrapping the Stuart

[46] On June 24 he uncharacteristically distanced himself from the administration, stating: "I disassociate myself, as I have publicly done on previous occasions, from the China policy which we pursued." Blum, *Drawing the Line*, p. 79.

[47] Kennan to Acheson, June 28, 1949, PPS Records, Box 13, File: China 1949, NA.

[48] "U.S. Policy and Action in Asia," July 18, 1949, Executive Secretariat Records, Secretary's Files, 1949–51, Box 8, Lot 53D444, NA.

[49] *New York Times*, July 2, 1949, p. 1.

[50] A State Department document from early July demonstrates the links between the need to explain China policy, problems in passing the Korean aid bill, and House opposition to Truman's foreign policy. See "White House Help on Korea Aid Bill," July 7, 1949, Executive Secretariat Records (Acheson), Secretary's Memos, 1949–51, Box 8, Lot 53D444, NA.

mission.[51] Poll data support Cabot's account, showing that in mid-June 1949 the public was relatively aware of events in China (75 percent claimed knowledge), and that those with an opinion opposed "sending an ambassador and having dealings" with a CCP government by a ratio of 2:1.[52] Another poll indicated that, by a 4:3 ratio, Americans supported a cessation of trade with China if it were completely conquered by Communists.[53]

The conclusions that State Department public opinion analysts reached about popular opposition to reconciliation with the Chinese Communists are entirely consistent with the approach presented here. A document from July 1949 reads: "These results apparently reflect the widespread distrust of dealing with any Communist regime—rather than considered opinion about our relations with China."[54] Since attitudes toward Communist regimes were relatively undifferentiated in the American public, the State Department had reason to believe that a softer policy toward the CCP would be dangerous to the administration's anticommunist reputation and to the domestic legitimacy of the administration's grand strategy, which so depended on maintaining that reputation.

The public did not want Truman to offer olive branches to the Chinese Communists, but it was not pushing for new pro-Chiang efforts either. As tensions over Berlin abated, support for assistance to Chiang dropped off in lockstep with support for military assistance to Europe. This change further suggests a general and simple view about the general threat of communism among the majority of American citizens. In late 1948, during the Berlin blockade, 60 percent of Americans wanted to continue or increase military aid to Chiang (even higher than the figure for assistance to Britain, France, and the Benelux countries). But in a June 1949 poll only 40 percent of the public approved of military aid to the KMT, while 48 percent disapproved.[55] These were similar to the figures cited above for military aid to Europe in spring 1949. Opposition to further assistance to Chiang and support for recognition of the Chinese

[51] John M. Cabot, July 18, 1973, Oral History, pp. 82–84, HSTL. Cabot was consul general in Shanghai in 1948–49.

[52] *Gallup Poll*, July 11, 1949 (the poll was conducted in mid-June), p. 831. While all groups opposed recognition, the ratio of approval to opposition was highest among those with a college education and lowest among those with only a grade school education.

[53] "Popular Opinion on U.S. Policy toward China," July 7, 1949, Foster Papers, Box 33, NA.

[54] Ibid.

[55] For public opinion on military aid to Chiang, see "Popular Attitudes toward U.S. Aid to China," June 28, 1949, Foster Papers, Box 33, NA; for the Brussels Pact countries, see "Popular Opinion on NAP and MAP," May 11, 1949, Foster Papers, Box 46, NA.

Communists were both positively correlated with education levels.[56] In other words, just as the more highly educated and wealthier citizens were most likely to take a long-term view about European security and accept economic sacrifices for future European stability, they were also most likely to comprehend and accept the logic of strongpoint defense and the possibility of creating Chinese Titoism over the long run.

Mao Leans to the Soviet Side

While Acheson considered and rejected the Stuart trip, Mao made his famous "lean to one side" speech in Beiping, blasting the United States and praising the Soviets.[57] In the West it has been argued that the lean-to-one-side policy extinguished any real hope for detente between the CCP and Washington for many years thereafter.[58] However, Chinese historians have countered that ten days after the speech, Mao sent Chen Mingshu to explain Mao's thinking to American officials in Nanjing. Chen's mission was to correct any misconceptions held by the Americans that the speech precluded improved relations with Washington. The meeting is cited as evidence that the United States, not Mao, was responsible for the lack of high-level contacts between the two sides in 1949. Some analysts had not found documentary evidence of the meeting in the United States, let alone proof that Mao's message was considered sincere by American officials. Therefore, the Chinese account has been called into question.[59]

Documentary evidence of the Chen-Stuart meetings does exist in the American archives. On or about July 12, 1949, Chen Mingshu visited Stuart and passed to him various memoranda relating to his discussions over the previous few days with top CCP officials, including Mao. With the important exception of a rather hostile and ideological message from Zhou Enlai, the tone of the memoranda was quite positive about the prospects of improved Sino-American relations. Chen told Stuart that "in politics, severity is necessary" and that Mao's lean-to-one-side speech was designed "for his own Party." Chen reported that CCP leaders em-

---

[56] This holds when we observe those respondents who were both aware of the Chinese Civil War and held an opinion about American policy toward China. See Polls 4 and 5 in Appendix A in this volume. Very similar results can be found in a November poll. See "U.S. Attitudes on Recognition," Nov. 30, 1949, Foster Papers, Box 33, NA.

[57] There is no evidence that Mao's speech figured into Acheson's decision. The telegram was probably drafted before the secretary knew of the speech. Otherwise it is difficult to explain why it was not mentioned in the return telegram.

[58] See, for example, Goncharov, Lewis, and Xue, *Uncertain Partners*, p. 54.

[59] For discussion and critique of the Chinese works along these lines, see ibid., pp. 54 and 309, n.77. For perhaps the only Western documentary analysis of the Chen-Stuart meetings, see Blum, *Drawing the Line*, pp. 84–85.

phasized the desirability of formal diplomatic relations between the United States and a Chinese Communist regime. Mao allegedly asked Chen to remind Stuart of a June 20 speech in which Mao had proclaimed that the CCP sought relations with all countries "on the basis of independence and sovereignty."[60]

In the last memorandum Zhou berated the ambassador for attempting economic coercion against China. He criticized the American role in China since the Marshall mission and praised the Soviet Union. Though generally negative from the American perspective, the memorandum does distinguish between good and bad periods in Sino-American relations and between friendly Americans, such as General Joseph Stilwell, and the "imperialists," like General Wedemeyer. Despite the abrasive general tone of the letter, Zhou reserved final judgment on Stuart. He praised Stuart for staying in China during World War II but criticized him harshly for his more recent activities. Zhou concluded by saying that Stuart would be judged by his future actions and that, if he wanted to visit Beiping in a private capacity, he might still be able to meet with a CCP leader.[61]

The Chen-Stuart meeting did nothing to restore Stuart's hope for improved relations with the CCP. But it appears that Washington analysts viewed the memoranda in a more positive light than Stuart, perhaps because they had a smaller stake in the Zhou message, which blasted the ambassador personally. Not privileging Zhou's negative comments, Washington analysts viewed the much more positive overall packet of memoranda as "indicative of the thinking of the Chinese Communists," including Mao.[62]

In any case, the lean-to-one-side speech did not destroy hope among American officials for improved relations with China, even if Chinese Titoism may have seemed a long way off. Some, like John Cabot in Shanghai, continued to discuss factions in the CCP, the regrettable effects that the refusal to go to Beiping had on pro-American forces in the CCP, and the need to avoid a belligerent attitude toward Communist-held areas in the future. Others, like the American ambassador to the Soviet Union, Alan Kirk, were exceedingly pessimistic about the prospects for Sino-American friendship or a Sino-Soviet split, but still saw practical benefits flowing from relations with the CCP and abandonment of the

---

[60] *FRUS: 1949*, Vol. 8, pp. 777–779.

[61] Ibid.

[62] For Stuart's July 13 reaction to the Chen visit, see Blum, *Drawing the Line*, pp. 84–85; and *FRUS: 1949*, Vol. 8, pp. 782–783. For the full cover sheet attached to the memoranda in Washington but not found in the *FRUS* series, see Sprouse to Jessup, Aug. 25, 1949, 893.00, China: Internal Affairs, LM69, Reel 17, frame 100, NA.

KMT.[63] Despite these analyses, the American leaders chose not to revisit the issue of high-level talks in Beiping.

THE MILITARY ASSISTANCE PROGRAM (MAP) AND THE CHINA DEBATE

After the Senate ratified the NATO treaty in July, the more expensive policies of military aid for Europe and Marshall Plan extensions were raised on the Hill. The foreign policy elite had come to a consensus as early as 1948 that for NATO to have teeth the United States would need to send military supplies to the future allies, particularly France.[64] Because all phases of the grand strategy were domestically controversial, MAP had to be phased in after the congressional approval of other key policies, such as renewal of the Marshall Plan and ratification of NATO.[65] On the same day that he signed the final NATO treaty into law (July 25), Truman requested $1.4 billion for MAP (an amount already reduced from the administration's preferred amount of $1.9 billion).

In many ways the MAP debate was a microcosm of the entire foreign policy process in the late 1940s. As Dean Acheson recalled:

> The heat generated by the Military Assistance Program . . . came from sub-
> terranean fires far deeper than any issues contained in the legislation itself—
> desire for economy and a balanced budget at a low level, an unwillingness to
> face and accept the responsibilities of power, the China bloc's belief that our
> interest and funds were excessively concentrated in Europe, and perhaps
> most of all, bitter resentment over the President's wholly unexpected victory
> in 1948.[66]

The proposed aid bill was controversial both because it was expensive and because large military outlays to allies in peacetime had no precedent

[63] See Blum, *Drawing the Line*, pp. 83–86. John Cabot in Shanghai described the decision not to send Stuart to Beiping as "disastrous," believing a Sino-Soviet split still to be likely. He warned, "[If] Communist moderation and tentative pro-Western moves are met by rebuffs, further pressures, trade limitations and vitriolic publicity . . . . then communists are likely to reason that modus vivendi with the West is impossible, and advocates of the course have likely to keep silent or be driven from power." For Kirk's August 26 analysis, see *FRUS: 1949*, Vol. 9, pp. 67–68. He called for recognition and "dignified aloofness."

[64] While there was dispute within the State Department and between State and the JCS as to how much emphasis should be placed on economic aid, military aid, and home defense, almost all top officials agreed that all three were valid pursuits. Gaddis, *The Long Peace*, pp. 61–67; and Kaplan, *A Community of Interests*, chaps. 2–3.

[65] Kaplan, *A Community of Interests*, pp. 42–43; Blum, *Drawing the Line*, pp. 126–127. In 1948 the administration omitted military assistance in omnibus aid bills in order to guarantee support for Marshall Plan allocations.

[66] Acheson, *Present at the Creation*, p. 307.

4.2. Political Cartoon about NATO and the Military Assistance Program. "What's The Hurry? We've Just Planted This Seed!" Edward Kuekes, 1949, *Plain Dealer* (Cleveland). Harry S Truman Library, in James N. Giglio and Greg G. Thielen, *Truman in Cartoon and Caricature* (Ames: Iowa State University Press, 1984), p. 77. Reprinted with permission of the publisher.

in American diplomatic history. Finally, as was noted above, the public had become less willing to support foreign aid after the Berlin blockade ended peacefully.[67]

The reaction to the MAP proposal on the Hill was severe. The Senate was upset.[68] Senator Vandenberg complained that the MAP program

[67] An August 1949 poll showed the public still divided on MAP. See "Monthly Survey," Aug. 1949, Foster Papers, Box 12, NA.

[68] Kaplan, *A Community of Interests,* pp. 43–49.

would make Truman "the number one warlord of the earth."[69] Under his leadership, the Senate voted to cut the program by a significant, but not earthshaking, $90 million. As before, Vandenberg suggested that the administration make some effort to fight communism in Asia, although he did not support the expenditure of significant resources for that purpose.[70] If the Senate was upset about foreign assistance, the more fiscally conservative House was livid. In August it voted to cut the appropriations in half.[71] The alliance that pushed the cut through on the floor was classically Asialationist: a hybrid mix of fiscal conservatives and supporters of China aid. The immediate reaction of bipartisan internationalists, including John Foster Dulles and Senator Tom Connally, was to suggest that money for China be added to a new version of the bill in the Senate.[72]

Senator William Knowland took the lead for the China Lobby, managing to secure an additional $75 million in military assistance for Chiang and for Asia more generally. Knowland used classic Asialationist tactics—criticizing European aid as unnecessary and wasteful, pointing to the severe paucity of assistance for Asia (only 2 percent of the original bill was for the Pacific), and tapping into the administration's own mobilizational rhetoric for Europe to underline its failure to defend all free peoples from communism. By threatening to publicize a minority report critical of the Asian phase of the bill, Knowland gained the compliance of nervous supporters of European aid. The China debate became a major point of contention in the Senate, receiving more attention than any other single issue in the program. This led the chair of the hearings, Senator Connally, to plead to his colleagues: "This bill relates to something besides China, you know. I do not think we should spend all our time on China."[73]

It took two months of debate and the announcement of a Soviet atomic explosion to get the Senate's $1.314 billion program approved in late September. The temporary crisis atmosphere caused by the Soviet explosion guaranteed passage of the bill and inspired Acheson's philosophical

[69] Vandenberg, ed., *The Private Papers of Senator Vandenberg*, p. 504.

[70] Kepley, *Collapse of the Middle Way*, p. 48.

[71] Acheson, *Present at the Creation*, pp. 309–313; and Doenecke, *Not to the Swift*, pp. 155–156.

[72] Blum, *Drawing the Line*, pp. 132–142.

[73] *Military Assistance Program: 1949*, Joint Hearings Held in Executive Session before the Committee on Foreign Relations and the Committee on Armed Services, 81 Cong., 1st sess. (hereafter cited as *MAP: 1949*). For reference to Europe, see pp. 116–118, 366. Pointing to the great disparities between Europe and Asia in the Senate bill Knowland said: "I'd like to know before we get all our eggs in the European basket what the Joint Chiefs propose to do or think should be done in the Pacific Area." He added: "[The Asian countries] are certainly menaced by the same Communist force which has been temporarily blocked in Europe." On the threat of a minority report, see p. 611; for the Connally quote, see p. 208.

statement: "An ill wind blows some good."[74] It also, however, meant that the administration would have to continue to support Chiang, however anemically, as Mao's forces prepared to drive all remaining KMT forces out of mainland China and declare the foundation of the People's Republic.

The August 1949 White Paper: Creating More Heat Than Light[75]

In order to prepare the American public and Congress for the fall of the Nationalists and the rise of the Chinese Communists, in February 1949 Truman and Acheson commissioned John Melby to draft a White Paper on the Chinese Civil War. Melby said that his orders from Truman were to "write the record and write it straight, no matter who is hurt; tell the truth."[76]

Truman obviously understood the damage that the domestic controversy over China policy was doing to the implementation of his preferred strategy. In June 1949 he viewed the White Paper's issuance as "one of our most important actions for some time to come."[77] Melby recalled: "We all believed this would call off the dogs, but of course it did nothing of the kind."[78] The paper, finally released in August, was an unmitigated disaster. The letter of transmittal that accompanied it was a political document, including a scathing attack on the Chinese Communists as tools of Moscow, a position that Melby recalls was not held by Acheson, who signed the ill-fated letter.[79] This diversion of attention muted the document's main points: that Chiang had failed because of his own corruption and that the CCP had come to power by exploiting nationalism and KMT ineptitude.

The White Paper received negative marks in the public, the press, and Congress. Immediately after its release, a poll showed that those in the public who had already heard of the report disapproved of its content by

[74] For a discussion of the Soviet explosion and its impact on the MAP debate, see Doenecke, *Not to the Swift*, p. 156.

[75] This apt phrase is borrowed from Gaddis, *Strategies of Containment*, pp. 102–103.

[76] Melby, Oral History, p. 168, HSTL.

[77] "Meeting with the President," June 13, 1949, RG59, Executive Secretariat Records, Secretary's Memos, 1949–51, Box 8, Lot 53D444, NA.

[78] Melby, Oral History, p. 168, HSTL.

[79] Melby recalls: "He [Acheson] didn't believe a word of that Letter of Transmittal. The Letter of Transmittal was one of those products of a committee . . . . Still, the letter was all anybody ever read, and Acheson had signed it thinking that it didn't make any difference. . . . That was his mistake, because it was what people latched on to." Ibid., pp. 167–168, HSTL. Allen Whiting reported to me that Philip Jessup claimed authorship of the letter of transmittal in a conversation he had with Whiting.

a margin of 2 to 1.[80] The press latched on to the White Paper's exposure of the administration's failure to oppose communism in Asia as it had in Europe. In the *New York Times,* Arthur Krock wrote: "The United States failed after World War II to follow the two-front wartime policy by which, though giving precedence to the reconquest of Europe, it fought an effective war in the Pacific at the same time. Military concentration on Europe was not permitted to preclude offensive tactics in the Pacific, but concentration on the Marshall Plan was permitted to preclude coming to grips with the post-war situation in China."[81] Of course, during World War II the resources available to Roosevelt far outstripped those available to Truman in the late 1940s.

THE DEVELOPMENT AND ABANDONMENT OF THE RECOGNITION STRATEGY

Under congressional, media, and popular pressure, in 1949 and 1950 Acheson continually rejected any notion that he was preparing to recognize the Chinese Communists, but the recollection of his major advisers and State Department documents clearly refute this claim. Melby recalls:

> Well, I think that when the final take-over took place—and Dean Acheson by that time was Secretary of State—when he was asked what American policy during the new regime [would be], he said, "Let's wait and see what happens when the dust has settled." But he was prepared at that time, as were a lot of other people, including some of our Allies, the British primarily, to recognize [the new regime]. This has been denied pretty consistently these days, but the fact is that at that time we were prepared to recognize.[82]

The State Department spent a good deal of time in 1949 considering the issue of recognition, as is demonstrated by various requests to the embassy in Moscow to analyze the benefits of recognition of the Soviet Union in 1933.[83] Recognition was viewed as desirable for a variety of reasons, including information gathering and the promotion of trade between occupied Japan and northern China. Moreover, other regional ac-

---

[80] *Gallup Poll,* Sept. 19, 1949. The interviews were done in mid-August. Thirty-six percent had heard or read something about the White Paper, and 64 percent had not. Of those who had read the document, 53 percent disapproved and 26 percent approved of its content.

[81] Krock, "Some Omissions from the White Paper," *New York Times,* Aug. 12, 1949, in Elsey Papers, Box 59, File: Foreign Relations—China, HSTL.

[82] Melby, Oral History, p. 164, HSTL.

[83] Tucker, *Patterns in the Dust,* pp. 177–178; *FRUS: 1949,* Vol. 9, pp. 66–68, 106–108. Ambassador Kirk encouraged formal recognition followed by "aloofness." He did not believe the United States could gain bargaining leverage by withholding recognition.

tors, including India, encouraged the United States to deal realistically with the Chinese Communists because, in much of Asia, the CCP was viewed primarily as a nationalist movement.[84]

In view of these factors, in an important September telegram embassy officials in China agreed that the United States should recognize the CCP, stating that there was little to gain by refusing to do so. As a matter of protocol, they did however want to wait for the CCP to approach the Americans to negotiate recognition.[85] Given the CCP's refusal to recognize the authority of the consulates and the continued detention of Ward and his staff, they believed that the United States could only await new Chinese approaches.[86] The Policy Planning Staff considered the embassy position to be the proper basis of American policy. Kennan and others believed that recognition should follow some CCP assurances of better treatment of American personnel. Dean Rusk added that recognition should at least await the control by the CCP of "substantially all of China."[87] But American officials knew the limits of holding off on recognition as a negotiating strategy. In order to use the prospect of recognition as a bargaining chip, it was important for the United States to establish agreement among its allies not to recognize the new regime hastily.[88] If other major Western powers recognized the Chinese Communists before the United States, the United States would lose bargaining power and trade opportunities with the mainland. Trade was considered important for both economic and strategic reasons. In early 1949, NSC 41 stated that increased Sino-American trade was considered a method of drawing the CCP away from Moscow. Moreover, trade with China

[84] For example, see reports about Indian attitudes in *FRUS: 1949*, Vol. 9, pp. 70–71.

[85] Jones (in Nanking) to Acheson, Sept. 1949, in ibid., pp. 71–72.

[86] In September, the embassy argued that "conciliatory gestures now of economic or diplomatic nature would not only be opposed by large portion of the American public but would simply be interpreted by CCP as bearing out Communist theory of inner weakness of USA." Telegram 1994, Jones to Acheson, Sept. 3, 1949, *FRUS: 1949*, Vol. 8, pp. 519–521. While encouraging recognition and negotiations if the CCP approached the United States, Nanking also stated, "At present it is difficult to see any basis for establishment of normal diplomatic relations between U.S. and Communist China." Jones (in Nanking) to Acheson, Sept. 4, 1949, *FRUS: 1949*, Vol. 9, pp. 71–72.

[87] See Kennan's statements in support of Telegram 1994 in "Discussion of Far Eastern Affairs in Preparation for Conversation with Mr. Bevin," Sept. 16, 1949, *FRUS: 1949*, Vol. 7, pp. 1204–1208.

[88] See Kirk to Acheson, *FRUS: 1949*, Vol. 9, pp. 67–68, 106–108; and Butterworth's negotiations with British representatives in September in Memorandum of Conversation, Sept. 9, 1949, and "Attitudes of Various Friendly Nations toward Recognition of a Chinese Communist Regime," Sept. 16, 1949, Office of Chinese Affairs, Film C0012, Reel 14, frames 421–430, NA.

would help the recovery of Japan, a strongpoint in the American grand strategy.[89]

From the various American documents on China policy written in the fall of 1949, one can distill four basic principles regarding recognition of the Chinese Communist regime: (1) the Communist regime should first control the vast majority of Chinese territory; (2) the CCP should approach the United States for recognition; (3) the CCP should demonstrate more civility toward American representatives and nationals in China (for example, by releasing Ward and his staff); and (4) the United States should withhold recognition for bargaining purposes, but only as long as it could dissuade Western allies from recognizing the Communists. As we will see below, by December 1949 the Chinese Communists controlled the majority of China, had approached the United States for recognition, and had released Angus Ward and his staff. Meanwhile America's closest ally, Great Britain, was preparing to break with Washington's line and recognize the CCP government, which it did on January 6, 1950.

Despite these changes, there still remained the problem of public and congressional opinion mentioned in the telegrams and memoranda in Washington. Acheson referred to this problem in September, stating that "there would be some difficulty in applying the policy set forth . . . in view of the attitude of the US public opinion and the Congress."[90] A November poll demonstrates that Acheson was correct about domestic opinion. As in June, opponents to recognition still outnumbered supporters two to one. Within the least-educated groups, the ones the administration would have the hardest time convincing through a strongpoint logic, the ratio was 3:1.[91] While no one in the administration seemed to believe that recognition equaled approval of the regime, officials realized that the public would likely equate the two. In order to counter that public view, Ambassador-at-Large Philip Jessup suggested a public campaign to push the traditional American Open Door or noninterference policy in China.[92] But in the hotly anticommunist atmosphere

[89] For the discussion of the positive political effects of Sino-Japanese trade, see *FRUS: 1949*, Vol. 9, p. 831. For their part, the Japanese hoped and expected that the United States would recognize the CCP early. See Tucker, *Patterns in the Dust*, p. 37. For a more general discussion of the benefits of trade, see Under Secretary's Meeting, Feb. 28, 1949, PPS Records, Box 13, File: China 1949, NA; and "Discussion of Far Eastern Affairs in Preparation for Conversation with Mr. Bevin," Sept. 16, 1949, *FRUS: 1949*, Vol. 7, pp. 1204–1208.

[90] "Discussion of Far Eastern Affairs in Preparation for Conversation with Mr. Bevin," Sept. 16, 1949, *FRUS: 1949*, Vol. 7, pp. 1204–1208.

[91] See Poll 6 in Appendix A.

[92] "Discussion of Far Eastern Affairs in Preparation for Conversation with Mr. Bevin." Sept. 16, 1949, *FRUS: 1949*, Vol. 7, pp. 1204–1208.

of postwar America, such a public education strategy would be of dubious value and, at best, slow in gaining results.

After "Liberation": China Stands Up and America Lies Low

On October 1, 1949, Mao Zedong announced the founding of the People's Republic of China in Beijing (renamed as the new PRC capital). In late September, Zhou Enlai had sent an emissary to the American consul general to explain the CCP's policy toward establishment of relations with all nations. Clubb was told that Mao was a pragmatist, not a radical, and was therefore flexible about relations with the West. On October 1, Clubb received a formal request for the establishment of diplomatic relations with the new country. As is discussed in Chapter 5, Mao would have accepted recognition and begun a dialogue on the establishment of diplomatic relations with any country that abandoned Chiang Kai-shek, treated Beijing as the sole legitimate government of China, and treated China "fairly." The CCP had clearly met one of the main criteria of the September telegram. Rather than acting on this request, as its own officials had earlier suggested, the State Department quickly released a statement reaffirming its recognition of the Nationalists and assuring Congress that it would be consulted before any change in recognition policy took place. In the same vein, Acheson took a tough line on Chinese communism in testimony to the Senate, arguing that the CCP was a "tool of Russian imperialism."[93]

On October 13, 1949, the State Department held a conference of influential consultants, including George Marshall, for the purpose of analyzing China policy. The meeting had been planned even before the formal founding of the PRC, and the results were predictable (in fact, they were predicted by Kennan).[94] The consultants clearly preferred cutting ties with the Nationalists and establishing relations with the CCP. The conference report reads:

> It was the majority view that a stabilization of relationships through quick
> recognition would be desirable from the standpoint of commercial consider-

[93] See Yao, *Cong Yalu Jiang Dao Banmendian*, p. 6; and Blum, *Drawing the Line*, pp. 144–156.

[94] In a September 20 memo about the planned conference, Kennan wrote: "I would suggest that pro-nationalist elements may claim that the list of invitees is stacked somewhat in the Department's favor. It might be advisable to invite a few people at least who are known to be hostile to the Department on the subject of China—those whose hostility is mixed with some degree of intelligence if possible." Kennan to Russell, PPS Records, Box 13, File: China 1949, NA.

ations, the ideological effect on the Chinese people, and to put the political orientation of the Chinese leadership toward the Soviet Union under a strain. This view was predicated on the assumption that the United States could secure from the Communist regime at least a working agreement on the treatment of nationals.[95]

While the approval of this course was nearly unanimous, perhaps most important was the fact that General Marshall concurred.[96] Truman and Acheson had the greatest respect for his opinion, particularly on China policy. But ten days earlier Truman had already rejected the notion of early recognition, pointing out that the United States did not recognize the Soviet Union for more than a decade after that nation was founded.[97]

Truman's actions were consistent with State Department domestic opinion analysis, which showed that, even among media commentators who accepted the inevitability of American recognition of the Chinese Communists, the majority were against "hasty recognition."[98] The Truman administration was also aware of the warnings in Congress, dating back to June 1949, that recognition of the CCP by the United States would threaten the consensus on the administration's general foreign policy. Public support for MAP had mostly recovered from its nadir in spring 1949, but from *both sides* of the aisle in Congress there was increasing pressure for ERP funding reductions.[99] Congressional representatives were merely following public opinion trends, which, from the end of the Berlin blockade until the outbreak of the Korean War, had grown increasingly tired of European aid.[100] For this reason, Truman met some

[95] "Summary of Some of the Views Expressed at Consultative Meeting on Problems of United States Policy in China," Oct. 13, 1949, PPS Records, Box 13, File: China 1949, NA.

[96] Ibid. The consultants later blasted a hard-nosed NSC draft paper, dated October 7, which called for a hostile posture toward the Chinese Communists and the defense of Taiwan. Instead they called for a hands-off Taiwan policy, recognition of the Communists, and trade with the mainland. See Wilds to Merchant, Oct. 19, 1949, Office of Chinese Affairs, Film C0012, Reel 15, frames 34–37, NA. That draft was also strongly criticized by the Far Eastern desk at State. See "Comments on Third Draft of NSC Policy Paper on Asia," Office of Chinese Affairs, Film C0012, Reel 15, frames 28–29, NA.

[97] "Meeting with the President," Oct. 3, 1949, PPS Records, Box 13, File: China 1949, NA.

[98] See, for example, "U.S. Attitudes on Recognition," Nov. 30, 1949, Foster Papers, Box 22, File: China: 1949–52, NA.

[99] For report on support levels for the MAP, see "Public Opinion on Military Aid to the Atlantic Treaty Countries," Feb. 27, 1950, Foster Papers, Box 46, NA. Once again, support for MAP positively correlated with education levels. For data on attitudes toward cutting ERP, see "Monthly Survey," Dec. 1949 and Feb. 1950, Foster Papers, Box 12, NA.

[100] "Monthly Survey," Mar. 1950, Foster Papers, Box 12, NA. The percentage believing the United States was spending too much on ERP increased from March 1949 (34 percent) through March 1950 (52 percent).

resistance on spending levels for ERP, even after cutting his initial requests for 1950 by 25 percent.[101]

Following the founding of the PRC and the Chinese approach for recognition, there seemed to be firm consensus at the State Department that recognition was the best policy for the United States. In an October 26 debate, advocates of both "carrot" and "stick" policies designed to encourage a Sino-Soviet split agreed on the desirability of recognition.[102] Because the impending British recognition weakened the argument against further American delay, in November the Policy Planning Staff abandoned its earlier wait-and-see position, arguing, "It is in our widest interest to bring about as rapidly as possible a normalization of relations with the Peking regime."[103]

The Angus Ward affair, which created new controversy in November when the CCP raised formal charges against the U.S. consul, was no small stumbling block. As part of their own domestic propaganda, the Chinese Communists had blasted the United States regularly in their rhetoric, and in late 1948 they had detained the American officials in Mukden, under Consul Angus Ward, ostensibly on suspicion of spying activities on behalf of the KMT. The historian Chen Jian argues that the Ward case was critical in the failure of the United States to recognize the Communist government in 1949. Chen cites Acheson's own comments that American recognition was out of the question until Ward was released.[104]

The Ward case was important to Sino-American conflict, but American archival evidence suggests that it served more as an irritant to an existing problem in China policy than as a prime cause of continued American intransigence toward Mao's government. As was demonstrated by the October consultative meetings, which occurred before the release of Ward, the Ward case did not change the administration's basic outlook on China policy in backroom meetings. It did, however, complicate somewhat the domestic political problems related to rapprochement with the Chinese Communists. In the media many saw the Ward case as reason to avoid haste in recognizing the PRC. But even this impact can be overstressed. The level of public opposition to recognition was consistent

[101] "Monthly Survey," Feb. 1950, Foster Papers, Box 12, NA.

[102] Butterworth argued that the $75 million allocated during the MAP hearings should not be spent on harassing the CCP. He and others advocated recognition instead. Rusk countered that the United States could recognize *and* harass. Blum, *Drawing the Line*, pp. 155–156.

[103] British recognition had been anticipated as early as October. See "Meeting with the President," Oct. 17, 1949, PPS Records, Box 13, File: China 1949, NA. PPS Document, Nov. 15, 1949, Office of Chinese Affairs, NA, cited in Blum, *Drawing the Line*, pp. 253–254, n.17.

[104] Chen, "The Ward Case."

throughout 1949 and was apparently unaffected by the level of salience of the Ward case, which was quite low before his publicly reported "conviction" and deportation in late November.[105]

For his part, in early 1949 Acheson tried to play down the significance of the Ward case with both the public and the president, countering rumors that the consul was being badly treated by his captors.[106] But the Ward case made Acheson's detente strategy difficult to sell to Truman. In mid-November, frustrated by the lack of progress on the release of Ward, Truman considered a naval blockade of the mainland and significant new appropriations to keep Hainan and Taiwan islands from falling to the Communists.[107] The State Department saw such actions as antithetical to its hopes for early rapprochement. Acheson met with the president on November 17, arguing strongly against a hostile posture toward the CCP.[108] The secretary paraphrased his discussion with Truman as follows:

> Broadly speaking there were two objectives to policy. One might be to oppose the Communist regime, harass it, needle it, and if an opportunity appeared to attempt to overthrow it. Another objective of policy would be to attempt to detach it from subservience to Moscow and over a period of time encourage those vigorous influences that might modify it. I pointed out that this second alternative did not mean a policy of appeasement any more than it did in the case of Tito. . . . I said that the consultants were unanimous in their judgment that the second course was the preferable one.[109]

Tito had also been hostile to the Americans before his late 1948 break with Moscow, and as in the Tito case, Acheson hoped the prospect of fruitful relations with the West would draw Mao away from Stalin.

Acheson's appeal was fabulously successful, as is demonstrated by Truman's late November correspondence with Maury Maverick, a former U.S. representative. Not only had Truman rejected the idea of punishing the Chinese Communists, he apparently accepted the idea that the United States ideally should recognize the CCP and use the promise of carrots to draw it away from Moscow. On November 19, Maverick wrote Truman of his opinions on China policy. He criticized the hard line taken in public hearings by Acheson, chastising the secretary for "suc-

[105] For media coverage, see "U.S. Attitudes on Recognition," Nov. 30, 1949, Foster Papers, Box 33, NA. For trends in attitudes toward recognition in 1949, see "Monthly Survey," Nov. 1949, Foster Papers, Box 12, NA.

[106] Tucker, *Patterns in the Dust*, pp. 14–15.

[107] See "Meeting with the President," Nov. 14, 1949, Office of Chinese Affairs, Film C0012, Reel 13, frame 244, NA; and Blum, *Drawing the Line*, pp. 163–164.

[108] "Memorandum for the President on the Ward Case," Nov. 17, 1949, Office of Chinese Affairs, Film C0012, Reel 13, frames 251–253, NA

[109] Dean Acheson, quoted in Blum, *Drawing the Line*, p. 164.

cumbing to mass newspaper agitation wherein everything that goes wrong is blamed on the 'Reds.'" Maverick wrote:

> The [present] position of the State Department does not gain the friendship of the new government of China, nor the Chinese people. Rather, our lecturing and smug attitude solidifies hostility to us with the Chinese people, whatever may be the future government of China. . . . I am inclined to believe that a way should be found to recognize the new government, or at least to negotiate. I understand the arrest of our consul and know it is bad. However, it . . . should not be permitted to get us out on the limb. . . . The new government is anxious for recognition. Also, we can make a friend out of China.[110]

To this letter Truman responded three days later:

> Your letter of the nineteenth is the most sensible letter I've seen on the China situation. I can't tell you how much I appreciate it. . . . There are so many crackpots who know all about what to do and who really know nothing about what to do, it is a pleasure to hear from somebody who has a little common sense in the matter.[111]

Acheson had clearly won a full-fledged convert to his realpolitik stance on China.

In late November, the Beijing government did fulfill the last requirement for swift recognition, releasing Ward after a show trial in which he was prosecuted for espionage.[112] The best chance for rapprochement after the scrapping of the Stuart mission fell in the period from the release of Ward to the CCP seizure of the American consulates in mid-January. Therefore it is instructive to view the pressures on the administration in that period. In late December 1949, despite the changes in China, the NSC reiterated its earlier line on recognition. NSC 48/1 and 48/2 state that "the United States should continue to recognize the National Government of China until the situation is further clarified."[113] But much had already been clarified by late December 1949. The CCP controlled most of the mainland, it had expressed an early desire for relations with the West, it had freed Angus Ward and his staff, and it was about to

[110] "Letter from Maury Maverick," Nov. 19, 1949, President's Secretary's Files, File: Foreign Affairs, China 1945–52, Box 173, HSTL.

[111] "Letter to Maury Maverick," Nov. 22, 1949, President's Secretary's Files, File: Foreign Affairs, China 1945–52, Box 173, HSTL.

[112] After the release, the PPS produced a memorandum stating that while continued nonrecognition would be useless, recognition would make the United States appear realistic in some quarters. Blum, *Drawing the Line,* pp. 162–165.

[113] NSC 48/1 and 48/2, Dec. 23, 1949, and Dec. 30, 1949, in *Documents of the National Security Council,* Film A 438, Reel 2.

receive recognition by America's most important ally, Great Britain. What was left to clarify?

THE PROBLEM OF FORMOSA (TAIWAN): ACCIDENTS OF GEOGRAPHY AND POLITICS

In his recollection of the case, John Melby claims that the island of Taiwan (Formosa), to which the KMT fled in 1949, was the last piece of dust that had not yet settled. Melby states that the failure of the United States to abandon the KMT and the related failure of the CCP to conquer Taiwan explains Acheson's inabiltiy to fulfill his goal of detente with the PRC in 1949–1950.[114]

In the first days of January, the recognition issue was tightly bound with the question of Taiwan. The agenda for a January 3 State Department meeting is revealing, stating that the "timing of recognition" would determine the advisability of an extension of ECA aid to Taiwan through June 1950.[115] This strongly suggests that the State Department was considering both recognizing Beijing and abandoning Taiwan in early 1950. This made sense because a prerequisite of meaningful recognition of Beijing was abandonment of the KMT on Taiwan. The administration would have to prepare the public and Congress for recognition before adopting any positive policy change toward Beijing. This slow campaign employed the public relations tactics developed by Acheson and Jessup in 1949: reference to the Open Door policy of noninterference in Chinese domestic affairs; appeals to Congress and the media that recognition of a government does not equate with a statement of approval; and evoking of the 1943 Cairo Declaration, which stated that the United States recognized Taiwan as part of Chinese territory.

Many problems relating to Taiwan were accidents of geography. Many sympathetic to the notion of strongpoint defense mistakenly believed that Taiwan was an integral part of the U.S. "island defense perimeter" in Asia. Moreover, the Communists had almost no experience in amphibious warfare and the United States maintained the world's strongest navy after World War II, so defense of the island seemed certain with only a minimum of effort by the U.S. Seventh Fleet. The low cost of Taiwan's defense also made it a popular proposal among fiscal conservatives attempting to paint themselves as more anticommunist than the administration.

[114] Melby, Oral History, p. 165, HSTL.
[115] Agenda for Meeting with the Secretary, Jan. 3, 1950, Office of Chinese Affairs, Film C0012, Reel 15, frame 8, NA.

The Debate over Taiwan and Recognition within the Administration

Unlike clearer strongpoint or peripheral areas such as Western Europe
and the Chinese mainland, Taiwan was not an easy case for strategic
analysts to decide. On the basis of an assessment by the Joint Chiefs of
Staff, in early 1949 the NSC developed the position that it would maintain throughout the next year and a half (NSC 37): keeping Taiwan from
Communist control was important, *but not vital* to America's global security position. While not part of the crucial Asian island defense perimeter, Taiwan was considered by many to be important to the defense of the
more important islands, especially the Philippines. But, the JCS argued:
"In spite of Formosa's strategic importance, the current disparity between our military strength and our many global obligations makes it
inadvisable to undertake the employment of armed force in Formosa."[116]
Given limited American military resources, military analysts in Washington believed that the prevention of Communist control of the island
should be attempted through economic and political means, not military
aid or direct military action.[117] Later in the year, the NSC decided that
the use of military force was doubly undesirable because, on political
grounds, American intervention would "enable the Chinese Communists
to rally support to themselves as defenders of China's territorial integrity and handicap our efforts to exploit Chinese irredentist sentiment
with respect to Soviet actions in Manchuria, Mongolia and Sinkiang
(Xinjiang)."[118]

Throughout 1949, amended versions of NSC 37 were drafted. Propo-
sitions for U.S. support of an independence movement or coup were considered and ultimately rejected by the State Department as the year progressed. This policy seemed imprudent because Taiwan lacked a strong
indigenous political movement and because American interference would
damage American prestige in an increasingly anticolonial Asia (particularly in China), while providing powerful propaganda ammunition for
the CCP.[119] As early as July 1949, State Department analysts apparently

[116] NSC 37/3, Feb. 10, 1949, in *Documents of the National Security Council*, Film 438,
Reel 1.

[117] See "Memorandum for the Secretary of Defense," Nov. 24, 1948, in *Documents of
the National Security Council*, Film 438, Reel 1; Schnabel and Watson, *History of the Joint
Chiefs of Staff*, Vol. 3, pp. 30–31. The Joint Chiefs argued that if Taiwan fell, the United
States could counter by redoubling efforts to strengthen air capabilities in Okinawa, the
Ryukyus, the Philippines, and Japan.

[118] NSC 37/8, Oct. 6, 1949, *Documents of the National Security Council*, Film 438,
Reel 1.

[119] See "The Position of the United States with Respect to Formosa," NSC 37/1 through
37/9, Jan. 19, 1949, through Dec. 23, 1949, in *The Documents of the National Security
Council*, Film 438, Reel 1; For the original formulations for a coup or internal revolution,
see National Security Council Meetings, Mar. 4, 1949, "Supplementary Measures with

had reconciled themselves "to the prospect of Formosa's [eventual] falling into the hands of the Chinese Communists."[120]

In late 1949, an intra-administration battle was forming on Taiwan policy. Secretary of Defense Louis Johnson seemed to be working behind the scenes with the JCS and General Douglas MacArthur to secure a commitment to the defense of Taiwan. Some members of this group were leaking their ideas and classified information to both the KMT government and the popular press.[121] Johnson, who many believed to be positioning himself for a run at the presidency, adopted a line consistent with Asialationism, advocating smaller federal budgets *and* increased military activity in and around China. Johnson found a ready ally in General MacArthur, who had long bemoaned the lack of attention to Asia and the high level of spending on Europe.[122]

On the other side of the debate, Acheson wanted to disengage from the Chinese Civil War and allow Taiwan to fall so as to speed rapprochement between the CCP and the West. In December 1949, while Acheson was waiting for the loss of the island, the JCS revised its views on the proper strategy to preserve a non-Communist Taiwan, advocating additional military assistance to the KMT.[123] Acheson soundly rejected this strategy, arguing that nothing short of direct military involvement would save Taiwan in the end and that any military aid would only do "further damage to our prestige and to our whole position in the Far East."[124] In a December 23 meeting between State Department and the JCS, Acheson argued:

Respect to Formosa," President's Secretary's Files, HSTL; Blum, *Drawing the Line*, pp. 36–37; and Tucker, *Patterns in the Dust*, p. 181.

[120] PPS 53, July 6, 1949, PPS Records, Box 13, File: China 1949, NA. Kennan himself was less sensitive to the nationalist feelings in China about Taiwan and therefore never accepted Acheson's concern that an active U.S. Taiwan policy would obstruct efforts to foster Titoism on the mainland. Reflecting that difference of opinion, Kennan often floated the idea of American intervention to secure the island as a strategic base, even if this meant physically ejecting the Nationalists from the island. See, for example, the June 23, 1949, annex to PPS 53.

[121] Butterworth offers clear evidence of this, claiming that it seems more than coincidental that a secret JCS report on military aid to Taiwan closely resembled a simultaneous request of aid from Taipei. Moreover, in early January, a top secret State Department "Policy Information Paper," designed to prepare foreign service officers for the fall of Taiwan, was leaked to the press through MacArthur's office. See Tucker, *Patterns in the Dust*, pp. 56, 190; and Tsou, *America's Failure in China*, pp. 529–531.

[122] See, for example, Blum, *Drawing the Line*, p. 173, which outlines Johnson and MacArthur's attempt to reverse the administration's position on the defense of Taiwan.

[123] See NSC 37/9, Dec. 23, 1949, *Documents of the National Security Council*, Film 438, Reel 1.

[124] Schnabel and Watson, *History of the Joint Chiefs of Staff*, Vol. 3, pp. 32–33; Blum, *Drawing the Line*, p. 166.

Assuming that by following the course recommended by the Joint Chiefs we can postpone the fall of Formosa for a year, we must ask what price we pay for that delay. I believe that, first, we will once more involve U.S. prestige in another failure for all to see; moreover, and of greater importance, we will excite and bring upon ourselves the united Chinese hatred of foreigners. . . . If it is at this price that we acquire an island essential to the defenses of the United States then it might be worth the price, but there does not appear to be demonstrated [in the JCS report] a claim that Formosa really breaches our defense.

At another juncture in the meeting, Acheson tied this argument into his hopes for Titoism in Mao's China: "Mao is not a true satellite in that he came to power by his own efforts and was not installed in office by the Soviet army. This situation, I pointed out, is our one important asset in China and it would have to be for a very important strategic purpose that we would take an action which would substitute ourselves for the Soviets as the imperialist menace to China."[125] Acheson sought to calm General Omar Bradley by saying, "From this it did not follow that we should let Formosa go and recognize the Chinese government." But such a conclusion did follow logically and, as we will see, was consistent with subsequent documents.

In his December 30 report to the president, Acheson included all of the arguments he made to Bradley but altered somewhat his language about recognition. He said: "U.S. military assistance enabling the Chinese National Government to continue the fight from Formosa would turn Chinese anti-foreign feeling against us and also place us in the position of *subsidizing attacks on a government that would soon be widely recognized*. . . . We had now extricated ourselves from the Chinese Civil War and it was important that we not be drawn into it again."[126]

The president approved Acheson's recommendations and ordered preparations to go public with the administration's hands-off policy toward China.[127] This effort was designed to refute what one State Department document on Taiwan referred to as increasingly frequent "public statements of visiting congressmen and public discussion of the desirability of [American] occupation of the island."[128]

[125] "Memorandum of Conversation by the Secretary of State: Meeting with the JCS," Dec. 23, 1949, *FRUS: 1949*, Vol. 9, pp 463–467.

[126] National Security Council Meetings, Memorandum for the President, Dec. 30, 1949, President's Secretary's Files, HSTL (emphasis added).

[127] There was, however, some residual hope among American officials in Taiwan that a withdrawal of military assistance would lead to the overthrow of Chiang Kai-shek and to a viable, pro-independence regime on the island. See Taipei to Secretary of State, Jan. 3, 1950, China: Internal Affairs, LM152, Reel 1, frame 10, NA.

[128] "Formosa," undated top secret document in 1950 files, Office of Chinese Affairs,

On January 5, 1950, Truman gave an enormously controversial speech announcing that the United States would neither intervene militarily in the Taiwan Straits nor provide military assistance to combatants in the Chinese Civil War. Citing the Cairo Declaration and the Open Door policy, Truman stated that Taiwan was part of China and that the United States sought no special privileges on Chinese territory. Coordinated with this speech was a massive State Department propaganda effort to downplay the importance of Taiwan and draw distinctions between recognition and approval of a government. During this campaign, Acheson tried to reverse the common misperception that Taiwan was part of the island defense chain. He is reported to have stated to Representative John Kee, chairman of the House Foreign Affairs Committee, that "there seems to be some magic that flows from the use of the term 'island' which seems to immediately give everyone the jitters, whereas, if Formosa had happened to be a peninsula we would probably have heard nothing more about it."[129]

Acheson described Taiwan to the press as but "a small part of the great question of the Far East." He preempted criticism from those who saw the rise of communism on the mainland as an entirely new situation calling into question the Cairo Declaration, at least in the absence of a peace treaty with Japan, which had controlled Taiwan from 1895 to 1945. Acheson stated: "We did not wait for a treaty on Korea. We did not wait for a treaty on the Kuriles." Acheson also took every opportunity to raise the issue of recognition of Beijing. He stated that, in the past, "everybody" recognized the KMT as the legitimate government of China, but that then it was "in control of a very large part of China." He also pointed out that the Beijing government "undoubtedly will soon be recognized by some other countries."[130] It seems rather clear that Acheson had more than cutting off military assistance in mind. He was, apparently, still attempting to lay the groundwork for the shifting of recognition from Taipei (Taibei) to Beijing.

The Congress and the Debate over Taiwan and Recognition

Believing the fall of Taiwan to be imminent, Acheson called leading pro-China representatives to his office to explain why Taiwan was part of China and why honoring the agreement at Cairo was the best long-term

---

Film C0012, Reel 15, frames 618–628, NA. The document must be from the first days of January because it discusses the impending recognition of Beijing by Great Britain.

[129] Acheson, quoted in Blum, *Drawing the Line*, pp. 179–180, 193.

[130] "For the Press: United States Policy with Respect to Formosa," Jan. 5, 1950, PPS Records, Box 15, File: China 1950–51, NA.

strategy to fight communism in Asia. Administration supporters on the Hill, such as Tom Connally of Texas, also began floating the notion of American recognition of the Chinese Communists in the Senate.[131] Acheson also offered strong cues that the United States was leaning in the direction of recognizing Beijing, mentioning the Cairo accord, the low standing of the United States in the eyes of the Chinese people, and "the realization of the fact that Burma, India, Great Britain, New Zealand, Australia, Canada, and doubtless a large number of other nations would be recognizing the Communist regime before the passage of any consider-able amount of time." Angered, Knowland promised to inform the American people of this "fatal policy."[132]

During the attacks on the administration's China policy in December and January, various representatives and senators, including William Knowland, Walter Judd, Kenneth Wherry, John Vorys, Charles 'Doc' Eaton, and H. Alexander Smith evoked the Truman Doctrine by pointing to inconsistencies between Truman's policy toward Greece and Turkey and his plan to write off Taiwan. The threat issued to Truman was that if he did not fulfill his obligations to "free peoples" in Asia, these members of Congress could sabotage future efforts in Europe, which they pointed out were supposedly designed to preserve human freedom.[133] Knowland went so far as to threaten aid to any third country that recognized the Beijing regime. On January 5, the *New York Times* wrote that Knowland "plainly threatened a prolonged and violent action against the Adminis-tration. He emphasized his membership in two Senate committees that have a vital power over the European Recovery Program and the Military Asistant Program for Europe."[134] Citing the obvious threat to the Eu-ropean Recovery Program posed by the China debate, Anne O'Hare Mc-Cormick of the *New York Times* stated: "We are obviously facing a domestic argument on Pacific policy that will make the debate on Atlan-tic policy seem like a model of agreement. For this argument will cut

[131] Princeton Seminars, July 23, 1953, Wire 3, p. 3, HSTL. The discussion here refers to a Jan. 11, 1950, *New York Times* article to this effect.

[132] "Meeting with Senators Smith and Knowland," Jan. 5, 1950, Acheson Papers, Box 65, HSTL.

[133] *New York Times*, Dec. 31, 1949, p. 1; *New York Times*, Jan. 5, 1950, p. 1, 18; and *Congressional Record*, 81 Cong., 2d sess., pp. 79–85. In the Senate, Knowland cried out: "Does the administration have less concern for human liberty in Asia than it does in Eu-rope? . . . Why no concern for the 400,000,000 people of China who have been dragged behind the Iron Curtain?" He questioned whether "the administration wants free men everywhere or whether it draws a color line on freedom." Also see Kepley, *Collapse of the Middle Way*, pp. 64–65.

[134] See *New York Times*, Jan. 5, 1950, pp. 1, 18; James Reston, "China Becomes Cen-tral Issue for U.S.," *New York Times*, Jan. 1, 1950, p. E3; and Tucker, *Patterns in the Dust*, p. 24.

across Party lines and turn former isolationists into red hot interventionists and vice versa."[135] Even Doc Eaton, an internationalist member of the House Foreign Affairs Committee and a supporter of Vandenberg's bipartisan efforts, responded to Truman's Taiwan policy by demanding that the administration use American forces, if necessary, to deny Taiwan to the CCP.[136]

Perhaps the biggest threat to the administration's grand strategy came when Arthur Vandenberg, the champion of bipartisanship for Europe, abandoned the administration's ship. In the domestic political heat created by Truman's January 5 speech on withdrawal from the Chinese Civil War, Vandenberg attacked the administration's Asia policies for undermining any remaining hope for continued bipartisanship in foreign policy.[137] The day after Truman's Taiwan speech, the *Washington Daily News* ran an article outlining the disillusionment of Vandenberg and others:

> The critical blow dealt the nation's bipartisan foreign policy in the white-hot battle over China was measured today in a flat decision by Senator Robert A. Taft that: "There is no such thing as a bipartisan foreign policy.". . . Altho the oratory may subside, the deep feeling will carry over into foreign policy questions quite outside the area of the Far East. . . . Coming up in the next few weeks will be such issues as continuation of the ECA program for Europe, bolstering the arms program under the North Atlantic Pact, and US membership in the new international trade organization. The fight to trim appropriations in this field seems certain to be more vigorous than last year.[138]

Since the legitimizing force behind the general foreign assistance program was anticommunism, the administration could not afford to be hypocritical on this issue.

Administration insiders at the *New York Times,* including James Reston, analyzed the administration's foreign policy dilemmas in an important series of articles about China policy. On January 1 the paper read: "If the State Department had its way it would probably recognize the Communists before many weeks passed. Mr. Truman, however, needs the support in Congress of anti-recognition Senators whose votes are felt to be necessary on other projects."[139] Truman could not afford to contradict the

[135] Anne O'Hare McCormick, "Effects on the Western Front of Far Eastern Policy," *New York Times,* Jan. 4, 1950, in Elsey Papers, Box 59, File: Foreign Relations—China, HSTL.

[136] *New York Times,* Jan. 5, 1950, pp. 1, 18.

[137] Ibid., Jan. 6, 1950, p. 1.

[138] *Washington Daily News,* Jan. 6, 1950.

[139] *New York Times,* Jan. 1, 1950, pp. 1, 16.

Truman Doctrine when he needed to continue to mobilize resources from a Congress described by Reston as "weary of well-doing, worried about expenses, baffled by the magnitude of the oriental problems, and bored with the Russians." On the same day, the "Week in Review" read:

> The United States has not yet publicly chosen its course. Official opinion has been divided. In the State Department and in the Joint Chiefs of Staff the feeling has been that aid to the Nationalists would not only be futile but would alienate India and other Far Eastern peoples. But in other circles it is argued that there is strong sentiment for the Nationalists and that refusal to aid them might jeopardize support for other areas of foreign policy, particularly in Western Europe. . . . The decision in principle was against direct and formal military aid to the Nationalists. Still, the high officials felt that Chiang should not be officially abandoned—as by recognition of Mao— and should be given some moral support and allowed to purchase American equipment with his remaining resources and perhaps with a little financial aid. Although this would tend to link the United States with a lost cause, it was regarded as the best way out in view of public opinion.

This article also pointed out that outspoken officials like Knowland and MacArthur were opposed to recognition of the CCP and abandonment of Taiwan by either the United States or its allies and that the general public would also strongly resent a transfer of recognition.[140]

In a January 8 article, Reston concisely addressed the problems of disengagement from China and the legitimation of the strongpoint defense strategy. Reston wrote: "Mr. Truman in his doctrine of 1947 did not say the United States would do what it could, when it could, and where it could, to block communism; he asserted flatly and broadly: 'I believe it must be the policy of the United States to support free peoples who are resisting attempted subjugation by armed minorities or by outside pressures.'"[141]

In these articles, journalists had touched on all of the connections in the argument here, including the central problem of public opinion. The Truman administration was being forced to choose between adopting its preferred China policy and guaranteeing sufficient funds for its grand strategy. Given the relative importance of Europe, the choice was ob-

---

[140] For both quotations, see ibid., p. E3, in Clifford Papers, Box 2, File: China 1948–50, HSTL. The relatively sympathetic Reston almost certainly had been granted briefings by someone in the administration. This was probably done to counter damaging leaks by Johnson and MacArthur.

[141] Reston, "Debate over China Shows Seven Misperceptions," *New York Times*, Jan. 8, 1950, Elsey Papers, Box 59, File: Foreign Relations—China, HSTL. Interestingly, in this article, Reston finds consensus between State and Defense on the issue of Taiwan, stating that their disagreement on the two departments' strategy revolve around their different missions. He posits that the mission of State is to prevent war, and Defense to win it if it occurs.

vious. Noting the connection between China and Europe, in Reston's January 8 article on China policy the editors embedded a political cartoon entitled "There Are Rumors," in which a man labeled "Congress" is sharpening an axe while a chicken labeled "ERP" looks on in terror.

On January 12, Acheson delivered his famous Press Club speech in San Francisco, in which he defined the American strongpoint global strategy, outlining the defense perimeter in Asia. From this perimeter he excluded Taiwan and South Korea. Rather than soothing political nerves through explanation, the speech only increased the volume of the cries of "Munich" on the floor of the Senate and House.[142] Perhaps most disturbing to the administration was the danger that Republicans, isolationists, and fiscal conservatives should actually support Truman's hands-off proposals on China and apply the same principles to Europe. On January 16, the *Washington Evening Star* ran an article noted by a top domestic adviser to Truman. The article read:

> [On Formosa policy] the Truman Administration [is] on the popular side. The "hands-off" and "let-them-stew-in-their-own-juice" doctrines are really "isolationist". . . . The Republicans must know this traditional position of the United States and how easy it is for the Truman Administration to revert to it. . . . The Republicans must know, too, that as far as popular issues are concerned, they can make more political hay by urging curtailment of spending in Europe than by urging increased involvement in Formosa and the Far East generally.[143]

Actually, administration opponents had a more complex strategy. They could threaten to cut any assistance to areas other than China unless the administration toughened its stand toward Beijing and Taipei. As Acheson recalled, if the administration did not comply, the opposition could cut other programs on principle, while if the administration did comply, they could take credit for forcing a tougher anticommunist stand toward China at relatively low additional costs, since Taiwan could be relatively cheaply secured.[144]

Public Opinion, Taiwan, and Recognition

In late 1949 and early 1950, trends in public commentary and public opinion suggested a hardening attitude over the fight against communism

---

[142] For examples of the use of the Munich analogy in Congress, see *New York Times*, Jan. 6, 1950, p. 1; and *Congressional Record*, 81 Cong., 2d sess., p. 79.

[143] David Lawrence, "No Political Gain Now by GOP Stand on Formosa Policy: More Popular Position Suggested in Pressing for Cut to Aid to Europe," *Washington Evening Star*, Jan. 16, 1950, in Elsey Papers, Box 59, File: Foreign Relations—China, HSTL.

[144] See Acheson's discussion of Taft's strategy in *Princeton Seminars*, July 23, 1953, Wire 2, p. 9, HSTL.

in Asia and an increasingly common belief that the loss of Taiwan would strongly compromise American security. As one State Department analysis stated: "Opinion . . . has now become almost unanimous in the conclusion that its loss to the Communists would be unfortunate for the U.S."[145] Another opinion analysis stated: "The discussion of Formosa has given further evidence of the widespread desire for a more positive approach in Asia. Many observers, while agreeing with the President, have asked: 'If not at Formosa, where do we draw the line against Communism in Asia?' "[146] In addition, judging from media comment, the belief in the possibility of Titoism in China was declining rapidly by early 1950.[147] This trend was strengthened by Mao's December visit to Moscow, which culminated in the February 1950 Sino-Soviet defense treaty.

Recognition of the Chinese Communists was complicated enough in terms of public opinion, but when a prerequisite of that recognition was the abandonment of an existing anticommunist regime, however unpopular, and the surrender of additional territory to "Communism," recognition became politically dangerous. In late 1949 and early 1950 public opposition to recognition increased from a ratio of 2:1 to 5:1 when the issue of abandoning Chiang for the Communists was included in the survey question.[148] All subgroups opposed the transfer of recognition strongly, but not with equal fervor. In a January 1950 poll, the higher the level of education of the respondent, the more likely he or she was to support recognition of the Communists over Chiang. But the majority of Americans were not college educated, and even the majority within that elite subgroup either failed to understand or accept the administration's strongpoint strategy.[149] Consistent with polls cited above, *New York Times* surveys showed that, in early 1950, recognition of the Chinese Communist regime would be widely

---

[145] "Monthly Survey," Dec. 1949, Foster Papers, Box 12, NA.

[146] "Monthly Survey," Jan. 1950, Foster Papers, Box 12, NA.

[147] "Monthly Survey," Dec. 1949, Foster Papers, Box 12, NA. While a February poll did show 50 percent approval (and 28 percent disapproval) of Truman's January decision to stop military aid to Chiang, these results seemed at odds with those from polls in which respondents simultaneously demanded a more positive strategy for the Far East. This variance may have to do with the wording of the questions. "A Summary of Current American Attitudes on U.S. Policy toward the Far East," Feb. 13, 1950, Foster Papers, Box 33, NA.

[148] A November poll showed that opponents of recognition outnumbered supporters by a ratio of more than 2:1. "U.S. Attitudes on Recognition," Nov. 30, 1949, Foster Papers, Box 33, NA. In late 1949, 76 percent had heard or read about the civil war in China; of these, those who opposed recognition of the Communists also outnumbered those who favored it by a ratio of more than 2:1. *Gallup Poll,* Jan. 11, 1950. A late January 1950 poll shows that opposition to recognition jumped to a ratio of 5:1 when the question included both abandoning of Chiang Kai-shek and recognition of the Communists. See "Summary of Current Attitudes," Feb. 13, 1950, Foster Papers, Box 33. Also see Kusnitz, *Public Opinion and Foreign Policy,* p. 24.

[149] See Poll 7 in Appendix A in this volume.

resented.[150] The American public may not have loved Chiang, but they still preferred him greatly to the Chinese Communists.

While the public was able to distinguish somewhat between the importance of Europe and Asia, the results were not impressive for the administration after a two-and-a-half-year effort to educate them on the subtleties of strongpoint defense. In November 1949, 43 percent of respondents in a Texas poll believed that it was as important (or more important) to fight communism in Asia as it was in Europe. The ratio of those choosing Europe over Asia decreased with the respondents' degree of knowledge about international affairs.[151] Given the public's inability to understand the strongpoint strategy, the fall of China was, as McGeorge Bundy and Herbert Feis described it in 1953, "a disaster to the country of the same magnitude as a depression."[152] As one journalist put it in 1950, "So much pain and passion is evoked in 'Who Lost China!' that the man from Mars would think that nothing less than a piece of American territory had been stolen."[153] State Department opinion analysts noted "deep public concern over the course of events in Asia and . . . a searching desire for a positive U.S. approach to the problems posed by the poverty, unrest and spread of Communism in that vast continent."[154] The need for a more coherent and anticommunist policy in Asia was clear, particularly if the administration was to improve the public's understanding of and support for foreign policy more generally. Without these trends in public opinion, Chinese Communism and the fate of Taiwan could not have become the leading issues in American partisan politics in early 1950.[155]

Taiwan and the Korea Aid Bill

The potential danger posed by the Asialationist opposition became clear in late January 1950 when the Congress dealt what Acheson described as

---

[150] New York Times, Jan. 1, 1950, p. E3.

[151] "Some Polling Results Indicating Less Popular Support for Active Policy in Asia than in Europe," Dec. 12, 1949, Foster Papers, Box 33, NA. Those who expressed a preference for one theater over another chose Europe by a ratio of 3:1, but they were outnumbered by those with no preference. Sixty-one percent believed that Europe was as important as or more important than Asia. For those with a clear priority in the informed group, the ratio was about 7:2 (Europe:Asia), while it was only 2:1 for the uninformed group.

[152] Princeton Seminars, July 22, 1953, Reel 3, p. 26, HSTL.

[153] "Who Lost China!" Washington Post, May 4, 1950, Elsey Papers, Box 59, File: Foreign Relations—China, HSTL.

[154] "Monthly Survey," Jan. 1950, Foster Papers, Box 33, NA. For a review of January commentary, see "A Summary of Current American Attitudes on U.S. Policy toward the Far East," Feb. 13, 1950, Box 33, NA.

[155] For evidence of the intensity of the China debate in January, see coverage in the New York Times, Jan. 1–6, 1950.

a "bitter and unexpected blow" to administration foreign policy.[156] As in June 1949, attempts to gain minimal assistance for Korea created controversy over China policy. In January, the administration raised a relatively small aid package ($60 million) for South Korea, from which the United States had withdrawn troops in spring 1949. The modest goal was to support the government as part of the UN program in Asia. As Robert Blum describes it, the bill failed to pass the House because of the opposition of an overlapping coalition of "economizers, Republican partisans, isolationists, and some members of the China bloc. The vote boded ill not only for Asian policy, but indicated that the broad bipartisan coalition that had supported American foreign policy was, after many false predictions of demise, finally crumbling."[157]

In the House debate, opponents argued that if the island stronghold of Taiwan could be written off as peripheral, so could the peninsula of Korea.[158] After the bill's initial defeat, Acheson called Vandenberg to the White House to "work something out." Vandenberg, like Acheson, described the vote as "shocking" and suggested the tried-and-true solution: extending aid to Chiang.[159] Attaching an amendment suggested by Smith and Knowland, the administration offered to extend the economic assistance bill to Chiang until June 30 (five days after the outbreak of the Korean War).[160]

The Korea bill passed its second time through the House. But once again, Capitol Hill had sent a clear message to the White House: while the administration could avoid significantly increasing its commitment to Chiang, when it wanted other interventionist programs it could not afford to write off Taiwan.[161] By reversing the hands-off China policy and continuing with $106 million in aid to the KMT (reported to have been used for weapons), the administration remained linked to Chiang and publicly hostile to Beijing.[162] Equally important, the issues of protecting

---

[156] Acheson, *Present at the Creation*, p. 358.

[157] Blum, *Drawing the Line*, pp. 184–185.

[158] Purifoy, *Harry Truman's China Policy*, p. 194.

[159] "Conversation with Paul Hoffmann," Jan. 20, 1950, and "Substance of Conversation with Vandenberg," Jan. 21, 1950, Acheson Papers, HSTL.

[160] An internal State Department document reads: "The reasons are primarily political. The President's opinion [of] February 8, 1949 is still controlling. . . . Shipments under the China $125 million dollar grant [should] be continued, but not expedited." China Shipments to Formosa, Jan. 12, 1950, Office of Chinese Affairs, Film C0012, Reel 15, frame 247, NA.

[161] On this point, see Westerfield, *Foreign Policy and Party Politics*, pp. 362–368.

[162] For press coverage of the China amendment and the use of its funds for military purchases, see Ickes, "Acheson vs. Acheson," Feb. 13, 1950, Elsey Papers, Box 59, File: Foreign-Relations—China, HSTL. Ickes argues that the United States shipped war supplies, including light Sherman tanks, from Philadelphia after the aid was extended by Acheson in late January.

the South Korean government and protecting Taiwan from Communist takeover were solidly linked on Capitol Hill.

THE EFFECT OF CHANGES IN CCP POLICY: A FUNDAMENTALLY NEW ENVIRONMENT OR MORE OF THE SAME?

On January 14, 1950, the CCP seized U.S. consular property in China (leading to the eventual withdrawal of American personnel from the mainland in the spring).[163] In the same month, Mao was in Moscow negotiating the Sino-Soviet Treaty of Friendship, a defense pact, which was signed in mid-February. It seems plausible that these policies of hostility to the United States and friendship with America's enemy would destroy any hope of rapprochement with Beijing or Titoism in China. They may also have forced a fundamental change in the strategic assessment of and policy toward Taiwan.[164] From American archival evidence, however, we can see that despite changes in CCP policies toward American representatives in China and toward the Soviet Union in early 1950, the State Department did not give up on the hope of fostering Titoism in China and abandoning Chiang Kai-shek. Although CCP belligerence hardly facilitated the process of rapprochement, the attacks had a bigger effect on the public than on the secretary of state. In fact, Acheson actually reduced the terms of recognition after these unwelcome events. After the British recognized the PRC in early January, there remained few strategic reasons to withhold American recognition.[165]

Acheson continued his patient efforts to prepare the public, Congress, and Asian allies for rapprochement with Beijing and abandonment of Chiang. He repeatedly emphasized the Open Door as the proper basis of American China policy.[166] Fully expecting the prompt fall of Taiwan to

[163] For a document discussing the linkage of the seizure of consular property and the decision to withdraw American personnel, see Memorandum for Lay, undated 1950 document, Office of Chinese Affairs, Film C0012, Reel 15, frame 18, NA.

[164] For this argument, see Garver, "Polemics, Paradigms," p. 9.

[165] For a compilation of evidence that Acheson considered and favored recognition, see the January 1973 Senate Foreign Relations Staff Study, "The United States and Communist China in 1949 and 1950: The Question of Rapprochement and Recognition" (Washington, D.C.: U.S. Government Printing Office, 1973).

[166] See, for example, "Remarks by Secretary Acheson: Office of Public Affairs, State Department," Jan. 23, 1950, p. 114 in Elsey Papers, Box 59, File: Foreign Relations—China, HSTL. Acheson argued: "For 50 years, it has been the fundamental belief of the American people . . . that the control of China by a foreign power was contrary to American interest. . . . We are [also] interested in stopping the spread of communism. . . . Now it is fortunate that this point that I made does not represent any real conflict. It is an important point because *people will do more damage and create more misrepresentation in the Far East by stating that our national interest is merely to stop the spread of communism than any other way*" (emphasis added).

Communist forces, Acheson and Truman tried to convince the nervous president of the Philippines, Elpidio Quirino, that the fall of Taiwan would not badly damage Philippine national security. In their February 4 meeting, Truman stated that "he did not regard Formosa in the hands of the Chinese Communists as a threat to the Philippines. It was flanked by bases in the Philippines and Okinawa as well as by our forces in Japan."[167]

Truman and Acheson's position was not just empty talk designed to reassure a worried foreign leader. An early 1950 State Department analysis of Taiwan's strategic significance is entirely consistent with the position presented to Quirino. It reads:

> While Formosa in hostile hands might thus bring the enemy bases some 40 miles closer [than the Chinese coast] to Okinawa and some 160 miles closer to the Northern tip of Luzon, any increased vulnerability of American bases resulting therefrom would appear to be offset by a corresponding increase in vulnerability of hostile bases to American attack. . . . Formosa played an important part as a base area in Japanese southward expansion in the early days of the war, but it should be noted that Formosa was thus useful to Japan when Japan enjoyed undisputed sea and air control of Far Eastern waters. . . . If Japan and Okinawa are firmly held, it would appear difficult for hostile forces to establish undisputed sea and air control of the water adjacent to and to the north of Formosa. Under these circumstances the maintenance of major [enemy] bases on Formosa would seem to present difficult if not insurmountable logistical problems [for the enemy].[168]

The document goes on to quote none other than Douglas MacArthur, who stated in March 1949: "There is no earthly military reason why we (i.e., the U.S.) should need Formosa as a base."

In January and February, intelligence reports from U.S. representatives in China continued to discuss factionalism in the CCP and the existence of strong, anti-Moscow forces in the party. American officials in Shanghai were contacted by a Mr. Zhou Mingxun, who, however sincerely, told them of various welcome trends in CCP foreign policy and domestic politics, including: trouble in Mao's negotiations in Moscow; an impending split in the CCP over the issue of relations with the Soviets; and the desire of certain groups to obtain assistance from the United States in the intraparty struggle to come, which Zhou argued might even devolve into civil war. Zhou Mingxun also stressed the widely held desire that the

[167] "Meeting at the White House: President Truman, President Quirino of the Philippines, Secretary Acheson," Feb. 4, 1950, Acheson Papers, Box 65, HSTL.
[168] "Formosa," undated top secret document in 1950 files, Office of Chinese Affairs, Film C0012, Reel 18, frames 618–628, NA. Because the document discusses the impending recognition of Beijing by Great Britain, it must be from the first days of January.

United States break relations with the Nationalists, because this was a policy all CCP factions opposed with equal vigor.[169] Reports through British intelligence were even stranger, going so far as to suggest the "admittedly bizarre" possibility of a Sino-Soviet war over Manchuria in 1950.[170] In retrospect we must question the accuracy or honesty of these accounts; for our purposes here it is worth noting that the Shanghai consulate had "strong reason to believe that Chou's [Zhou Mingxun's] approach [was] genuine."[171]

As John Melby reports, even the signing of the Sino-Soviet pact in February did not disabuse Acheson and many China experts in the State Department of their beliefs about CCP independence from Moscow.[172] Neither did CCP policies toward Moscow alter Acheson's hopes of abandoning Taiwan. In mid-February, Acheson considered using an old sore point with the KMT to cut off support of Chiang. Since late 1949, the KMT air force had been bombing Shanghai with American-built planes strongly resembling those of U.S. general Claire Chennault's "Flying Tigers." State Department officials had complained bitterly about this practice, arguing that it was a blatant attempt by Chiang to drag America into the Chinese Civil War and a great hindrance to American businesses trying to function in the region.[173] In strongly worded telegrams American officials on the mainland complained of the "use of U.S. aviation equipment to bomb the Chinese civilian population," with the result of "damage . . . to our position in China" and the dissipating of the "beneficial effect of the President's statement of January 5 regarding Formosa."[174]

Acheson initially proposed using the Shanghai bombings as a pretext

[169] Shanghai to Secretary of State, Jan. 21, 1950, China: Internal Affairs, LM152, Reel 1, frame 400, NA.

[170] Memorandum for the Record, Feb. 7, 1950, Office of Chinese Affairs, Film C0012, Reel 15, frame 112. The memorandum includes a discussion of Chinese troop buildups in Manchuria.

[171] The consulate advised caution, however, in the American response, with which "high officers" in the State Department agreed. See Shanghai to Secretary of State, Jan. 21, 1950, and State Department to Shanghai, China: Internal Affairs, LM152, Reel 1, frames 400–405, NA. In early February, American officials decided that an internal CCP revolt was not going to happen in the very near future, but still believed that Nationalist elements in the CCP might still rise to the fore as "Soviet imperialism" put ever increasing pressure on China. See analysis by John Davies, Feb. 2, 1950, Office of Chinese Affairs, Film C0012, Reel 15, frames 110–111, NA.

[172] See Melby, Oral History, pp. 166–167, HSTL. He did say, however, that for those in the State Department with such intellectual predispositions, the Sino-Soviet treaty supplied confirming evidence of their beliefs.

[173] See "Taipei to the Secretary of State," Feb. 9, 1950, Decimal File 293.1141/2–950, Box 1205, NA.

[174] Sprouse to Merchant, Feb. 16, 1950, Decimal File 293.114/2–1650, Box 1205, NA.

to break relations with Chiang but eventually abandoned this approach. [175] His language regarding this affair is most revealing. After warning Taipei about bombing Shanghai, the State Department received a response paraphrased by Acheson as "telling us to go to hell." The secretary inquired of top Far Eastern Affairs officials whether this note *"gave us a chance* to get out of Formosa and withdraw aid from the Nationalists." He was told that an analysis of that matter was forthcoming, to which he responded: "Fine, fine, I just wanted to make sure that you are thinking about it."[176] The tone of Acheson's statements suggest a person who long wanted to abandon Chiang Kai-shek and was searching for a domestically palatable pretext under which he could carry out that wish.

In early March, State Department officials clearly understood the contradiction between continued relations with Chiang's regime and Acheson's most "basic policy" toward China: "the avoidance of actions [that] will deflect upon ourselves the righteous wrath of the Chinese people which if unobscured so surely will be concentrated on the Russians."[177] Addressing the contradiction in a memorandum for Acheson and Rusk, Livingston Merchant stated:

> It is necessary it seems to me, however, that we should be clear in our minds in which direction we are moving in order to give a consistent emphasis in our daily actions to the policy which is fundamental. This, I take it, would be regaining our complete freedom of maneuver and disassociation in the Chinese mind with the Kuomintang as rapidly as events at home and abroad permit.[178]

Another State Department analysis in March strongly criticized the continued shipping of arms to Taiwan after Truman's January 5 pledge to the contrary. It reads:

> The United States can repair to some degree the damage to its prestige in China and restore pro-American sentiment within mainland China only by taking forthright and public steps to disassociate itself from the National Government and to prevent the flow of arms and military supplies from the United States to Formosa.[179]

[175] Blum, *Drawing the Line*, p. 194.

[176] Hackler to Merchant, Feb. 17, 1950, China: Internal Affairs, LM152, Reel 1, frame 886, NA (emphasis added).

[177] Merchant to the Secretary, Mar. 2, 1950, PPS Records, Box 14, File: China 1950–51, NA.

[178] Given those domestic and international constraints, Merchant believed that the administration should not shift recognition from Taipei to Beijing but should instead continue to distance itself from Taiwan's politics. Merchant to the Secretary, Mar. 2, 1950, PPS Records, Box 14, File: China 1950–51, NA.

[179] Untitled document, Mar. 16, 1950, Office of Chinese Affairs, Film C0012, Reel 15, frames 562–569, NA.

These documents support several aspects of the argument here: despite the seizure of American consular property in China and the Sino-Soviet pact, the Truman administration still preferred a Tito strategy toward China; State Department officials understood the gap between preferred grand strategy and actual policy toward China; and domestic hurdles were the most important factors in preventing the State Department from implementing that preferred grand strategy.

Although for domestic reasons Acheson did not pursue active policies such as recognition, he did manage to fight off calls for more active anti-communist options in Taiwan. On February 17, Acheson explained to a KMT advocate of Taiwanese separatism why U.S. assistance to such a movement would not be in the American national interest.[180] In late March, Acheson continued his appeal to the Senate Foreign Relations Committee based on background material produced by the China Affairs desk. In support of American nonintervention in China, Acheson said: "The island of Formosa is not a great question in American foreign policy, *but it may become a very great question if it obscures or changes or interferes with what we are trying to do in regard to China.*"[181] Continuing in this vein, Acheson appealed: "Why should we reverse our entire objectives as regards China in order to fight the Chinese for an island that is not vital?"[182] Adopting a Churchillian realpolitik tone, Acheson stated, "Whoever runs China, even if the devil himself runs China, if he is an independent devil that is infinitely better than if he is a stooge of Moscow."[183]

In April the State Department continued to consider improvement of relations with Beijing. Clubb had remained the U.S. consul general in Beijing (though he was still accredited to the KMT government). On April 10 he visited the "alien affairs office" to discuss differences of opinion over the improvement of relations. The CCP made it clear to him that discussion of improvement in bilateral relations would follow U.S. disassociation from Taipei and recognition of Beijing. Clubb paraphrased the CCP position as follows: "As long as United States continue to support Chiang Kai-shek talk of working an improvement in general situation was ridiculous. . . . If general problem of 'support to Chiang Kai-shek' is cleared up by recognition of Peking regime there might be approach to solution of particular problems otherwise not."[184]

---

[180] "Memorandum of Conversation: Secretary Acheson and L. K. Little, Inspector General of Customs, Republic of China." Feb. 17, 1950, Acheson Papers, Box 65, HSTL.

[181] Tucker, *Patterns in the Dust*, p. 193 (emphasis added).

[182] Kepley, *Collapse of the Middle Way*, p. 77.

[183] Tucker, *Patterns in the Dust*, p. 194.

[184] Clubb to Sprouse via British Embassy, Apr. 11, 1950, Office of Chinese Affairs, Film C0012, Reel 15, frames 106–107, NA.

Recognition was, however, out of the question. In late March the administration was under attack by McCarthy for hiring Communists and by the Taftites, who threatened to cut $500 million from Marshall Plan aid. In this climate Acheson promised the Senate Foreign Relations Committee that there was "no immediate prospect" of recognition of Beijing, although he hoped America could remain "flexible" on this issue. In order to gain bipartisan support for the next round of aid bills, an ailing Senator Vandenberg wrote a letter of support to ECA chief Paul Hoffman. Consistent with his earlier strategy during MAP and ERP debates, Vandenberg also requested a review of Far East policy. Truman responded with gratitude to Vandenberg's letter to Hoffman, adding the standard arguments about the Chinese Civil War and the fact that it was fundamentally a Chinese affair. Vandenberg stated: "Certainly we cannot fundamentally divide at home in respect to foreign policy and expect to have much authority abroad."[185] Working with Vandenberg, the administration was able to halve the proposed cuts to the ECA bill, but the lessons of this episode were now familiar to the administration: do not expect consensus on European policy without demonstrating some consistency between anticommunist policies in Europe and Asia.

NSC 68 AS A STRATEGIC SHIFT AND AS A MOBILIZATIONAL DOCUMENT

Mobilizational difficulties would only get worse for the administration in the months before the Korean War. In NSC 68 American strategists prescribed a massive increase in American security spending, including a tripling of the defense budget. Commissioned in January and completed in April 1950, this document was designed mainly to respond to the Soviet's breaking of the American nuclear monopoly. But it was also designed to mobilize the government and public behind the budgetary hikes called for by the NSC in light of increasing Soviet power. The difficulty in selling any increases to the public in early 1950 was as severe as in 1947. In November 1949 polls, the public rejected the notion of higher taxes even though the government was spending more than it took in. When asked how the government could cut expenditures, the second most common answer (next to cutting payrolls) was to cut aid to Europe.[186] As the *New Republic* lamented in January 1950, "Rarely has the mood of public opinion been so unprepared for the actions that America must take."[187]

---

[185] Kepley, *Collapse of the Middle Way*, pp. 73–77.
[186] *Gallup Poll*, Nov. 30, 1949.
[187] *New Republic*, Jan. 6, 1950, cited in McLellan, *Dean Acheson*, p. 218.

Throughout 1950 the administration struggled to maintain the existing levels of European assistance and in the spring required the influential voice of Dwight Eisenhower to prevent cuts in the existing defense budget.[188] While NSC 68 apparently convinced even the fiscally conservative secretary of defense Louis Johnson that there was a need for additional defense spending, Truman knew he would have more trouble with Congress. In the first half of 1950, the American public was searching for new purpose and resolve in foreign policy.[189] But that same public was also tired of the opportunity costs of containment strategies, especially European aid.

It was in this strange political environment that McCarthyism and Asialationism were breeding. Acheson recalled that in 1950, while the administration was under attack for "appeasement" in China, Congress was threatening to cut any international package it presented on the Hill.[190] In March congressional leaders were demanding a Far East pact similar to NATO, which would include additional assistance to Taiwan.[191] In a late April meeting with Truman, his newly appointed Republican adviser, John Foster Dulles, said the following: "It was important that there should be some affirmative action in the field of foreign affairs which would restore the confidence of the American people that the government had a capacity to deal with the Communist menace. My impression was that many Americans had lost confidence as a result of what had happened, particularly in the East." Truman agreed with Dulles, saying that "in talking yesterday with Secretary Acheson yesterday he had expressed much the same point of view."[192]

Rather than accepting public lethargy and smallish funds from Congress, Acheson favored a reassessment of American strategy and a propaganda campaign to mobilize the American public around higher foreign policy expenditures.[193] It was with this in mind that NSC 68 had been commissioned in January 1950. The final version of the document, finished in April, did not mention dollar amounts, but it was widely understood that the suggested figure for defense alone ranged from $45 billion to $50 billion. Despite Acheson's desire to raise the defense budget, the domestic political drive to reduce international spending led Truman to

[188] Hammond, "NSC 68," pp. 332–337.

[189] Ibid., pp. 336–337. For evidence that the American public wanted a tougher policy toward Moscow, see Wells, "Sounding the Tocsin," p. 128.

[190] Princeton Seminars, Reel 5, Track 2, p. 8, HSTL.

[191] See Memorandum for the Secretary of State from Lucius Battle, Mar. 9, 1950, Acheson Papers, Box 65, HSTL.

[192] Dulles in "Memorandum of Dulles' Conversation with the President," Apr. 28, 1950, Acheson Papers, Box 65, HSTL.

[193] Pollard, *Economic Security and the Origins of the Cold War*, p. 237.

shelve NSC 68 until after the outbreak of the Korean War.[194] As he did
with the Clifford-Elsey report in 1946, Truman decided that the American public was not yet ready to take on the responsibilities that NSC 68
was demanding.

Even before the final draft of NSC 68 was completed, Acheson met
privately with individual congressional leaders to discuss the need for a
new American security effort and the difficulties in mobilizing the public
for such an effort. In March the internationalist Republican Christian
Herter "wondered whether it would be possible to bring about among
our American people a realization of the seriousness of the situation
without some domestic crisis, something concrete to which your appeal
could be tied, such as a break in diplomatic relations [with the Soviets]."
Acheson stated that, rather than the United States creating international
tension, the administration could merely wait for the Communists to attack somewhere around the globe.[195] In April, Senator Estes Kefauver
(D.-Tenn.) also expressed concerns about public confusion and apathy
toward international affairs. The minutes read: "Senator Kefauver referred to Congressional and public doubts as to where our foreign policy
was really leading and thought that these doubts might be even more
serious next year unless a clear and simple sense of direction was given to
the people. He mentioned particular objection to the appropriations for
foreign aid when benefits to farmers and other domestic groups were
being reduced." Kefauver expressed concern whether "what [Acheson]
had in mind could be expressed in simple enough terms to American and
other peoples to capture their imagination." Acheson responded, "We
were trying and would continue to try to make clear the direction we
were working."[196]

The problem with the United States in 1950 was not that it lacked
power potential along the measures traditionally considered by neoreal-
ists, but that it lacked the political ability to activate that potential into
projectable power. In 1953 Acheson reminisced at length about NSC 68
and the lack of American political power in 1950:

[194] For further evidence that Acheson wanted to raise the defense budget, see Johnson
and Acheson Conversation, June 5, 1950, Acheson Papers, HSTL.

[195] He mentioned the possibility that the Chinese Communists would attack Taiwan
with Soviet planes as one scenario that might arouse the public's attention to the Cold War.
Acheson did not advocate any American military response to such an attack, but he did
seem to think that the attack itself would create a fervor in the United States. "Conversation
between the Secretary and Representative Herter," Mar. 24, 1950, Acheson Papers, Box
65, HSTL. Other potential points of international conflict mentioned by Acheson were
West Berlin, where he expected Soviet-sponsored youth riots in May, and Austria, where he
thought the Soviets might withdraw from the Austrian treaty negotiations, "thus bringing
down the iron curtain on that area."

[196] Subject: North Atlantic Community, Apr. 4, 1950, Acheson Papers, Box 65, HSTL.

Now suddenly . . . we haven't got the monopoly of the atomic bomb. This great thing that Churchill says is [sic]—has policed the world has disappeared. . . . You have got to make a colossal effort. . . . [NSC 68] spelled out what this meant in terms of our societies. We produce so much more aluminum than they do that there isn't any two ways about it. What do we do with it? We put it on the front of automobiles, we throw it all over the place. They put more aluminum into airplanes. . . . The totality of their armament production vastly exceed ours. We have an army that is nothing at all. It costs us twenty times their army. Every one of our boys has three hundred dollars a month. . . . They have a fellow with a bayonet and a blanket. . . . All of the power of this very primitive world is creating something that in a very short time is going to knock the daylights out of our world although we can do colossally more. Now, what are the elements of policy? . . . Now why do you do this [write the document]? Do you do it to get a Ph.D.? What are you trying to do? You are trying to get people to move into action. . . . You had to move into the field of Congress, public opinion, and do something about it.[197]

Acheson's account underscores the problem with measuring national power by economic resources and population without considering political will. It also shows how simplification of threats and some ideological crusading help gather essential support to adapt to straightforward shifts in the international balance of power, such as the loss of a nuclear monopoly.

NSC 68 was designed to do just that. Because of its sometimes crusading rhetoric, the document is viewed by John Gaddis and others as marking the end of the strongpoint defense strategy advocated by Kennan.[198] Much like the Truman Doctrine, NSC 68 stated that "a defeat of free institutions anywhere is a defeat everywhere."[199] It also introduced the concept of "rollback."[200] But the document was not primarily aimed at readjusting the attitudes of career foreign policy officials, and there is strong evidence that it did not. The language of the document is at times flowery and moralistic, uncharacteristic of previous NSC working papers.[201] Even after the outbreak and escalation of hostilities in Korea, in secret memoranda key figures in Nitze's own Policy Planning Staff questioned the implications of NSC 68 for actual policy formation, arguing

---

[197] Princeton Seminars, Oct. 10, 1953, Reel 2, Track 2, pp. 12–14, HSTL.

[198] Gaddis, *Strategies of Containment*, chap. 4.

[199] For an analysis of this aspect of NSC 68, see Wells, "Sounding the Tocsin."

[200] For the full text see, NSC 68, Apr. 7, 1950, *FRUS: 1950*, Vol. 1, pp. 234–292.

[201] For example, in discussing communism, it reads, "The system becomes God and submission to the will of God becomes submission to the will of the system." NSC 68, as cited in Gaddis, *Strategies of Containment*, p. 107.

that history, including recent events in Korea, did not support some of the document's more dramatic conclusions.[202]

The drafters of NSC 68 themselves fully expected, in fact suggested, that parts of the document be presented to the public through declassification.[203] Although Truman refused any public disclosure of the document itself, Acheson and others based their public statements and speeches on the language of NSC 68 throughout the spring of 1950.[204] In a quotation often misapplied by scholars to the Truman Doctrine, Acheson analyzes the reasons that NSC 68 was sometimes simplistic, crusading, and moralistic in tone:

> The task of a public officer seeking to explain and gain support for a major policy is not that of the writer of a doctoral thesis. Qualification must give way to simplicity of statement, nicety and nuance to bluntness, almost brutality, in carrying home a point. . . . In the State Department we used to discuss how much time that mythical "average American citizen" put in each day listening, reading, and arguing about the world outside his own country. Assuming a man or woman with a fair education, a family, and a job in or out of the house, it seemed to us that ten minutes a day would be a high average. If this were anywhere near right, points to be understandable had to be clear. If we made our points clearer than truth, we did not differ from other educators and could hardly do otherwise.[205]

Although this statement could apply to either the Truman Doctrine speech or NSC 68, it is important to emphasize that Acheson was referring to the latter, since, unlike the Doctrine speech, NSC 68 is often viewed as a wholly sincere policy paper and an actual shift in thinking about how America should ideally respond to changes in the world.

If anyone was a true believer in the crusading sections of NSC 68, it was the document's principal author, Paul Nitze. But even Nitze himself at times stated that the document was aimed at the general populace. In defending the paper's crusading implications to a critical fellow drafting committee member, Nitze said, "If we had objectives only to repel invasion and not to create a better world the will to fight would be less-

[202] One such document argues that, while the administration might need to "oversimplify Soviet intentions in appealing to Congress and the people for support, . . . the NSC [should not] become 'hoisted by our own petard.'" *FRUS: 1951*, Vol. 1, p. 166. For others, see pp. 163–178, 180–181.

[203] Princeton Seminars, Oct. 10, 1953, Reel 3, Track 1, p. 1, HSTL. Also see "First Meeting of the Ad Hoc Committee on NSC 68," May 2, 1950, *Documents of the National Security Council*, Supplement 4, Reel 4.

[204] Acheson, *Present at the Creation*, pp. 374–376. Acheson writes, "Throughout 1950, the year my immolation in the Senate began, I went about preaching . . . [the main] premise of NSC-68."

[205] Ibid., p. 375.

ened."[206] Similarly, the document itself comes close to the thesis here, when it states: "Our fundamental purpose is more likely to be defeated from lack of will to maintain it, than from any mistakes we may make or assault we may undergo because of asserting that will."[207] It was decided that an overactive security strategy was less dangerous than an underactive one.

A careful reading of the document demonstrates that, while the suggested peacetime increases were revolutionary, many of the basic strategic notions in the paper were not entirely new. Only once does the term "rollback" appear, for example, and radical notions, such as preventive war, are rejected explicitly. In addition, the possibility of Titoism spreading among Soviet satellites is explicitly addressed.[208] Perhaps the best test of Nitze's real beliefs were his prescriptions for policy, which, with the exception of levels of defense spending, differed little from Kennan's on two critical occasions in 1950: Nitze was among the very few who warned against crossing the 38th parallel in Korea in October 1950; he was also at the forefront in keeping the conflict limited later in the year, heading up a study that advised Truman to mask from the American public the involvement of Soviet pilots over Korean airspace.[209]

NSC 68's Effect on Public Opinion

The public effort by Acheson and others apparently paid off to some degree. By May 1950 support for military assistance to Europe was at an all-time high (61 percent). As we would expect, this jump in approval was accompanied by the high salience of international communism and a strongly heightened sense that America would soon be at war. At the same time, citizens opposing recognition of Beijing outnumbered those who approved of it by a ratio of 2.5:1 (a two-year high).[210] The concurrence of these trends does not appear coincidental. After the Korean War began, public support for anticommunist measures in Korea, Europe, and Taiwan increased together. In the low-mobilization days of January, most Americans seemed willing to cut off military assistance to Chiang,

[206] Gaddis, *Strategies of Containment*, p. 108.

[207] NSC 68, *FRUS: 1950*, Vol. 1, p. 265.

[208] Ibid., pp. 247, 281, 284. I am grateful to Adam Condron for pressing me to reread these sections.

[209] Nitze, *From Hiroshima to Glasnost*, pp. 106–108; Halliday, "A Secret War."

[210] "Monthly Survey," May 1950, Foster Papers, Box 12, NA. Expectations of war in two and ten years both jumped sharply from March to April 1950 to their highest points since the Berlin blockade. For the June 2, 1950, poll on attitudes toward recognition, see the memorandum for Mr. Russell, dated Sept. 11, 1950, Foster Papers, Box 33, File: China 1949–52, NA. Forty percent opposed recognition and 16 percent supported it.

but in July a majority of respondents (58 percent) said that the United States should "go to war with Russia" if Taiwan were attacked by Communist forces. As State Department opinion analysts put it, the American public came to support the defense of Taiwan because of the "general increase of popular willingness since the Korean War to take positive action against Communist aggression wherever it may appear."[211]

NSC 68 and the Assessment of Taiwan's Strategic Value and the Chances for CCP Titoism

In the literature on Chinese-American relations in 1950, it has been argued that the Truman administration had a change of heart toward Taiwan in the first half of 1950, particularly since the completion of NSC 68 in April.[212] In this account the intervention in the Taiwan Straits at the beginning of the Korean War was understandable given the administration's earlier change of attitude about the island's strategic importance. These analyses correctly note that many documents suggest intensified interest in the defense of the island among officials in both the military and the State Department. The majority of these documents were drafted after the hiring of Dulles as an adviser in April 1950 and the appointment of the hard-line cold warrior, Dean Rusk, to the position of assistant secretary of state for the Far East in the same month. In order to bolster their case for a new commitment to Taiwan, in spring 1950 Dulles, Rusk, and the military noted the Sino-Soviet Treaty of February 1950, the presence of Soviet planes on the mainland, and the general strategic importance of Taiwan to the security of the Philippines and Southeast Asia.[213] As the JCS put the case to Rusk and Acheson on May 5, 1950: "The Joint Chiefs of Staff consider that the United States and the USSR are now, to all intents and purposes, engaged in war—except for armed conflict. Further, they consider that the aggressive operations of the Chinese Communists, supported by Soviet aid, constitute an increasing threat to the already greatly weakened United States position in the Far East." The document then calls for a reconsideration of Taiwan policy by the National Security Council.[214]

Beginning in May, Rusk and Dulles joined forces with Louis Johnson

[211] "Public Attitudes concerning Formosa," Sept. 26, 1950, Foster Papers, Box 33, File: China 1949–52, NA.

[212] See, for example, Chang, *Friends and Enemies*, pp. 70–76; Gaddis, *The Long Peace*, p. 88; Cumings, *Origins of the Korean War*, chap. 16, esp. p. 539.

[213] See, for example, "Renewed Proposals by Service Attaches in Hong Kong and Taipei for Further Military Aid to Chinese Nationalists," Apr. 26, 1950, Decimal File 794A.5/4–2650, Box 4258, NA.

[214] Rusk to Acheson, May 5, 1950, Decimal File 794A.5/5–550, Box 4258, NA.

in the Defense Department and some members of the uniformed military, including Douglas MacArthur, to push for increased military assistance and, if possible, a defense commitment for Taiwan. Various documents demonstrate that Johnson and Rusk carefully prepared a united position to present to Acheson in the hope that he would alter the China policy that had been in place since Truman's January 5 speech.[215] On May 29, MacArthur weighed in with his now famous argument that Taiwan was an "unsinkable aircraft carrier and submarine tender" of vital importance to regional security.[216] On May 30, Rusk finished his memorandum for Acheson, which strongly suggested a reconsideration of Taiwan policy. Rusk emphasized international changes that followed Truman's January 5 speech: the Sino-Soviet pact of February 14, 1950; "Soviet dismemberment designs on Communist China"; and Beijing's recognition of Ho Chi Minh. One proposed American response was to persuade Chiang to accept a UN trusteeship protected from the People's Liberation Army (PLA) by the American Seventh Fleet.[217] Another option was to neutralize Taiwan with or without UN trusteeship. This more aggressive option was discussed in memoranda that were written on May 18 by Dulles and that were attached to Rusk's May 30 memorandum for Acheson.[218]

It is important to emphasize, however, that even if Acheson had agreed with these proposals, the reconsideration of Taiwan policy was itself largely related to fears about domestic consensus on foreign policy. In a May 30 meeting, Rusk emphasized the disillusionment of "world opinion and U.S. opinion" with the passive nature of American foreign policy in East Asia. Rusk argued that Taiwan "presents a plausible place to 'draw the line' and is, in itself, important politically if not strategically."[219] In early June, Rusk discussed with Acheson the need to reconsider policy toward China and Taiwan because, "It is of vital importance to the national interest that we establish our policies toward the Far East on a broad bi-partisan basis as soon as possible." He continued: "It should not be too difficult to maintain a bi-partisan approach toward

[215] See, for example, Burns to Rusk, May 29, 1950, Decimal File 794A.5/5–2950, Box 4258, NA.

[216] Schnabel and Watson, *History of the Joint Chiefs of Staff*, pp. 39–40. This could not have come as a complete surprise; the State Department long suspected MacArthur of opposing U.S. policy toward Formosa. See Strong to Sprouse, Mar. 30, 1950, Office of Chinese Affairs, Film C0012, Reel 15, frames 574–575, NA.

[217] Rusk to Acheson, May 30, 1950, Office of Chinese Affairs, Film C0012, Reel 15, frame 696–712, NA.

[218] For Dulles's May 18 memorandum, see Finkelstein, *Washington's Taiwan Dilemma*, pp. 307–309. For discussion of its inclusion in Rusk's May 30 memorandum to Acheson, see Cumings, *Origins of the Korean War*, Vol. 2, p. 538.

[219] Memorandum, May 31, 1950, Decimal File 794A.00/5–3150, Box 4254, NA.

Japan, Korea, the Ryukyus, the Philippines, and Southeast Asia. We have not yet achieved bi-partisanship toward the main elements of the China-Formosa problem."[220]

Acheson's reply or replies to Rusk's memoranda are not available, so we cannot be certain of their impact on the secretary. Evidence from Britain suggests that Acheson was indeed exploring new ways to keep Taiwan out of Communist hands in early June. Acheson's discussion with the British, however, was apparently limited to the plausibility of UN protection for Taiwan and did not include Dulles's more radical scenario for unilateral American neutralization of the island.[221] Since the UN scheme would require the cooperation of Chiang Kai-shek and key UN members, such as Britain, all of whom would be opposed, this proposal was a nonstarter. Acheson very well may have known the British would oppose such a plan. He may then have raised it with them in hopes that their explicit opposition to the plan would silence some critics of American Taiwan policy within the administration.

Although the evidence for the argument that Acheson had a change of heart in June is very limited, there is a good deal of documentary data suggesting that the Rusk-Dulles effort to reverse Taiwan policy did not succeed until after the outbreak of war in Korea.[222] As stated above, it is clear that administration officials expected Taiwan to be attacked by the Chinese Communists in 1950 and that they expected the attack to be successful. This expectation was only confirmed by the PLA's seizure of Hainan island in April 1950.[223] A May State Department "Intelligence Estimate" is particularly revealing. It rejected the notion that, politically, the loss of Taiwan would hurt the United States and assist Beijing. It stated that although "the fall of Taiwan would slightly increase Chinese capabilities . . . [it] would in general be adverse to the Chinese Communists because economic difficulties could no longer be blamed upon the blockade and air raids, and attributed to the U.S." Without directly mentioning American recognition of Beijing, the document also pointed out that the "disappearance of the Chinese Nationalist Government . . . would partially eliminate the basis for the present divergence between the policies of the US and UK toward China" and that the fall of Taiwan "could contribute to a worsening of relations between the Chinese Com-

[220] Rusk to Acheson, June 9, 1950, PPS Records, Box 14, File: China 1950–51, NA.

[221] Cumings, *Origins of the Korean War*, Vol. 2, p. 538. I am grateful to Walter LaFeber for helpful comments on Acheson's meetings with British representatives.

[222] For a recently published argument along these lines, see Finkelstein, *Washington's Taiwan Dilemma.*

[223] As one May 17, 1950, report from Taipei to Acheson stated: "In opinion of attaches and myself fate of Taiwan sealed. Communist attack can occur between June 15 and end July." Taipei to Secretary of State, May 17, 1950, Decimal File 794A.00/5–1750, Box 4254, NA.

munists and the Kremlin."[224] A key difference between the Intelligence Estimate and other documents can be found in its introduction, which states: "As an intelligence estimate it does not deal with the possible domestic repercussions in the United States or any international repercussions of such consequences."[225] When those factors are bracketed off, American analysts seem much more like their British counterparts.

Leading State Department officials familiar with China also wrote scathing critiques of the approach advocated by Rusk, Dulles, and Johnson. Having returned to Washington with the rest of American consular personnel earlier in the spring, on June 16 Clubb dismissed the notion of a UN trusteeship of Taiwan because "other members on whose support we should have to rely [are inclined] to support the entry of the Chinese Communists into UN bodies . . . instead of becoming involved in sharper quarrels with those communists." He continued:

> The consensus of opinion by informed American observers [is that] . . . only the direct intervention of American armed forces would save the island from ultimate Communist invasion. Such intervention would be *contrary to existing policy.* . . . At some time and place the issue with International Communism must be joined, but the present question [is] whether Formosa is the time and the place, whether our existing military resources are to be committed to that sector in the international arena . . . . Unilateral intervention would probably weaken the moral position of the United States, which has already taken a categorical stand against intervention in Formosa particularly and against intervention in the domestic affairs of other States generally. The political reaction in China itself would probably be such as to tend to consolidate the hold of Communism on the Chinese people, and the hold of the USSR on China. . . . And in Asia generally there would develop new suspicions of our motives—and our *bona fides.*[226]

By its reference to "existing policy" Clubb's memorandum suggests strongly that as late as nine days before the North Korean invasion there had not been a change in Taiwan policy.

Other officials also weighed in against the May 30 Rusk memorandum. In a point-by-point mid-June analysis, leading State Department

[224] Intelligence Estimate 5, May 19, 1950, Office of Chinese Affairs, Film C0012, Reel 15, frame 711–720, NA. The document also did not analyze the purely military implications of the fall of Taiwan. The authors did cite the potentially negative political consequences of KMT collapse for Southeast Asia. But they also noted that Truman had argued that Taiwan was part of China. Therefore, in analyzing the meaning of American passivity on Taiwan, the CCP could not draw conclusions about American resolve in defending other areas, such as Southeast Asia, that were clearly not considered part of China.

[225] Intelligence Estimate 5, May 19, 1950, Office of Chinese Affairs, Film C0012, Reel 15, frame 711–720, NA.

[226] Clubb to Rusk, June 16, 1950, Decimal File 794A.00/6–1650, Box 4254 (emphasis added).

officials directly took on the notion that Taiwan was the place where the United States should begin taking a strong stand against Chinese Communism. They stated:

> In the eyes of the Chinese and other Asiatics Formosa is Chinese territory, a view confirmed by . . . statements by the President and the Secretary. Thus, when the Chinese Communists move against Formosa, they will be moving against what is in effect Chinese territory and it would be difficult to picture such action as 'aggression'. . . . It would seem more advantageous to take a stand [against Communist aggression] in non-Chinese territory.[227]

They attack the notion that the Taiwan issue is linked with the security of French and British colonies in Southeast Asia on any grounds other than psychological ones. The lengthy document states: "In sum it would appear that this course of action [active retention of Formosa] would create an enduring obstacle to bettering United States relations with China, regardless of the regime in that country." Making similar arguments about the Cairo declaration, another June document rejects American involvement in the fostering of a Taiwan independence movement.[228] These documents suggest that Acheson had access to very different opinions on the Taiwan question than he was getting from congressional representatives, uniformed officers, the Defense Department, and Rusk and Dulles. He apparently agreed with those opinions. As late as June 23, Acheson informed the press that the United States had no intention of reversing its nonintervention policy toward Taiwan and the Chinese Civil War.[229]

In fact, in early June the State Department was still considering informal recognition of Beijing as well as admission of the PRC to the United Nations (something Britain strongly preferred).[230] While not planning to disown the Taipei regime in the short term, State Department officials proposed making an announcement stating, "[The] Peiping [Beiping] regime exercises certain *de facto* control in parts of China. . . . The United States will therefore hold that regime responsible . . . wherever its authority extends." As one analyst stated, "This would not amount to *de facto* recognition (although the press will probably so construe it)" but

[227] Memorandum by PDS and WWS, circa June 15, 1950, Office of Chinese Affairs, Film C0012, Reel 15, frames 661–696, NA.

[228] Connors to Allison, June 6, 1950 (declassified Dec. 1993), Decimal File 794A.00/5–350, Box 4254, NA.

[229] Tucker, *Patterns in the Dust*, p. 187.

[230] For evidence of British preferences on PRC admission to the UN, see Memorandum of Conversation, June 16, 1950, China: Internal Affairs, LM152 Reel 18, frames 863–869, NA.

"would be desirable in helping to educate public opinion to a more realistic attitude toward the problem." Another legal analyst stated that the suggested wording would "make it possible to begin to connect our recognition policy, in regard to China, with the factual state of affairs in that country." The language used in these documents strongly implies that the public's simplistic attitude toward the problem of U.S. relations with China was the main stumbling block to implementation of Acheson's realist preferences about China policy.[231]

THE OUTBREAK OF THE KOREAN WAR AND THE REVERSAL ON TAIWAN

On June 25, 1950, North Korea launched a massive invasion of the South, conjuring up images of Hitler's invasion of Czechoslovakia in President Truman's mind. The need to demonstrate Western resolve by defending the Republic of Korea required the application of significant force by the United States and other UN allies on the Asian mainland. Truman's decision to enter the Korean War has been covered ably and thoroughly elsewhere. Various scholars emphasize the following important factors in Truman's decision: the nature of the invasion (a carefully planned and massive armored assault); the fear of appeasement after Munich; and the need to draw the line against communist advance somewhere in order both to reassure European allies and to mobilize the American public behind greater levels of defense spending and military assistance abroad.[232]

At the first Blair House meeting, where Truman decided to respond with force in Korea under the auspices of the United Nations, the president also decided to act unilaterally to send the American Seventh Fleet to block the Taiwan Straits. Scholars in the past have argued that the Taiwan decision was based at least as much in American domestic politics as it was in international strategy.[233] David Finkelstein takes a different approach. He argues that, while Acheson and Truman never accepted the reassessment of Taiwan's strategic importance before the outbreak of

---

[231] See Yost to Perkins, June 1, 1950; Perkins to Rusk, June 2, 1950; Perkins to Rusk, June 6, 1950; and Tate to Rusk, June 6, 1950; all in China: Internal Affairs, LM152, Reel 18, frames 818–833, NA.

[232] May, *"Lessons" of the Past*; Paige, *The Korean Decision*; Foot, *The Wrong War*; and Stueck, *The Road to Confrontation*; Cumings, *Origins of the Korean War*, Vol. 2, chap. 2, offers the historical backdrop for Washington's view that ROK defense was politically, if not strategically, critical.

[233] For examples, see Stueck, *The Road to Confrontation*, pp. 196–198; Westerfield, *Foreign Policy and Party Politics*, pp. 368–369; Donovan, *Tumultuous Years*, p. 206; and Kusnitz, *Public Opinion and Foreign Policy*, p. 43.

war in Korea, they did so once the war in Korea began. In other words, the war context made Taiwan strategically more valuable.[234] Although the available evidence is sparse, it does not fully support this latter conclusion. On the contrary, there is reason to believe that Truman and Acheson had not changed their minds about the strategic significance of Taiwan even after the outbreak of war in Korea.

But the evidence on this issue is mixed. In his memoirs, Truman claimed that the blocking of the straits was designed to prevent anything that might "enlarge the area of conflict" at the outset of the Korean War.[235] This, of course, is syllogistic reasoning. It begs the question why the United States would oppose the spread of communism to Taiwan on June 25 when it had fully anticipated the fall of the island throughout the spring. At the onset of the Korean War, the administration did not think the Chinese or the Soviets would become involved in the fighting. In fact, this is a major reason that the administration risked both sending ground troops into Korea and allowing them to cross the 38th parallel.[236] While Taiwan became more important as Chinese intervention seemed increasingly likely in the fall, this factor was not part of the administration's calculations in June. Criticizing the JCS in his memoirs, Acheson explicitly denies that strategic reassessments of Taiwan's importance affected Truman's decision to block the straits in June.[237] Memoranda by officials other than Acheson in summer 1950 suggest that the secretary's stubborn view that Taiwan lacked critical strategic importance was not universally shared in the State Department.[238] But, as we have already seen, such disagreements were not unique to the period following the outbreak of war in Korea.

The United States might have blocked the straits in order to reassure Asian allies of American resolve. On June 30, Acheson accepted congratulations on his Taiwan decision from the Norwegian ambassador to

[234] Finkelstein, *Washington's Taiwan Dilemma.*

[235] Truman, *Memoirs,* Vol. 2, p. 337.

[236] See, for example, General Omar Bradley's analysis at the June 25, 1950, Blair House meeting, in which he argued that Korea was a good place to demonstrate American resolve because the Soviets were not yet ready for war. *FRUS: 1950,* Vol. 7, p. 158.

[237] Acheson, *Present at the Creation,* p. 422. Acheson writes; "At the end of July the Joint Chiefs, interpreting President Truman's order not to permit an attack on or from Formosa as a change in view regarding its strategic importance (*which was not the idea at all*), recommended a military survey team to report on the state of its defenses" (emphasis added).

[238] A July 12, 1950, State Department review ordered by Rusk, however, does suggest that the Korean War and the possibility of global conflagration did require a "reconsideration of our attitude toward Formosa." Office of Chinese Affairs, Film C0012, Reel 15, frame 0012, NA. American ambassadors around the world were instructed to adopt this line with the governments to which they were accredited. See "Eyes Only Ambassador," July 12, 1950, Office of Chinese Affairs, Film C0012, Reel 15, frame 595, NA.

Washington, who argued that intervention in China comforted Asian allies, particularly the Philippines.[239] But, as discussed above, the secretary and the president had already attempted to prepare the Philippine leadership for the fall of Taiwan in the February meeting with Quirino. Also, Truman and Acheson understood that, while the intervention in Korea was popular in Europe and Asia, the intervention in the Taiwan Straits was not. Further support of the discredited Chiang regime appeared imperialistic to the increasingly anticolonial populations in the region.[240] In Europe, the intervention in the Chinese Civil War seemed a rejection of the more realistic approach announced by Washington in January, one in which American resources earmarked for Europe would not be wasted in fighting Chinese Communists. There was clear disagreement over Taiwan policy between the United States and its two most important allies, Britain and France.[241] Attempting to minimize the impression of antinationalism and limit the damage to its hopes for rapprochement with Beijing, the administration stated publicly that the purpose of the intervention in the straits was not only to protect Taiwan from attack but to prevent any armed conflict initiated from either side of the straits.[242] As was the pattern over the preceding three years, it seems that the administration intervened in the Chinese Civil War only to the minimum degree necessary to guarantee consensus on its other policies.

There is also evidence that domestic pressure was crucial in the Taiwan decision. Acheson claims that in the anteroom before the first Blair House meeting, Louis Johnson invoked General MacArthur's prestige to insist on parallel action in Taiwan if the United States were to intervene in Korea. Acheson wrote:

> The full group invited was assembled at Blair House. While waiting for dinner to be announced, Secretary Johnson asked General Bradley to read a memorandum that he had brought from General MacArthur on the strategic importance of Formosa. I recognized this as an opening gun in a *diversionary argument* that Johnson wished to start with me. Evidently another did also, for when General Bradley had finished, the President announced

[239] "Ambassador Morgenstierne (Oslo) to Acheson," *FRUS*, Microfiche Supplement, June 30, 1950, fiche 36 of 59.

[240] "Present Position Respecting American Relationship to Formosa," July 14, 1950, Office of Chinese Affairs, Film C0012, Reel 15, frame 599, NA.

[241] See, for example, "Principal Objectives of Discussion with the British and French Respecting Formosa," Aug. 31, 1950, Decimal File 794A.5 MAP/8–3150, Box 4258, NA. For a clear statement of the British position on American China policy in the early phases of the Korean War, see "Message from Mr. Bevin" Aug. 16, 1950, and Memorandum of Conversation (with Franks et al.), Aug. 28, 1950, PPS Records, Box 14, File: China 1950–51, NA.

[242] For the June 27, 1950, statement by the president, see Truman, *Years of Trial and Hope*, pp. 338–339.

that discussion of the Far Eastern situation had better be postponed until after dinner when we would be alone.[243]

The fact that Johnson still felt it necessary to raise this issue argumentatively once again suggests that the Rusk-Johnson effort of late May and early June had been unsuccessful. Moreover, Acheson saw Johnson's discussion of Taiwan's strategic significance in the Korean War context as "diversionary" rather than banal or obvious. This also suggests that the outbreak of war in Korea had not changed Acheson's analysis of Taiwan's strategic importance.

While Acheson most likely had already drawn up plans to block the straits in the hours before his presentation at Blair House, he could have easily anticipated Johnson's line of attack. He merely needed to recall the debate over the Korean aid bills of January 1950 and June 1949. More recently, just days before the outbreak of the Korean War, there were media reports that MacArthur was about to blast the State Department publicly if it did not agree to assist in Taiwan's defense.[244] Acheson could not see these threats as unfounded. On June 22 the State Department received a secret telegram via Dulles and Johnson stating that MacArthur believed the fall of Taiwan "would be a disaster of the utmost importance."[245] This perception combined with the threat of political attacks by MacArthur and the China Lobby would make it impossible for the administration to justify sending American combat troops into a strategically peripheral area like Korea while standing idly by as the Communists seized Taiwan.

Truman and Acheson had learned the lesson that, because of domestic constraints on grand strategy, nothing significant could be done in Europe, let alone Korea, without assistance to Chiang and public hostility toward Beijing. Moreover, as Nancy Tucker argues, after the administration's earlier compromise on the Korean aid bill there was a firm link in American domestic politics between Korea and Taiwan.[246] In addition to legitimizing the sending of American forces into Korea, the blocking of the straits would provide a line of American resolve against communism that might impress the American public even if efforts in Korea failed. Since one important goal of the Korean intervention was to stand up to communism somewhere, Taiwan provided a good complement to the

[243] Acheson, *Present at the Creation*, pp. 405–406 (emphasis added).

[244] See *Human Events*, June 21, 1950. Political columnist Frank Hanighen wrote: "It is reliably reported to this column that General MacArthur will give his views on the Far Eastern situation via an international broadcast, if the State Department does not yield to his desire to defend Formosa." *New York Times*, June 19, 1950, p. 1, reported that MacArthur was to request emergency military assistance for Taiwan.

[245] Dulles to Acheson, June 22, 1950, Decimal Files 794A.00/6–2250, NA.

[246] Tucker, *Patterns in the Dust*, p. 197.

Korea policy. Not only was Taiwan a highly salient point of anticommunist resistance in the minds of the American public, as an island it provided a more easily defended position than anywhere on the Asian mainland. If success in Korea was doubtful, success in Taiwan was almost guaranteed.[247]

The addition of Taiwan to the area of containment during the Korean War would lend much-needed consistency to American grand strategy. In reference to Truman's problems with Asialationism, a contemporary observer remarked: "The strongest language used by Christ while on earth was used by Him in denouncing hypocrites."[248] Unfortunately for Sino-American relations, the potential for being accused of hypocrisy was great during an expensive mobilization drive backed by an ideological crusade. To avoid this crippling charge, the administration needed to demonstrate some degree of consistency between rhetoric and practice. Truman could not adopt a hands-off policy toward Taiwan, let alone a conciliatory policy toward Beijing, if he hoped to guarantee support for the Korean War and, more generally, to transform the fervor over Korea into broad popular support for larger security policy budgets.

[247] As one participant recalled to Acheson in 1953: "[In 1950] Formosa looked as though it would be as good a place to stand as any other. After all, there you could make sea and air power available. Well, then you'd get this build up domestically which would increase your capability and you'd have a better shot at the thing [balancing against the Soviets]." Unidentified speaker addressing Acheson in the Princeton Seminars, July 23, 1953, Wire 2, p. 3. At Blair House, General Bradley had insisted that America "draw the line" somewhere in order to demonstrate and increase American resolve against expanding Soviet power. Bradley in *FRUS: 1950*, Vol. 7, p. 158. Clearly, as an island, Taiwan provided an ideal place to draw such a line. On December 5, 1950, when expulsion from Korea seemed a real possibility, General Bradley discussed the added value of a stand in Taiwan. He said: "We may fail in Korea but if so, we must draw the line on Formosa. People could not understand why we changed so much if we yielded entirely." *FRUS: 1950*, Vol. 3, p. 1736.

[248] Hugh Butler, quoted in Doenecke, *Not to the Swift*, p. 179.

CHAPTER 5

The Real Lost Chance in China: Nonrecognition, Taiwan, and the Disaster at the Yalu

SINCE CHINA was viewed as a sideshow for American grand strategy, Truman and Acheson wanted to prevent the compromises on their preferred China policy from cutting too deeply into resources reserved for core security programs. On the surface it may seem that they were highly successful. They managed to limit the value of China aid packages, and they ensured that the distribution of assistance funds was slow. Using the Seventh Fleet to block the Taiwan Straits was a relatively simple operation. Moreover, Truman tried to minimize the political risks of the deployment by proclaiming that its purpose was to prevent attacks from either side, not just attacks on Taiwan by the mainland.

But in the context of the Korean War, earlier compromises on China policy proved much more costly than the casual observer might have guessed. In light of the documentary evidence from China and the United States, we can detect a causal link between two key American China policies of 1949–50—nonrecognition of Beijing and the blocking of the Taiwan Straits—and the disastrous escalation of the Korean War that occurred when China crossed the Yalu in the fall of 1950. To demonstrate this link, below I offer a new version of the "lost chance" in China thesis, arguing that while friendship between China and the United States was precluded by their ideological differences, peace between the two nations was not. A plausible argument can be made that Sino-American combat in Korea could have been avoided if the United States had recognized Beijing and had honored Truman's January pledge to stay out of the Chinese Civil War.

This chapter has two purposes. The first is to demonstrate that apparently mild forms of hostility, such as those that Washington pursued toward the Chinese Communists, can lead to costly and unintended outcomes, especially during international crises such as the Korean War. The first half of the chapter does not, therefore, test the theoretical approach presented in Chapter 2. Instead it demonstrates the historical importance of the policies explained with that approach in Chapters 3 and 4. The

Sections of this chapter are derived from previously published articles. They are Christensen, "Threats, Assurances" and "A Lost Chance for What?"

second half of the chapter returns to the book's theoretical approach, demonstrating that in both July and December 1950 mobilizational politics related to the implementation of NSC 68 prevented the United States from pursuing China policies that might have limited the intensity and duration of the Korean War.

TRUMAN, MAO, AND THE LOST-CHANCE DEBATE

The question of whether the Truman administration wasted a chance for friendly relations with the Chinese Communists has spawned as much scholarship and debate as any issue in the history of China's foreign relations. Those who support the lost-chance thesis point to Mao's pragmatism, the ideological differences between Mao and Stalin, and the highly nationalistic nature of Chinese communism. In its original and simplest form, the lost-chance thesis posits that Mao could have befriended either camp in the Cold War. American belligerence, not ideological hardwiring, determined Mao's hostility toward Washington and alliance with Moscow. Those who reject the lost-chance thesis point to Mao's ideological hatred and distrust of the United States and the CCP's desire to secure spiritual as well as practical leadership from Stalin.[1]

Scholarship on documentary evidence from China suggests that the critics of the lost-chance thesis are basically right. Given Mao's fundamental mistrust of the United States and early affinity for Moscow, it would have been impossible for Washington to woo the Chinese Communists away from the Soviets and toward the Western camp. In fact, Mao's "lean to one side" policy seemed set in stone as early as the 1930s.[2] While some have argued that modified American behavior in 1948–49 might have changed Mao's fundamental perceptions of America, Chinese archival materials demonstrate that Mao would have been extremely suspicious of the Americans, even if the United States had adopted maximally conciliatory policies: cutting aid to the KMT and recognizing the Communists in 1949.[3]

A major limitation of the original lost-chance debate is its focus on the possibility for amicable relations or alignment between the United States and China. A large number of other potential outcomes fall between Sino-American alignment, as witnessed after 1972, and direct military

[1] For early lost-chance arguments, see Kolko and Kolko, *The Limits of Power*, chap. 20; Tuchman, "If Mao Had Come to Washington"; and Gurtov, *The United States against the Third World*, p. 142. For arguments stressing Mao's ideology and the inevitability of Sino-American conflict, see Tatsumi, "The Cold War and China"; and Goldstein "Sino-American Relations, 1948–50."

[2] Sheng, "America's Lost Chance in China?"

[3] The documentary evidence is discussed at greater length below.

conflict, as occurred in Korea in 1950. Just because there was no chance for friendship does not mean that there was no chance for peace. The same holds true for Sino-Soviet relations. There is a spectrum of possibilities between the high level of Sino-Soviet cooperation in Korea and the out-and-out enmity of the late 1960s. In 1950 the Chinese Communists were going to ally with the Soviets regardless of American behavior; but the tightness of the Sino-Soviet alliance still may have depended in large part on American actions.

The original lost-chance debate too often focused on Washington's ability to replace the Soviets as a friend and benefactor. In the early 1980s scholars began to address the lost-chance question more subtly, asking whether Sino-American relations could not have been somewhat better, even if they could not have been friendly.[4] But despite these contributions, there has not been enough exploration of just how American policies, if different, might have reduced conflict between the two sides. This is not coincidental. The lack of documentary evidence on the Chinese side rendered speculation highly problematic. Using such evidence— including Mao's military and diplomatic manuscripts—below I analyze Mao's attitudes toward the United States in order to determine whether there was a lost chance for peace between the United States and China in 1949–50. I conclude that, while Mao viewed the United States as unquestionably hostile to the CCP in this period, he believed that American hostility might manifest itself in more or less threatening ways. American recognition of Beijing and abandonment of Chiang Kai-shek would not have provided a panacea for the many ills facing Sino-American relations. Still, those policies might have prevented the escalation of the Korean War in fall 1950.

Mao's Attitudes toward the United States in Early 1949

In January 1949 Mao advised the Central Committee of its responsibilities in bringing the civil war to a successful conclusion. Mao's assessment of the American threat was a central element in his presentation. His view of America's future policies toward China was complex. On the level of intentionality, Mao saw the United States as unalterably hostile to his revolution. He saw no chance for friendship with Washington. On the other hand, he viewed the United States as a somewhat rational actor that eventually would recognize the futility of armed intervention in China. He went so far as to speculate that the United States might end direct military assistance to the KMT and then recognize the CCP

---

[4] Hunt, "Mao Tse-tung and the Issue of Accommodation with the United States"; Stueck, *The Road to Confrontation;* and Tucker, *Patterns in the Dust.*

regime. Still, Mao believed that even if the United States withdrew entirely from the civil war and recognized the Communists, Washington would still support covertly all available domestic opponents to his regime.

Despite intermittent notes of caution, Mao's talk was generally quite optimistic.[5] He believed that American leaders, relative newcomers to "imperialism," were becoming wiser, recognizing the futility of significant assistance to Chiang Kai-shek. Therefore, in the future, Mao believed the United States would likely limit its activities to subversion. Mao said:

> In our strategic planning, we have always calculated in the possibility that the United States would directly send troops, occupying several coastal cities and engaging in warfare with us. We still must not dismiss this type of possibility. . . . *But, as the Chinese people's revolutionary strength increases and becomes more resolute, the possibility that the United States will carry out a direct military intervention also decreases, and moreover, in the same vein, the American involvement in financial and military assistance to the KMT may also decrease.* In the past year, especially in the past three months, the multiple changes in and unsteadiness of the American government's attitudes prove this point. *Among the Chinese people and in the Party there still exists a mistaken viewpoint which overestimates the power of American imperialism. It is essential [that we] continue to uncover and overcome [this tendency].[6]*

Although he was hardly calling for laxity among his military forces, Mao's major purpose in this section of the speech was to allay fears within the party that the United States was about to invade Communist-held areas.

The optimism about the United States in Mao's speech should not be overstated. Mao believed that the United States would modify its behavior, but he believed this reflected a moderation in strategy, not a change in American intentions. He continued:

> The China policy of the American imperialists has changed from pure support of the KMT's military opposition to the Communist Party to a two-sided policy. This [policy] consists of, on the one hand, supporting the remnant KMT military forces and regional warlords [so as] to continue to

[5] In his book, which focuses on Mao's strategy of deterring the United States, Zhang Shuguang appropriately concentrates on the more cautious and vigilant sections of Mao's January 1949 talk. See Zhang, *Deterrence and Strategic Culture*, chap. 2.

[6] See *Mao Zedong Junshi Wenxuan: Neibuben*, pp. 326–332 (emphasis added). Mao's talk was apparently sincere. He expressed similar beliefs in a telegram to Stalin. See "Mao Zedong to Stalin," Jan. 13, 1949, in Westad, "Rivals and Allies," p. 27. The Russian document was translated by Maxim Korobochkin.

oppose the People's Liberation Army; [and] on the other hand, dispatching their running dogs to infiltrate the revolutionary camp, [so as] to organize a so-called opposition party and to break up the revolution from the inside. When the People's Liberation Army is about to achieve victory throughout the country, they may not even hesitate to use the method of recognizing the People's Republic, adopting a legitimate position [in China], and thereby implementing this policy of "internal break up." We need to increase our vigilance toward this imperialist conspiratorial plot, and resolutely smash it.[7]

Counter to the earlier versions of the lost-chance thesis, conciliatory American moves would not have changed Mao's beliefs about America's opposition to his revolution. Consistent with his overall ideology, Mao attributed Washington's hostility to an imperialist national character. He associated any potential American conciliation in the future with environmental constraints—increased CCP power—rather than a change of heart in Washington.[8] But for our purposes, the chairman's statements also demonstrate that, in his mind, there was a scale of hostility ranging in declining order from direct military involvement on the side of domestic adversaries, to military aid to domestic adversaries, to recognition of a Communist China followed by subversive activities. In early 1949 Mao believed that, faced with growing CCP strength and KMT collapse, the United States was rationally moving down the scale to the strategy of subversion.

Mao's Calculations after Crossing the Yangzi (Yangtze)

The acquiescence of the U.S. Pacific Command to Chinese victories in Shanghai and Tianjin in spring 1949 demonstrated that Mao's first and most important prediction about the United States was basically correct: the United States was not going to involve itself directly in defending the remaining KMT forces on the mainland. The historical importance of Mao's predictions should not be underestimated. In April 1949 Mao decided to cross the Yangzi despite the warnings of Stalin's emissary, Anastas Mikoyan, that such an action should not be taken hastily, lest the United States enter the Chinese Civil War.[9] It was the crossing of the Yangzi that drove Chiang's government to Taiwan and ended the KMT's reign on the mainland.

After seizing Nanjing, Mao was impressed that the American embassy

[7] See *Mao Zedong Junshi Wenxuan: Neibuben*, pp. 326–332.

[8] In Jonathan Mercer's theoretical terms, Mao believed American withdrawal was situational, not dispositional. See Mercer, *Reputation in International Politics.*

[9] Goncharov, "Stalin's Dialogue with Mao Zedong."

did not flee to Canton along with the KMT government. Mao stated on April 28:

> We should educate our troops to protect British and American residents . . . as well as foreign ambassadors, ministers, consuls, and other diplomats, especially those from the United States and Britain. Now the American side is asking a third party to contact us for the purpose of establishing diplomatic relations. We think that, if the United States and Britain can cut off their relations with the KMT, we can consider the question of establishing diplomatic relations with them. . . . The old U.S. policy of assisting the KMT and opposing the CCP is bankrupt. It seems that its policy is turning to one of establishing diplomatic relations with us.[10]

Mao was actively considering the establishment of relations with the United States and, on April 30, he stated that the CCP would establish diplomatic relations with any country that broke with the KMT, removed its forces from China, and treated China "fairly."[11]

Various Communist Party actions were in accord with these statements. As discussed in Chapter 4, in April, Yao Yilin sought trade ties through Clubb's offices in Shanghai. In May and June, Huang Hua responded positively to the overture from Ambassador Stuart's office. These policies were not a sign of CCP factionalism, as was previously believed by many foreign analysts. It is clear that Mao directly controlled Huang's mission to the American embassy in Nanjing. In fact, a May 10 telegram from Mao to the Nanjing Municipal Bureau gives specific instructions to Huang Hua about what issues were to be raised with Stuart regarding the establishing of diplomatic relations with a CCP government. Huang was ordered to be firm and to emphasize that American support for the KMT, not the lack of American aid to CCP-held areas, was the main stumbling block to improved relations.[12] Huang's apology for the Stuart incident, complaints about American relations with the KMT, and offers of detente all represented the CCP line, not simply the view of a minority faction under Zhou Enlai.[13]

The events of April through July convinced the CCP leadership that, while Mao may have been right that the United States would not enter

[10] "CCP Military Commission Instructions regarding English, American, and Foreign Nationals and Diplomatic Personnel. . . ." Apr. 28, 1949, in *Dang De Wenxian*, 1989, no. 4, p. 43.

[11] See the internally circulated history by Yao, *Cong Yalu Jiang Dao Banmendian*, pp.2–3; a text of the speech, made in the name of Li Tao, can be found in *Mao Zedong Xuanji*, Vol. 4, pp. 1460–1461.

[12] "Some Issues to Which Huang Hua Should Give Attention When Speaking with Stuart," May 10, 1949, in *Mao Zedong Waijiao Wenxuan*, pp. 87–88.

[13] Chen, *China's Road to the Korean War*, chap. 2; Yao, *Cong Yalu Jiang Dao Banmendian*, p. 2.

the Chinese Civil War directly, in the near term American distancing from the KMT was likely to be extremely limited. Despite the Huang mission and the CCP's July dispatch of Chen Mingshu, the United States rejected rapprochement with the CCP. Stuart did more than refuse to meet with Mao in Beiping, he also failed to respond satisfactorily to Huang Hua's main criticism of American behavior: that the United States was still actively involved in the civil war on the side of the KMT.[14] Despite Stuart's assurances that American aid to Chiang was small and decreasing, Chinese Communist leaders believed that American involvement with Chiang Kai-shek was even greater than it actually was.[15] For example, a leading Chinese Communist, Bo Yibo, reports that in July 1949 Chinese leaders believed (falsely) that the American and British navies were participating directly in the KMT naval blockade of China's southern and eastern ports.[16] In a July 1949 report, Deng Xiaoping argued that China's experience "in the last month or so" had shown that forcing the "imperialists" to submit to CCP control of China would not be simple.[17] Although the United States had not intervened to prevent PLA control of coastal cities, in the CCP's mind it had not come far down Mao's ladder of hostility. The CCP still believed that the United States would only recognize the KMT, would continue to grant the KMT economic and military aid, and would remain actively involved in military harassment of Communist-controlled coastal areas.

After the Founding of the Republic: Mao's Attitudes and Expectations about the United States

Some authors argue that Mao did not seek recognition from the United States in 1949 and that he did not plan to do so for years to come.[18] This is correct if, by this, we mean that Mao was not going to revise the goals of his revolution in order to persuade the Americans to recognize the PRC. But the CCP was willing to accept, and in fact formally requested, recognition from the Western powers. The CCP's actions, party documents, and leaders' memoirs all suggest that Mao would have accepted

[14] For Huang Hua's own recollections of the offer by Zhou Enlai and the American response, see Li Xiaobing's translation of Huang Hua's account, entitled "My Contacts with John Leighton Stuart."

[15] For Stuart's assurances, see ibid.

[16] Bo, *Ruogan Zhongda Juece yu Shijian de Huigu,* Vol. 1, pp. 38–39. This misperception was understandable because the United States had equipped the Nationalists' navy.

[17] Bo, *Ruogan Zhongda Juece yu Shijian de Huigu,* Vol. 1, pp. 38–39.

[18] Zhang, *Deterrence and Strategic Culture,* chap. 2, esp. pp. 26–27; Cohen, "Conversations with Chinese Friends."

recognition from all countries, including the United States, albeit with suspicion and on China's terms.

Mao's metaphor for China's policy toward foreign powers in 1949–50 was to "sweep China clean before inviting guests." The CCP was to eliminate all imperialist power in China before allowing real foreign influence to return to the mainland. But despite the image of foreigners flying out of China like swept dust and a virulent anti-American propaganda campaign, Mao's strategy did not preclude direct relations with Western powers.[19] As discussed in Chapter 4, while Mao was preparing to announce the founding of the People's Republic, the CCP sent an emissary to the American consul general, O. Edmund Clubb, in order to explain again the CCP's attitude toward establishing relations with outside countries. On October 1, 1949, Clubb was given the same request for the establishment of relations as other foreign representatives in China.[20]

The Chinese conditions for accepting recognition and beginning a dialogue that would lead to diplomatic relations were not extremely arduous. In a December 1949 telegram regarding the establishment of relations with Burma, Mao laid out the two conditions for establishing relations with nonsocialist countries. The recognizing country must be willing to break diplomatic relations with the KMT and to enter a negotiation process to hammer out the terms of diplomatic exchanges.[21] In his memoirs, Bo Yibo states that in late 1949 Mao had consistent criteria for the establishment of relations with any country: the recognition of the sole legitimacy of the PRC and respect for Chinese sovereignty. Bo emphasizes that "it is self-evident that Western countries were included under this principle."[22] Huang Hua made similar statements about CCP preconditions in midyear.[23] In Mao's hierarchy of nations there were distinctions between typical nonsocialist countries, such as Burma, and "imperialist" countries, such as Britain and the United States. In fact, on December 16 Mao is reported to have said to Stalin that China should

[19] For an outline of the "sweep" strategy, see Han and Xue, eds., *Dangdai Zhongguo Waijiao*, chaps. 1 and 2. Huang Hua stated that while the strategy meant that China was not anxious to acquire diplomatic recognition from the West, neither did the strategy preclude high-level contacts such as the proposed meeting of Stuart and Zhou Enlai in Beiping. See Huang, "My Contacts with John Leighton Stuart," p. 50; and Yang, "The Soviet Factor," pp. 31–34.

[20] See Yao, *Cong Yalu Jiang Dao Banmendian*, p. 6; and Blum, *Drawing the Line*, pp. 144–146.

[21] See "Telegram concerning the Establishing of Relations with Burma," Dec. 19, 1949, in *Jianguo Yilai Mao Zedong Wengao*, Vol. 1, p. 193.

[22] Bo, *Ruogan Zhongda Juece yu Shijian de Huigu*, pp. 39–40.

[23] In "My Contacts with John Leighton Stuart," p. 50, Huang writes, "We were willing to establish relations with all countries on the basis of equality."

not rush to be recognized by Britain and other imperialist powers.[24] But it is significant to note that Britain recognized China and established official contacts in January 1950 despite Britain's long history of imperialism in China.

For practical purposes, a nation could establish high-level contacts merely by recognizing the CCP as the sole legitimate government, halting assistance to Chiang, and sending a team of representatives to negotiate the formalizing of relations. The British did this successfully in January. Although Britain fell far short of meeting Mao's terms for the exchange of ambassadors, the British still were able to dispatch a team of representatives to Beijing and to undertake long-term negotiations over the details of "unequal treaties" and other matters. These types of contacts, while not ideal, still provide direct channels of communication, which are critical in times of crisis.

But even if such contacts had been possible between Washington and Beijing, there is no reason to believe that friendship and significant economic relations would have flowed from them. Given what we now know about his deep-seated caution about the United States, Mao would have been extremely suspicious of the motives behind American recognition. But these concerns apparently would not have led him to denounce American attempts to establish more normal relations. While in Moscow, rather than worrying about the possible negative effects of recognition by nonsocialist countries, Mao seemingly welcomed the possibility, decreeing that, when nonsocialist countries agree to recognize China, the Chinese media should announce the news promptly.[25] Three days later, Mao discussed plans for increased trade with the West, including the United States, although in no sense did he believe that the West would or should supplant the Soviet Union as China's main economic partner.[26] Even after Mao made his decision to enter the Korean War and troops

[24] "Conversation between Stalin and Mao," Dec. 16, 1949, in Rozas, Chen, and Weathersby, trans., "Stalin's Conversations."

[25] See "Telegram concerning the Establishing of Relations with Burma," Dec. 19, 1949, in *Jianguo Yilai Mao Zedong Wengao*, Vol. 1, p. 193. It is possible that Mao was hoping to use the recognition of China by nonsocialist countries as leverage against Stalin in his appeal for a Sino-Soviet defense treaty. One Russian analyst argues that British recognition combined with Truman's policy of disengagement from Taiwan in early January made Stalin so worried about potential Chinese Titoism that he finally agreed to the Sino-Soviet defense treaty. See Zubok, "To Hell with Yalta!" p. 25.

[26] See Mao's Dec. 22, 1949, telegram, entitled "Concerning the Issue of Preparing a Trade Treaty with the Soviet Union," in *Jianguo Yilai Mao Zedong Wengao*, Vol. 1, p. 197. Party archivists have pointed to these December telegrams as evidence that Mao was open to relations with the West, but that the West, and in particular the United States, was not accommodating. See the editors' postscript in ibid., pp. 777–778.

had begun crossing the Yalu, Mao still held some outside hope that a major blow to UN forces (the killing of tens of thousands of troops) might compel the Americans to open diplomatic talks with the PRC.[27] In 1949–50, Mao saw no contradiction between diplomatic contacts and severe forms of mutual hostility.

The Potential Effect of U.S. Recognition on Sino-Soviet Relations

There is a good deal of evidence that the Soviets expected the development of American relations with the CCP. In May 1950, after returning from Moscow, UN Secretary General Trygve Lie informed Acheson that the Soviets had walked out of the UN in January 1950 only because they fully expected the United States to recognize the PRC in the short term. Stalin thought that if the Soviets made a principled stand at the UN, they could "take a bow for helping get the Chinese Communists into the Security Council."[28] The Soviets may secretly have wanted to prevent Chinese entrance, but they also would have liked to take credit for that outcome if it were viewed as inevitable. There is documentary evidence from China demonstrating that, in January, China and the Soviet Union were carefully coordinating their efforts regarding the UN.[29] While in Moscow Mao seemed hopeful that, at a minimum, the PRC would soon enter the Security Council, actually directing Liu Shaoqi to ready a PRC delegation to the UN.[30]

While the Chinese and the Soviets may have anticipated improved relations with the United States in early January, for their part, the Soviets felt that any improvement in Sino-American relations was detrimental to Soviet interests.[31] If Lie's account is correct, by protesting at the UN the Soviets were only trying to take credit for what they falsely saw as an inevitable outcome. We now know from Russian archival discoveries and interview research that Stalin actually feared improved relations between Beijing and Washington. From all accounts Stalin's cognitive biases

[27] "Telegram to Peng Dehuai and Gao concerning Strategic Issues in the Korea," Oct. 23, 1950, in ibid., pp. 588–589. It is important to note that Mao did not seem to put much hope in this prospect. See Christensen, "Threats, Assurances."

[28] "Memorandum of Conversation," May 29, 1950, in *FRUS*, microfiche supplement, Secretary's Memoranda of Conversation, 1947–52, fiche 36 of 49.

[29] See Mao's Jan. 7, 1950, telegram to Zhou Enlai and the Central Committee regarding a joint Sino-Soviet strategy to assail the KMT position in the Security Council. *Jianguo Yilai Mao Zedong Wengao*, Vol. 1, pp. 219–220.

[30] "Telegram to Liu Shaoqi concerning Sending Our Representatives to the United Nations," Jan. 13, 1950 in *Jianguo Yilai Mao Zedong Wengao*, Vol. 1, pp. 235–236.

[31] Goncharov, "Stalin's Dialogue"; Zubok, "To Hell with Yalta!" p. 25.

about Mao's Titoism were even stronger than the Americans' oft-cited bias that Mao was a tool of Moscow. Stalin believed that Mao was a Titoist nationalist or, even worse, a rival leader of international communism.[32] Mao's own later reflections about relations with Moscow in this period fully conform with the evidence from Russia. Mao's 1959 internal review of Sino-Soviet relations states that, until 1951, when the Chinese were fully engaged in Korea, the Soviets "doubted that ours was a real revolution."[33]

Even though American recognition of China in the period December 1949–January 1950 would not have made Mao view the United States as a friendly power, it may have indirectly damaged Sino-Soviet relations. Stalin almost certainly would have objected vigorously to Chinese contacts with Washington. Fearing Chinese Titoism, the Soviets put a great deal of pressure on Mao to shun any overtures from the United States. They pointed to American support for the KMT as a reason to reject any such overtures.[34] Interestingly, Acheson was well aware of this problem. On January 23, American intelligence officers informed Acheson of the potentially divisive effects of American recognition on Sino-Soviet relations, concluding that the "Soviets could not brook American recognition."[35]

Stalin's protestations and pressure would have appeared to Mao as increased Soviet interference in China's sovereign affairs, particularly if the United States had already broken relations with the KMT. Mao, however, clearly did want to prove to Stalin that he was no Tito. Although the Chinese evidence suggests otherwise, it is possible that Mao would have denounced American attempts at recognition in order to curry favor with Stalin. But even in the event that Mao decided to buckle to Soviet pressure and react belligerently to such an American overture, this episode would have exacerbated existing tensions between the two sides, tensions that an internal CCP history chalks up to Stalin's "great power chauvinism."[36] In 1958, while berating the Soviet ambassador to

---

[32] Goncharov, "Stalin's Dialogue." As Kathryn Weathersby's archival discoveries suggest, Stalin agreed to Kim Il-sung's attack on South Korea largely because he did not want the Chinese to supplant the Soviets as leaders of the international communist movement. See Weathersby, "New Findings on the Korean War," p. 14.

[33] "An Outline for a Talk on the International Situation," in *Jianguo Yilai Mao Zedong Wengao*, Vol. 8, pp. 599–603. Also see Yao, *Cong Yalu Jiang Dao Banmendian*, p. 22.

[34] Goncharov, "Stalin's Dialogue"; and Goncharov, Lewis, and Xue, *Uncertain Partners*, chap. 4.

[35] Peiping to Secretary of State, Jan. 23, 1950, China: Internal Affairs, LM152, frame 490, NA.

[36] For discussions of Mao's reservations about Stalin's early demands on China, see Han and Xue, eds., *Dangdai Zhongguo Waijiao*, chaps. 1 and 2; and Shi, *Zai Lishi Juren de Shenbian*, chap. 14.

China, Mao claimed that he was deeply offended by Soviet paternalistic condescension on such matters as early as the January 1949 Mikoyan mission to China.[37]

TAIWAN, U.S. RECOGNITION POLICY, AND THE ESCALATION OF THE KOREAN WAR

In the Western literature on the Korean crisis, it is widely held that there were two failures of coercive diplomacy in Korea that led to Sino-American conflict on the peninsula in fall 1950.[38] China first failed to deter the Americans' crossing of the 38th parallel in October 1950. The United States then failed to dissuade Mao from entering Korea in force in October and November: either the United States was too soft—the American diplomatic and military posture failed to deter Chinese entrance; or the United States was too tough—moving American troops close to the Chinese border threatened Chinese security. The documentary evidence from China suggests that we should focus mainly on Beijing's failure to deter American troops from crossing the 38th parallel. Once they had done so, no mixture of American threats and reassurances, short of voluntary withdrawal of U.S. forces from North Korea and the Taiwan Straits, would have dissuaded Mao from attacking American troops. America could not have deterred Chinese attack with clearer threats of escalation, and MacArthur could not have reassured Mao by maintaining a buffer zone between American forces and the Yalu border.[39] Therefore we should study more carefully the reasons that Mao was so sensitive about America's move into North Korea and why China was unable to deter it.

China's Deterrence Failure: October 1950

The standard interpretations of the Chinese failure to deter the United States from crossing the 38th parallel in October are straightforward and stand up well to the documentary evidence. The tragedy was based both in American misperceptions about how Chinese weakness would affect Beijing's calculations and in poor communication channels between the two capitals. In calling for the unconditional surrender of North Korean troops (on October 1) and crossing the 38th parallel (on October 7), the

---

[37] "A Discussion with the Soviet Ambassador to China, Yudin" July 22, 1958, *Mao Zedong Waijiao Wenxuan*, pp. 322–333.

[38] For a review of the literature on the Korean crisis and a detailed analysis of Mao's decision to enter the war, see Christensen, "Threats, Assurances."

[39] Ibid.

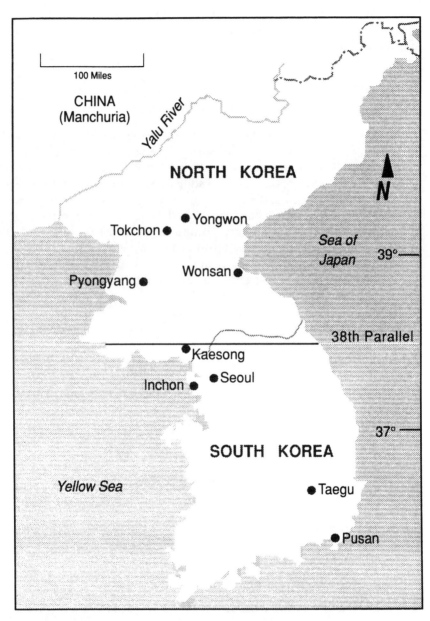

5.1. Map of Korea

Americans believed that China's vulnerability would probably preclude Chinese entrance into the war. However, as Allen Whiting argued, it was China's vulnerability that precipitated its October 19 crossing of the Yalu.[40] Although the Chinese attempted to deter the American crossing, the lack of direct communications meant that their warnings were both too weak and too late to reverse the American decisions.[41] In September and October the United States was emboldened in Korea both by MacArthur's stunning success at Inchon and by China's military, economic, and political weakness.[42] In late September, Marshal Nie Rongzhen and Premier Zhou Enlai voiced deterrent warnings. These statements were accompanied by movements of Chinese troops in and around Manchuria. On the night of October 2, Zhou called Indian ambassador K. M. Panikkar to a midnight meeting. Zhou gave him a message to pass to Washington: if U.S. forces crossed the 38th parallel, China would enter the war.[43] Considering these warnings to be bluffs, Americans crossed the parallel on October 7.

The Chinese faced several serious problems in their effort to deter the Americans. First, the United States had solid realpolitik incentives to cross the parallel. Second, without direct diplomatic relations it was difficult for Beijing to communicate a message strong and authoritative enough to deter implementation of the American strategy. Third, the clearest Chinese warning came only after the American decision to cross the 38th parallel had been made.

In American strategic planning, Korea was considered a region of little geostrategic significance. American troops were withdrawn from Korea in spring 1949 because the manpower was considered better spent elsewhere. After the DPRK (Democratic People's Republic of Korea) attacked the South on June 25, 1950, Truman dispatched American forces in order to punish aggression and save the American reputation for resolve against communist expansion. The decision to intervene was not based in a reevaluation of the strategic significance of Korea.

But if the goal of the war was simply to restore the international

[40] Whiting, *China Crosses the Yalu.*

[41] On problems of diplomatic signaling see Zelman, "Chinese Entrance into the Korean War," passim; George and Smoke, *Deterrence in American Foreign Policy,* pp. 188–190; Lebow, *Between Peace and War,* pp. 148–149, 178; and Kalicki, *Patterns of Sino-American Conflict,* pp. 56, 211–217.

[42] The Inchon landing of Sept. 15, 1950, reversed American fortunes in Korea by successfully dividing North Korean troops at the waist of Korea. The forces south of the 38th parallel were trapped and the forces north of it were in disarray. For discussion of the invasion, see Appleman, *South to the Naktong,* chap. 25. For a discussion of American perceptions of Chinese weakness in the fall of 1950, see Tsou, *America's Failure in China,* pp. 573–574; and Foot, *The Wrong War,* pp. 80–81.

[43] See Whiting, *China Crosses the Yalu,* pp. 108–109.

boundary at the 38th parallel, the United States would find itself back in the position it was in before 1949, assisting South Korea at the expense of other more important strategic goals worldwide. Dean Acheson had initially opposed crossing the parallel, but as early as July 10 he put the American dilemma this way: "In the longer run, if we should succeed in reoccupying the South, the question of garrisoning and supporting it would arise. This would be a hard task for us to take on, and yet it seemed hardly sensible to repel the attack and then abandon the country. I could not see the end of it."[44] In fall 1950 the American defense budget was still tightly constrained: the Korean War mobilized the American public behind higher military spending levels, but the most significant NSC 68 increase did not occur until after the Americans crossed the parallel and met the massive Chinese counteroffensive.[45] Given this budgetary constraint, a decision to settle for a ceasefire near the 38th parallel in October 1950 would have cut deeper into resources earmarked for Europe than the ultimate decision to do so in 1953. In short, budgetary limits made the 38th parallel a difficult place to stop in October 1950. Moreover, American political commentators were clamoring for the American military to pursue North Korean troops across the parallel, and the American public agreed.[46]

In mid-September when MacArthur succeeded so fantastically by landing forces at Inchon and cutting the overextended North Korean forces in half, the Americans were faced with a tempting opportunity to break out of Acheson's dilemma by destroying the North Korean military once and for all. In late September, the North Korean army was in retreat and disarray; destroying the North Korean forces quickly and totally would serve to reduce the need for long-term American assistance to South Korea, punish aggressors, and quiet domestic critics of the administration's foreign policy.[47]

Given the importance of these American goals in Korea, only a strong and clear warning from China might have reversed Truman's course. The Zhou-Panikkar communique did not meet this criterion. Washington lacked direct contacts in Beijing and had received unreliable messages

[44] Acheson, paraphrasing a July 10, 1950, letter to Paul Nitze, in *Present at the Creation*, pp. 450–451. In a June 28 NSC meeting, Acheson and Truman both opposed crossing the 38th. See Executive Secretariat Records, Box 13, Memoranda of Conversations, NA. The Joint Chiefs and the Defense Department argued that the 38th parallel was a geographically infelicitous position to assume a permanent defense, and that a halt there would permit renewed military instability in Korea and lead to exorbitant American expenditures. See Foot, *The Wrong War*, p. 71; and Gaddis, *The Long Peace*, p.99.

[45] Hammond, "NSC 68," pp. 351–363.

[46] "Monthly Survey," Sept. and Oct. 1950, Foster Papers, Box 12, NA.

[47] Stueck, *The Road to Confrontation*, pp. 228–231; Gaddis, *The Long Peace*, pp. 98–99; Foot, *The Wrong War*, pp. 69–70; and Kaufman, *The Korean War*, chap. 3.

from mainland sources before, so it questioned Zhou's authority.[48] In addition, Washington questioned the credibility of the messenger, Panikkar, viewing him as a gullible Communist sympathizer.[49] The October 3 communique was the most direct Chinese deterrent threat, but it came only after Truman had authorized MacArthur's crossing of the parallel (September 27) and the UN had called for Pyongyang's capitulation (October 1). So, the Chinese statement was more of a compellent than a deterrent threat. As Thomas Schelling and others have argued, because the status quo is more difficult to change than to maintain, it is more difficult to compel action than it is to deter it.[50]

Although many have questioned Truman's failure to heed China's earliest warnings, even the most critical scholars understand the difficulties the Truman administration faced in reading Chinese signals of resolve in early October. For example, in his psychological critique of deterrence theory, Richard Ned Lebow suggests that Truman and Acheson may have fallen victim to "defensive avoidance" of early Chinese deterrent signals, but he concedes that "given the American reading of the military situation, it was not altogether unreasonable for them to dismiss Chou En-lai's warning as a bluff."[51]

The American Failure of Coercive Diplomacy: October–November 1950

Historians and political scientists generally view the first bilateral deterrence failure as a tragedy of bad timing and poor signaling, but responsibility for the second set of deterrence failures in November 1950 has been firmly laid on Truman's and MacArthur's shoulders. Scholars point out that, even after UN forces met Chinese troops in limited fighting south of the Yalu (October 25–November 7), American leaders continued to disregard Chinese security concerns and underestimate Chinese military strength and political resolve. The United States chose to advance despite clear deterrent signals and sufficient time to digest them: the Chinese had already demonstrated their resolve by fighting American troops in northernmost Korea in late October, and the Americans had weeks in which to digest the meaning and implications of the early Chi-

---

[48] Witness the misleading Zhou Mingxun contacts in early 1950.

[49] For Truman's discussion of his mistrust of Panikkar, see Truman, *Memoirs*, Vol. 2, p. 362.

[50] For the theoretical and practical distinctions between deterrence and compellence as forms of coercion, see Schelling, *Arms and Influence*, pp. 69–92; and George and Smoke, *Deterrence in American Foreign Policy*, pp. 200–201.

[51] Lebow, *Between Peace and War*, p. 178.

nese engagements.[52] Chinese troops broke off operations from November 5 to November 7 and disappeared into the Korean countryside. Seventeen days later, MacArthur began his final offensive to the Yalu and quickly met a massive Chinese counteroffensive (November 26) that drove UN forces back across the 38th parallel.

Each of the two correctives scholars have suggested for American policy in November is based on one of the two core concepts of deterrence theory: credibility of threat, and reassurance. As Schelling has argued persuasively, all effective deterrent threats contain both elements. If the threat is not credible because the deterrer lacks capability or resolve, then deterrence attempts will be ineffective. But of equal importance is the deterrer's reassurances to the target that the threat is conditional. Unless the target believes a punitive attack is contingent on the target's behavior, then it has no incentive to comply with the deterrer's demands.[53]

In threat-based accounts, such as MacArthur's, China is portrayed as insufficiently fearful of American punitive air attacks on the mainland. Because of this confidence, it is argued, Mao viewed the risks of large-scale entry into Korea as permissibly low. Thus, more direct U.S. threats of strategic bombing on the Chinese mainland might have dissuaded the Chinese from the counteroffensive of late November.[54]

The second and far more common critique of American deterrent policy centers on the failure of the Americans to reassure Mao that Chinese interests and territory would not be violated by UN forces in Korea. Advocates of reassurance policies argue that U.S. leaders mistakenly assumed that China saw no real threat of direct invasion from America. So, they contend, when Acheson and others did make reassuring statements toward China, they placed too much emphasis on border region issues, such as continued Chinese access to Yalu River hydroelectric facilities.[55] More important, by disregarding Washington's September directives to keep non-Korean troops away from the Manchurian border, MacArthur physically threatened China in a manner Mao could not ignore. Various analysts suggest that America should have reassured China about its territorial concerns with clearer actions, giving more explicit guarantees of Chinese sovereignty and establishing a buffer somewhere between the

[52] George and Smoke, *Deterrence in American Foreign Policy*, pp. 222–231; Zelman, "Chinese Intervention," pp. 9–10; Lebow, *Between Peace and War*, pp. 178–184.

[53] Schelling, *Arms and Influence*, chap. 2.

[54] Halperin, *Limited War in the Nuclear Age*, pp. 50–53; Kugler, "Assessing Stable Deterrence," p. 53; Twining, *Neither Liberty Nor Safety*, pp. 53–54. For more conditional discussions of the utility of deterrent threats, see Zelman, "Chinese Entrance," pp. 27–28; George and Smoke, *Deterrence in American Foreign Policy*, pp. 220–221; Farrar, "A Pause for Negotiations," p. 77; and Betts, *Nuclear Blackmail and Nuclear Balance*, pp. 34–36.

[55] For criticism of Acheson's anemic reassurances, see Whiting, *China Crosses the Yalu*, pp. 151–152, 158–162. In accord is Jervis, *Perception and Misperception*, p. 46.

American forces near Pyongyang and Wonsan and the Chinese border.[56] They argue that a buffer would have ensured both South Korean and Chinese security and might have prevented an avoidable and tragic escalation of war in late November.

The meaning of China's disengagement in early November is central to deterrence theory analyses of the crisis. While MacArthur argued that Mao's disengagement was part of a plot to prepare a massive assault on UN forces in the winter,[57] those who attribute defensive intentions to China argue that the disengagement demonstrated China's desire to deter a larger war.[58] They recognize that the stealth employed by the Chinese troops during disengagement worked against the goal of deterring the Americans, but some suggest this was an unintended and tragic consequence of Chinese tactical vulnerability to American air superiority.[59]

How one views the disengagement depends on one's assumptions about China's political and military goals in Korea. China's minimum and maximum goals in entering the war also determine the accuracy of our assessment of American policy and the chances for peace. But, as Allen Whiting first cautioned, only Chinese government documents can offer us solid evidence about Chinese intentions. Without them, the arguments rest on speculation. When presenting the Chinese documentation below, at appropriate junctures I also analyze relevant documentary findings from the Russian archives. These sometimes differ in important ways from the Chinese documents. While there is significant overlap and

[56] For discussions of the potential effectiveness of a buffer in this period, see Whiting, *China Crosses the Yalu*, pp. 155, 160–162 and passim; Stueck, *The Road to Confrontation*, p. 251; George and Smoke, *Deterrence in American Foreign Policy*, p. 222–231; Zelman, "Chinese Intervention," p. 27; Orme, "Deterrence Failures," pp. 109–110; Schelling, *Arms and Influence*, pp. 54–55; Kalicki, *Pattern of Sino-American Crises*, pp. 57–64.

[57] For the MacArthur argument, see Spanier, *Truman-MacArthur Controversy*, p. 149. For a related argument, see Cohen and Gooch, *Military Misfortunes*, pp. 171–172; Cohen and Gooch argue correctly that Mao saw the crossing of the 38th parallel as the *casus belli* and that Mao's military objective was to drive American forces completely off the peninsula. Arguing that China had adopted a "compellence" strategy is Segal, *Defending China*. Segal, however, does not specify whether Mao initially wanted to compel U.S. withdrawal from North Korea alone or from the entire peninsula. Neither Cohen and Gooch nor Segal utilizes documentary evidence from China.

[58] See, for example, Camilleri, *Chinese Foreign Policy*, p. 38; Gurtov and Hwang, *China under Threat*, pp. 53–62; Whiting, *China Crosses the Yalu*, pp. 160–162; George and Smoke, *Deterrence in American Foreign Policy*, p. 228; Zelman, "Chinese Intervention," pp. 4, 10; Orme, "Deterrence Failures," pp. 109–110.

[59] Zelman, "Chinese Intervention," pp. 13–14, 31; George and Smoke, *Deterrence in American Foreign Policy*, pp. 228–231. On the trade-offs between Chinese stealth and deterrence, see Schelling, *Arms and Influence*, pp. 54–55; and Orme, "Deterrence Failures," pp. 111–112; and George and Smoke, *Deterrence and American Foreign Policy*, pp. 229–230. On how Chinese disengagement affected U.S. Army field assessments, see Appleman, *South to the Naktong*, p. 756.

agreement in the documents, the Russian evidence sometimes calls into question the completeness or veracity of the available Chinese documentation, particularly from the first few days of October. But, as we will see, even where they differ from the Chinese documents, the Russian materials support the argument presented here as strongly as the Chinese documents, and in some cases even more strongly.[60]

Mao's Opening Strategy: The Telegrams to Stalin and Zhou

The October telegrams to Stalin and Zhou Enlai (see Appendix B for full texts) demonstrate that Mao entered Korea in October for the general reasons offered by Whiting in his classic account of the case: China felt threatened by the American presence in North Korea.[61] In the October 2 telegram to Stalin, Mao offers a domino-theory explanation for why China must stand up to the United States.[62] But Mao's fears were even deeper than Whiting and other Western analysts have perceived. The October 13 telegram to Zhou Enlai demonstrates that Mao was afraid not only of an immediate American push beyond the Yalu, but also of the long-term economic and domestic political implications if he hedged against that eventuality by placing standing forces on the Manchurian border. Even if the Americans did not attack Manchuria in the short term, their presence in North Korea would tie down Chinese defense forces in the border region. This would be fiscally expensive and also politically dangerous, because the American presence near North China would embolden domestic counterrevolutionaries while the dual-purpose military forces needed to combat them were occupied on the border. An American presence in North Korea would embarrass the regime, encourage counterrevolutionaries, and weaken the regime's military capability to deal with opponents at home.[63] In the October 13 telegram to Zhou, Mao refers to the cost of passive defenses and concern about the hydroelectric plants on the border; these references demonstrate that, contrary to MacArthur's and Whiting's claims, these factors did play an important role in Mao's thinking. Acheson's emphasis on the plants in his reassurance statements was not misplaced. Yet, given Mao's additional fear of growing American arrogance and falling dominos, Whiting is still correct in arguing that Acheson's reassurances were insufficient.[64]

---

[60] Whiting, *China Crosses the Yalu*, p. 172.

[61] Ibid., passim.

[62] For a discussion of domino psychology, see Jervis, "Domino Beliefs and Strategic Behavior," pp. 20–50.

[63] On the prohibitive expense of passive defenses in Manchuria, see Hao and Zhai, "China's Decision," p. 104.

[64] Whiting, *China Crosses the Yalu*, chap. 8.

The Crossing of the Parallel as a Triggering Event

Both secondary sources and documents from early October suggest that the American crossing of the 38th parallel on October 7, 1950, was the triggering event that convinced Mao to enter the war in force. An authoritative Chinese history describes Zhou's attempt to deter American crossing of the 38th parallel as the last chance to solve the Korean crisis peacefully.[65] The timing of Chinese actions fits this account. Mao's initial decision to enter the war (October 2) was made the day after MacArthur called for the surrender of all North Korean forces on both sides of the parallel. Mao gave his initial orders to form the Chinese People's Volunteers on October 8, the day after American troops began crossing the parallel. On the same day he informed Kim Il-sung of China's intention to enter the war.[66]

There is, however, strong evidence that China had prepared to enter the Korean War even before Inchon. As Chen Jian writes, in July and August, PLA and civilian leaders argued that China must prepare to do battle with the United States in Korea. On August 4 some even favored helping the North Koreans destroy the American forces before the United States was able to reverse the tide of battle in its favor. On the basis of this evidence, Chen argues that Zhou Enlai's deterrent message may have been only a delaying tactic. Even if the United States had stopped behind the 38th parallel, China would still have prepared to attack American forces in South Korea.[67]

It should be noted, however, that, from early August until the Inchon landing, Chinese military and civilian leaders were basing their analysis on the assumption that the United States would reverse the course of the war and that it would then attempt to defeat and occupy North Korea. The Chinese predictions turned out to be impressively accurate. Mao and his advisers anticipated that MacArthur would break out of the Pusan perimeter by landing at a port near the 38th parallel or in North Korea itself. They also assumed that the United States would then attack North Korea with the purpose of unifying the peninsula. They were incorrect in only one key prediction: that if China did nothing to stop American ad-

[65] Xu, *Di Yi Ci Jiaoliang*, p. 23. The author is a PLA officer and a leading military historian at China's National Defense University.

[66] See "The Directive concerning the Formation of the People's Volunteer Army," Oct. 8, 1950, and "Telegram to Kim Il-sung concerning Sending the Volunteer Army to Enter Korea for Combat," Oct. 8, 1950, in *Jianguo Yilai Mao Zedong Wengao*, Vol. 1, pp. 543–545.

[67] Chen, *China's Road*, chaps. 4–5. Chen attributes the aggressive strategy both to defensive motivations and to Mao's revolutionary goals, but he emphasizes the importance of the latter.

vances in Korea, an attack on China would follow. For our purposes it is important to note that even the most aggressive Chinese plans were based primarily in defensive motivations rather than expansionist goals. The fears expressed by Zhou Enlai and military leaders in August were not so much that South Korea might survive, but that North Korea would eventually be defeated and that the Americans could then attack China.[68] Russian sources reveal that, as early as July 2, 1950, Zhou Enlai told the Soviet ambassador that *if the Americans crossed the 38th parallel,* then Chinese forces would have to enter the war.[69]

If the United States stayed behind the 38th parallel and pledged to remain there, Chinese leaders would have been surprised, and would have remained wary, but their defensive concerns might have been reduced because North Korean survival would have seemed much more likely than it did after American forces crossed the parallel.[70] Moreover, even in the event that Chinese leaders wanted to attack American troops stopped south of the 38th parallel, it would have been a very difficult and risky operation. The lines of communication would have been much longer and American defensive positions harder to overrun than was the case when American forces were overextended in North Korea and closer to the Chinese border in October and November 1950. To launch any offensive across the 38th parallel the Chinese would have required a great deal of material support from the Soviet Union, in particular airplanes and artillery.[71] As discussed below, impressive levels of Soviet support in these areas were forthcoming after the United States crossed the 38th parallel and China entered the war, engaging American troops. But it is highly doubtful that Stalin would have repeated his earlier mistaken decision to assist Kim Il-sung's June invasion by encouraging China to attack American forces that had merely restored the prewar status quo in Korea. Not only would this be militarily more dangerous than either Kim Il-sung's initial attack on South Korea or Mao's later attack on American forces in North Korea, but, on political grounds, it would be more difficult to mask Soviet involvement or to portray such a Chinese attack as defensively motivated.

Russian documents help resolve this question. As early as July 5, Stalin

---

[68] Ibid., chap. 4.

[69] Bajanov, "Assessing the Politics of the Korean War," p. 89.

[70] In such an instance Chinese forces might have entered North Korea anyway, but most likely to assist in defending against future American air or ground attacks. In this way Chinese participation in Korea would have been more like Chinese participation in the Vietnam War in the 1960s.

[71] This issue is discussed further below in the context of Mao's plans for an offensive against American forces near Pyongyang and Wonsan. For Chinese leaders' recognition in August that they would need Soviet assistance before launching a knockout blow to American forces in Korea, see Chen, *China's Road,* pp. 150–151.

apparently agreed to assist Chinese troops if they entered Korea in support of Kim Il-sung's forces. In Stalin's July 5 plan, a large force of nine Chinese divisions would form near the Yalu border and prepare to attack American forces "in case the enemy crosses the 38th parallel."[72] On October 1, as MacArthur called for the surrender of DPRK troops on both sides of the parallel, Stalin asked Mao to rush a smaller contingent of five divisions to the 38th parallel to help protect DPRK troops setting up defensive positions north of that line, "thereby providing for the defense of the 38th parallel."[73] In both of these plans Stalin's goal was to prevent American domination of North Korea, not to guarantee North Korea's domination of the South. As Alexandre Mansourov's analysis of Russian documents makes clear, Stalin's concern about American crossing of the 38th parallel was the main reason he decided to arm large numbers of Chinese forces and to encourage them to fight the Americans.[74] Without that Soviet support, China simply could not have launched an offensive so far from its borders.

Although Stalin appears to be the most powerful actor in this story, since he was unwilling to send Soviet ground forces into battle, Stalin relied heavily on the resolve of the Chinese Communists to take the fight to the Americans. But Mao was no puppet, so China's own decision to enter the war is vital. Both Russian and Chinese documents support the argument that China's final entrance into the war was triggered by the American decision to invade North Korea. Where the two accounts differ is on the issue of just when Chinese fears led to Chinese resolve. Citing a late-night October 2 message (received early October 3) from Mao to Stalin, which was found in the Russian archives, Mansourov portrays the CCP as paralyzed by the fear of war with the United States and apparently unwilling to send troops to Korea. This differs from the Chinese October 2 telegram from Mao to Stalin, in which Mao appears resolute from the start (see Appendix B). But according to both Russian and Chinese sources, Mao spent the first weeks of October convincing nervous Politburo members of the dangers of inaction in Korea and the need for bold Chinese intervention. In both the Chinese and Russian accounts, on October 13 Mao sent a telegram to Zhou Enlai in Moscow reporting the final Politburo decision to enter the war. And in both the Chinese and Russian versions of communications between Stalin and Mao, Mao expresses strong defensive concerns relating to American occupation of North Korea as the main reason for Beijing's final decision.[75]

[72] Stalin to Zhou Enlai, July 5, 1950, in Weathersby, "New Russian Documents," p. 43.
[73] Stalin to Mao Zedong and Zhou Enlai, in Mansourov, "Stalin, Mao, Kim, and China's Decision to Enter the Korean War," p. 114.
[74] Mansourov, "Stalin, Mao, Kim, and China's Decision to Enter the Korean War."
[75] The lobbying to the Politburo by Mao and Peng Dehuai in early October is discussed

But why was the American invasion of North Korea so frightening to Mao and the CCP Politburo that they would enter a war in a foreign country against the forces of the world's strongest power? A careful study of this question reveals the importance of Truman's earlier policy toward Taiwan. Mao's suspicions about American intentions had been growing since June, when at the outset of the Korean War, Truman reversed his policy of noninterference in the Chinese Civil War and blocked the Taiwan Straits. This guaranteed a sanctuary for Chinese "counter-revolutionaries" (Chiang Kai-shek's Kuomintang), provided a base for future American air attacks against the mainland, and suggested to Mao that America might at any time go back on its word and invade Chinese territory.[76]

As part of the compromise on the Korean aid package in January 1950, the Truman administration again offered an economic aid package to Chiang Kai-shek, which he promptly spent on military supplies.[77] But despite America's continuing assistance to Chiang, before June 27, 1950, Mao and his military advisers did not expect that the United States would

---

below. For the Chinese version of the October 2 and October 13 telegrams, see Appendix B. For analysis and presentation of the Russian documentation, see Mansourov, "Stalin, Mao, Kim, and China's Decision to Enter the Korean War." Although Mansourov's account calls into question the veracity and importance of the Chinese version of Mao's October 2 telegram to Stalin, there are important commonalities between Mansourov's version of events and the relevant Chinese documents and memoirs on the Korea decision. In Mansourov's account, the Soviet leaders expressed disappointment and surprise when, on October 3, they learned of Mao's decision not to fight, because it was a reversal of earlier and more resolute stands taken by Mao. In other words, before October 3, Russian leaders had come to believe that Mao's strategic thinking was fully consistent with the October 2 document from the Chinese archives. Moreover, in the Russian document, Mao emphasized domestic resistance in China to a more resolute stand, not his own doubts, as the cause for Chinese reticence. As in the Chinese document, in the Russian telegram Mao discussed the need to arm Chinese troops so that they could eventually fight Americans in Korea. He forecast that eventuality with a high degree of certainty. It is possible that Mao sent both messages and that each archive has featured the one that portrays its national leader in command of events. In other words, Mao may have first expressed the opinion that China should enter the war, as is demonstrated by the Chinese telegram, and then, later the same day, expressed new reservations based on his discussions with other CCP leaders, as is demonstrated by the Russian evidence. It is more likely that Mao wrote down his strategic plan in the Chinese telegram of October 2 but did not send it because he needed first to overcome resistance in the Politburo and because he wanted to bargain for the maximum amount of Soviet assistance by pretending to be uncertain but ultimately persuadable on the issue of intervention. In any case, well-connected Chinese scholars assure me that the Chinese version of the October 2 telegram (in Mao's own handwriting) indeed exists in the Chinese archives but may not have been sent.

[76] Hong, *Kangmei Yuanchao Zhanzheng Huiyi*, p. 1; also see Hao and Zhai, "China's Decision," p. 101.

[77] See Chap. 4 in this volume.

escalate its hostility toward the PRC.[78] Mao had no reason to doubt Truman's publicly stated promise of January 5 that the American military would stay out of the Chinese Civil War. Mao's belief about American passivity must have been confirmed in the spring when the PLA successfully routed KMT forces on Hainan Island without sparking American intervention. After this, the PLA began preparations for an assault on Taiwan itself.[79]

Mao's analysis of America's military intentions may also have been reflected in his reported confidence that the United States would not intervene to stop Kim Il-sung from unifying Korea by force in June 1950. According to Russian sources uncovered by Kathryn Weathersby, Mao backed Kim's plan to attack because he did not believe the United States would get involved over "such a small territory as Korea." According to this account, although Mao believed the United States would send Japanese troops to help the ROK, he did not predict American intervention.[80] Another study of Russian materials states that Mao believed that America would not intervene because a Korean war would be a civil war, and Washington would allow the Koreans to fight it out on their own.[81] If these accounts are accurate, when Kim did invade in June 1950, Mao must have been doubly shocked: not only would the United States intervene quickly and effectively in Korea, it would intervene in the Chinese Civil War by blocking the Taiwan Straits. In two days the United States had climbed to the highest rung on Mao's ladder of escalation, reversing earlier promises of restraint toward China and demonstrating a willingness to fight in civil wars on the Asian mainland.

Others make a more complicated argument about Mao's risk assessment, positing that Mao predicted the United States might act to save South Korea. But in these accounts Chinese leaders did not foresee that this would lead the United States to intervene in the Taiwan Straits. Either portrayal of Mao before June 25 supports the thesis here.[82] Whether viewed as confident or cautious, Mao did not expect Kim's invasion to cause the United States to protect Taiwan militarily.[83]

---

[78] Chen, *China's Road*, pp. 89 and 102. Chen cites early 1950 documents drafted by General Su Yu, who believed that America lacked the capability to intervene in Asian civil wars for the next five years.

[79] He Di, "The Last Campaign to Unify China."

[80] Weathersby, "New Findings on the Korean War," p. 16.

[81] Holloway, *Stalin and the Bomb*, p. 277.

[82] Goncharov, Lewis, and Xue, *Uncertain Partners*, chap. 5; and Xu, "New Materials on the Origins of the Korean War."

[83] Stalin apparently had a very different take on the probable outcome of a war in Korea. Given the withdrawal of American forces in 1949 and Acheson's exclusion of Korea from the American defense perimeter, Kim was able to convince Stalin that America would not intervene effectively on the peninsula. Cautious about China's increasing importance

While the United States tried to portray the navy's actions as a mere preserving of the status quo in China, the Chinese viewed it instead as a reversal of U.S. policy and a military intervention on behalf of the CCP's domestic rivals on Taiwan. The day after the announcement of Truman's decision to block the straits, Mao stated to the Central People's State Conference: "Truman proclaimed on January 5th of this year that America would not interfere in Taiwan; now he has proven that was false. Moreover, at the same time [he] tore up all international agreements [stating that the U.S. would] not intervene in China's civil war. By doing this America has exposed its own imperialist face."[84] In the Chinese leaders' mind, the Americans now were clearly not beyond invading Chinese territory and allying fully with the KMT in its civil war efforts.[85] Later in the Korean War, the reputational damage done to the United States would strongly affect Mao's attitudes about promises of American restraint in northern Korea. Especially after the Americans crossed the 38th parallel, the CCP leaders did not trust American reassurances, so they dismissed out of hand British and Indian proposals for a buffer zone between U.S. forces and the Chinese border.[86]

Given Mao's sharpened perception of American duplicity and expansionism, Truman's decision to cross the 38th parallel itself triggered Mao's decision to enter Korea in force. With the expansion of American military operations in Korea, Mao became fully convinced that a war between American and Chinese forces was inevitable regardless of the details of subsequent American coercive diplomacy.[87] Moreover, the American presence in both Taiwan and North Korea meant that China would always face the unacceptable threat of a two-front war. From bases in both Taiwan and North Korea the United States could attack

---

for international communism, Stalin approved of and provided ample supplies for Kim Il-sung's attack on South Korea. According to recent accounts, by doing so Stalin apparently hoped not only to reduce Mao's influence in Pyongyang, but also to cause the Americans to block the Taiwan Straits, thereby threatening China and driving Mao firmly into the Soviet camp. By intervening in Korea and blocking the straits, the United States proved Stalin's predictions to be only half right. See Weathersby, "Soviet Aims in Korea," p. 31; also see Goncharov, Lewis, and Xue, *Uncertain Partners*, chap. 5.

[84] "Talk at the Eighth Meeting of the Central People's State Conference," June 28, 1950, in *Jianguo Yilai Mao Zedong Wengao*, Vol. 1, p. 423.

[85] For Mao's vitriolic statements about the blocking of the straits, see Hong, *Kangmei Yuanchao Zhanzheng Huiyi*, p. 1; Hao and Zhai, "China's Decision," p. 101; Chai and Zhao, *Banmendian Tanpan*, pp. 81–82; Ye, *Chubing Chaoxian*, pp. 3–6, 93; Bo, *Ruogan Zhongda Juece yu Shijian de Huigu*, p. 43. For Mao's public discussion of American duplicity, see Tsou, *America's Failure in China*, p. 561.

[86] Chai and Zhao, *Banmendian Tanpan*, pp. 72–74.

[87] For Mao's belief in the inevitability of war after the Taiwan blockade and the crossing of the 38th parallel, see Hao and Zhai, "China's Decision," pp. 103–108; and Ye, *Chubing Chaoxian*, p. 93.

both of China's main industrial bases—Shanghai and Manchuria—at any time of Washington's choosing. Peng Dehuai explained this danger to the Politburo while rallying support for Mao's decision to enter Korea with significant forces. In his efforts to encourage Chinese intervention in Korea, Stalin also played up the threat to China posed by American occupation of Taiwan.[88]

Mao was not, however, eager to enter the war, particularly after the Soviets initially appeared to renege on their promise of early air support for Chinese forces in North Korea. According to Chinese scholars, from October 10 to 12 Mao reconsidered his October 2 decision in the light of lingering doubts in the Chinese Politburo and the Soviets' claim that, for technical reasons, they were unable to supply air cover for his troops in Korea during the earliest phase of Chinese intervention. Mao is said to have paced the floor for sixty hours, distraught over the weighty implications of his decision. He eventually decided to intervene with all the force he could muster because he could not see how else to ensure China's long-term security.[89] In his October 13 and 14 telegrams to Zhou Enlai in Moscow, Mao reconfirmed the decision to enter Korea in force, even without initial Soviet air support. Chinese troops began crossing the Yalu on October 19.[90]

Mao's Risk Analysis

Contrary to the threat-based accounts discussed above, an October 2 telegram to Stalin found in the Chinese archival collections demonstrates

[88] Chai and Zhao, *Banmendian Tanpan*, pp. 81–82; Ye, *Chubing Chaoxian*, pp. 3–6, 93; Wang and Wang, *Kongzhan Zai Chaoxian*, p. 107. For Stalin's proddings, see Mansourov, "Stalin, Mao, Kim, and China's Decision to Enter the Korean War," p. 101.

[89] For the documentary evidence of Mao's final decision, see his October 13–14 telegrams to Zhou Enlai in Moscow, in Appendix B. For analysis of Mao's decision, see Hao and Zhai, "China's Decision"; Chen, "The Sino-Soviet Alliance"; Christensen, "Threats, Assurances"; Chen, "China's Changing Aims during the Korean War"; Hunt, "Beijing and the Korea Crisis"; Zhang, *Deterrence and Strategic Culture*, chap. 4; and Goncharov, Lewis, and Xue, *Uncertain Partners*, chap. 5.

[90] The October 13 and October 14 telegrams to Zhou Enlai in Appendix B provide evidence that Mao's original threat assessment was reconfirmed. Mansourov calls into question the Chinese portrayal of Stalin as weakly committed to providing air cover for Chinese troops in Korea. But the Russian documents he and Weathersby present demonstrate that the first engagements of American aircraft by Soviet pilots occurred only on November 1, a full twelve days after Chinese troops began pouring across the Yalu. This Russian evidence strongly supports the Chinese version of events in October. Russian air support during the first days of China's entrance into the war was not as great as Mao had hoped. But, Mansourov correctly notes that this did not mean Stalin lacked resolve. The Chinese drew the wrong inferences from Soviet delay. Stalin was willing but simply not able to meet all of China's air cover demands in the last two weeks of October. See pp. 168–169 in this text.

that Mao fully considered the possibility of an American declaration of war and bombardment of "many major cities and industrial targets" in China (see Appendix B). Mao did not discuss atomic weapons, but he clearly envisioned massive conventional strategic bombing.[91] Mansourov's study of Russian documents portrays a CCP even more concerned with the threat of an American declaration of war than the Chinese documents reveal. In the Russian version of Mao's October 2 message to Stalin, Mao reveals that Central Committee members believed that China should not enter the war in Korea because open warfare with the United States would delay China's economic development and create popular discontent. Mansourov argues that in the early days of October Stalin failed to convince the CCP that Chinese entrance into Korea was wise. Stalin used two arguments for this purpose: first, he argued that the United States was not ready for a world war, so China need not fear that America would launch a direct attack on a Soviet ally; second, if America was indeed ready for a world war, 1950 was the best time for the communist bloc to fight such a war. In Mansourov's account, the final decision by Mao and the Central Committee to enter the war was not driven by Stalin's reassurances but by the fear engendered by American forces crossing the parallel on October 7 and by Stalin's clever threat to acquiesce fully to American domination of Korea if China did not send in ground troops.[92] While the discrepancies between the Russian and Chinese versions of events on October 2 and October 3 remain an interesting puzzle, the Russian account supports strongly the argument that Mao and the CCP Politburo entered the Korean War fully aware of the threat of American retaliation against the Chinese mainland.

Some scholars suggest that Mao's statements to Stalin about American bombing and declaration of war may have been a ploy to get the Soviets more involved in Korea by triggering the Sino-Soviet defense treaty.[93]

---

[91] It is not clear why Mao did not mention atomic bombs. It is possible that, as Nie Rongzhen had suggested, Mao saw atomic weapons as inappropriate in the largely agrarian Chinese arena. Richard Betts speculates that Mao may have been informed by the Soviets that the U.S. atomic stockpile was then small, and that America lacked operational plans for using atomic weapons against targets outside the Soviet Union. Betts, *Nuclear Blackmail and Nuclear Balance*, pp. 34–36. It is also possible that even the documents available in the West have been subject to deletion; sections about atomic deterrence may have been deleted except in collections at a very high level of classification. It is widely believed among China scholars that the original telegram to Stalin contains words that have been deleted from the series cited here.

[92] See Mansourov, "Stalin, Mao, Kim, and China's Decision to Enter the Korean War." For the telegram, see pp. 114–115.

[93] Goncharov, Lewis, and Xue, *Uncertain Partners*, pp. 178–179. When analyzing the October 2, 1950, telegram, the authors focus on the importance of the document for Sino-

But other evidence demonstrates that Mao's stated fears were sincere. Peng Dehuai reports that he and Mao discussed the threat of American bombing with the Chinese Politburo and that Peng had prepared Chinese forces for such an eventuality.[94] Beijing's fear of American bombing never diminished in the first months of U.S. operations. On November 22, two days before MacArthur's final drive north, the Central Military Commission warned South China forces that American pilots flying under the guise of Chiang's air force might make bombing runs against Chinese targets.[95]

Mao had every reason to believe that America would launch such an attack. Declassified American documents show that the State Department plotted a "calculated indiscretion" by the American ambassador to India, Loy Henderson, stating that if China attacked in Korea or the Taiwan Straits "the United States will consider itself at war, and not only deal with such Chinese forces as may be met in the field but also strike at the bases of Chinese power."[96] A Chinese account of the war claims that Beijing indeed received such a warning via India in August.[97]

Rather than deterring Mao, the risk of bombing seems to have led him toward more aggressive military objectives in Korea than he might otherwise have pursued. In the telegram to Stalin, Mao reasoned that as long as Chinese and American forces faced each other in Korea, American bombing of the mainland was a threat. His fear that China would be tied down in Korea while the United States attacked the Chinese mainland led him to conclude that the best strategy was to drive all foreign forces out of Korea as quickly as possible.[98] With America out of Korea, Mao thought, any subsequent American attacks on the Chinese mainland would be of a more tolerable scope and duration. Mao's conclusions were not far off the mark. In December, when American officials considered options related to total withdrawal from Korea, they discussed just such limited, punitive assaults on China as the proper response, but no one in Washington advocated an all-out war with China, which was considered the "second team" of the communist world. Moreover, Dean Rusk implied that tougher military sanctions would be brought against

---

Soviet relations rather than as a true representation of Mao's plans for and fears about war in Korea.

[94] Chai and Zhao, *Banmendian Tanpan*, p. 98.

[95] See "Telegram from the Central Military Commission concerning the Tightening of Air Defenses," Nov. 22, 1950, in *Jianguo Yilai Mao Zedong Wengao*, Vol. 1, p. 677.

[96] See Davies Draft, July 11, 1950, and Herbert Feis's note on Memorandum by John Davies, entitled "Calculated Indiscretion to Be Committed by Ambassador Henderson," July 12, 1950, PPS Records, Box 14, File: China 1950–51, NA.

[97] Han and Song, *Dongya Heping yu Hezuo*, p. 16.

[98] See the October 2 telegram to Stalin in Appendix B. On the adverse economic consequences of a two-front war, see Hao and Zhai, "China's Decision," p. 108.

China if UN forces stayed on the peninsula than if they withdrew.[99] Aside from reducing the risk of punitive strikes against China, total expulsion of UN forces from the Asian mainland would eliminate the necessity of expensive standing defenses in Korea similar to those Mao contemplated for Manchuria.

Chinese strategic vulnerability not only led Mao into the Korean War; it also counseled him to adopt extremely aggressive military policies designed to ensure total victory. Since what Mao feared most was a local military deadlock in Korea while China remained vulnerable to American bombing, he tried to eliminate the possibility of such a deadlock by seeking total destruction of American forces in Korea.[100] Mao consistently rejected any notion of deterrence or local military compromise from October 1950 through January 1951. While his goals were not based primarily on a desire for rollback in Korea, his minimum defensive needs led him to reject the notion of a buffer anywhere in Korea, north or south of the 38th parallel. Maintaining such a defensive line would have carried many of the costs of passive border defense in Manchuria and would also sustain the risk of a future two-front war with the United States. MacArthur's strategy of explicit and authoritative bombing threats would have been worse than ineffective. Assuming that when deterrence failed the United States would have carried through on its earlier threat and bombed China, such a strategy might have triggered the Sino-Soviet defense Treaty and sparked a third world war.

Mao's Rejection of Buffer Zones

Mao's October 2 telegram to Stalin and October 14 telegram to Zhou Enlai clearly demonstrate that Mao had no intention of allowing American troops to remain permanently below the Pyongyang-Wonsan line. If MacArthur had not sent UN forces north of that line, Mao would have attacked them in Pyongyang and Wonsan after a six-month build up of planes and artillery.[101] So even if MacArthur had adopted the most con-

---

[99] In a discussion with Acheson, Dean Rusk clarified American options. If Americans withdraw voluntarily or are forced out of Korea, the United States might continue with "harassing tactics" against China. If, however, American troops are to stay in Korea for the long haul, the United States must "make it in the interest of the Chinese Communists to accept some stabilization by making it so costly for them that they could not afford not to accept." See Memorandum of Conversation, Dec. 27, 1950, in *FRUS: 1950*, microfiche supplement.

[100] See the October 2 telegram to Stalin in Appendix B.

[101] See the October 14, 1950, telegram to Zhou Enlai in Appendix B. One sentence in this translation might lead one to the conclusion that Mao had not yet decided on a future attack on American urban positions. Mao states, "After six months we will once again

ciliatory of reassurance strategies—never engaging Chinese troops north of Pyongyang and Wonsan in late October, maintaining the largest of the various proposed buffer areas, and forgoing the November 24 offensive—Mao still planned to attack American troops in force.

Mao's October 23 telegram to Marshal Peng Dehuai in the field provides further evidence that a buffer would not have prevented a wider war. This telegram also demonstrates that Mao's earlier telegrams to Stalin and Zhou Enlai in Moscow were not just tough posturing designed to influence the Soviets. In this cable Mao claimed that China was not ready to take on urban positions, so he ordered guerrilla tactics to destroy any UN reinforcements that were heading for Pyongyang and Wonsan, as well as cities in South Korea. In the same passage, Mao lists cities such as Pyongyang, Wonsan, Seoul, Taegu, and Pusan as areas that Chinese forces were not yet prepared to assault. But he claims that "after we possess planes and artillery . . . [we will] open up the cities one by one."[102] Even before the first Sino-American skirmishes in late October, Mao sought total victory in Korea and placed no value in a northern buffer. In fact, his plans for targeting cities in southernmost Korea for future attack show that, once he entered the war, Mao placed no importance on the 38th parallel itself. His goal was to drive all foreign forces from the peninsula.

In the October 23 telegram Mao made an unusual reference to a strategy of coercion: he mentioned the possibility of "compelling" the United States to enter diplomatic talks with China. But Mao did not seem to place great hope in this prospect. Moreover, he viewed such an American reversal as possible only *after* the destruction of multiple enemy divisions. Mao displayed no hope of deterring such escalation.[103]

While MacArthur was dangerously misguided in believing that the threat of escalation would force Beijing to back down in Korea, he was right on this key point: China was indeed secretly preparing for a massive drive to destroy all UN forces in Korea. Launching such an attack, of

---

discuss the issue of attacking." Here, Mao certainly means "the issue" of China's material preparation at that time, not whether or not, ultimately, China should attack the cities. Additional statements within this document and Mao's later cables to his commanders in the field, discussed below, demonstrate Mao's conviction that China must attack those cities after a Chinese buildup. Note the statement, "After in the air and on the ground we enjoy a state of overwhelming superiority over enemy forces, then we will go back and attack Pyongyang and Wonsan, etc." Also note the end of the document's fourth paragraph, calling for a future "big battle."

[102] "Telegram to Peng Dehuai and Gao Gang concerning Questions of the Korean Strategic Situation," Oct. 23, 1950, in *Jianguo Yilai Mao Zedong Wengao*, Vol. 1, pp. 588–589.

[103] Ibid.

course, would have been risky and preparations arduous.[104] There are, however, three good reasons to believe that the attack would have occurred if the Americans had stopped and declared victory at Pyongyang and Wonsan: Chinese forces would have grown in strength with Soviet assistance; American forces would have remained small because the U.S. defense budget would have remained tightly constrained; and Mao would have been willing to run risks because the status quo would have seemed unacceptably threatening.

The Soviets were very careful to keep their own planes and pilots near the Chinese border when engaging American planes, but Soviet pilots did enter the Korean War soon after Chinese forces crossed the Yalu. Moreover, as the Korean War progressed, the Soviet Union provided China significant military aid in the form of artillery and aircraft, the weapons Mao specified as necessary for launching an offensive against fixed American positions. In fact, according to one report the Soviets provided 70,000 pilots, gunners, and technicians during the course of the war.[105] It is possible, however, that generous Soviet military assistance would not have been forthcoming if MacArthur had not driven toward the Yalu in late November. The Soviets might not have provided the weapons Mao wanted, fearing escalation if Mao attacked. But there is a significant amount of evidence that suggests otherwise. According to American documents, the Soviets had agreed to a program to increase Chinese air power as early as July. Russian documents reveal that, on July 5, Stalin had promised Mao that he would try to provide air cover for Chinese troops sent to North Korea for the purpose of repelling American forces that might cross the 38th parallel. Russian documents also demonstrate that as early as November 1, more than three weeks before MacArthur's final drive north, Soviet pilots began shooting down American planes to protect Chinese troops in North Korea and their supply lines in Manchuria. Days before MacArthur's offensive, Acheson noted direct Soviet air activity along the Yalu border.[106]

---

[104] I am grateful to Allen Whiting for encouraging me to explore this question.

[105] Mao specified planes and artillery in his October 2 telegram to Stalin, cited above. For their part, the Chinese had begun building up the PLA air force in early 1950 in preparation for an attack on Taiwan. See the May 31, 1950, report in *Nie Rongzhen Junshi Wenxuan*, p. 324. For the full extent of Soviet military assistance to China during the Korean War, see Goncharov, Lewis, and Xue, *Uncertain Partners*, pp. 200–201; and Halliday, "Air Operations in Korea," pp. 149–170. These authors point out that the Soviets would give enough arms to supply sixty-four infantry divisions and twenty-two air divisions. By summer of 1951 the Soviets had even transferred to China two air divisions of their highly advanced MiG-15 fighters. By war's end the Chinese and North Koreans may have lost as many as 2,000 aircraft. For the head count on Soviet personnel, see Weathersby, "New Russian Documents," p. 35, n. 11.

[106] In July 1950, American intelligence reported Sino-Soviet agreements for the transfer of 200 planes. See Office of Chinese Affairs, Film C0012, Reel 15, frame 605, NA. For the

Although Stalin apparently was unable to fulfill Mao's request for extensive air cover for Chinese troops during the first two weeks that they crossed the Yalu (October 19–November 1), this did not demonstrate a fundamental lack of resolve on Stalin's part. By early November 1950 the Soviets were already engaged in the conflict and were willing to fulfill their earlier promises to supply both air cover and military assistance as long as Chinese troops were willing to do the fighting on the ground. According to Russian sources, before MacArthur's offensive Stalin was feverishly supplying the Chinese and Koreans with weapons, planes, and pilot training. On November 15 he even agreed to transfer to China advanced MiG-15 fighters.[107] If Stalin had refused such assistance for the six months in which Mao planned to prepare an offensive, Stalin would have risked damaging his relations with both Mao and Kim Il-sung, whose capital would have been permanently surrendered to the West. In comparison to a decision to assist China in attacking American forces that had never crossed the 38th parallel, a decision to assist in a Chinese attack on American forces in North Korea carried far fewer military and political risks, while inaction in the latter instance would have cost Stalin far more in terms of his alliance relations.

Military power is relative, and before the Chinese intervention American forces in Korea were still not very strong. Moreover, they almost certainly would not have been beefed up if China had not counterattacked in November. If MacArthur had declared victory in Pyongyang, it is doubtful that the American defense budget would have increased enough to allow for substantial increases in deployments in Asia. The defense budget had risen after the initial Korean attack, but the largest jump in defense spending associated with the Korean War and NSC 68 would not occur until after the Chinese intervention in force. After the initial North Korean attack on the South, the budget jumped from about $14 billion to $25 billion. The second large jump took place only in December, when the budget increased by another $17 billion.[108] As the

---

Russian document, see Stalin to Zhou Enlai, July 5, 1950, in Weathersby, "New Russian Documents," pp. 43–44. For presentation and analysis of the Russian documentation on extensive Soviet air activity in November, see ibid. and Mansourov, "Stalin, Mao, Kim, and China's Decision to Enter the Korean War." While Mansourov portrays Stalin as firm and prompt in his offering of air cover, Weathersby portrays him as nervous but still "finally" willing to provide pilots and planes by November 1. The minutes of Acheson's November 21, 1950, meeting with French ambassador Bonnet read: "[Acheson] said that we found the Soviet air activity rather serious in that four of our large B-29's had been destroyed by aircraft that attacked from across the border and immediately returned to safety." Executive Secretariat Records, Lot 53D444, Box 14, NA.

[107] For documentation and analysis of extensive Soviet military assistance and pilot training programs for Chinese and Korean troops in the weeks before MacArthur's offensive, see Weathersby, "New Russian Documents," pp. 34, 48–50.

[108] For a discussion of defense budget increases from June to December 1950, see Ham-

president himself realized, it was the continuing tensions with China that allowed Truman to push his NSC 68 defense budgets through the Congress.[109]

Without the larger budget, increasing the standing forces in Korea would have cut directly into America's ability to strengthen European defenses, a task considered central to American grand strategy. In his own defense to the Senate, MacArthur argued that with the force levels available in November he would not be able to withstand a concerted Chinese attack if the Chinese had as little as two or three months to assemble forces.[110] In my discussion with army historians at West Point, all but one agreed that MacArthur could not have held a defensive line in North Korea against a moderately well-armed attacker that was willing to suffer heavy casualties.[111]

An attack on standing American forces still would have been extremely risky for Mao, but one must remember that he saw the status quo as even more risky for all the reasons offered above. Mao believed that America's blocking of the Taiwan Straits and crossing of the 38th parallel meant that war was inevitable. Moreover, he believed that an extended Cold War preceding the American attack would drain Chinese resources and undercut CCP legitimacy.[112] Mao also surmised that, if given sufficient time, America would only strengthen its forces in Korea. So, despite the risks, it seems fair to argue that Mao would have attacked American forces given the lack of more attractive options.[113]

The Disengagement: Was China Still Trying to Deter?

Mao's strategy in mid-November provides another reason to believe that Mao would not have settled for the status quo if American troops had

mond, "NSC 68." While the outbreak of the Korean War is widely considered the cause of the explosion in the defense budget from $14 billion to nearly $50 billion, the biggest increase would not occur until after the Americans met the Chinese counteroffensive in late November. See Stueck, "The Korean War"; and Jervis, "The Impact of the Korean War."

[109] 72nd Meeting of the National Security Council, Nov. 24, 1950, President's Secretary's Files, HSTL.

[110] For MacArthur's arguments, see Spanier, *Truman-MacArthur Controversy*, pp. 130, 149; and Rees, *Korea: The Limited War*, Part 1, p. 137.

[111] This issue arose in the question and answer period following a presentation I made to members of the social science faculty at the U.S. Military Academy, West Point, New York, Apr. 26, 1993.

[112] Hao and Zhai, "China's Decision"; and Christensen, "Threats, Assurances," pp. 135, 138.

[113] For additional evidence that Mao recognized the vast superiority of American forces in 1950 but still planned a spring offensive after a six-month buildup, see Lei, "Kangmei Yuanchao Zhanzheng Ji Ge Zhongda Juece de Huiyi."

remained anywhere in North Korea. The meaning of China's November disengagement is a key factor in many accounts of Chinese and American deterrence failure. Authors analyzing the potential for American reassurance policies often assume that the Chinese disengagement was part of a deterrent strategy designed to give the United States time to reconsider a final drive to the Yalu. The stealth of the operation led America to view China as weak and irresolute, but this was an unintended consequence. In this account it is presumed that China believed it had already demonstrated military power and a willingness to use it in late October; it hid its forces only to prevent attrition from American air force sorties.

However, evidence about Marshal Peng Dehuai's field strategy in November invalidates such interpretations of the Chinese disengagement. In his memoirs, Peng claims that the Chinese commanders released UN prisoners of war to add to the impression that the Chinese forces were cutting their losses and abandoning Korea. This, Chinese leaders hoped, would encourage MacArthur's arrogance and ease China's first major military victory on the peninsula.[114] Peng's account should be viewed with some suspicion. He was politically hounded in China from 1959 until his death in 1974, and his memoirs were actually a Cultural Revolution "confession," in which he had every reason to claim credit for what might have been a stroke of luck. However, the documentary evidence strongly supports Peng's account. On November 18, 1950, one week before MacArthur's offensive, Mao sent a telegram to Peng celebrating the American misperception of China's troop strength. Mao knew that MacArthur falsely believed Chinese forces in Korea to consist of only 60,000 or 70,000 troops, when actually there were at least 260,000. Mao told Peng that this was to China's advantage and would assist Chinese forces in destroying "tens of thousands" of enemy troops. In the same telegram, Mao instructed Peng to release prisoners of war.[115]

[114] See Hao and Zhai, "China's Decision," pp. 113–114; Cohen and Gooch, *Military Misfortunes*, pp. 171–172. See also Peng, *Memoirs of a Chinese Marshall*, p. 476.

[115] See "Telegram to Peng Dehuai and Others concerning the Release of Prisoners of War," Nov. 18, 1950, *Jianguo Yilai Mao Zedong Wengao*, Vol. 1, p. 672. In fact, according to a recent Chinese memoir, Peng hoped that the Americans would get the false impression that the Chinese troops had entered Korea only to protect the electrical facilities on the Yalu. See Du, *Zai Zhiyuan Jun Zongbu*, pp. 84–85. Mao's general strategy of hiding his troops did indeed lead the Americans to grossly underestimate the Chinese forces in Korea. It is not clear whether the strategy of feigning retreat in mid-November worked, however. On November 17 Acheson believed that Chinese forces were increasing, not decreasing, in number. See "Memorandum of Conversation with Sir Mohammed Zafrulla Khan, Foreign Minister of Pakistan," Nov. 17, 1950, p. 2, Executive Secretariat Records (Dean Acheson), Lot 53D444, Box 14, NA. One Russian document suggests that China may have had more than 300,000 troops in Korea by mid-November. See "Zhou to Stalin," Nov. 16, 1950, in Weathersby, "New Russian Documents," p. 49.

Once the Americans had crossed the 38th parallel and China had entered the war, buffer zones and the 38th parallel itself became irrelevant for Mao. The same was true for Stalin, particularly after China's early successes in the counteroffensive. In early December, Stalin discouraged peace negotiations and encouraged Chinese efforts to cross the 38th parallel. Mao also clearly hoped for early escalation of the conflict in December so that he could drive the Americans completely out of Korea. A December 3 telegram to his commanders in Korea sheds light on Mao's early intentions in the war. In it Mao instructed his units to surround enemy forces in one area, but not to attack them. The strategy was to allow them to call for help, thus attracting additional enemy forces and exposing them to Chinese attack.[116] On December 13 Mao instructed Peng to cross the 38th parallel and attack near Kaesong. Mao told Peng that, for political reasons, China had to ignore American and British calls for a firebreak at the 38th parallel.[117] On December 21 Mao warned Peng that the Americans were trying to play up the significance of the 38th parallel so as to "trick us into a halt in fighting." He worried that a ceasefire would only provide the American troops a chance to reinforce themselves. Mao instructed Peng to launch an attack against scattered Republic of Korea (ROK) units south of the parallel, but to leave American and British forces untouched in Seoul. The goal was to destroy the UN's Korean allies. Mao argues that then, "the Americans will have fallen into isolation, and cannot stay in Korea for long."[118]

On December 24, 26, and 29, Mao altered his plans somewhat. He instructed Peng to scrap his earlier orders to penetrate enemy lines and scatter UN forces. Mao decided that American and ROK consolidation of concentrated and fixed defensive positions between the 37th and 38th parallels was advantageous to the Chinese and should be encouraged. Mao was still planning for a massive final offensive in the spring, even though the logistical lines were even longer than they would have been if UN forces had held up in Pyongyang and Wonsan in October. Given the difficulties inherent in launching an offensive so far from China's borders, Mao recognized that the total destruction of UN forces would be easier if they were stationary and further north, where Chinese supply lines would be shorter and the terrain more advantageous for the offen-

[116] See "Telegram to Peng Dehuai and Others concerning the Destruction of Enemy Reinforcement Troop Deployments," Dec. 3, 1950, in *Jianguo Yilai Mao Zedong Wengao*, Vol. 1, p. 705. For documents on Stalin's attitudes in December, see Weathersby, "New Russian Documents," pp. 52–53.

[117] "Telegram to Peng Dehuai concerning the Necessity for Our Forces to Cross the 38th Parallel," Dec. 13, 1950, in *Jianguo Yilai Mao Zedong Wengao*, Vol. 1, pp. 722–723.

[118] "Telegram to Peng Dehuai and Others concerning the Situation in the Korean Battlefield and Our Army's Deployments," Dec. 21, 1950, in ibid., pp. 731–732.

sive. Therefore, Mao canceled plans that might drive UN forces south to the narrow and more easily defendable Taegu and Pusan areas. Mao celebrated the arrival of General Matthew Ridgway in Seoul, because Ridgway had indicated that he would not abandon the capital. On December 29 Mao told Peng that it would be better if Ridgway did stay in Seoul after the current campaign: "We are not now afraid of the enemy [forces] entrenching themselves in Seoul and north of the 37th parallel, we only fear that they will abandon that line and hold out in the narrow region of Taegu and Pusan."[119]

The problem facing Peng in late December was that Mao was also calling on him to strike one more major blow against UN forces before resting and regrouping in preparation for the spring offensive. Mao claimed that this last victory of the current campaign was necessary to destroy "the old influence" that "the so-called 38th parallel" still held on people. The only way to destroy this image was to strike another major attack across the parallel before retreating for a two-month rest and resupply period.[120] Peng did attack and win a major victory in early January, but this victory also drove American troops out of Seoul and behind the 37th parallel, exactly what Mao had warned against.[121] From their relatively safe southern bases, the Americans launched fierce counterassaults in late January that took heavy tolls on overextended Chinese troops and rendered them permanently incapable of expelling UN forces.[122] Until the meaning of these defeats sunk in, Mao's strategy had been to expel all forces from Korea relatively quickly. It was not until February that Mao began to shift to a long-term attritional war strategy.[123]

[119] "Telegram to Peng Dehuai and Others concerning the Advantage to Our [Future] Destructive Attack If Enemy Forces Concentrate Themselves," Dec. 24, 1950, in ibid., p. 733; "Telegram concerning the Falling Back, Resting, and Regrouping of the Entire Army's Main Forces after the Conclusion of the Second Campaign," Dec. 26, 1950, in ibid., pp. 734–735; and "Telegram to Peng Dehuai concerning Fighting the Third Campaign to Its Conclusion and Preparing for the Spring Offensive," Dec. 29, 1950, in ibid., pp. 741–742.

[120] See "Telegram to Peng Dehuai concerning Fighting the Third Campaign to Its Conclusion and Preparing for the Spring Offensive," Dec. 29, 1950, in *Jianguo Yilai Mao Zedong Wengao*, Vol. 1, pp. 741–742.

[121] Jonathan Pollack asserts that rather than being driven south by the New Year attack, UN troops "simply outran the CPV [Chinese People's Volunteers'] offensive." This suggests that Peng had not intentionally disobeyed Mao's orders. See "The Korean War and Sino-American Relations," p. 225. For a Russian document on the strategic problems created by the seizure of Seoul by Communist forces in early January, see "Mao to Stalin," Jan. 8, 1951, in Weathersby, "New Russian Documents." p. 53.

[122] Mid-January 1951 is widely considered a turning point in the war. See Pollack, "The Korean War and Sino-American Relations," p. 226; Brodie, *War and Politics*, p. 80; Foot, *The Wrong War*, p. 129; and Kaufman, *The Korean War*, pp. 144–148.

[123] Mao would later employ attritional methods in the hopes of compelling the Ameri-

The Importance of American Nonrecognition of the PRC
and Protection of Taiwan in Korea

The only chance of avoiding significant Sino-American conflict in Korea was missed in late September and early October, before American troops crossed the 38th parallel. This failure was at least partially due to the poor communication channels available to leaders in Beijing and Washington. There is evidence that suggests some possibility for successful deterrence if Chinese threats had been better communicated. Before Inchon, civilian and military leaders wanted to avoid actions in Korea that might cause a Chinese or Soviet entry and sap America's strategic reserves in an area of little geostrategic value. On September 8 the NSC viewed favorably the crossing of the 38th parallel, "provided MacArthur's plans could be carried out without risk of a major war with the Chinese Communists or the Soviet Union."[124] Even after Inchon, on September 27 Truman authorized MacArthur to proceed north only if he was certain that there would be no significant Soviet or Chinese intervention in Korea.[125] The qualifications in Truman's September 27 orders demonstrate that his willingness to go north was not unconditional. Moreover, in his memoirs Truman himself recalled that the lack of direct and reliable communication channels caused him to discount the Zhou-Panikkar communique of early October.[126] Documentary evidence from 1950 supports his recollections.[127] This implies that Truman might have placed more weight on a more clearly communicated threat. Finally,

---

cans to leave the peninsula. This is demonstrated by an internal party analysis of Mao's strategic thinking. See Zhang and Yao, *Jiji Fangwei Zhanlüe Qianshuo*, 61–63. In February and March 1951 the optimistic tone of Mao's communiques turned sour as he instituted stopgap military measures, such as a rotation system for exhausted Chinese troops. See the Feb. 7, 1951, letter to Zhou Enlai announcing the beginning of the troop rotation system and the somber March 1 telegram to Stalin in *Jianguo Yilai Mao Zedong Wengao*, Vol. 2, pp. 104–105, 151–153.

[124] See Meeting of the National Security Council, Sept. 8, 1950, President's Secretary's Files, HSTL.

[125] For an account of the Sept. 27, 1950, authorization, see Kaufman, *The Korean War*, pp. 85–86.

[126] Truman said: "One problem was that we lacked any direct contacts with the Peiping regime through diplomatic channels." Truman, quoted in Zelman, "China's Intervention," p. 15; Also see Truman, *Memoirs*, Vol. 2, *Years of Trial and Hope*, p. 362.

[127] See McConaughy to Rusk and Jessup, Oct. 12, 1950, Office of Chinese Affairs, Film C0012, Reel 15, NA. It concludes: "Panikkar's Mephistophelian quality is not limited to his spade beard." Significantly, McConaughy called into doubt a message from Panikkar stating that the Chinese believed that America's action in Korea was "a screen for a conspiracy to attack China."

while backing down to Chinese threats might have injured American reputation for resolve internationally, the Americans had hedged their bets by not making the unification of Korea a stated war aim in the United Nations. In early November, Acheson said to the NSC: "Politically we have tried to keep the military conquest of all of Korea from being a war aim. In the UN we have never allowed any resolution to require expelling communists from all of Korea. . . . Therefore, politically we are not committed to the conquest of all of Korea if something short of that can be worked out that is satisfactory."[128]

It is, however, impossible to determine with certainty whether better communications would have prevented the disaster in North Korea. Given the American incentives to end the Korean problem once and for all, Truman might very well have ignored even the most direct Chinese warnings. By deciding to discount the weak and indirect October 3 warnings from Beijing, Washington squandered the last chance for peace. Once Americans crossed the 38th parallel on October 7, no coercive or reassuring acts by Truman or MacArthur could have prevented a wider war.

The history of Mao's Korean War decision making demonstrates the vital importance of the two American policy problems discussed in Chapters 3 and 4: Truman's inability to abandon Chiang Kai-shek and his related failure to establish working relations with Beijing. For both political and strategic reasons, Truman's June decision to protect Chiang intensified Mao's sense that any long-term American presence in North Korea would threaten his new nation's security. The possibility of a future two-front war against the United States not only led Mao to fight but also counseled him to adopt an extremely offensive strategy designed to drive the Americans completely off the Korean peninsula. Finally, the lack of direct government-to-government channels complicated China's last genuine attempt to deter an expansion of the Korean conflict (Zhou's meeting with Panikkar).[129] Truman's assistance to Chiang and his lack of contacts in Beijing were rooted in the American domestic politics of Cold War mobilization. These two policies played a more important role in Korean War escalation than the details of American military operations

[128] Meeting of the National Security Council, Nov. 10, 1950, President's Secretary's Files, HSTL.

[129] In his book, *China's Road to the Korean War*, Chen Jian argues that even if Zhou had successfully deterred American crossing of the 38th parallel, Mao would have ordered attacks on American troops eventually if they remained anywhere on the peninsula. I disagree on this critical question, but it should be noted that Chen agrees that America's Taiwan policy in June was a major element in Mao's threat perception during the Korean War.

or the nuances of Truman's coercive threats and assurances in fall and winter 1950.

MOBILIZATION POLITICS IN AMERICA'S CHINA POLICY DURING THE KOREAN WAR

The politics of mobilization in Washington also affected American China policy after the initial Korean War decisions of June 1950. The need to keep the public and Congress on board behind NSC 68 prevented the United States from allowing the PRC representation in the UN in July 1950. American leaders believed that Beijing's entry into the UN might put a strain on Sino-Soviet relations. At a minimum it would have provided a better channel of communication between Beijing and Washington in the second half of 1950. The politics of selling NSC 68 also prevented the United States from negotiating an early peace settlement with China in December, after the Chinese counteroffensive stunned American troops. It is, of course, impossible to certify that these strategies actually would have limited warfare, and evidence from the Russian and Chinese archives suggests that there was little chance to restrain China in Korea after the United States crossed the 38th parallel. But it is still instructive to note that the pursuit of a negotiated settlement was precluded on the American side not by straightforward strategic considerations but by the two-level logic of long-term mobilization for containment of the Soviet Union.

Chinese Representation in the United Nations and NSC 68 Mobilization

In July 1950 Prime Minister Jawaharlal Nehru of India attempted to broker a Korean War settlement between Washington, Moscow, and Beijing. The conditions of peace would be admission of the PRC into the UN and Security Council resolutions calling for a return to the prewar status quo in Korea. Kennan believed that the Chinese were receptive to the plan, but the Soviets were not satisfied with a simple return to the prewar borders in Korea. Kennan believed, therefore, that American acceptance of Nehru's plan provided a good opportunity to create a foreign policy split between Beijing and Moscow that might foster Chinese Titoism. The Soviets rejected the Indian plan, insisting on PRC admission to the UN before the beginning of any negotiations on Korea. As Kennan put it at the time, calling the Soviet bluff and allowing the Chinese Communists into the UN unconditionally in July and August "might place the Soviet government before the dilemma of returning to the Security Council and publicly disagreeing with the Chinese Communists in the UN about Korea or remaining outside the Security Council while the Chinese Communists were in it, thus producing a very strange and embarrassing situation for themselves."[130] A July 13 telegram from Stalin to Zhou and Mao suggests that Kennan very well may have been right. The telegram demonstrates that, at a minimum, Stalin was most unhappy about the Indian proposal and a simultaneous peace overture by the British ambassador in Moscow. Instead of pursuing the diplomatic route in the UN, for the second time in eight days Stalin rather cantankerously urged the Chinese to prepare troops for eventual combat in Korea.[131]

In top-level administration meetings throughout July, Kennan raised the possibility of allowing Chinese Communist admission to the UN. But he was attacked by the Republican John Foster Dulles who believed that such a strategy would be damaging not on international or reputational grounds, but on domestic political ones. In his diary for July 17, 1950, Kennan wrote:

> I was shouted down on this. Mr. Dulles pointed out that if we were to do this it would look like as though we were retreating on the Chinese Communist issue in the belief that we were thereby buying some Russian concessions about Korea; and that it would therefore look to our public as though we had been tricked into giving up something for nothing. I recognized the force of this and realize that nothing can be done; but I hope that some day history will record this as an instance of the damage done to our foreign policy by the irresponsible and bigoted interference of the China Lobby and its friends in Congress.[132]

In this debate each adviser was doing his job. Kennan, the politically insulated foreign policy adviser, was proposing a realpolitik diplomatic strategy that might serve to end an American military action in an area of little strategic significance (Korea) and that might create divisions in the alliance opposing the West. Brought on board as a watchdog to guarantee bipartisan support for Truman's grand strategy, Dulles was reminding the administration what limits the domestic political environment placed on administration action if it still wanted to mobilize resources under NSC 68. Sensitive to public and congressional opinion on foreign policy, Dulles knew that any policy that appeared to appease the Chinese

---

[130] Kennan, *Memoirs*, Vol. 1, pp. 491–493, citing his diary from 1950.

[131] See Stalin to Zhou Enlai and Mao Zedong, July 13, 1950, in Weathersby, "New Russian Documents," p. 44. Unfortunately, we lack similar documentation about Chinese attitudes toward these proposals.

[132] Kennan, *Memoirs*, Vol. 1, p. 493.

Communists would undercut public support for anticommunist policies elsewhere, including Europe.

The poll data from 1950 suggest that Dulles was correct. Even before the outbreak of hostilities in Korea, the public opposed seating the Chinese Communists in the UN by more than a 5:1 ratio.[133] After the outbreak of hostilities, a July State Department opinion analysis states that commentators nationwide viewed Nehru's plan as "appeasement of the most despicable sort."[134] As in 1949 and 1950, public support for increased foreign aid was driven by a reaction to communism, not to geographic imperatives. By midsummer 1950, support for military aid to Asia rivaled that for aid to Europe and, in an August poll, 55 percent viewed stopping communism in Asia as "equally important" to stopping it in Europe.[135] Lest the administration was not fully aware of these trends in public opinion and their implication for China policy, in July Senator Tydings raised a bill in the Senate that asked the President to "instruct the United States representatives in the Security Council to exercise the veto of any proposal to admit Communist China to membership in the United Nations."[136]

In the dialogue between Kennan and Dulles—the administration's leading international and domestic political analysts of foreign policy—Dean Acheson played arbiter. Acheson sided with Dulles, and while Kennan lamented the implications of Dulles's analysis, he grudgingly recognized its accuracy. Kennan wrote:

My view [toward admission of the PRC] was rejected by Dulles primarily on the ground that it would confuse American public opinion and weaken support for the President's program looking toward the strengthening of our defenses, and this position was eventually upheld by the Secretary. I said that I could very well understand this but that I shuddered at the implications of it; *for it implied that we could not adopt an adequate defense position without working our people into an emotional frenzy, and this emotional state, rather than a cool and unemotional appraisal of national*

[133] *Gallup Poll*, July 10, 1950. The poll was conducted in early June.

[134] "Monthly Survey," July 1950, Foster Papers, Box 12, NA.

[135] Support for military aid to Asia was 69 percent in October 1950. While not reaching the same plateaus, support for military aid to Chiang increased along with support for military aid for Europe. Popular support for military aid for Europe increased 22 percent from March 1950 to March 1951, reaching 80 percent. Page and Shapiro, *The Rational Public*, pp. 211–214. While popular support for military aid to Chiang was extremely low in late 1949 and early 1950, a majority of respondents (54 percent) supported military aid to Chiang in January 1951; 32 percent were opposed. For the 1949–1950 data see Tucker, *Patterns in the Dust*, p. 161. For the January 1951 poll, see *Gallup Poll*, Jan. 29, 1951.

[136] For the text of Senate Resolution 345, see "Memoranda on the Position of the United States with Respect to China," Nov. 20, 1950, in *Documents of the National Security Council*, Supplement 3, Reel 3, "Mill Papers."

interest, would then have to be the determinant of our action. . . . It seemed further to imply that the basis of our policy in the Far East from here on out would be an emotional anticommunism which would ignore the value to ourselves of a possible balance between the existing forces on the Asiatic continent.[137]

Kennan's earlier analysis was logical but failed to take into account domestic constraints. By August, Kennan had begun anticipating such responses to his policy advice. For example, he conditioned his own suggestions for a ceasefire in Korea and peace talks with the Russians with the statement: "So much for our national interest in the abstract. There remains the fact that United States public opinion, aroused by the Korean aggression, and confused by the partisan attacks on the Administration is not prepared for this type of policy. . . . It would mean pouring oil on the fires . . . [caused by the argument] that our Far Eastern policy has been overly lenient to communism."[138]

Because he was mobilizing resources for much more than just the war in Korea, Truman was facing many of the difficulties he faced in 1947. But in late 1950 the problems were more intense because of the size of the defense increases he was requesting, the high salience of communism under the new McCarthyite onslaught, and the increased public attention to Asia after the "loss" of China and the outbreak of war in Korea. Although Truman's initial decision to intervene in Korea itself met with wide public and congressional support, if anything, the existence of a new area of Communist advance amplified the more general attacks on Truman's foreign policy. Senator Joseph McCarthy and his allies approved of a forceful response to the North Korean attack but blamed the administration's Eurocentrism and past appeasement of China for the American setbacks in Asia.[139] General MacArthur also became more, not less, political in wartime, making a trip to Taiwan with an unauthorized escort of three squadrons of jet fighters. While on the island, the general publicly attacked "the threadbare argument by those who advocate appeasement and defeatism in the Pacific that if we defend Formosa we alienate Continental Asia."[140] This thinly veiled attack was clearly leveled at Kennan, Acheson, and Truman. These criticisms had an effect on

---

[137] Kennan, *Memoirs*, Vol. 1, pp. 495–496 (emphasis added).

[138] Kennan to Acheson, Aug. 21, 1950, Acheson Papers, Box 65, HSTL.

[139] Joseph McCarthy quoted in Purifoy, *Harry Truman's China Policy*, p. 211.

[140] "General MacArthur's Message on Formosa," Aug. 17, 1950, Acheson Papers, Box 65, HSTL. A recently declassified document removes any doubt that the trip was not only unauthorized but was opposed by Truman, Acheson, and General Bradley, though not, apparently, by Johnson. See Meeting with the President, Aug. 3, 1950, Policy Planning Staff Records (hereafter cited as PPS Records), Box 14, File: China 1950–51, NA.

the public and almost certainly contributed to the defeat of many of Truman's fellow Democrats in the interim elections.[141]

In the first few months of the war, Truman had not yet mobilized sufficient funding to pay for the proposed increases in military aid to Europe and American defense spending. A large part of the initial increase was absorbed by the operations in Korea. After that initial jump in the budget, the administration viewed public and congressional support for any additional increases as extremely weak.[142] In the summer, sympathetic leaders on the Hill were warning Acheson that the public was critical of Truman's foreign policy because it lacked moral purpose. Senator Kefauver said Truman's grand strategy seemed like "a series of temporary expedients with no long-term forward looking design." He continued: "The lack of enthusiasm in Congress to grant funds (for foreign affairs) . . . is traceable to a sense of frustration and lack of understanding as to the purpose behind our policies. A bold new program involving herculean efforts to achieve some form of clear political ties among the free nations of the world would make foreign aid programs easier to sell."[143]

Kennan's schemes for compromises and the balancing of Chinese and Korean Communists against Soviet ones were hardly the stuff of moral bracers or herculean efforts. While logically sound, such realist strategies would not sufficiently inspire the public to rally around Truman's massive new defense programs. Since Truman viewed the NSC 68 spending levels as vital to American survival, he could not accept any policy that would call into question the president's sincerity and leadership in the global anticommunist struggle. Kennan's proposal to allow Beijing's entry into the UN was just such an unacceptable policy.

Aside from negating whatever possibility there may have been for a negotiated settlement in Korea and the exposing of Sino-Soviet differences, the failure to allow PRC admission to the UN had one major cost not considered by Kennan. It meant that the United States still lacked direct high-level contacts with Chinese officials. As I argued above, this condition was another major price of maintaining domestic consensus about grand strategy during mobilization. The lack of communications would complicate Chinese attempts at deterrence in the Sino-American

---

[141] The Democratic Party lost twenty-nine congressional and six Senate seats in the November elections. See "Congress and the Presidency," in Congressional Quarterly, *Congress and the Nation*, p. 63.

[142] See, for example, the skepticism over future budgets and the November tax bill in the minutes of the October 5 meeting of Acheson, Marshall, Nitze, Snyder, Harriman, and others in the microfiche supplement of *FRUS*, 'Secretary's Memoranda of Conversations, 1947–52."

[143] Memorandum of Conversation, Aug. 14, 1950, Acheson Papers, Box 65, HSTL.

crisis over Korea in early fall 1950. These weak deterrent attempts constituted the last chance for peace before the United States crossed the 38th parallel and triggered Mao's decision to escalate the Korean conflict. The importance of direct communication channels to American leaders would be demonstrated again in November and December, when Acheson and others expressed frustration that there were no established channels in which to carry out secret negotiations that might not embarrass the Truman administration domestically as it geared up for rearmament.[144]

After the Chinese Counteroffensive: The Continuing Inability to Negotiate

In Europe, since the early days of the Korean War, the possibility that the United States would concentrate its resources in Asia excessively and thus damage its global strategic position had been a major concern. On July 8, 1950, Acheson sent the following message to embassies in Europe: "We must dispel the feeling in Europe which followed [the] initial relief over our vigorous action in Korea that we may now become overcommitted in [the] Far East and overlook [the] continued importance [of] Europe in [the] struggle against Communism. With this in mind you should take every opportunity to indicate that as [a] result [of the] Korean situation US leadership will be even more vigorous and confident, with a view to instilling resolve."[145] In high-level meetings with the State Department on July 12, the British made it clear that their first priority in Korea was no longer to demonstrate resolve, but to prevent the Americans from expending their power in an unimportant arena or from triggering World War III.[146]

After the Chinese counteroffensive in late November, these concerns exploded into near panic in London, especially after Truman publicly hinted at the possibility of atomic weapons being introduced into the

---

[144] See the minutes of the tense meeting of Acheson, Nitze, Jessup, and others in Acheson's office on Dec. 2, 1950, Acheson Papers, HSTL. Ambassador Gross said: "The question at the outset is how to establish contact with the Chinese Communists, where to get in touch with them, and who should serve as an intermediary. He said Sir Bengal Rau (of India) was the most obvious intermediary and that, while he was often unreliable, he was the best available." At this meeting, Nitze advocated secret negotiations while America maintained an outward posture of firmness. Such a strategy required direct contacts with the Communists, however. Also see Meeting of the National Security Council, Nov. 10, 1950, President's Secretary's Files, HSTL.

[145] *FRUS: 1950*, Vol. 3, p. 130.

[146] Ibid., p. 1658.

war. Within three days of the Chinese counteroffensive, the extent of the UN debacle in Korea became clear in the West. The Europeans, in particular the British, became extremely worried that the Americans were about to enter a prolonged, full-scale war with China and, perhaps, the Soviet Union. In early December, Prime Minister Clement Attlee raced to Washington to propose alternatives to further escalation, including a ceasefire accompanied by regional peace talks involving the Soviets and the Chinese Communists. Attlee argued that, at a minimum, the United States should allow the Chinese Communists into the UN, because then the allies "could use arguments based on the principles of the United Nations which were not so effective when they are outside the club."[147] Attlee also suggested negotiations at the UN based on the Cairo Declaration, since that document did more than just grant Taiwan to China; it also renounced aggression as a means of gaining territory.[148]

Acheson and Truman explained to Attlee the intricacy of the two-level game in which the American leadership found itself. Through a long dialogue they convinced Attlee that by continuing to take a resolute stand in Asia, more, not less, assistance would be available for Europe because the American government would be able to mobilize more from its citizenry. Alternatively, negotiated compromise would seem like appeasement and squelch the fire behind the American rearmament effort. The mobilization power lost by extinguishing the American anticommunist crusade would far outweigh any material resources saved by withdrawing from the Korean conflict or the Taiwan Straits.

The minutes of the discussions are very revealing of the American position in the late 1940s and deserve careful attention.[149] Truman and Acheson tried to employ various strategic arguments for why the United States should reject a compromised settlement in Korea, none of which convinced the British leaders, who had come prepared with convincing counterpoints for these shaky justifications. In the first meeting on December 4, Truman and Acheson attempted to persuade Attlee that a demonstration of continued American resolve in Korea and Taiwan was important, lest nervous allies question American fortitude and cut deals with the increasingly powerful Communists. As a corollary to this argument they equated Chinese Communists with Soviet Communists, calling the CCP puppets of the world communist movement. This monolithic communist argument meant that, by standing up to the Chinese Communists, the United States was also standing up to the Soviets. This would

---

[147] Ibid., p. 1763.

[148] "Truman-Attlee Talks," Dec. 7, 1950, Meetings in the Secretary's Office, Acheson Papers, HSTL.

[149] The meetings with Attlee, Dec. 4–7, 1950, are found in *FRUS: 1950*, Vol. 3, pp. 1698–1787.

prevent nervous Asians from cutting deals with Moscow. Attlee aptly described this analysis of tumbling Asian dominoes as "the bandwagon psychology."[150]

Attlee, however, was not buying this line. He began refuting this argument with a logic that the Americans could not counter. First, he argued that while the international interpretation of American actions was important, the major issue abroad was not American reputation for resolve, but the fear that America could not act with restraint. America appeared imperialistic in Asia. Europeans feared that the United States was sapping its strength in a strategic backwater, leaving insufficient raw power to guarantee Western defense if the Soviets attacked. The British particularly focused on the issue of the American intervention in Taiwan, which they believed was alienating Asian opinion and leading to an undesirable wave of neutralism among potential Asian allies.[151] In Europe, they argued, the real concern was not with resolve, but capabilities. The West should save its best punches for the defense of Europe. Attlee also criticized the argument about monolithic communism, citing the precedent of Tito as well as the clear strands of nationalism in the Chinese revolution. Since Attlee was not so much concerned about American or British reputation for resolve, and did not view Beijing as a puppet of Moscow, he suggested a regional peace settlement even if the United States and Britain "lost face" in the process. This would allow the West to concentrate on the real enemy—the Soviets—and do so in Europe, the arena of greatest strategic importance.[152] Moreover, Sir Oliver Franks, the British ambassador, argued against continuation of the American policy of "friction" with Beijing, since it would only tighten the Sino-Soviet alliance, which was based on "coincidence of Chinese and Russian views, not Chinese subservience to Russian views."[153]

The British arguments destroyed the American leaders' assumptions and undercut their conclusions, and Acheson and Truman retreated on almost all of their opening positions. On the issue of American reputation in Asia, Truman admitted: "Asiatic governments seem to condone [the] Chinese action in Tibet and Korea and blame the U.S. for all that

[150] Ibid., pp. 1711–1714. Subsequent statements by Acheson and later State Department analyses demonstrate that Acheson was less than genuine in this opening approach. As late as March 1951, the Policy Planning Staff discussed the ways in which American support of Chiang Kai-shek was acting to prevent the rise of Titoism in China. "Effect within China and Other Asiatic Countries of United States Backing of Chiang Kai-shek," Mar. 29, 1951, PPS Records, Box 14, File: China 1950–51, NA.
[151] "Truman-Attlee Talks." Dec. 4–7, 1950, Memoranda of Conversations, Acheson Papers, Box 65, HSTL.
[152] FRUS: 1950, Vol. 3, pp. 1710–1716.
[153] Sir Oliver Franks quoted in "Truman-Attlee Talks," Dec. 5, 1950, Memoranda of Conversations, Acheson Papers, Box 65, HSTL.

happens."[154] This admission, consistent with NSC documents from late 1949, suggests that America was not taking a tough line toward China simply to impress third parties in Asia.[155] On the issue of Asian neutralism, Acheson conceded that "the Asians would probably do that anyway and he did not think that we should pay a price for Asian opinion."[156] In fact, Truman was afraid that the Asians would be lackadaisical, not panicky, in the face of Communist advances. He said that the United States should make "special efforts to convince non-communist Asia of the nature of the threat which confronts it and to urge upon the governments concerned the need for concerted action to resist communist aggression in that area."[157] Clearly, by December 1950, concern over Asian opinion about American resolve was not the driving force behind American actions in Korea or Taiwan.

On the possibility of Titoism and the danger of world war, Truman conceded to Attlee that the longer the United States could avoid major war, the more likely it would be that "people behind the Iron Curtain will object to Stalin's iron rule."[158] Similarly, Acheson called "correct" Franks's analysis of the "virulent nationalism" in the CCP, the fragile nature of the Sino-Soviet alliance, and the high costs of the American policy of friction toward China.[159] Thereby, Acheson admitted that, even after the Chinese counteroffensive, the administration still did not consider the communist bloc to be a monolith.[160] Acheson also stated that the administration agreed with Attlee's analysis of the CCP, the potential for a Sino-Soviet split, and the strategically peripheral nature of the Asian mainland. In response to Attlee, Acheson said: "Returning to the Prime Minister's remarks on China, he thought that he would not find much disagreement among the President's advisors on many of the fundamental points. He pointed out that he had probably been more bloodied by announcing these views than anyone else. . . . The question was not whether this was a correct analysis but whether it was possible to act on it."[161] Like Kennan's analysis of Asia, Attlee's portrayal of Chinese independence from Moscow may have been logical, but it was not possible to

[154] *FRUS: 1950,* Vol 3, p. 1716.

[155] See the discussion of NSC 48/1 and 48/2 in Chap. 4.

[156] "Meeting in the Secretary's Office," Dec. 5, 1950, Memoranda of Conversations, Acheson Papers, Box 65, HSTL.

[157] *FRUS: 1950,* Vol. 3, p. 1717.

[158] Ibid., p. 1729.

[159] "Truman-Attlee Talks," Dec. 5, 1950, Memoranda of Conversations, Acheson Papers, Box 65, HSTL.

[160] This was consistent with State Department analyses after the North Korean attack but before Chinese intervention. See "The Likelihood and Possibilities of Overt Aggression by China," Sept. 19, 1950, Office of Chinese Affairs, Film C0012, Reel 15, frame 132, NA.

[161] *FRUS: 1950,* Vol 3, p. 1732.

implement any policy based on it without crippling other aspects of grand strategy.

With the simpler arguments shot down, Acheson, Truman, and others began explaining the more complicated two-level problem that the administration faced. Acheson knew that any public compromise or conciliation with Beijing would destroy the momentum of the expensive rearmament program under NSC 68. The secretary and the president sought to convince the prime minister that, counterintuitively, a tough stand toward the PRC would allow for more American assistance for Europe than would a policy of conciliation in Asia. Acheson said:

> Before coming to the long range considerations regarding China, there was one important thing which ought to be mentioned and that was the attitude of the American people. . . . As the President said yesterday no Administration in the United States could possibly urge the American people to take vigorous action in its foreign policy on one ocean front while on the other ocean front they seemed to be rolled back and to accept a position of isolation. . . . This would affect our attitude toward other things.[162]

Acheson's own records from the meetings read as follows:

> The Secretary then went on to develop our general thought. Foreign policy in the East and Western Europe cannot be separated. We must have a single foreign policy for both sides of the world. He touched on the problem of American public opinion, pointing out that he was not referring to vociferous extremists but to the sound judgment of reasonable people. *If we surrender in the Far East, especially if this results from the actions of our Allies, American people will be against help in the West to those who brought about the collapse. In order to avoid this outcome we must take a steadfast position in the Far East. He pointed out that he was not falling back on the glib catchword "my public opinion won't let me." He was, however, appraising an important factor, namely the trend of general American thinking. He pointed to the size of the effort here in terms of taxes, military service, etc.*[163]

Acheson was addressing all of the international and domestic problems facing leaders who are mobilizing massive domestic resources for grand strategy. In such circumstances, carrying popular opinion is no longer an issue of mundane domestic politics, but one of national security.

It was in this light that Acheson clarified the administration's strategy toward China over the past three years. He pointed out that the need to

---

[162] Ibid.

[163] "Truman-Attlee Talks," Dec. 4, 1950, Memoranda of Conversations, Acheson Papers, Box 65, HSTL (emphasis added).

reject conciliation in order to guarantee mobilization for Europe did not require all-out war with the mainland. Acheson said:

> We must link this [the China] problem with the problems of Europe. Whether there was a cease-fire or not a possible line is one not necessarily involving us in the bombing of the Chinese and similar military action *but merely stating that our attitude is one of hostility.* . . . It may be a decade before the American people are ready to forget [PRC hostility to the United States].[164]

Truman, backing these statements by Acheson fully, said, "We could not separate our discussion from the political problems we face. Mr. Acheson had brought out the need to carry our people with us."[165] Throughout the leaders' conversations, Truman intermittently interceded to remind the prime minister that popular and congressional funding for grand strategy was not guaranteed, that the China bloc was vocal and influential, and that the administration's policies would suffer if there were any hint of appeasement in Asia. For example, when discussing the possibility of ceasefire negotiations and PRC admission to the UN, Truman's response was that "this certainly would not be good from the point of view of maintaining our position in American opinion."[166] The concern about public opinion was not simply an episode of electoral politics. Rather, as Acheson put it, it reflected the need to "get our people behind the effort [in Europe and Asia] and to draw on the power from the United States which actually is the only source of power."[167]

Other key administration officials weighed in to support the thrust of Truman's and Acheson's arguments. Discussing the deployment of American forces to Europe, General George C. Marshall, the new secretary of defense, added that the "situation is much like that in 1940. The hesitation of the members of Congress is very important unless you can show that there is a real basis for going forward."[168] Averell Harriman summed up the administration's position most clearly: "The question was one of the organization of the Free World and the re-establishment of its morale. This could be accomplished only by strong action with a demonstration of strength in the Far East to the limit of our capacity and especially by pressing on with our NATO plans. . . . From a realistic

---

[164] *FRUS: 1950*, Vol. 3, p. 1733.

[165] Ibid., p. 1734.

[166] Ibid., p. 1736.

[167] Ibid., p. 1734.

[168] Truman then referred to the fact that he had been unable in the past to implement conscription in peacetime, having been rejected seven times by Congress since the end of World War II. Ibid., pp. 1749–1751.

point of view, he [Harriman] did not think that we could carry the American people in their support of NATO without common action in the East."[169] Clearly, domestic political concerns were behind the fact that the administration could no longer make public distinctions between strongpoints and peripheral interests. Europe was still the most important strategic area, but success there required the demonstration of allied cooperation and anticommunist resolve in Asia.

In discussing Taiwan, at times Generals Bradley and Marshall as well as civilian advisers attempted to convince Attlee of the island's strategic importance. Marshall discussed the military "unsoundness" of allowing Taiwan to fall to the Communists, but Truman would chime in with the more compelling argument that "it was not sound from the political point of view here [in the United States] and that he had to consider the political situation here."[170] In late 1950, arguments for protecting Taiwan included saving some face if the Chinese drove the United States completely from Korea. Also, as Mao recognized, the island could be used for attacks against the mainland if all-out war between the PRC and America ensued. But a Korean peace settlement which preserved the ROK could be portrayed abroad as a military victory for the United States. Such a settlement would reduce the reputational value of Taiwan and the future chance of war between the United States and the PRC. As Bradley recognized in 1952, when the Korean fighting had stabilized: "If we are not going to war with Communist China, then what do we do with Formosa? How long can we hope to hold the situation? We might be wasting all the money we are spending there. We have said many times and still say that the loss of Formosa would be bad but . . . not be so bad as to justify sending U.S. troops there to hold it."[171] Of course, if as Attlee suggested, the removal of American forces from the area of Taiwan was part of a negotiated peace in Korea, then the American dilemma over Taiwan would be solved. The offensive need for Taiwan would disappear with the end of the war and the United States would then have every reason to withdraw. Moreover, as we saw from the Chinese documents above, the removal of American forces from the Chinese Civil War probably would have been effective in convincing Mao that a negotiated peace was in accord with Beijing's security needs, since it would remove the threat of a two-front war erupting from the conflict in Korea. But a settlement would not solve the domestic problem cited by Truman. As

[169] Ibid., p. 1770.
[170] Ibid., p. 1770. Earlier in the meetings, Truman had stated: Formosa was "quite a political issue in the U.S. since Chiang had many converts here." Ibid., p. 1732.
[171] General Bradley in an Apr. 9, 1952, meeting of the JCS, NSC, and State Department in *FRUS: 1952–54*, Vol. 14, p. 39.

Acheson summed up the administration's China policy in 1950 to Attlee: "This was not a question of logic, but the very integrity of the people."[172] If America was to act logically in countering Soviet communism in Europe it would have to behave somewhat illogically by countering Chinese communism in Asia.

The British entourage fully grasped the nature of America's China policy in 1950. Acheson was arguing that the United States must stay hostile toward China, but that because the Asian mainland was strategically unimportant the United States should also avoid full-scale war with China. Sir Oliver Franks critically distilled the American position: "It seemed to him [Franks] that the United States was seeking a middle way between branding the Chinese [Communists] as aggressors and negotiating with them. In this policy we end up merely by harassing them."[173] This was precisely the American position and had been since 1947.

Of course, all of these discussions with Attlee might have been an example of disingenuous salesmanship to a savvy foreign leader. Perhaps the administration did not actually perceive the domestic difficulties in increasing the defense budget, did not tie these issues to China policy, and moreover, saw continued resolute action in Asia as justified on straightforward strategic grounds. However, documents from National Security Council and State Department meetings from November and early December suggest that the domestic political arguments assumed by the administration in the Truman-Attlee meetings reflected the true thinking of American foreign policy leaders.

In early November the Policy Planning Staff under Nitze discussed the potential fallout of an American withdrawal from the Asian mainland and the husbanding of resources to protect more important areas. The document argues that while such an action would "alleviate the present crisis" with China in Korea, it was undesirable: "In the first place, the American people would be confused and humiliated by a decision of this character. It would be a body blow to morale at the center, the maintenance of which is essential if we are to win the world-wide struggle in which we are engaged."[174] The document went on to discuss the negative effects on Free World allies. Of course, this justification would fall apart when in December those allies rushed to Washington pleading for such a settlement.

On November 24 Truman gathered his domestic and international advisers to discuss the campaign to market the massive increase in the defense budget. General Marshall, citing the difficulties of peacetime mobil-

---

[172] *FRUS: 1950*, Vol. 3, p. 1732.

[173] "Truman-Attlee Talks," Dec. 4, 1950, Memoranda of Conversations, Acheson Papers, Box 65, HSTL.

[174] Draft memo by Davies, Nov. 7, 1950, *FRUS: 1950*, Vol. 7, p. 1082.

ization in America, stated, "We had never before tried to raise and maintain troops prior to the outbreak of a war." Acheson pointed out that the world was bipolar and that the United States was the "only force in the world capable of opposing Soviet aggression." Because the government must mobilize resources, the administration's public relations was now vital to American security. According to the minutes of the meeting, the president said: "We will not have a sound position if we can't state the facts and make a proper appearance in the press, which is not too friendly to the administration anyway. The President said that he feels this is a matter of vital importance involving our survival or destruction."[175] Later in the meeting Truman argued that the rearmament must continue no matter what the outcome in Asia. Nearly all present at the meeting seemed to agree that this would not be easy.

While agreeing with the need for more military spending, one official, Air Force Secretary Stuart Symington, was critical of the administration's efforts to date. He claimed that administration experts knew of the need for across-the-board increases as early as January 1950 (when NSC 68 was commissioned) but implied that Truman had imprudently waited until late 1950 to actually push for the major increases. Truman exploded at this insinuation. Truman's angry response to Symington sums up the history of the two-level mobilization game the administration played from 1945 to 1950. It also demonstrates the relationship between domestic support for grand strategy and Sino-American tensions. The minutes read:

> The President questioned whether Mr. Symington may have forgotten that this is a democracy. He recalled that in 1945 we faced a debacle in which we could foresee a situation we would have to meet but could do nothing about it. The President said that he had tried to get a backlog of trained men, but that after the war everybody thought the whole thing was over and there was no sense in preparing for a military situation which we might never encounter. Then Secretaries Acheson and Marshall started on the European Recovery Plan after initiating the Greek-Turkey aid program, and with those we were able to meet the situation despite a hostile Congress. Subsequently it got to the point where Congress thought we were throwing money away, and began to cut the programs. The only thing that stopped that was Korea, which we met in the best way we could. Now, the President said, we are trying to get an arrangement that will prevent all-out world war and be prepared for it if we can't prevent it. . . . The President feels this is a very difficult situation which may very easily blow up. *For instance, if the Chi-*

[175] 72nd Meeting of the National Security Council, Nov. 24, 1950, President's Secretary's Files, HSTL.

*nese Communist threat evaporates, the president questions that you could
go through with a $45B program.*[176]

The outbreak of the Korean War itself, while helpful, was not sufficient
to rally support for the administration's full rearmament program. The
administration had indeed had trouble raising taxes for security policy in
the months after the outbreak of war in Korea. Treasury Secretary John
Snyder stated in October: "The tax bill was coming up in November and
we were going to have a very difficult time with it. . . . Pressure from
Congress had really been to get through tax reduction measures rather
than tax increases."[177]

While there is no evidence that Truman intentionally caused the escalation of the Korean conflict (although, as he spoke to Symington, Mac-
Arthur was implementing the disastrous American offensive to the Yalu),
it is clear that he could not afford an openly negotiated settlement of the
Korean War involving Beijing if he hoped to gain congressional support
for the $45 billion defense budget. The public made almost no distinction
between the Soviet and Chinese Communists. As stated in Chapter 4, in
July the majority of Americans would have approved war with Russia if
the CCP had attacked Taiwan. In December, 81 percent of respondents believed that the CCP had "entered the fighting on orders from
Russia."[178] As Kennan reflected on a regional peace proposal involving
the PRC and the Soviet Union: "For this . . . we were totally unprepared.
This was at the height of the McCarthyist hysteria. The China Lobby, in
particular, was in full cry. There were violent differences in Congress
over Far Eastern policy. No attempt could be made to give final definition
to that policy, and especially to discuss it with the Russians, without
blowing the domestic political situation sky-high."[179]

As the administration prepared for the arrival of the British entourage,
strong messages emanated from Congress that compromise in Asia would
not be tolerated. Republican senators were preparing a bill, which ultimately failed, stating that any agreement reached by Truman and Attlee
in the December meetings must be ratified by the Senate as if it were a
treaty.[180] On the Senate floor on December 4, Knowland again exploited
the language of the Truman Doctrine speech in order to preempt any
negotiated settlement with Beijing. He stated: "Are we to take the posi-

[176] Ibid.

[177] Memorandum of Conversation, Oct. 5, 1950, Executive Secretariat Records, Lot
53D444, Box 14, NA.

[178] "Gallup Poll on Red China and the UN," Dec. 28, 1950, Foster Papers, Box 33, File:
China 1949–52, NA.

[179] Kennan, *Memoirs*, Vol. 2, p. 28.

[180] Acheson, *Present at the Creation*, p. 481.

tion that human freedom is less worth supporting in Asia than it is in Europe?"[181]

Further evidence that Acheson was sincere in his meetings with Attlee can be found in the internal briefings Acheson held for administration officials about the proceedings. Acheson's tone in these briefings is not one of a person who just sold a bill of goods, but of one who had merely stated the unpleasant facts to the British. While the purpose of the briefings was to explain the previous day's proceedings, there is no hint that the president or Acheson had been disingenuous in presenting the political problems of mobilization. The minutes read in a matter-of-fact fashion: "In the meeting in the Secretary's office last night the Secretary informed the British that we could not separate our foreign policy into two compartments—the Far East and the European. . . . The Secretary went on to say that Americans would not accept surrender in the Far East in accord with the desire of some of our allies who have urged us to be conciliatory in the Far East. *Americans demand that we must be vigorous everywhere.*"[182]

It is not clear what would have resulted if Truman and Acheson had agreed to negotiate a broad settlement of the conflict along the lines suggested by Attlee, which included "Formosa, a seat in the UN, and recognition."[183] There is some spotty evidence in the American archives that the Chinese in December would have been willing to negotiate a ceasefire in Korea, but only if the United States reasserted its January position on the Chinese Civil War and abandoned Taiwan. On December 9 James Reston passed a message from Beijing via Indian ambassador Rau stating that China might negotiate if the United States reasserted the Potsdam and Cairo Declarations.[184] Documents from Russia suggest that this effort was not genuine, however, and that the last real chance for a short-term settlement, however small, evaporated after the Chinese counteroffensive proved so successful. In the October 23 telegram to Peng Dehuai, Mao seemed willing to negotiate a peace settlement with the Americans after significant but limited Chinese military victories. But after the stunning military achievements of Chinese forces in late November, neither the Chinese nor the Soviets were in the mood to negotiate a true compromise. It appeared they could simply grab what they wanted on the field of battle. Zhou's initial proposal for a negotiated peace, drafted December 7,

---

[181] Knowland quoted in Kepley, *Collapse of the Middle Way,* p. 119.

[182] Meeting in the Secretary's Office, Dec. 5, 1950, Memoranda of Conversations, Box 65, HSTL (emphasis added). Attending this meeting were Acheson, Webb, Matthews, Jessup, Rusk, Merchant, Nitze, Perkins, Harriman, Kennan, and McWilliams.

[183] Ibid.

[184] Memorandum for the Files, Dec. 10, 1950, Memoranda of Conversations, Acheson Papers, Box 65, HSTL.

demanded total American withdrawal from both Korea and Taiwan, PRC replacement of the ROC government in the United Nations, and PRC and Soviet participation in the Japanese peace treaty. This entirely unacceptable proposal was never sent but still demonstrated the bravado of the Chinese after their military successes. In fact, the document apparently was not sent because Stalin convinced the Chinese leaders that only vague peace proposals should be made until after Communist forces had seized and secured large areas south of the 38th parallel. Such a diplomatic strategy would prevent the Americans from raising public counterproposals and thereby gaining international sympathy before they had lost their hold on South Korea.[185]

It is clear from the Russian document that the Indian proposals in July held out a much more serious chance of limiting warfare than the Indian proposals in December. If Kennan's July proposal for an unconditional admission of the PRC into the Security Council had been accepted by the rest of the administration, at a minimum there would have been direct contacts between the two sides in early October, and at a maximum the United States might have been able to foster tensions between Beijing and Moscow in UN peace negotiations. Whether American concessions at various points would have led to peace or not, for our purposes it is important to understand the main reasons why the administration rejected all such overtures in 1950. Not only could the administration not compromise with Asian Communists, it had to struggle against popular pressure for punitive military and economic measures against China. Although it was capable of resisting pressures for strategic bombing, the administration folded to domestic pressure on economic war, agreeing to an across-the-board, unilateral trade embargo and assets freeze on the PRC. In private, administration leaders considered such an embargo to be useless at best, and at worst, damaging to vital trade for the British Commonwealth and Japan and to hopes of gaining a tacit ceasefire agreement in Korea.[186]

THE AFTERMATH OF ESCALATION

Before the Panmunjon armistice of July 1953, the bitter battles between the Chinese and American forces during the Korean War claimed the lives of tens of thousands of Americans and hundreds of thousands of Chinese, including Mao's son. This disaster sealed the poor relations be-

---

[185] See various Sino-Soviet communications on Dec. 7, 1950, in Weathersby, "New Russian Documents," pp. 52–53.

[186] Almost all the justifications for the trade embargo were domestic. See the Dec. 14, 1950, document in *FRUS: 1950*, Vol. 6, p. 681.

tween the two sides for years to come. Moreover, the American reversal over Taiwan placed the United States in the unsettling position of protecting the KMT from CCP attack. The Taiwan issue, still important in the 1990s, would become the major focal point of Sino-American tensions through the 1950s, leading to two major crises (1954–55 and 1958) that tested the Eisenhower administration's doctrine of nuclear brinkmanship.

While in the middle and late 1950s different forces were at work in determining American policy toward China, the degree of mutual animosity and the remaining issues of contention all stem from the period discussed above. The degree of tension and conflict between the United States and China can be traced to the problems the Truman administration had in mobilizing public support for an expensive but moderate grand strategy. The two-level dynamics prevented the administration from establishing working relations with Beijing and thereby prevented crisis communication that might have allowed the Chinese to deter the disastrous American crossing of the 38th parallel. Moreover, these dynamics prevented Truman from exploiting the real potential for discord between Beijing and the Soviets. Of course, ideology still mattered. A true friendship or alliance between Washington and Beijing is hard to imagine in this period. But there is increasing evidence that Mao's relations with Moscow were rocky from the start and that Mao was willing to establish relations with any country that would abandon the KMT and accept the CCP victory in the Chinese Civil War.[187] Breaking with the KMT and establishing direct contacts with the CCP alone likely would have been enough to prevent the Korean debacle. Moreover, successful American abandonment of Chiang would have precluded the next two crises in the Taiwan Straits.

[187] For new evidence of the tense relations between Mao and Stalin as early as the negotiations for the Sino-Soviet Treaty of Friendship, see the fascinating memoirs of Mao's Russian language interpreter, Shi, *Zai Lishi Juren Shenbian.*

CHAPTER 6

Continuing Conflict over Taiwan: Mao, the Great Leap Forward, and the 1958 Quemoy Crisis

IF THE EARLY Sino-American conflict was linked with Truman's efforts to mobilize America for the Cold War, one might ask why relations did not improve later in the 1950s. After two years of deadlock at the 38th parallel and wrangling over the terms of prisoner-of-war exchanges, the Korean War had finally ground to a halt in July 1953 with the signing of the Panmunjon armistice.[1] By then, because both CCP control over the mainland and American Cold War internationalism had become more-or-less accepted realities in American public life, there should have been an opportunity to place American China policy on a more realistic basis.[2]

One central problem was that a noncommunist Taiwan became the accepted status quo in American strategic thinking while it did not in the minds of the CCP. This problem was exacerbated by the fact that Eisenhower's "New Look" Doctrine placed a strong emphasis on nuclear deterrence, so preserving America's reputation for resolve became an even more essential plank of the American security platform.[3] Since reputation for resolve is built on defense of the status quo, Taiwan remained important to American grand strategy. When China tested America's unofficial commitment to Chiang in 1954 by attacking KMT positions on offshore islands in the Taiwan Straits, Washington assisted Taipei and signed the Mutual Defense Treaty with the Republic of China (ROC).[4] Of course, one could argue that the roots of this conflict can be found in Truman's earlier decision to block the straits. If America had disowned Chiang in 1950, Taiwan would no longer have been an issue of Chinese sovereignty or of American resolve.

---

[1] Foot, *A Substitute for Victory*.

[2] The American internationalist policy was, however, continuously challenged throughout the 1950s in traditionally isolationist sections of the Midwest and South. See Snyder, *Myths of Empire*, chap. 7; Also see Lerche, *Uncertain South;* and Hero, *The Southerner in World Affairs*.

[3] For a comprehensive review of Eisenhower's New Look doctrine, see Gaddis, *Strategies of Containment*, chap.5.

[4] For coverage of the 1954–55 crisis, see Stolper, *China, Taiwan, and the Offshore Islands*, chaps. 1–7; Xu, *Jinmen Zhi Zhan*, chap. 4; He, "Evolution of the People's Republic of China's Policy"; Lewis and Xue, *China Builds the Bomb*, chap. 2.

The motivations for Mao's 1954 attack on the offshore islands are fairly clear and have been explored in detail both in the United States and in China: Mao hoped that by attacking in the straits he could dissuade the United States from including Taiwan in new multilateral defense arrangements in Southeast Asia (specifically, SEATO, the Southeast Asia Treaty Organization). The attack was essentially a test of American resolve toward the defense of Taiwan. Mao was warning that any nation signing a defense pact with Taiwan ran a risk of war with Beijing.[5] Mao's attempt backfired. If anything, the attack caused Eisenhower and Dulles to make a clearer and earlier commitment to Taiwan's security than they otherwise would have preferred.

But the simple strategic probe explanation for China's 1954 attack cannot explain the 1958 crisis in the Taiwan Straits. This crisis occurred after the Americans already had made clear commitments to Taiwan. Below I first offer a brief overview of the history of the crisis and the domestic political setting in China at the time. I then present and test various explanations for Chinese behavior during the crisis, including my own two-level explanation.

THE 1958 TAIWAN STRAITS CRISIS: A BRIEF OVERVIEW

The Military and Diplomatic Events

On August 23, 1958, the PLA forces in Fujian Province began a three-day intensive shelling of the heavily fortified, KMT-held islands of Quemoy and Matsu (Jinmen and Mazu), the former just two miles off the mainland port of Amoy (hereafter Xiamen), the latter near Fuzhou. The initial artillery attack was rather ferocious, with tens of thousands of shells falling on the islands in the first few days. On August 24 and 27, the PLA broadcast calls for surrender to ROC troops on the islands. Shelling decreased markedly in the following days, but it became apparent that the PLA was attempting to use its artillery and navy to blockade the island. The PLA attack had clearly been planned well in advance: troop levels and air assets were increased rapidly in the Xiamen area starting in the middle of July.[6]

The Chinese attack triggered a two-month crisis with the United States during which American war planners prepared for some hair-raising contingencies, including tactical nuclear strikes against Chinese airfields near

---

[5] See, for example, works cited in note 4 above.

[6] For details, see Halperin, "The 1958 Taiwan Straits Crisis"; Pollack, "Perception and Action in Chinese Foreign Policy," Vols. 1–2; Lin, *Yi Jiu Wu Ba Nian Taiwan Haixia Weiji Qijian Meiguo Dui Hua Zhengce*; Xu, *Jinmen Zhi Zhan*, chap. 5; and Ye, *Ye Fei Huiyilu*.

Xiamen and as far up the coast as Shanghai.[7] One early-August State Department document describes Joint Chiefs' plans to defend Quemoy and Matsu with "nuclear strikes deep into China," which, while designed to destroy military targets, would also lead to "millions of non-combatant casualties."[8] Given Chinese restraint and very good American analysis of Chinese deployments and military plans, the risk of such horrific escalation was limited and short-lived. But because the United States had such aggressive contingency plans and the Chinese were allied with the Soviets, the crisis was obviously extremely dangerous for China and the United States alike. Military errors or misreadings of the other's motives or maneuvers could have led to significant escalation both regionally and globally. In fact, American leaders at the time feared that the American public had little idea how dangerous the standoff was and therefore was unprepared for the implications of escalation.[9]

The initial American military response to the attack was quick, though politically ambiguous. Having observed the buildup of PLA forces over the preceding weeks, the United States was not caught entirely off guard by events in the area. Fearing the reputational consequences both in Taiwan and elsewhere if America failed to assist its ally, Eisenhower ordered an increased American naval presence near Taiwan. Not only did Eisenhower upgrade the combat readiness of the Pacific Seventh Fleet, he augmented the local fleet with ships from the Sixth Fleet, recently deployed in the Middle East during the July 1958 crisis over Lebanon and Iraq. Within two weeks the United States had assembled in the region the largest nuclear navy witnessed to date.[10]

Despite the military muscle sent to the region, Washington did not initially announce any plans to assist in the defense of the islands, which had an ambiguous status under the 1954–55 Mutual Defense Treaty. That treaty allowed for American defense of the islands only if an attack on them was considered part of a phased attack on Taiwan. Fearing that the KMT might exploit a stronger American commitment by dragging the United States into a war with China, the United States did not commit publicly to defending the islands until September 4, when Secretary of

---

[7] Halperin, "The 1958 Taiwan Straits Crisis," pp. 55–84. During the crisis a conventional plan for such attacks was also developed; see pp. 140–143. One apparent problem from the Western side was that Washington was not certain whether the Chinese Communists had acquired atomic weapons from the Soviets.

[8] Memorandum from Gerard C. Smith [director of the PPS] to Mr. Herter, Aug. 13, 1958, S/P-58231–3A, NARA Release Date Feb. 14, 1995, in "Document of the Month," Aug. 9, 1995, National Security Archive, Gelman Library. I am grateful to Judith Reppy for bringing this document to my attention.

[9] Eliades, "Once More unto the Breach," p. 353.

[10] For details of American deployment decisions in the first week of the conflict, see Halperin, "The 1958 Taiwan Straits Crisis," pp. 135–136.

State Dulles made a firm statement of American resolve at Newport, Rhode Island.[11]

On September 6, the Chinese premier, Zhou Enlai, publicly agreed to hold ambassadorial-level talks with the United States in Warsaw. In this period, September 5–8, the Soviets weighed in on the side of the Chinese Communists. Their foreign minister, Andrei Gromyko traveled secretly to Beijing, and the Soviets made various public and private warnings to the United States about the dangerous consequences of an attack on the Soviets' ally. The degree and timing of Soviet support has been a source of controversy. Some have been impressed with Soviet allegiance to China, while others, including Chinese historians, argue that Soviet bluster and offers of military assistance came only after the worst danger had passed.[12]

The Sino-American meetings in Warsaw, begun on September 15, were the first direct discussions between the two governments in several months. With the resumption of direct talks, the crisis seemed to be winding down. Washington became increasingly convinced that the PLA was not attempting to take the islands by force. Beijing was clearly taking measures both diplomatically and militarily to avoid escalating the conflict.[13] The remaining immediate challenge for the Americans was to break the blockade. This would ensure that KMT forces on the island would not be choked off from their supply base in Taiwan. The United States adopted naval convoys and successfully broke the blockade by the end of September, delivering hundreds of tons of cargo to the islands in a matter of days.[14]

While this success solved the immediate crisis for the Americans, the volatile conditions that could lead to future crises remained. As a proposal for a more permanent solution to the problem, the United States urged the KMT to withdraw its forces from the islands once it could do so without appearing to retreat under duress. The islands were considered symbolically important to Eisenhower but militarily unimportant to the defense of Taiwan. As long as the KMT was not physically driven from the islands, Eisenhower believed that neither reputational nor military damage would be suffered by the KMT or the United States.[15]

[11] Ibid., pp. 200–204; and Eliades, "Once More unto the Breach," p. 350.

[12] Arguing that the Soviets gave minimal assistance and did so late in the crisis is Zagoria, *Sino-Soviet Conflict*, pp. 211–217. For a counterargument, see Segal, *Defending China*, pp. 130–132. For a critical Chinese review of Soviet policy, see Wei, "Gromyko's Recollections of Talks with Chairman Mao concerning the Taiwan Situation Are Incompatible with Reality," in *Xin Zhongguo Waijiao Fengyun*, pp. 135–138.

[13] For reviews of the talks, see Young, *Negotiating with the Chinese Communists;* and Wang, *Zhongmei Huitan Jiu Nian Huigu.*

[14] Halperin, "The 1958 Taiwan Straits Crisis," pp. 297–304.

[15] Eliades, "Once More unto the Breach," pp. 362–364.

Because his party's legitimacy on Taiwan was largely based on the notion of reunifying China under KMT rule in the future, and because the offshore islands were a salient link to the mainland, Chiang Kai-shek predictably rejected the American plan. More surprising was the CCP response to the American efforts. The CCP declared a lengthy ceasefire in early October and, later in the month, adopted a merely symbolic policy of shelling every other day. But the Chinese Communists firmly rejected overtures from the United States about demilitarization of the islands. Late in the crisis, not only did Beijing take a belligerent diplomatic position at Warsaw, it even took active diplomatic and military steps to *help ensure that the KMT stayed on the islands.* (These actions are discussed further below.) Mao clearly feared that a KMT withdrawal would assist the United States in implementing a "two-China policy," under which Taiwan would be severed permanently from the mainland's control. There was one crucial issue on which Mao and Chiang agreed: Taiwan was an inseparable part of China.

For all intents and purposes, by the middle of October the crisis ended without any significant change in the pre-crisis status quo. KMT forces remained on the island, as they do to this day, and for many years China sporadically shelled the islands. Although new crises would heat up in 1962 and 1996, the level of tensions has never again reached the level that it did in 1958.

The International Context

The crisis occurred in a volatile two-year period in regional and international politics. In the spring and summer of 1957 the KMT increased force levels on the tiny offshore islands to 110,000, while the United States decided to introduce nuclear-capable Matador missiles to the area.[16] The KMT troops used their bases on the islands for sporadic blockades of ports and other harassment of Chinese assets in the coastal region, espionage against the CCP, and propaganda warfare designed to weaken the CCP's hold over the coastal population.

In 1958 Sino-American relations were also rocky. Talks at Geneva, established in 1954, had broken off ostensibly over the attempt by the United States to replace a U.S. ambassador with a subambassadorial representative. In a late June ultimatum, the Chinese threatened to break off talks permanently if the United States did not restore ambassadorial-level representation within fifteen days. In a complex turn of events, including

[16] For a brief overview of the 1957 buildup, see George and Smoke, *Deterrence in American Foreign Policy*, p. 372.

a conscious effort by China to ignore American conciliatory moves, no agreement was reached and talks broke off until mid-September 1958.[17]

If Sino-American relations appeared as icy as ever, Sino-Soviet relations, at least on the surface, appeared quite positive. Mao had severe reservations about Khrushchev's 1956 de-Stalinization speech, but in the same year he publicly supported Khrushchev in the suppression of uprisings in Eastern Europe. Mao also tacitly supported the Soviet leader against rivals within the Communist Party of the Soviet Union (CPSU) during Khrushchev's 1957 struggle with the so-called Anti-Party Group. In November 1957 the Soviets celebrated the 40th anniversary of the Bolshevik Revolution by hosting Communist leaders from around the world. In the few months before the conference, the Soviets demonstrated their ability to launch a multistage intercontinental ballistic missile (ICBM) and to place a man-made satellite in space (Sputnik). Attending the festivities in Moscow, Mao hailed the Soviet achievement, praising Soviet leadership of the Communist camp, and proclaiming confidently that the United States was a "paper tiger" and that "the East wind prevails over the West wind." For their part, in November 1957 Soviet leaders signed an agreement to help the Chinese develop nuclear weapons, complete with a promise to transfer a sample bomb sometime in the future.[18]

It is doubtful that Mao ever felt as confident about relations with the Soviets as his 1957 rhetoric suggested, but his reservations were hidden by optimistic statements and diplomatic congratulations on Soviet achievements. By August 1958, however, relations had become strained, and diplomatic niceties were put in the closet. Relations had soured markedly in the spring and early summer of 1958 when the Soviets refused to transfer key weapons systems, suggested a joint Sino-Soviet naval fleet, and requested the construction, on Chinese soil, of radio transmitters for Soviet submarines. Arriving on July 31 for four days of consultation, Khrushchev met an icy reception in Beijing. The meetings between the two Communist leaders were extremely rancorous. Mao interrogated Khrushchev about the joint fleet issue and other Soviet policies that the chairman viewed as an unacceptable infringement on Chinese sovereignty.

As 1958 progressed, Chinese foreign policy rhetoric and behavior to-

---

[17] See Young, *Negotiating with the Chinese Communists*, pp. 139–141; and Wang, *Zhongmei Huitan Jiu Nian Huigu*.

[18] For coverage of Sino-Soviet relations 1956–58, see Zagoria, *Sino-Soviet Conflict*; for Chinese accounts see Han and Xue, eds., *Dangdai Zhongguo Waijiao*, chap. 10. Relevant Chinese memoirs include, Li, *Waijiao Wutaishang de Xin Zhongguo Lingxiu;* and Liu, *Chushi Sulian Ba Nian*. Li was the Foreign Ministry translator during the 1950s. Liu was China's ambassador to the Soviet Union from 1955 to 1963.

ward other countries became increasingly harsh. In the spring the Chinese delegation suddenly withdrew from Yugoslavia and Beijing accused Tito of revisionism.[19] During the July–August Middle East crisis, the party-controlled media railed against American and British intervention in that region and promised Chinese support for the Arab peoples. In the press the CCP directly linked American imperialism in the Middle East with American policy toward Taiwan, calling for American withdrawal from both regions.[20] In July and August tensions in the straits increased when Mao ordered a beefing up of artillery and air power in Xiamen and the KMT military went on alert and increased its air activities over the mainland.[21]

The Domestic Context

In 1958 Mao adopted a radical new domestic economic and political agenda, the various aspects of which fall under the umbrella term "the Great Leap Forward." Although it was implemented in different phases, the plan in its entirety amounted to a second revolution in China. By the end of 1958 all agriculture was communized, wage and other incentives were abolished in the rural and urban sectors of the economy, massive industrial drives with fantastically high targets and bizarre production methods were launched, women were sent to work in the fields and factories, and labor was militarized through the enrollment of half the Chinese population in the "people's militia." The stated goal of the movement was for China to surpass leading Western economies, such as Great Britain, in a matter of several years.

The Great Leap Forward started out more mildly in the winter and spring of 1958 and then became much more radical through the summer and early fall. In the earliest phase, which occurred between harvests, the party mobilized idle labor to work on large construction projects, such as the erection of dams and irrigation systems. In July 1958 Mao launched the first large-scale production drive, focusing on steel output. Also in early summer 1958, a new form of agricultural organization, "the people's commune," was tested in selected areas of the country, mainly in Henan province. At the Beidaihe Party Conference in August, Mao decided to launch the most radical phase of the Leap. With the Henan model as a guide, in early September he ordered the nationwide commu-

[19] For coverage of Sino-Yugoslav relations in 1958, see Wu, *Zai Waijiaobu Ba Nian de Jingli*. Relevant to the thesis here, Wu, former ambassador to Belgrade, surmises that his removal from office was related to domestic politics in China rather than to any grand strategic vision.

[20] See the various front-page stories to this effect in the *Renmin Ribao* in the second half of July 1958.

[21] For excellent and concise coverage, see Xu, *Jinmen Zhi Zhan*, pp. 211–215.

nization of agriculture, new and fantastically high industrial targets (including the doubling of steel production in a single year), as well as the "everyone a soldier" campaign (*quanmin jiebing*), which mobilized the entire work force around a military theme.[22]

ALTERNATIVE EXPLANATIONS FOR CHINESE BEHAVIOR DURING THE CRISIS

Given this international and domestic context, why did China launch the attacks in the Taiwan Straits? Scholars have disagreed about Mao's political and military objectives in attacking the offshore islands. Below, I briefly compare my own two-level approach with the leading explanations for Chinese behavior in the current literature. I then present my own approach in more detail and provide evidence that it has more explanatory power than the alternatives. It should be noted, though, that the approaches are not all mutually exclusive. Actors can have multiple goals and motives in a crisis, and Mao is certainly no exception. But even if the available evidence does not clearly reveal a single motive, a careful study should at least suggest which motives were primary and which secondary in Mao's strategy.

International Explanations

CHINA UNDER THREAT

In the West and in China, various security-related explanations for the PLA attack have been offered. The most straightforward argument stresses the threat posed by the KMT forces on the offshore islands, which lie but a few kilometers from the Chinese mainland. The KMT had increased the forces on Quemoy and Matsu in 1957 (to 110,000 troops) and used the island bases to send spies onto the mainland and to harass the port of Xiamen. In addition, the islands could be used for a base of attack by the KMT in the event that the United States increased its "imperialist" activities toward China. In this thesis, the placement and test-firing of American Matador missiles on Taiwan, Washington's apparent refusal to continue with ambassadorial-level talks between the two governments, and America's July intervention in the Middle East are all viewed as signals to Mao that the United States was becoming more aggressive globally and in the region. In this portrayal, China attacked in the straits as part of Mao's "active defense" strategy. His primary goal

[22] For a detailed discussion of the Great Leap strategy, see Schoenhals, *Saltationist Socialism*. For frank Chinese accounts see Xie, *Dayuejin Kuanglan;* and Liu and Wu, eds., *Dayuejin he Tiaozheng Shiqi de Guomin Jingji.*

was to minimize or destroy the KMT military presence off China's shore and to send a tough message to Washington about Beijing's outrage over recent American policies.[23] A corollary to this hypothesis is that the militia drive was consistent with Mao's fear of invasion. The "everyone a soldier" campaign was not cynical manipulation for domestic purposes but a further manifestation of Mao's perception of an increased threat from the United States and the KMT.[24]

THE STRATEGIC PROBE: TESTING AMERICAN RESOLVE

An almost opposite argument about Chinese goals and risk analysis is provided by the strategic probe thesis. In this thesis, held by the Eisenhower administration itself at the time, Mao is portrayed as probing American resolve, which he viewed as unclear or weak.[25] After Sputnik, Mao may have been so encouraged by the Soviets' perceived lead in the strategic arms race that he felt the Americans would not dare counter Beijing's attempts to settle the Taiwan question. As a result, Mao sought to test the American commitment to Chiang by attacking the offshore islands. The offshore islands were a good place to begin a probe because American commitment to them was not clearly spelled out in the 1955 Mutual Defense Treaty. If the Americans backed down, then China would continue to push until it had "liberated" the offshore islands and then, perhaps, Taiwan. If, however, the Americans supported the KMT claims to the islands, then China could still back down and avoid war. In this account, the strong American response surprised and disappointed Mao and led him to abandon a more aggressive military posture.[26]

THE SOVIET FACTOR: MAO SEEKS TO DEMONSTRATE INDEPENDENCE AND GAIN MORE ASSISTANCE

Another possibility is that Mao had become anxious that the Soviets were taking China for granted, so Mao needed to demonstrate his independence in foreign affairs by creating a crisis without Moscow's permis-

[23] Chen, "Paoji Jinmen Neimu"; Gurtov and Hwang, *China under Threat*, chap. 3. Gurtov and Hwang argue that Mao wanted to weaken KMT forces on the island, not to seize the islands themselves. Also see Zhang, *Deterrence and Strategic Culture*, chap. 8. Zhang argues that, seeing a longer-term threat from Taiwan and the United States, Mao adopted an "active deterrence" strategy, so as to warn Chiang and the United States about the consequences of future attacks on the PRC.

[24] See Zhang, *Deterrence and Strategic Culture*, p. 253.

[25] For a carefully researched review of the administration's position throughout the crisis, see Eliades, "Once More unto the Breach."

[26] George and Smoke, *Deterrence in American Foreign Policy*, chap. 12. Halperin and Tsou, "The 1958 Quemoy Crisis," p. 273. For various versions of the probe thesis, see Sigal, "The 'Rational Policy' Model." For a critique of the probe thesis, see Pollack, "Perception and Action in Chinese Foreign Policy,' Vol. 1, pp. 19–26, 138.

sion. This would serve two purposes. First it would demonstrate to Moscow that Mao could not be controlled. Second, it would draw the Soviets closer to the Chinese by creating a Sino-American crisis that the Soviets could not afford to ignore. This would prevent the Soviets from abandoning China and perhaps lead to an increase of Soviet assistance to its ally.[27]

THIRD WORLD SOLIDARITY: HELPING IRAQ AND LEBANON

Beginning in the 1980s the standard Chinese scholarly line on the 1958 attack on Quemoy changed. In the earlier account, Mao's main purpose was to punish Chiang's troops for making incursions on the mainland. In Chinese accounts of the 1980s and early 1990s, Mao was primarily seeking to assist the populist struggles in Lebanon and Iraq by drawing American naval forces away from the Middle East and toward China. Here Mao is portrayed not merely as a Chinese nationalist but as someone truly dedicated to anti-Western revolutions around the world.[28]

Psychological Explanations

PAPER TIGERS, SPUTNIK EUPHORIA, AND THE OVERCONFIDENT MAO

Related to the probe thesis is the argument that Mao felt China or the socialist camp enjoyed strategic superiority in 1958. In this account, Mao is considered sincere in his 1957 rhetoric about Sputnik and the east wind prevailing over the west wind. Mao's attack in the straits and the militia campaign may have resulted from a distorted worldview, in which Mao believed that China was in a strong military position and could seize the offshore islands and Taiwan with some ease. Consistent with this explanation are Mao's various pejorative statements about American power in 1957–58, in which he referred to the United States as a paper tiger.[29]

---

[27] See, for example, Ulam, *Expansion and Coexistence,* pp. 617–618.

[28] My determination of this line is based partially on my interview research in 1990–91. For published versions, see Li, "The Politics of Artillery Shelling," pp. 36–38; Ye, *Ye Fei Huiyilu,* pp. 656–657; and Liu, *Chushi Sulian Ba Nian,* p. 72; also see the entry in Yan, ed., *Shijie Zhengzhi Jingji yu Guoji Guanxi Cidian.* For a somewhat revised version of the argument, see Xu, *Jinmen Zhi Zhan,* pp. 202–220; and Liao, "1958 Nian Mao Zedong Juece Paoji Jinmen de Lishi Kaocha." Xu argues that Mao initially planned the attack on Quemoy in July largely in order to help solve the Middle East crisis, but that by the time he actually ordered the attack in late August, the crisis had dissipated. In late August, Xu argues, Mao was mostly interested in the domestic mobilizational value of renewed tensions with the United States in the Taiwan Straits.

[29] Those I interviewed in China sometimes raised the possibility that Mao had lost touch with both domestic and international realities during 1958. For a qualified version of the "overconfident Mao" thesis, see He, "The Evolution of the People's Republic of China's

Also consistent with this position are Mao's pie-in-the-sky targets for the Chinese economy during the Great Leap. The Chinese leader may simply have been in a manic, optimistic frenzy that manifested itself in both the international and domestic arenas.

Domestic Political Explanations

FACTIONAL AND BUREAUCRATIC STRUGGLE

In official Soviet history it was argued that the Taiwan Straits crisis was pushed by a radical faction in the Communist Party who preferred international tension and radical economic strategies. This group was purportedly battling more realistic party elements who preferred peaceful coexistence and moderate economic strategies.[30] Such a factional analysis would be consistent with some Western analyses of the Great Leap Forward, which argue that the campaign resulted from the ascendance of a radical planning group within the CCP and the decline of more moderate party elements.[31]

THE TWO-LEVEL MOBILIZATION THESIS

My thesis is that international and domestic factors were integrally related and, in combination, led Mao to seek tensions short of war with the United States.[32] Because of his growing fear of abandonment or exploitation by an increasingly powerful Soviet Union, Mao believed that China needed to increase its own power in relation to both the West and the Soviet Union. The Great Leap Forward, particularly its most radical phases in the summer of 1958, was an effort to transform China, over the

Policy," p. 237. Arguing that Mao was apparently sincere in his "paper tiger" statements and that he was surprised that the Americans responded so strongly in the straits is Pollack, "Perception and Action in Chinese Foreign Policy," Vol. 1, pp. 171–178.

[30] See Borisov and Koloskov, *Soviet-Chinese Relations*, pp. 152–153.

[31] For a factional analysis of the decision for the Great Leap, see Chang, *Power and Policy in China*, pp. 76–80. For an account focusing on the differences within the CCP bureaucracy, see Bachman, *Bureaucracy, Economy and Leadership in China*. For the competing "Mao in command" approach, see Teiwes, *Leadership, Legitimacy and Conflict in China*.

[32] A number of authors have discussed the relationship between the Great Leap Forward and the attack in the straits, but, as Jonathan Pollack points out, it has not been explored in depth. Pollack, "Perception and Action in Chinese Foreign Policy," Vol. 1, pp. 7, 41. For examples, see Dutt, *China and the World*, pp. 43–44; Schurmann, *Ideology and Organization in Communist China*, pp. 480–482; Vogel, *Canton under Communism*, chap. 6; and Solomon, *Mao's Revolution*, pp. 361–368.

course of several years, into a great power with nuclear weapons and an advanced industrial base.

The problem for Mao is that his earlier attempts in 1955–56 to gain popular acquiescence to increased government control of the economy had largely failed. Mao therefore attempted to replicate the wartime conditions of the anti-Japanese and civil war period, during which common people sacrificed greatly for the communist cause without much material reward. To mimic those heady, nationalistic days, Mao needed international tension and a sense of national danger. Although Mao certainly did not want war with the United States in the short term, he saw benefit in a carefully controlled crisis environment within which he could mobilize the Chinese people to sacrifice for the Great Leap. Therefore Mao launched a circumscribed attack on KMT positions in the Taiwan Straits, creating a crisis atmosphere. But from the onset, Mao was careful to avoid escalation. While the Great Leap itself was an economic and humanitarian disaster, Mao's careful manipulation of conflict with the United States and the KMT was actually a great political success. During that crisis Mao successfully communized agriculture and mobilized the Chinese masses to work harder for less remuneration.

Below I separate the explanation here into distinct parts. First I analyze the connection between the international challenges facing China and Mao's decision to launch the Great Leap Forward. Then I analyze the political hurdles facing Mao in attempting to mobilize the Chinese people behind the massive self-strengthening effort. I conclude this section with a discussion of how Mao exploited and manipulated international tensions in order to get over those domestic political hurdles.

The International Challenge and the Origins of the Great Leap: Mao's Growing Fears about Soviet Power and Chinese Backwardness

From 1950 to 1958, the PRC had adopted a grand strategy that relied heavily on the Soviets for economic and military aid. The Soviets had apparently asked for too much in return. During the 1954–55 Taiwan Straits crisis the CCP leadership was uncomfortable relying on Soviet assistance to counter American threats. While continuing to seek aid from the Soviets, in 1955 Mao advised the Chinese military to develop its own modern weapons capabilities. It was at this time that Mao also launched the Chinese atomic weapons program.[33]

For Mao the continuing decline of China in relation to both Western and other socialist bloc countries dictated change in China's grand strat-

---

[33] For the pressures that led to Mao's January 1955 decision to seek atomic weapons, see Lewis and Xue, *China Builds the Bomb*, chaps. 2, 3.

egy. By early 1958 Mao had become disillusioned with the Sino-Soviet alliance and Soviet assistance programs. As the Soviets recovered from World War II and assumed a more equal position with the United States, Mao believed that China was able to rely less, rather than more, on its Soviet ally, which was seeking cooperation with the United States on issues such as nuclear proliferation. As a developing, nonnuclear power, the Chinese would not benefit from a superpower condominium. By 1958 the Chinese clearly feared that, if they fell further behind, the Soviets might then cut separate deals with the United States without regard to their weaker ally. Moreover, in 1958 Mao also worried that the Soviets would treat China as they had their Eastern European satellites. The fears of abandonment and exploitation underpinned Mao's critique of strategic concepts promoted by Khrushchev, such as "nuclear nonproliferation" and "peaceful coexistence."[34] In addition, Soviet assistance and economic strategies were proving increasingly unsuitable to Chinese conditions. The trademark Soviet overemphasis on centralized heavy industry had created bottlenecks and had only exacerbated the problem of capital accumulation shortages in the countryside, where some 80–90 percent of the Chinese population resided.[35]

Evidence from the mainland demonstrates that, despite public enthusiasm about the Sino-Soviet alliance, Mao was extremely disillusioned with Moscow before the more radical phases of the Great Leap Forward were implemented.[36] Despite his optimistic rhetoric about the prevailing east wind, Mao feared that the Soviets' new Sputnik delivery capabilities would marginalize China as a Soviet security asset. As Vice Minister of Defense Xiao Jinguang recalls, when the Soviets demonstrated their "shocking" new capabilities to a Chinese military entourage in late 1957, the Chinese felt relatively backward and resolved themselves to "struggle hard" to close the gap between China and its ally.[37]

Beijing had apparently been skeptical from the start about the Soviets' 1957 agreement to transfer atomic weapons. In his memoirs, the former Chinese ambassador to Moscow, Liu Xiao, states that in 1957 Beijing viewed the nuclear agreement with Moscow as a side payment for support of Khrushchev in his struggle against the Anti-Party Group.[38] Mao must then have doubted that the Soviets would honor the agreement after Khrushchev won his internal struggle and after Sputnik marginalized the

---

[34] For Mao's criticisms, see ibid., pp. 67–68; also see Clemens, *The Arms Race and Sino-Soviet Relations*, pp. 33–34.

[35] Zagoria, *Sino-Soviet Conflict*, passim.

[36] Relevant memoirs include Li, *Waijiao Wutaishang de Xin Zhongguo Lingxiu;* and Liu, *Chushi Sulian Ba Nian.*

[37] Xiao, *Xiao Jinguang Huiyilu*, Vol. 2, pp. 174–176.

[38] Liu, *Chushi Sulian Ba Nian*, pp. 45–46.

Chinese as military allies. The memoirs of Mao's Russian interpreter, Li Yueran, support this interpretation. Li argues that by early 1958 Khrushchev's domestic position was stable. Thereafter, Sputnik became the biggest factor in Sino-Soviet relations. Li writes of Mao's relations with Khrushchev in 1957–58:

> Before 1958, Khrushchev's [domestic] political position was not secure, and the East and West [blocs] had entered a Cold War posture, so Khrushchev paid the utmost attention to Sino-Soviet relations, struggling to obtain the support of the CCP and Mao for himself [Khrushchev] and the CPSU. . . . [By New Year's Day 1958] Khrushchev was already completely consolidated in his [domestic] position and the Soviets had also created an intercontinental missile. Under these conditions, Khrushchev assumed the attitude that he needn't have many misgivings about China and Mao. The Western media openly recognized that "the Soviet Union had become a country immune to other nations' attack; it no longer mattered that it was communist, socialist, or anything else, attacking it would be unwise." Thereupon, Khrushchev wanted to create detente with the US; [but] toward China he was anxious. From the time of these developments on, Khrushchev and Malinovsky both made statements disadvantageous to Sino-Soviet friendship.[39]

In Beijing's view, the Soviet acquisition of a secure, second-strike capability and the relative decline of Chinese power within the alliance carried a dual danger: the Soviets were less likely to support China and more likely to treat China like a weak satellite.

The Chinese fears were well founded. From late 1957 Khrushchev seemed less willing to buy Chinese support through direct assistance. In their November 1957 meeting in Moscow, Khrushchev discussed with Mao the return of Soviet experts working in China.[40] By March 1958 the Soviets had decided to renege on their promise to transfer atomic weapons to China. They began employing delaying tactics to mask this secret decision.[41] Even when the Soviets honored weapons transfer commitments, they shared only technology at least two generations behind their own.[42]

As John Lewis and Xue Litai argue, in June 1958 when Mao predicted Chinese atomic capability within ten years, he still hoped for and would have happily accepted Soviet assistance.[43] In fact, China received Soviet

[39] Li, *Waijiao Wutaishang de Xin Zhongguo Lingxiu*, pp. 177–178.
[40] Ibid., p. 151.
[41] Lewis and Xue, *China Builds the Bomb*, p. 61.
[42] For this general Soviet policy in the 1950s, see Lewis and Hua, "China's Ballistic Missile Programs," p. 13.
[43] Lewis and Xue, *China Builds the Bomb*, p. 71.

military assistance, including gaseous diffusion equipment and naval vessels, through the early part of 1959. At the urging of Soviet experts in China, the Chinese military even requested nuclear submarine technology from the Soviets in June 1958.[44] But while Mao still harbored hopes for Soviet assistance, he relied less and less on their coming to fruition. In January 1958 he is reported to have stated that the Soviet nuclear deterrent was an "unreliable" factor for Chinese security and referred bitterly to the ungenerous terms of Soviet assistance during the Korean War.[45] In February 1958 CCP meetings, Mao is said to have pushed for more independence from the Soviets in weapons production.[46] In the spring Chinese military leaders argued that China would obtain nuclear weapons only when its own scientists and technicians could develop them.[47] The new push for independence in nuclear weapons programs was consistent with an overall theme of the Great Leap Forward, self-reliance (*zili gengsheng*).

By July, when Mao apparently created the final guidelines for the enlarged Chinese nuclear program, disillusionment with the slow pace and limited scope of Soviet assistance was clearly evident. Mao reportedly stated to his military leaders: "In the process of developing nuclear weapons we should not imitate other countries. Instead our objectives should be to 'catch up with world levels,' and to 'proceed on all phases [of the nuclear program] simultaneously.'"[48] As summer progressed, the Chinese seemed even more cynical about the value of future Soviet assistance. After the Soviets refused simply to transfer nuclear submarine technology and instead suggested a joint production plan, Mao exploded at the Soviet ambassador to China, P. F. Yudin. He summed up his displeasure with the Soviets dating back to the 1930s. Focusing on the period 1957–58, he claimed that his discussion of a fraternal relationship between the CCP and CPSU in October 1957 was "merely talk"

---

[44] The Chinese made the request for nuclear subs on June 28. The request was denied by the Soviets at the same time that they requested the creation of a joint Sino-Soviet fleet. This sparked an angry reaction from Mao, who called in the Soviet ambassador for a dressing down on July 22. For evidence of the Chinese requests, see *Mao Zedong Waijiao Wenxuan*, p. 634, n. 177. For the minutes of the Mao-Yudin meeting of July 22, see "Discussion with the Soviet Ambassador to China, Yudin," in ibid., pp. 322–333. For a discussion of these matters in English, see Lewis and Xue, *China's Strategic Seapower*, chap. 1.

[45] Quan, *Mao Zedong yu Heluxiaofu*, p. 97. The Soviets asked for repayment, at "market prices," for their weapons transfers.

[46] Clemens, *The Arms Race and Sino-Soviet Relations*, p. 32.

[47] Zagoria, *Sino-Soviet Conflict*, p. 170.

[48] "The Guidelines for Developing Nuclear Weapons," point 4, in Lewis and Xue, *China Builds the Bomb*, p. 70. The document is not dated, but Lewis and Xue deduce persuasively that it was drafted during the May–July 1958 meeting of the Central Military Commission.

(*zhibuguo shi koutoushang shuoshuo*). He stated that in fact relations between the parties were more like "a father and a son, a cat and a mouse." He complained bitterly that the Soviets never believed in the Chinese and that they would not give up control of nuclear technology to the Chinese because they "only trust Russians." After canceling the request for nuclear submarines, Mao summed up his disdain for Soviet arrogance by saying: "[You think that] naval nuclear subs are sophisticated technology and contain secrets. [You think that] Chinese people are clumsy. If you give it to us, problems could emerge. . . . You have never trusted the Chinese. Stalin was very untrusting of us. Chinese people are viewed [by you] as . . . a backward people. You say Europeans look down on Russians, I think Russians look down on the Chinese."[49] A week later, on Army Day (August 1), Marshal He Long spoke with regret about China's past tendency to solve its problems "purely from the military point of view and [by hoping] for outside aid instead of relying on the mobilization of the masses."[50]

Mao's fear of being looked down upon by the Soviets was surely important in his decision to accelerate the Chinese nuclear program in summer 1958. In a June 21 meeting with the Central Military Commission, Mao previewed his general plan for an accelerated development of atomic weapons, including hydrogen bombs and intercontinental missiles. His justification for such a massive effort was made not in military terms but in political ones. He argued: "If you do not have such [big] things, others say you do not count for anything."[51] It is important to note his use of the general term "others" (*renjia*), rather than "the United States" or "the imperialists." In the context of the budding disputes with the Soviets over joint military cooperation, Mao seemed to be including the Soviets among those who glorified such capabilities and looked down upon those who did not have them.

Perhaps more important than Soviet duplicity in arms transfer agreements was Mao's fear that the Soviets would begin treating China as a puppet regime or satellite. As the gap between Soviet and Chinese power grew in the 1950s, the Soviets also increased their demands on their Chinese allies. These intensified Mao's concern about Soviet "great power chauvinism," which dated back to his initial meetings with Stalin in 1949–50.[52] Mao's fears peaked in the first half of 1958, when the Soviets

---

[49] "Discussion with the Soviet Ambassador, Yudin," July 22, 1958, in *Mao Zedong Waijiao Wenxuan*, pp. 322–324.

[50] Marshal He Long in *Renmin Ribao*, Aug. 1, 1958, cited in Lewis and Xue, *China Builds the Bomb*, p. 71.

[51] "We Should Produce Some Atomic Bombs and Hydrogen Bombs," June 21, 1958, in *Mao Zedong Junshi Wenji*, Vol. 6, p. 374.

[52] Han and Xue, eds., *Dangdai Zhongguo Waijiao*, pp. 30–32. The book points to the

requested a joint naval fleet and the stationing of Soviet submarine radio stations on Chinese territory.[53] In their meeting with Yudin, Mao, Peng Dehuai, and Zhou Enlai treated these requests as violations of Chinese sovereignty.[54] During their summit in early August 1958, Mao accused Khrushchev of using the proposal for a joint naval fleet as an opening wedge in an attempt to seize the Chinese coastline. Mao chastised Khrushchev: "What do you mean by a joint navy? . . . What do you consider mutual consultation? Do we still have sovereignty? Do you plan on seizing our entire coastal region? . . . Go ahead and seize all of it!"[55] Mao is reported to have feared that by demanding bases at Chinese ports, Khrushchev wanted to "kill two birds with one stone: vying with the United States for the Pacific and encircling China."[56]

On the issue of the submarine radio stations, Mao also took a stubborn line: the stations could be built on Chinese soil only if the capital for the project were supplied by China. Mao's concern was clear. He stated: "The money has to come from the Chinese side, it can not come from the Soviet side. [The transmitting station] can be jointly used. . . . If the Soviet side puts on a lot of pressure, then do not answer [the Soviets], delay a while and then speak, or we will discuss it for a while at the [Party] Center and then respond."[57] Although he was not averse to Soviet technology transfers, he wanted no strings attached. He feared Soviet proposals to provide the bulk of the capital for the project. For the construction to be acceptable to Mao, ownership and control had to be Chinese.

Soviets' duplicity in negotiations over the Manchurian railways and port facilities in 1949–50. The authors argue that China had to accept this humiliation at this time because of the clear and present hostility that America was demonstrating toward Beijing at the time. For evidence that the initial meetings between Stalin and Mao were rocky at best, see Shi, *Zai Lishi Juren Shenbian*, chaps. 13–14. Mao later claimed that Stalin had asked for a joint naval fleet in 1950. Mao refused and argued with Stalin. See "Discussion with the Soviet Ambassador, Yudin," July 22, 1958, in *Mao Zedong Waijiao Wenxuan*, p. 331.

[53] For a review of Soviet requests for basing rights, see Li, *Waijiao Wutaishang de Xin Zhongguo Lingxiu*, pp. 167–168; Han and Xue, eds., *Dangdai Zhongguo Waijiao*, pp. 112–114; and "Discussion with the Soviet Ambassador, Yudin," July 22, 1958, in *Mao Mao Zedong Waijiao Wenxuan*, pp. 328–333. For early Western discussion of the tensions in Sino-Soviet relations that preceded the mass communization drive, see Zagoria, *Sino-Soviet Conflict*, chaps. 4–6; Griffith, *The Sino-Soviet Rift*, esp. pp. 16–18; and Clemens, *The Arms Race and Sino-Soviet Relations*, pp. 40–41.

[54] "Discussion with the Soviet Ambassador, Yudin," July 22, 1958 in *Mao Zedong Waijiao Wenxuan*. For further discussion of the Yudin meeting, see Lewis and Xue, *China's Strategic Seapower*, pp. 13–14; and Cong, *Quzhe Fazhan de Suiyue*, pp. 348–350.

[55] Li, *Waijiao Wutaishang de Xin Zhongguo Lingxiu*, p. 170.

[56] Mao as paraphrased by Zhu, "Soviet Strategic Inferiority," p. 30; also see Quan, *Mao Zedong yu Heluxiaofu*, pp. 124–130.

[57] "Comments on the Request by the Soviet Union to Build a Long-Wave Radio Transmitter in Our Country," June 7, 1958, in *Jianguo Yilai Mao Zedong Wengao*, Vol. 7, pp. 265–266.

We should not underestimate the importance of the Soviet requests in Mao's assessment of China's security environment. In a September 1959 analysis, Mao reviewed the rocky history of Sino-Soviet relations dating back to 1949; about Sino-Soviet relations in 1958 he wrote: "At the Sino-Soviet talks in Beijing in August, there occurred the incidents related to the [proposals for] a joint navy and 70% [Soviet] capitalization of the radio transmitter. We resisted this *assault*."[58] It is clear that by using the term "assault" (*jin gong*, sometimes translated as "offensive"), Mao viewed Soviet pressure with the utmost seriousness. This is not to say that the Soviets became China's number one enemy as early as 1958, but rather that Soviet weapons advances appeared to increase Soviet demands on China and reduce dangerously China's importance in the Sino-Soviet alliance. As a political history of China points out, the combination of fast-paced Soviet economic growth (in relation to that of the United States) and the development of the ICBM "seriously endangered" Sino-Soviet relations.[59]

Mao's Grand Strategy

With its emphasis on long-term industrial and military modernization, the Great Leap Forward was viewed by Mao as the best way to launch China into the league of self-sufficient nuclear and industrial powers.[60] This would help China improve relations with both the West and the Soviets. As one Chinese history puts it: "At this time [early 1958] all Chinese Communist Party leaders urgently felt that only by raising economic performance and closing the gap with America in military science and technology could [China] establish forces effective in expelling American imperialists, and [avoid] falling under the control of the great power chauvinism of the Soviet leadership."[61]

It was actually during Mao's 1957 trip to Moscow that the term "Great Leap Forward" began appearing in CCP newspapers.[62] In his reflections on the early decisions leading to the Great Leap policies, then–finance minister Bo Yibo remembered that, particularly after his November 1957 trip to Moscow, Mao decided that China needed to stand up more actively against American imperialism. While not defending the di-

---

[58] "An Outline concerning the International Situation," Sept. 12, 1959, in ibid., Vol. 8, pp. 599–603 (emphasis added).

[59] Chen, ed., *Xin Zhongguo Sishiwu Nian Yanjiu*, pp. 242–243.

[60] For all its disasters, the Great Leap did succeed in mobilizing tens of thousands of peasants for uranium prospecting and mining. These projects provided the raw materials for China's first nuclear bomb. See Lewis and Xue, *China Builds the Bomb*, pp. 87–88.

[61] Xu, *Jinmen Zhi Zhan*, p. 223.

[62] Chen, ed., *Xin Zhongguo Sishiwu Nian Yanjiu*, pp. 178–179.

sastrous form that Great Leap policies took, Bo still states that, given China's backward place in the international balance of power, the general notion of a Great Leap was basically a good one.[63]

From its initial and less radical phases through the high tide of August and September, the CCP argued that the Great Leap was necessary for international security reasons. The initial stated goal of the economic drive was to surpass Great Britain within fifteen years on key industrial indicators, especially steel production. The *People's Daily* of February 3, 1958, stated that China had to compete successfully with capitalist countries if it were to stand up to imperialism.[64] Mao certainly saw the West as his biggest enemy, but his strategic concerns were not limited to the West. As Marshal Liu Bocheng reported, by late June 1958 Mao was not only discussing surpassing the British and the Americans economically and militarily but was also explicitly listing the Soviets as a rival that must be overtaken by China.[65] Fearing that China was lagging behind both the West and the Soviet Union, in July and again in August Mao upgraded his plan for fast-paced industrial growth. Mao's grand strategy was designed (however poorly) to launch China into the class of great world powers.[66]

In order to develop an advanced industrial base and modern weapons, Mao would need capital, something China sorely lacked. Although the Great Leap strategy suffered from various utopian ideological assumptions and poor planning, the basic notions of substituting peasant labor for capital when possible and accumulating significant capital through rural taxation were not, in and of themselves, economically irrational.[67] In 1950 the U.S. Central Intelligence Agency (hardly poisoned by communist utopianism) expected China eventually to try just that. CIA analysts predicted that China would seek capital from the countryside when

---

[63] Bo, *Ruogan Zhongda Juece yu Shijian de Huigu*, Vol. 2, pp. 717–718.

[64] Xie, *Dayuejin Kuanglan*, p. 36. Xie quotes the first reason for the Great Leap given by the Feb. 3 *Renmin Ribao*: "If we do not employ the fastest pace in implementing (national) construction, and if we do not energetically surpass the economies of the developed capitalist countries in the shortest time possible, then we cannot view our national security as completely guaranteed."

[65] *Liu Bocheng Zhuan*, p. 664.

[66] In each phase of the Great Leap, improving China's international position was a major impetus for Mao's policies. He felt that both the United States and the Soviet Union were "looking down" (*kan buqi*) at China. See Pei, "Yi Jiu Wu Ba Nian Ba Da Er Ci Huiyi," p. 240. For Mao's growing disappointment with Soviet "great power chauvinism" throughout the 1950s, see Han and Xue, eds., *Dangdai Zhongguo Waijiao*, esp. pp. 30–32 and 111–114.

[67] Riskin, *China's Political Economy*, pp. 118–119. Riskin traces the basic notions of the Great Leap to rejection of Soviet-style planning and the influence of respected international development economists such as Ragnar Nurske. Also see Cheng, *China's Economic Development*; Xie, *Dayuejin Kuanglan*; and Liu and Wu, eds., *Dayuejin he Tiaozheng Shiqi de Guomin Jingji*, chap. 1.

Soviet assistance proved wanting. These analysts only wondered how the CCP would muster the necessary political consensus for such a program when its traditional political base was in the rural areas.[68]

Along with nuclear weapons, Mao's leading national power indicator was steel production. In mid-July 1958 Mao launched a massive drive to increase steel output. At the August Beidaihe conference, Mao called for a doubling of Chinese steel output in one year. This second push for increased steel production led to the infamously wasteful policy of creating backyard furnaces in rural areas in order to produce iron and steel locally.

In late August and early September Mao launched the most radical phase of the Great Leap Forward: the nationwide communization of agriculture and the militarization of the work force. Mao's program called for the ultimate sacrifice for the greatest percentage of Chinese citizens: surrender of their remaining small, private plots and household property. Because most of China lived in the countryside and China was short of capital, Mao needed the peasants to work harder for less. In an August edict, implemented in early September, the peasants were ordered to form communes and work brigades that would perform labor-intensive capital construction as well as tilling. In addition, "bourgeois" incentive programs such as providing small private plots and piece-rate wage systems were abolished.[69] To further control consumption under the new "supply system," peasants were required to eat in public mess halls. As one Chinese history puts it, Mao believed that a technologically underdeveloped China needed to answer the Soviet launching of Sputnik by first launching an "agricultural Sputnik."[70]

The Domestic Hurdles to Mobilization: The Great Leap Forward as Social Revolution

If one employs the standards offered in Chapter 2, the description of Mao's strategy as novel and controversial should raise little debate. Al-

[68] In January 1950, CIA China analysts seemed impressively prescient. See "Review of the World Situation: CIA 1–50," Jan. 18, 1950, in Intelligence Files, Central Intelligence Reports, Box 250, HSTL. They wrote; "During this period, [1950–60] progress in industrialization will depend on extensive capital accumulation. Assuming that the bulk of it does not come in the form of Soviet or other foreign investment, which seems likely, most of this capital will have to come from the scanty surpluses of China's small-scale agriculture. Consequently . . . Chinese Communist Administrative efficiency and peasant loyalties will be severely tested by the problem of extracting this agricultural surplus and using the proceeds as capital for industrialization."

[69] For a detailed discussion of the Great Leap strategy, see Schoenhals, *Saltationist Socialism*; Xie, *Dayuejin Kuanglan*; and Liu and Wu, eds., *Dayuejin he Tiaozheng Shiqi de Guomin Jingji*.

[70] Quan, *Mao Zedong yu Heluxiaofu*, p. 116.

most every aspect of the Great Leap communization was unprecedented in Chinese history. The militarization of civilian life, the mobilizing of women into the work force, and the creation of public mess halls are just a few of its novel aspects. The Great Leap Forward was nothing short of a social revolution. But it was more than a social oddity; it was an enormous physical and economic burden on the average Chinese citizen. There is no evidence that Mao actually knew the program would lead to tens of millions of hunger-related deaths, but he did know that the communization program would require massive sacrifice by the majority of Chinese. He said that "three years of hard struggle" were necessary so that China could become a leading economic and military power in the longer term.[71]

HIGHER TAXES IN PEACETIME

For the pre-Deng era, the best indicators of tax burden on the Chinese citizenry are the accumulation rates of state capital. This figure represents not only what percentage of output the government took in but also how much of that revenue was used on investment rather than consumption. State capital accumulation rates rose sharply from 24.9 percent of total production in 1957 to 43.8 percent in 1959 (the 1958 jump was smaller because the most radical phase of the Great Leap did not begin until the 1958 fall harvest).[72] In a country as underdeveloped as China in the 1950s, such an increased burden is almost unconscionable when one considers the marginal value of the added taxes on poor peasants and workers.

Compounding the burden on the average citizen, the newly accumulated capital was directed toward heavy industry, capital construction, and atomic weapons development, budgetary items that do not quickly improve the average citizen's standard of living.[73] This investment strategy was consistent with Mao's hope that, within a decade, the Great Leap would make China a power to be reckoned with in both the Western and socialist camps. A review of Chinese economic statistics for the period shows that the Great Leap was designed to increase heavy indus-

---

[71] For Mao's recognition that the Great Leap would require at least three years of great sacrifice by the Chinese people, see his August 17 speech at Beidaihe in MacFarquhar, Cheek, and Wu, *The Secret Speeches of Chairman Mao*, pp. 402–403. For another reference to the "three years of bitter struggle" (*ku zhan san nian*), see Mao's discussion with reporters in September 1958 in *Jianguo Yilai Mao Zedong Wengao*, Vol. 7, pp. 429–433.

[72] Hsiao, *The Government Budget and Fiscal Policy*, p. 140; and Schoenhals, *Saltationist Socialism*, p. 91.

[73] In 1957, 55 percent of industrial production was in the light industries, while 40 percent was in heavy industries. By 1960 the figures were 33.4 percent for light industry and 66.6 percent for heavy industry. Similarly, in 1958 and 1959 the percentage of new capital reinvested in heavy industries increased while the percentage dedicated to consumer industries dropped sharply. See *Zhongguo Tongji Nianjian*, pp. 56–62.

TABLE 6.1

Reported Increases in Chinese Light
and Heavy Industry, 1957–1959
(overall output as a percentage of 1952 output)

	Light Industry	Heavy Industry
1957	183.3	310.7
1958	245.0	555.4
1959	298.9	822.8

Source: *Zhongguo Tongji Nianjian*-1990 (China statistical yearbook: 1990), p. 57.

try, not consumer-oriented light industries (see Table 6.1). These statistics are not accurate because they do not capture the poor quality and exaggerations of local reporting during the Great Leap. They do, however, accurately represent the skewing of government policy toward heavy industry because government targets largely guided the patterns of exaggeration.

Earlier, less ambitious efforts to increase state control of production in 1955–56 led to urban strikes and a drop in rural economic growth.[74] This "Little Leap Forward" involved the collectivization of agriculture and the reduction of wage incentives. Although relatively few people went on strike or lashed out directly against the party in this period, a large number simply refused to work as hard without the normal material incentives. As one Chinese expert reflected on early 1956: "In a country like China [in the 1950s] there are two ways to protest government policy: one is to rise up, the other is to sit down. In 1956 relatively few people rose up, but relatively many sat down."[75] Such behavior did not threaten the state directly, but it did undercut the state's goal of increasing capital accumulation.

In the second half of 1956, after the economic slowdown was evident, particularly in the countryside, small private plots were returned to the peasants and additional material incentives were offered to rural and urban workers. While production rose, so did consumption, nontaxed income, and the percentage of state revenues paid out in wages. As a result, state expenditures for capital construction fell in 1957.[76] Openly frus-

---

[74] The strikes were reported by Anita Chan in a talk at the Columbia University East Asian Institute in 1990. She cited the cause of the strikes as a drop in workers' real wages during the first five-year plan. For supporting data, see Schoenhals, *Saltationist Socialism*, pp. 107–108. My interview research in 1990 supports these accounts. However, interviewees stressed that, while worker discontent was high in 1956, strikes were relatively rare. Workers most commonly protested by using safer and more subtle tactics, such as work slowdowns, rather than overt and organized protest.

[75] Interview, Beijing, China, 1990.

[76] The combined government expenditures for basic construction and working capital was 15 billion yuan in 1956. It actually dropped to 14 billion yuan in 1957. By 1959 the

trated, Mao harkened back to the days of the anti-Japanese struggle and the civil war, when people worked harder for less because they were dedicated to the CCP military cause.[77] Paraphrasing Mao at the August 1958 Beidaihe Party Conference that launched the communization drive, a party historian writes: "During the war period, who received salary payments? The revolution killed so many people, and there was no price asked [in return]. Why can't we have this now?"[78] By reinstating the guerrilla economics of the civil war period the CCP was attempting to maximize capital accumulation during the initial period of "hard struggle."[79]

But unlike the earlier period, in 1958 Mao did not perceive China as under immediate military threat, and Mao did not want to fight a war in the near term. The Great Leap was a long-term mobilization effort, not a response to a pressing crisis. Even according to Mao's hopelessly optimistic plan, it was only after several years that China would stand up as a significant power and gain worldwide recognition and respect. In the near term Mao did not expect or desire war. One week before the attack on Quemoy, Mao said that American alliances worldwide were primarily for defensive purposes and that therefore China was relatively safe for the time being. Mao stated: "In our propaganda we say that [imperialism] is an aggressor because it launches aggression against nationalism and socialism, but [we] should not see this as anything alarming. It will only attack us under one circumstance: that is, if we're in great disorder, and are overthrown by counterrevolutionaries. . . . As for those imperialist treaties, they're not so much for offense as for defense."[80]

---

government would spend over 35 billion yuan in these two categories. See Hsiao, *The Government Budget and Fiscal Policy*, p. 31. For additional evidence of the financial cost of salary payments in the second half of 1956, see Xie, *Dayuejin Kuanglan*, p. 5. For statistics on dropping levels of consumption in 1956 and rising levels in 1957, see *Zhongguo Tongji Nianjian: 1990*, p. 62. For a breakdown of state capital expenditures on fixed capital and the amounts on liquid capital in the period, see ibid., p. 47. For a general overview, see Riskin, *China's Political Economy*, p. 91; and Chang, *Power and Policy*, pp. 28–36.

[77] At the August 1958 Beidaihe conference Mao made reference to the need to bring back the selfless spirit of this earlier period and to abolish "bourgeois" incentives. For a cogent discussion of this trend in Mao's thinking, see Shi, "Mao Zedong Dui Shehuizhuyi Fazhan Jieduan Lilun de Gongxian he Shiwu"; and Zhou, "Renmin Gongshe he Shehuizhuyi Jianshe de Kongxiang Lun."

[78] Quoted in Shi, "Mao Zedong Dui Shehuizhuyi Fazhan Jieduan Lilun de Gongxian he Shiwu," p. 49.

[79] Schoenhals, *Saltationist Socialism*, pp. 90–100; For data on worker dissent, see p. 107–108; Liu and Wu, eds., *Dayuejin he Tiaozheng Shiqi de Guomin Jingji*, chap. 1; and interview research conducted by the author.

[80] Mao's draft speech for the August 17 session of the Beidaihe Party Conference in MacFarquhar, Cheek and Wu, *The Secret Speeches of Chairman Mao*, pp. 401–402.

In fact, it was the lack of a direct threat from the West that allowed China to concentrate on its internal long-term construction, including a ten-year nuclear program. From 1956–58 military spending on standing forces dropped 18 percent in absolute terms and shrank 40 percent as a share of budget expenditures, as Mao emphasized long-term economic and technological investment over immediate buildups.[81] However, the average Chinese citizen was not to benefit from the peace dividend. Although as early as 1955 Mao called for a cut in current military expenditures, he did so to increase long-term research and development, most of which is not included in the official defense budget. Obtaining the bomb alone was expensive. By one estimate, in order to develop its first atomic bomb, by 1964 China had spent more on the bomb than on the entire defense budget for 1957 and 1958 combined.[82]

Manipulating Conflict, Militarizing Society, and Selling the Program

The political problem for Mao was that he needed to mobilize capital and labor for the industrial and atomic programs. Since the nation was not under direct threat, it should have been difficult to justify such heavy burdens on China's impoverished citizenry. The Great Leap Forward was designed to solve this problem by combining an intensified version of the 1955–56 "Little Leap" economic program with the militant political fervor of the anti-Japanese and civil war period. To imitate that period, the communization process in the majority of areas involved the militarization of village life. The threat to China and the related need for vigilance, unity, and sacrifice was used to justify land seizure and extremely high government accumulation rates. As one party history describes the communes: "The entire commune work force was drawn up along military lines, organized into work units with squads, brigades, platoons, barracks, etc. Under the commune's united command, industrial and agricultural production was carried out implementing the methods of large organized armies fighting a war."[83] The commune program was painted as part of a national war effort built on the notion of local militias and a "people's war." By winter 1958, 300 million Chinese had enrolled in the people's militia.

The "everyone a soldier" campaign was the linchpin of Mao's two-level strategy. By militarizing labor, the movement linked the threat of foreign invasion with less dramatic agricultural and industrial goals. The movement was not designed to prepare China for war but to create the siege

[81] Hsiao, *The Government Budget and Fiscal Policy*, pp. 38–42.
[82] Lewis and Xue, *China Builds the Bomb*, pp. 107–108.
[83] Zhou, "Renmin Gongshe he Shehuizhuyi Jianshe de Kongxiang Lun," p. 47.

6.1. A Militarized Work Brigade in a People's Commune in Rural Hebei Province in the Summer of 1958. The photograph originally appeared in *China Pictorial*, no. 100, 1958, p. 9.

mentality necessary to extract massive sacrifices from the Chinese public. As Mao stated cynically at Beidaihe about the militia drive: "Producing that many guns is probably a waste, since we are not at war. But a little waste is still necessary. 'Everyone a soldier' helps build morale and courage."[84] Rather than a response to new international realities, the militarization of society was designed explicitly to replicate the selfless domestic political climate of the anti-Japanese war period.[85]

Needless to say, it is difficult to militarize an entire society without the clear presence of an enemy. So Mao chose to legitimize the campaign to the public by reference to the "American imperialists."[86] In July 1958 the

[84] Mao, Aug. 18, 1958, in MacFarquhar, Cheek, and Wu, eds., *The Secret Speeches of Chairman Mao*, p. 404.

[85] See Mao's August 30 speech at Beidaihe, in ibid., pp. 430–441.

[86] I surveyed CCP propaganda from various sources, including national and local newspapers and provincial party journals (see bibliography for a listing). A major propaganda theme during the early communization movement was the need for military organization to increase production and thereby, repel American invasion and liberate Taiwan. See, for example, the Sept. 7, 1958, *Renmin Ribao*, with the heading, "All the Nation's People Mobilize, Struggle to Resolutely Oppose the American Military Provocation!" Articles include reports that workers and peasants were forming militias and promising to increase production as a means of countering American threats. They were employing slogans such as, "Whatever the motherland needs, we will provide!" and "Each additional ton of steel

CCP orchestrated massive rallies ostensibly to denounce American imperialism in Lebanon and to call for a renewed struggle to "liberate" Taiwan from the "American puppets," the KMT. During these rallies, speakers linked economic production goals with the nation's ability to fend off American imperialism. Typical of the media coverage of the rallies, a daily newspaper reported: "The Shanghai workers, possessing a glorious history of opposing imperialism, will use outstanding production achievements to fulfill the production goals of the Great Leap ahead of schedule, to increase the forces of peace, and to assist the Arab people."[87] When the Middle East crisis wound down in mid-August, Mao conveniently created new tensions in the Taiwan Straits to replace it as a cause for public mobilization. In late August, at the same party conference that created nationwide communization policies and radically increased production and capital accumulation targets, Mao ordered a limited assault on KMT positions in the Taiwan Straits.[88] Mao knew at the onset that he was indirectly attacking the United States.[89] Although there was no change in the previously existing status quo, the true victory was won when the United States came to the aid of KMT forces. In September Mao could add salience to the anti-Chiang, anti-U.S. campaign begun in July by pointing to joint U.S.-KMT operations in the straits.

Mao did not want war, just conflict. Conflict short of war would guarantee popular consensus for his broad economic strategy without wasting the mobilized resources on actual warfighting. As a Chinese military history argues about Mao's decision to attack in late August: "Based on the [international and domestic] situation from late August on, the military activities adopted by the People's Liberation Army toward Quemoy flowed mainly from considerations of the internal political struggle, the needs of economic construction, and Chinese-American bilateral relations."[90] Consistent with the position taken here, the author, Colonel Xu Yan, argues that Mao needed to legitimize his radical economic construction plan. In order to form communes and increase both production and accumulation he formed the people's militia. In order to form the people's

means more power to liberate Taiwan!"; also see Xie, *Dayuejin Kuanglan*, pp. 100–106; and Pollack, "Perception and Action in Chinese Foreign Policy," Vol. 1, pp. 220–227.

[87] *Wenhui Bao*, July 19, 1958, p. 1. One can turn to any national newspaper and find similar reporting of rallies in major cities around the country. These rallies were clearly carefully organized and manipulated by the party to mobilize support for concurrent demands for increased production.

[88] Schurmann, *Ideology and Organization*, pp. 480–81. For a colorful discussion of the anti-American rallies in Beijing in July 1958, see Deutscher, *Russia, China and the West*, pp. 160–161.

[89] See "Comments concerning the Cessation of Military Exercises at Shenzhen and Preparation for Attack on Quemoy," Aug. 18, 1958, in *Jianguo Yilai Mao Zedong Wengao*, Vol. 7, p. 348.

[90] Xu, *Jinmen Zhi Zhan*, pp. 220–221.

6.2. Political Cartoon Depicting Steel Worker Repelling an American Imperialist and Chiang Kai-shek. "Steel Is Power," *People's Daily*, September, 9, 1958. The skewered person with the Republic of China symbol on his back is Chiang Kai-shek.

militia and to mobilize the peasants and workers, he exploited conflict with the United States.[91]

Secret speeches published in the West reveal that, before the assault on Quemoy, Mao strongly desired tensions with the West in order to mobilize the public. At the Beidaihe conference in August, Mao ordered both the commune drive and the attack in the Taiwan Straits. During the August 17 session Mao stated baldly:

> In our propaganda, we say that we oppose tension and strive for detente, as if detente is to our advantage [and] tension is to their advantage. [But] can we or can't we look at the situation the other way around: is tension to our comparative advantage [and] to the West's disadvantage? Tension is to the West's advantage only in that it will increase military production, and it's to our advantage in that it will mobilize all [our] positive forces. . . . *[Tension]*

[91] Ibid., pp. 215–224. Xu argues that, from its inception at the July military conference, the notion of the people's militia was "subordinated" to the "more important" goals of the commune drive and the Great Leap Forward.

can help us increase steel as well as grain production. It's better if the United States and Britain withdraw from Lebanon and Jordan later [rather than sooner]. Don't make the Americans seem kind-hearted people. Every extra day they stay is an additional advantage to us. [We can] capitalize on the United States' mistakes and make an issue of it. American imperialism will become a target of public criticism, but in [our] propaganda we can't talk like this. We still have to say [they] should withdraw immediately. . . . As for the embargo, the tighter the better; the longer the UN refuses to recognize us the better. We have experience [in this]. During the anti-Japanese war, Chiang Kai-shek and He Yingqin [KMT minister of war, 1930–44] refused to give us supplies and money. We raised [the slogan of] unity and self-reliance, developing production on a large scale. . . . It was like that then, so it's to our advantage now to have various countries put an embargo on us. . . . *To have an enemy in front of us, to have tension is to our advantage.*[92]

Mao would arrange to keep an enemy in front of China by attacking in the straits one week later, drawing massive American naval forces into the region. In fact, the final order to attack was made at the same time (August 21) that the Middle East crisis was finally being resolved in the UN.[93] Clearly Mao needed a new conflict to replace the Middle East crisis as a mobilizing theme.

On the first day of shelling and during the ensuing crisis, which lasted until late October, Mao adopted the same tone he used in his August 17 speech. Wu Lengxi, then head of the Xinhua News Service, claims that, on August 23, Mao underscored the sections of his August 17 speech that are quoted above. He paraphrases Mao as saying: "The bombardment of Jinmen [Quemoy], frankly speaking, was our turn to create international tension for a purpose."[94] On September 5, the day after the United States first publicly committed itself to defending the offshore islands, Mao told the State Supreme Council: "War mobilizes the people's spiritual state. . . . Of course we do not now have war, but under this type of

[92] "Talks at the Beidaihe Conference (Draft Conference): August 17, 1958" in MacFarquhar, Cheek and Wu, eds., *The Secret Speeches of Chairman Mao*, pp. 402–403 (emphasis added). Words in brackets are in the original translation.

[93] On August 21 a political settlement of the Middle East crisis was found, and Dag Hammarskjold arranged for the phased withdrawal of Western forces from the region. On this day, Mao met with the Fujian regional commander, Ye Fei, at Beidaihe and ordered the August 23 attack in the straits. For the influence of events in the Middle East on Mao's decisions, see Xu, *Jinmen Zhi Zhan*, p. 220. For a discussion of the August 21 meeting between Mao and Ye, see ibid., pp. 224–226; and Ye, *Ye Fei Huiyilu*, pp. 654–655.

[94] Wu, "Inside Story of the Decision Making during the Shelling of Jinmen," pp. 208–209. Wu states that Mao's immediate purpose was to "teach America a lesson" and that his deeper purpose was to "make the Americans nervous and mobilize the people of the world to join our struggle." While mobilization is central to Wu's account of Mao's strategy, he portrays Mao as more of an internationalist than a nationalist.

6.3. Political Cartoon Depicting Grain and Steel Production as Forces for National Defense. *People's Daily,* September 15, 1958. The characters on the wall simply read "China."

armed antagonism [short of war], [we] can mobilize all [our] positive forces."[95] Mao continued with his two-level analysis, harkening back to the heady days of the anti-Japanese and civil war period. As he had on August 17, Mao compared Dulles to the KMT military leader He Ying-qin because both had tried to combine embargoes and military pressure to break the spirit of the Chinese Communists. He claimed that such methods by the Americans would only help China carry out the Great Leap Forward.[96] In reference to the educational value of American and

[95] Mao's speech at the Supreme State Conference, Sept. 5, 1958 in *Mao Zedong Sixiang Wansui!,* p. 233. The book is a Red Guard collection of Mao's speeches smuggled from the mainland. The collection is generally considered credible and accurate.

[96] Mao's speech at the Supreme State Conference, Sept. 5, 1958, in ibid., p. 234.

British forces in the Middle East, he said: "If you want to oppose aggressors, it is difficult to [do] if you do not have a [concrete] object, target, and opponent."[97] Mao's September statements have been interpreted as a retrospective attempt to find something good about an imprudent decision to attack in the straits.[98] But the consistent themes in Mao's statements before, during, and after the initiation of the crisis belie this interpretation. It appears that mobilization of the population behind increased production was precisely Mao's goal in attacking in the straits.

Further evidence that Beijing was manipulating conflict for domestic mobilization is provided by Zhou Enlai's October 5 discussion of the Sino-American crisis with the Soviet attache in Beijing. Zhou said:

> ter the Quemoy artillery rang out, it served to mobilize the people of the world and especially the people of China. In every corner of the globe a wave of anti-Americanism was uncovered that surpassed in width and scope that of the Lebanon Incident. . . . Chiang Kai-shek's remaining on Quemoy and Matsu and America's continuing intervention carry great benefits. They can serve to educate the people of every country, especially our own Chinese people.[99]

Such statements by Mao and Zhou are consistent with mass media propaganda that constantly drew connections between American imperialism generally, the American threat to China in particular, and the need for China to fulfill the production goals of the Great Leap Forward.[100] For this purpose, in September and October central and provincial party

[97] "Discussion of the International Situation at the Fifteenth Supreme State Conference," Sept. 5, 1958, in *Mao Zedong Waijiao Wenxuan*, p. 344.

[98] See, for example, Pollack, "Perception and Action in Chinese Foreign Policy," Vol. 1, pp. 176–177.

[99] "The Situation in the Taiwan Straits and Our Policy," Oct. 5, 1958, the record of a discussion with the temporary Soviet charge d'affaires for the Soviet Union in China, from *Zhou Enlai Waijiao Wenxuan*, pp. 262–267. It is important to note that this discussion begins with a more cryptic statement by Zhou about straightforward goals in the straits. Zhou said, "We originally prepared to move in two steps: first we would regain the offshore islands, second we would liberate Taiwan." It is not clear what the term "originally" (*ben-lai*) refers to here. It could refer to the original plan for the 1958 attack on Quemoy, or to the general, long-term strategy for liberating Taiwan from which this episode diverges. Only this one unclear sentence is devoted to the goal of liberating the offshore islands and Taiwan, while two paragraphs are dedicated to the mobilizational value of a continuing American presence in the straits and KMT presence on the offshore islands. In any case, the Soviets came to believe that the Chinese goal in 1958 was to manipulate tension in order to mobilize the population. See Pollack, "Perception and Action in Chinese Foreign Policy," Vol. 1, p. 177.

[100] I surveyed the following national newspapers for July–October 1958: *Renmin Ribao*, *Wenhui Bao*, *DaGong Bao*, and *Guangming Ribao*. The most explicit links between international conflict and production goals were made in September and October 1958.

journals called on local cadres to militarize the work force behind an anti-American theme.[101]

Perhaps the most convincing evidence that threat manipulation was central to the commune program comes from Henan province, where the early test communes were created in July. If the use of the militia movement and anti-Americanism were central to Mao's mobilization strategy during communization, we would expect anti-American propaganda to have been particularly militant in Henan as early as July, and this is precisely what a review of the *Henan Daily* at that time reveals. While in July mass rallies protesting U.S. intervention in the Middle East were taking place all over China, in Henan the protests were much more closely tied to production goals and the transformation of rural society than in other areas, where steel production was more often the focus of mobilization. The July 27 front-page story read:

> We Chinese are bearing the burden of protecting world peace. If the imperialists do not stop their invasions, we will resolutely launch movements to strike them back. In the autumn farm management movement, the hoe is our weapon, the weeds are comparable to the American and British imperialist armies, we will resolutely eradicate all weeds. Achieve an even bigger autumn bumper crop, speed the socialist Great Leap Forward on all fronts, support our Middle Eastern brothers![102]

At the "July 1" commune, one of the first in all of China, the link between international tension, military social organization, and increased production goals was very clear. The *Henan Daily* reported:

> The "July 1" agricultural cooperative . . . unanimously decided to form immediately a great labor army from the entire cooperative's labor force of 9,000. Everyone also passed a resolution stating that the entire body of collective members will now adopt a combat style of work, striving to achieve a thousand jin of ginned cotton and three thousand jin of millet per mu. . . . [Depending on the] immediate strategic necessity (*yidan xingshi xuyao*), our labor army is [also] a staunch combat army, coming to counterattack invaders, and protecting peace.[103]

---

[101] The Sept. 1, 1958, edition of *Hongqi*, the Party Central Committee journal, likened the Great Leap to a war on nature in which workers would be militarized. A mass army prepared for American attack would have the proper organizational skills to carry out this economic war in peacetime. In 1958 the Party Central Committee of each province and autonomous region created a monthly journal for party cadres (see bibliography for a complete list). For examples of the use of the American threat to mobilize the masses in these, see the September and October issues of *Shangyou* (Guangdong Province) and *Qianjin* (Shanxi Province).

[102] *Henan Ribao*, July 27, 1958, p. 1.

[103] Ibid.

These mobilizational tactics in rural Henan presaged similar nationwide propaganda during the concurrent crisis in the straits, the national communization drive, and the "everyone a soldier" campaign in early September. In fact, in its September 1 issue the national party journal, *Hongqi* (Red flag), referred directly to the Henan communes as national examples, and in particular to their military organization and anti-imperialist fervor. During the nationwide "everyone a soldier" campaign, the propaganda at the local level closely resembled the earlier Henan model of using the American threat to increase production and sacrifice. As Roderick MacFarquhar reports from eyewitness accounts in far off Yunnan province, in early fall communization and production drives were "interwoven with the Taiwan Straits crisis in the minds of Chinese cadres," creating an "overheated atmosphere of militance and nationalism."[104] In light of this clear pattern of mobilizational propaganda both before and after the outbreak of conflict and Mao's own cynical statements at Beidaihe, it seems hardly coincidental that the most radical phases of the Great Leap coincided with the Taiwan Straits crisis.

THE TWO-LEVEL THESIS VERSUS THE ALTERNATIVE HYPOTHESES

China under Threat?

As discussed above, just one week before the attack on the straits, Mao saw little threat from the United States or its allies in Asia. He viewed America's alliances as "defensive" in nature. At the Beidaihe Party Conference Mao stated plainly that the CCP must portray the United States as threatening in its propaganda but that there was little reason to believe this was the case. Moreover, Mao said that although the CCP should continue to preach the language of detente, Beijing actually preferred tension as a mobilizing tool to increase production. Rather than being threatened by America's actions in the Middle East, Mao seemed to welcome the intervention because it supplied a domestically exploitable international issue. Moreover, exploitation of the Middle East crisis came at low cost and risk to China because it was occurring far from the East Asian region.[105]

By the middle of 1957 the KMT had finished most of its significant strengthening of forces on Quemoy and Matsu, and the United States had already announced its intention to introduce Matador missiles to the area. This makes one wonder why Mao did not attack earlier if KMT

---

[104] MacFarquhar, *Origins of the Cultural Revolution*, Vol. 2, p. 115.

[105] See Mao's August 17–20 speeches at the Beidaihe conference in MacFarquhar, Cheek, and Wu, *The Secret Speeches of Chairman Mao*.

buildup was his concern. The KMT did use the offshore islands in block-
ading the port of Xiamen, but these largely naval operations could be
carried out easily from bases on Taiwan.[106] Moreover, American military
operations in the region before the shelling could hardly be seen as threatening to China.[107] As Jonathan Pollack argues, the "U.S. response to the
[PLA's Fujian] buildup . . . could not have been construed as evidence of
substantial increases in the U.S. military presence."[108] We know from his
statements at the Beidaihe conference that Mao did not believe the Americans were preparing for an offensive against China in 1958. His cutting of
the current 1958 defense budget is also consistent with his analysis at
Beidaihe.

Perhaps most damning to the "China under threat" thesis is Mao's
telegram to Peng Dehuai on July 27, delaying a planned attack on
Quemoy. In this telegram Mao states that he has decided that China
should be patient and cautious in choosing a time for attack. But rather
than fearing an attack from the KMT on military grounds, Mao in fact
welcomed that attack on political grounds. Mao states: "The Middle East
situation will take time to be resolved, so we have time. What is the need
for anxiety? We will temporarily not attack. Eventually the day of attack
will come. If the enemy attacks [first] at Zhangzhou, Shantou, Fuzhou,
[and] Hangzhou, that would be most wonderful."[109] In the document
Mao also claimed that Chinese strategists must keep "politics in command" (zhengzhi guashuai).

Another piece of evidence against the threat thesis is Mao's handling of
the issue of restoring ambassadorial-level talks in June and July. On June
30, China leveled an ultimatum stating that if the United States did not
restore ambassadorial-level talks within two weeks all talks would be
broken off. Dulles responded affirmatively to the Chinese request on July
1, one day after the two-week ultimatum was made. He secretly made
detailed arrangements for Jacob Beam, an American ambassador, to meet
with the Chinese in Warsaw. In his internally circulated memoirs, a high-
level foreign ministry official admits that Beijing simply refused to recognize the American response, which fulfilled all of Beijing's requests.[110]
Beijing's refusal to accept the American conciliation supports the thesis

[106] Stolper, China, Taiwan and the Offshore Islands, p. 125.

[107] For a description of American military moves in the region before August 23, see
Halperin, "The 1958 Taiwan Straits Crisis," p. 65.

[108] Pollack, "Perception and Action in Chinese Foreign Policy," Vol. 1, p. 103.

[109] "A Letter to Peng Dehuai and Huang Kecheng concerning Ensuring the [Best] Opportunity for Attacking Quemoy," July 27, 1958, in Jianguo Yilai Mao Zedong Wengao,
Vol. 7, p. 326; also printed as "It is necessary to resolutely support the principle of fighting
only battles of certain victory," in Mao Zedong Junshi Wenxuan: Neibuben, p. 364.

[110] Liu, Chushi Sulian Ba Nian, pp. 65–71. Liu was ambassador to Moscow at the time.

that Mao preferred tension with the West and undercuts the notion that
he would have preferred a reduction in tensions. Moreover, it shows that
Mao's strategy of conflict manipulation preceded both the Middle East
and Taiwan Straits crises.

Mao may have wanted to reduce the number of KMT troops on the
offshore islands because he saw large deployments as threatening to
China in the long run. Mao almost certainly would have welcomed some
reduction of KMT forces on the islands. But Mao's dismissive statements
about the threat from America and his hopes that the KMT would attack
first in the crisis suggest that a threat from the KMT was not a primary
force behind Mao's decision to shell and that reduction of KMT forces on
the offshore islands was, at best, a secondary goal of Mao's strategy.

A Strategic Probe?

As Pollack argues, it seems highly unlikely that the CCP was engaged in a
strategic probe in August and September 1958.[111] The probe hypothesis
implies that Mao believed that China or the socialist camp as a whole was
ascendant in 1958 and that China was in a position to exploit the West's
strategic decline by escalating in the straits if Washington backed down.
But the military details of the straits crisis do not support this thesis. The
timing and pattern of the attacks and the balance of forces in the region
are not consistent with the probe hypothesis. Even if the Americans had
abandoned Chiang in the fall of 1958, there was little the PRC was prepared to do to exploit that eventuality. Moreover, rather than probing for
America's reaction by attacking until America responded, Mao sought to
avoid Sino-American escalation at the outset by limiting the duration and
type of attacks leveled on Quemoy.

The first key issue is the timing of the attacks. The period from late
August through early September is the heart of typhoon season, the worst
time for Beijing to initiate a probing strategy. This fact was not over-
looked by the local military commander, Ye Fei, who from the middle of
August had encountered great difficulty with transportation and logistics
because of typhoons.[112] Although artillery positions were relatively unaffected by the wind and rains in August and September, these conditions
greatly complicated the preparation of air, sea, and land operations necessary to seize the offshore islands, let alone Taiwan. Moreover, even in the
best of weather, the PLA lacked landing equipment sophisticated enough

[111] Pollack, "Perception and Action in Chinese Foreign Policy," Vol. 1, pp. 138–139.
[112] Ye, *Ye Fei Huiyilu*, p. 651; Xu, *Jinmen Zhi Zhan*, p. 216.

TABLE 6.2
Number of Shells Fired Daily at the Offshore Islands, August 23–30, 1958

Aug. 23	40,000 (shells)	Aug. 27	11,660
Aug. 24	36,000	Aug. 28	12,730
Aug. 25	3,213	Aug. 29	16,200
Aug. 26	3,580	Aug. 30	400

Source: Halperin, "The 1958 Taiwan Straits Crisis," p. 160.

to ensure an easy breach of the formidable KMT defenses on the offshore islands.[113]

Second, the pattern of attacks in the straits suggests that Mao's goals were not altered by American behavior. Morton Halperin reveals that Mao restrained his forces within three days of the initial shelling. Halperin's report on the pattern of shelling fired from the mainland in the first eight days is reproduced in Table 6.2.[114] As Pollack points out, this deescalation occurred a week before any firm American diplomatic or military response to the crisis. It was not until September 4 that Dulles delivered the Newport Declaration, linking the security of the offshore islands with that of Taiwan. Pollack argues that, although Chinese restraint came decidedly early in the crisis, "there is, however, no known instance of an early and authoritative American threat having been communicated either privately or publicly to the PRC [by Washington]."[115] It is clear from American sources that Washington consciously avoided sending any clear deterrent warnings to Beijing in the first days of the conflict. Washington feared such a commitment might encourage either foot-dragging or rash behavior by the KMT.[116]

For his part, Mao was clearly afraid of American reprisals *even before the initial attacks.* We now have Chinese evidence that PLA restraint in the early days of the crisis was planned on August 21 during Mao's meeting with Commander Ye Fei. It was at this meeting that Mao decided upon a three-day limit on the fiercest shelling. In fact, the CCP leaders were so concerned about America's becoming involved that Lin Biao even suggested warning Washington in advance so that American advisers might not be killed in the initial assault (a suggestion Mao rejected).[117]

[113] Xu, *Jinmen Zhi Zhan,* p. 218.

[114] Halperin's account, based on the CINCPAC Taiwan Diary, is corroborated by Ye, *Ye Fei Huiyilu,* and by Lin, *Yi Jiu Wu Ba Nian Taiwan Haixia Weiji Qijian Meiguo Dui Hua Zhengce.*

[115] Pollack, "Perception and Action in Chinese Foreign Policy," Vol. 1, p. 139.

[116] See Halperin, "The 1958 Taiwan Straits Crisis," pp. 200–204; and Eliades, "Once More unto the Breach," p. 350.

[117] Ye, *Ye Fei Huiyilu,* pp. 650–656.

Mao's military telegrams also demonstrate extreme caution. On August 18, Mao strongly warned Peng Dehuai that China's air force must not fly past the offshore islands (*JinMa xian*).[118] In the Chinese sources the confident Mao of prevailing east winds is nowhere to be found.

Of course, Mao was acutely interested in how the United States would respond to the shelling. In this sense he clearly was probing America's commitments to the KMT. Wu Lengxi states that Mao intently watched reports of American naval and diplomatic activities and adjusted his military and propaganda strategies accordingly. Early in the crisis he instructed Wu not to begin the media propaganda campaign until America had responded to the initial shelling. But far from hoping that America would not stand firm in the crisis, Mao appeared pleased that the United States intervened in late August and early September. Mao was not trying to determine just how much land the United States would allow China to seize but was probing for the best and safest way to create tensions short of war to further his political goals.[119]

Did Mao Intend to Take the Islands?

In both the strategic probe and the China under threat theses, one potential motive for the PLA attack might have been to wrest the offshore islands from KMT control. The goal of such an action would have been to eliminate the military threat from the islands or to move one step closer to the eventual recovery of Taiwan, or both. Mao may have backed away after observing America's response to the initial shelling. This scenario seems logical and consistent with a broad overview of the history, but the evidence from China suggests that, while Mao considered recovering the islands, it was not his primary goal in attacking in the straits.[120] Therefore, China's failure to recover the islands should not be seen as a great defeat for Mao or a great victory for American deterrence.

Mao at least considered the seizure of the islands when he ordered the

[118] See "Comments concerning the Cessation of Military Exercises at Shenzhen and Preparation for Attack on Quemoy," Aug. 18, 1958 in *Jianguo Yilai Mao Zedong Wengao*, Vol. 7, p. 348. In this same telegram Mao also orders the halt to military exercises near Canton for fear of frightening the British.

[119] Wu, "Inside Story of the Decision Making during the Shelling of Jinmen," pp. 209–210. On September 4, Mao and the Central Committee believed that America's response was perfect given their mobilizational goals. Although they had sent forces to the region, American leaders had made it clear that they were not eager to fight a war over the offshore islands. While Wu's account of events fits the mobilization model almost perfectly, it should be noted again that Wu saw Mao's mobilizational efforts as aimed at "the people of the world," not just the Chinese people.

[120] See Zhang, *Deterrence and Strategic Culture*, chap. 8.

initial massive attack on Quemoy in August.[121] A military history paraphrases Mao as saying: "After the first period [of attack], the enemy might decide to withdraw troops from the islands or, under great duress, continue to struggle; at that time, based on our view of the situation, we will decide whether or not we will consider landing on the islands to do battle."[122] In this portrayal, Mao clearly considers seizing the islands. However, the highly circumscribed language about the option of amphibious attack suggests that recovery of the islands was not a primary goal at the onset of China's military operations.

Mao's military strategy also suggests that, in late August, invasion of the islands was not Mao's primary military goal. As Pollack argues, Mao never brought his most effective forces (including air power) to bear in the conflict. Mao demonstrated such restraint even before America's September 4 commitment to assist Chiang in defending the islands.[123] Ye Fei's account corroborates Pollack's analysis. Ye argues that in late August commander Han Xianchu suggested to him that he should use bombing runs to attack the islands. Ye replied that Mao had never mentioned "landing on and liberating" the islands as a military goal, so such bombing runs were unnecessary. Moreover, since bombers would need fighter escort, such attacks might risk confrontation with American planes over the straits, which Mao had warned against on August 21.[124]

It is of course possible that Mao hoped that shelling alone would compel KMT withdrawal from the islands and make armed invasion unnecessary. The PLA did broadcast two surrender calls to the islands on August 24 and 27 and successfully blockaded shipments to the island in early September.[125] There is little doubt that Mao would have accepted the

[121] For Mao's initial orders, see Xu, *Jinmen Zhi Zhan*, p. 215.

[122] *Dangdai Zhongguo Jundui de Junshi Gongzuo* (shang), p. 394. Also see Wu, "Inside Story of the Decision Making during the Shelling of Jinmen," pp. 211–212. Wu also portrays Mao as considering the recovery of the islands, but not as particularly eager to do so. He says, "Mao told me we were not unwilling to take over Jinmen [Quemoy] and Mazu [Matsu]."

[123] Pollack, "Perception and Action in Chinese Foreign Policy," Vol. 1, p. 211. Pollack writes, "For example, there was virtually no effort (outside of a few isolated strafing incidents) to employ air power against the garrison, even though MIG's on August 24 had proven their capability to deliver 500 pound bombs. . . . The longest range PLA artillery pieces, with capabilities up to 16 miles, were not even used until Sept. 17."

[124] Ye, *Ye Fei Huiyilu*, pp. 656–663.

[125] We should doubt the sincerity of the surrender calls however. The second surrender call included Taiwan as an area that the PLA was sure to liberate in the near future. Linking the territorial issues probably only made the forces on Quemoy and Matsu more resolute than if the PLA had only targeted Quemoy and Matsu, barren islands to which the KMT troops likely had no allegiance. Moreover, whereas by September 2 the PLA shelling had successfully halted all KMT shipments to the islands, some American officials and military officers in the region complained to Washington that this was not so much the result of PLA

islands if they were abandoned by the KMT and that he would have tried to get the most propaganda mileage possible from the PLA victory. As one military scholar explained, as an institution the PLA would have liked to seize the islands as a symbol of its contribution to the Great Leap Forward. Moreover, Mao could have used seizure of the islands to demonstrate to his people that China's stock was truly on the rise.[126] Even if China had successfully recovered the islands, the atmosphere in the straits still would have been tense and Mao could have attempted to use the ensuing crisis to mobilize the public.

A quick military victory would have carried various political and security benefits. But there are reasons to believe that it would not have served Mao's purposes as well as the actual outcome. Given his broader political objectives, the value of a quick victory was no match for the domestic political value Mao tapped from the extended international crisis that followed the PLA attack. In the domestic political environment, a weak and irresolute enemy is less likely to mobilize the public than a more stubborn and powerful one. Moreover, recovery of the offshore islands would have carried real international costs for the PRC. Available data from August do not demonstrate that Mao was concerned about the negative repercussions of recovering the islands at the very beginning of the crisis, but Chinese actions and statements show that such concerns were paramount in September and October. A KMT retreat from Quemoy and Matsu would move the Civil War enemy much further (100 miles) from the mainland, making it harder to attack in the future. Whether it destroyed Chiang Kai-shek's legitimacy on Taiwan or not, the delinkage of Taiwan from the mainland would only further the cause of Taiwanese separatism. Because this factor was ignored, Chinese behavior during the crisis puzzled observers in China, the Soviet Union, Eastern Europe, and the United States. These analysts wrongly assumed the attack was designed, at a minimum, to compel Chiang's forces to abandon the offshore islands.[127]

Late in September, after the Americans successfully assisted the KMT in breaking the artillery blockade of the offshore islands and Sino-American talks had been reestablished in Warsaw, the Americans offered what they considered conciliatory proposals on a settlement of the

---

activities as it was the KMT's feigning of helplessness in an effort to drag the Americans further into the conflict. See Halperin, "The 1958 Taiwan Straits Crisis," passim.

[126] Interview with military scholar, Beijing, China, 1993.

[127] For Chinese confusion, see Ye, *Ye Fei Huiyilu*, pp. 656–657. For Soviet confusion, see Talbott, trans. and ed., *Khrushchev Remembers*, pp. 262–263; for East German confusion, see Liu, *Chushi Sulian Ba Nian*, p. 65; for American confusion, see Young, *Negotiating with the Chinese Communists*, pp. 188–190.

crisis.[128] They suggested either demilitarization of the offshore islands under UN supervision or a World Court decision on the future of the islands. The Americans were trying to find some face-saving way to get Chiang to remove his army from the offshore islands so as to prevent him from dragging the Americans into an all-out war with the CCP. Beginning on September 30, the Chinese responded to these proposals with increasingly hostile rhetoric and demands for complete American withdrawal from the Taiwan region. Rather than trying to weaken the American conditions for KMT withdrawal from the offshore islands, the Chinese became confrontational and made sweeping demands on the United States.[129] This behavior puzzled Kenneth Young, an American foreign service officer at the time. Young could not understand why the Chinese seemed to be refusing KMT withdrawal from the islands precisely at a time when the American bargaining position was so strong.[130] Such a hostile posture by the Chinese Communists was not consistent with Young's perception of Beijing's major goal in the crisis: to destroy the threat posed by KMT forces on the islands.

Beijing's refusal to accept a compromised settlement is, however, consistent with the domestic politics thesis offered here, which argues that Mao did not so much want territory as he did military tensions short of war. There is documentary and other evidence to support this conclusion. According to Khrushchev's memoirs, Mao denied that the PLA ever intended to liberate the islands. Mao is reported to have said: "All we wanted to do was show our potential. We don't want Chiang to be too far away from us. We want to keep him within our reach. Having him [on Quemoy and Matsu] means we can get at him with our shore batteries as well as our air force. If we'd occupied the islands we would have lost the ability to cause him discomfort any time we want."[131]

On October 5, Zhou Enlai informed the Soviet military attache that, for reasons related to popular mobilization, Beijing hoped that the crisis might be prolonged without a change in the status quo ante. Zhou said: "After discussion in the Party Central Committee, we still consider it best to make Chiang Kai-shek continue to remain on Quemoy, Matsu, and the offshore islands. The United States wants to remove itself from Quemoy

---

[128] Talks were reestablished on September 15. Zhou Enlai agreed to talks in a speech on September 6, which was laced with accusations of American imperialism. Zhou managed to agree to talks without reducing the domestic war siege mentality. In his speech he said: "To make a further effort to safeguard peace, the Chinese Government is prepared to resume the ambassadorial level talks between the two countries. But the danger of war created by the United States is not lessened thereby." For an English translation of Zhou's speech, see Young, *Negotiating with the Chinese Communists*, pp. 150–151.

[129] Ibid., pp. 182–190.

[130] Ibid.

[131] Talbott, trans. and ed., *Khrushchev Remembers*, p. 263.

and Matsu, but we will not allow this. . . . In this way, when we want to create a period of tension we can attack Quemoy and Matsu a bit."[132] To conclude the conversation, Zhou stated: "If America is unable to persuade Chiang's military to withdraw, we will have achieved our objective."

Still, we must consider the possibility that the Chinese Communists might not have objected to KMT withdrawal from the offshore islands as much as they opposed an American role as broker in what was considered a "domestic conflict." But Mao's statement to Khrushchev and Zhou Enlai's discussion with the Soviet attache do not reflect any such conditionality in the CCP's desire to prolong the conflict. Moreover, there is even stronger evidence that Beijing wanted the KMT to remain on the islands, no matter what the circumstances of withdrawal. In early October, the Chinese defense minister, Peng Dehuai, unilaterally announced a one-week ceasefire. As long as American boats did not bring supplies to the offshore islands, the PLA would not attack the islands. He stated that, as of October 20, the PLA would shell only on odd days of the calendar. Finally, and most important, Peng asked the KMT forces on the islands to remain and even offered to send supply boats from the mainland to ease their living conditions.[133] Xiao Jinguang cites the fear of a two-China outcome as driving Peng's actions.[134] This behavior strongly supports the thesis that Mao preferred prolonged tensions and Chiang's remaining on Quemoy and Matsu to all other outcomes.

Was Mao Trying to Draw the Soviets into the Conflict on Beijing's Side?

There is significant evidence that Mao neither expected nor wanted Soviet assistance in the crisis. Consistent with earlier analyses, Chinese evidence suggests that Mao already strongly mistrusted the Soviets by August 1958, so his attack can hardly be considered a test of the alliance.[135] Moreover, Mao's entire propaganda line about the crisis was that it was a Chinese domestic political affair in which the American imperialists were meddling. Russian sources suggest that, short of retaliation for a full-scale American strategic nuclear attack on the mainland, Soviet military

---

[132] "The Situation in the Taiwan Straits and Our Policy," Oct. 5, 1958 (The record of a discussion with the temporary Soviet charge d'affaires for the Soviet Union in China), in *Zhou Enlai Waijiao Wenxuan*, pp. 265–266.

[133] Pollack, "Perception and Action in Chinese Foreign Policy," Vol. 1, p. 237.

[134] Xiao, *Xiao Jinguang Huiyilu*, pp. 160–161.

[135] Gurtov and Hwang, *China under Threat*, p. 91.

intervention in the crisis would have been viewed by Mao as unwarranted interference in China's internal affairs.[136]

As early as November 1957, Mao had warned Khrushchev against interfering in Chinese foreign policy without an explicit request from Beijing. Mao's interpreter recalls the following argumentative exchange between Khrushchev and Mao at that time:

> Khrushchev: "Whatever socialist country might receive attack by the imperialists, we will quickly retaliate against them."
> Mao: "This way of talking is incorrect. Every country is independent. You must first see if they have invited this or not."[137]

As discussed above, Mao's concern about Soviet interference in China was heightened in the spring and summer of 1958.

During the Taiwan Straits crisis Mao's ambassador in Moscow warned Beijing that Khrushchev might use the crisis as a pretense to increase Soviet involvement along the Chinese coast. This would allow the Soviets and the Americans to continue to split the Asian Pacific into superpower spheres of influence. Fearing this, Ambassador Liu Xiao cabled Beijing:

> The current Soviet position toward the tension in the straits and the goal of the military measures they are considering have become clear. Khrushchev wants to exploit the tense situation in the Taiwan Straits in order to bring the question of the Taiwan Straits within the scope of Soviet-Western and, in particular, Soviet-American world hegemony and to alter the balance of military power between the United States and the USSR in the Asian Pacific region.[138]

Chinese officials seemed more worried about increased Soviet involvement than they did desirous of increased Soviet support. In fact, Mao rejected a mid-September Soviet offer to station Soviet interceptor squadrons near the Taiwan Straits, accusing Khrushchev again of compromising Chinese sovereignty.[139]

While stirring his own population into a war-scare mentality, Mao made no effort to play up the international significance of the straits crisis abroad, something one would expect if he were hoping for more allied assistance. In fact, Chinese leaders played down the possibility of escalation with China's nervous allies. On September 10, Mao telegraphed Ho

[136] Zubok, "Khrushchev's Nuclear Promise," pp. 219, 226. Russian documents reveal that Mao did not want Soviet assistance even in the case of U.S. tactical nuclear strikes on the mainland. Khrushchev was angered by Mao's attitude, which seemed to be in direct contradiction with the 1950 Sino-Soviet defense agreement.

[137] Li, *Waijiao Wutaishang de Xin Zhongguo Lingxiu*, p. 152.

[138] Liu, *Chushi Sulian Ba Nian*, p. 70.

[139] Lewis and Xue, *China's Strategic Seapower*, p. 17; Liu, *Chashang Chibang de Long*, pp. 150–152.

Chi Minh, stating: "The Americans fear fighting a war, so as for now, it is very unlikely that large-scale fighting will start up. Accordingly, your country can carry out business as usual."[140] In early October, rather than trying to increase Soviet concern, Zhou tried to reassure Moscow that the United States and China would not become involved in war. On October 5, Zhou said: "The situation has already become clear. The United States knows that we are not preparing to do battle with it. . . . Not only will we not attack it [the American military], we do not even intend to liberate Taiwan in the near future. We also know that America is not preparing to do battle with us over [the] Quemoy issue."[141] Clearly, the Chinese were not trying to exaggerate the tension in the straits in order to receive more military and economic assistance from the Soviets.

In February 1988 the *New York Times* reported Andrei Gromyko's recollections of the 1958 Taiwan Straits crisis. Gromyko claimed that he made a secret trip to Beijing on September 5, where Mao revealed a bizarre and dangerous plan in the event of American attack. Mao supposedly told the Soviets that, in such an instance, the Chinese would withdraw troops deep into the Chinese heartland. This would draw American forces inland, where they would be exposed to Soviet air power and perhaps even nuclear attack. Gromyko's report seems fantastic. Chinese Foreign Ministry reports of the straits crisis verify only that Gromyko made the secret trip. The Chinese dispute all the other claims by Gromyko, stating that Mao merely thanked the Soviets for warning the United States against invading China. Mao did not ask for any additional Soviet assistance beyond Moscow's general warning to the United States, which, in the Chinese view, came only after the most dangerous period of the crisis had ended.[142]

Rather than drawing the Soviets in, Mao was more likely trying to demonstrate his foreign policy independence from Moscow by attacking in the straits. This probably was one of the secondary goals of Mao's attack. But Mao did not need to attack in the straits to demonstrate Chinese independence. Mao had argued cantankerously with Khrushchev in early August, rejected all of his proposals for military cooperation, and sent him packing for Moscow on the most unfriendly of terms. If Khrushchev had not yet grasped the message that Mao was not a

---

[140] "Telegram to Ho Chi Minh regarding the Taiwan Situation, etc." Sept. 10, 1958, in *Jianguo Yilai Mao Zedong Wengao*, Vol. 7, p. 413.

[141] "The Situation in the Taiwan Straits and Our Policy" Oct. 5, 1958, in *Zhou Enlai Waijiao Wenxuan*, pp. 265–266.

[142] For the Gromyko story, see *New York Times*, Feb. 22, 1988, p. 1. For the Chinese rebuttal, see Wei, "Geluomike Guanyu Taiwan Jushi Tong Mao Zhuxi Tanhua de Huiyi yu Shishi Bu Fu," pp. 135–138. More recent Russian sources support the Chinese version of events; see Zubok, "Khrushchev's Nuclear Promise," pp. 219, 226.

puppet of the CPSU, it is unclear how an attack on KMT positions would have convinced him.

Was Mao a Victim of His Own Propaganda about Prevailing Winds and Paper Tigers?

After Sputnik, Mao made his oft-cited comment about the east wind prevailing over the west wind and portrayed the United States as a paper tiger. Of course, if Mao believed the socialist camp was dominant in 1958 and that the United States was not dangerous, then he might also have believed that advancing in the straits was relatively safe and painless. There is however significant evidence that Mao did not accept his own propaganda at face value in 1957–58.

It is important to note that in November 1957 Mao viewed Sputnik only as a symbol of the superiority of socialism and a harbinger of a more advantageous balance of power to come. He fully realized that the Soviet Union and China still trailed the West in the international balance of power. This is why, in November 1957, Mao said that within ten years the Soviet Union could surpass the United States and within fifteen years China could surpass the United Kingdom in power potential. In late 1957 Mao was like a structural realist in his obsession with relative material capabilities, particularly steel production. He saw such capabilities as crucial in international politics but did not foresee the socialist world surpassing the West for at least a decade, even after implementing the most aggressive of development programs.[143] Although his prediction for the future was optimistic, this optimism does not suggest that, as early as 1958, Mao believed he could safely challenge the United States.

In Moscow in November 1957, Mao was confronted about his paper tiger theory by the Polish leader, Wladyslaw Gomulka, who was justifiably afraid of Mao's apparent underestimation of American might. Mao reassured Gomulka: "We are talking about the state of the people's morale. Every day imperialism bares its fangs somewhere; if you fear it, does it then begin to behave? Therefore, we say that strategically we should show it contempt [and say] it has nothing extraordinary, it's a paper tiger. But, in a concrete situation, you must treat it seriously, not lightly. This is respecting it tactically."[144] As with most of Mao's public pronouncements and actions in international affairs at this time, it appears that Mao's paper tiger thesis was aimed as much at domestic audiences as it was international ones.

---

[143] See Li, *Waijiao Wutaishang de Xin Zhongguo Lingxiu*, pp. 162–163.
[144] Ibid., p. 156.

What was the Role of Straightforward Domestic or Factional Politics?

After the founding of the PRC, there were clear differences of opinion within the CCP about development strategies and foreign affairs.[145] But Mao's opinion generally ruled the day. Although the ultimate disasters of the Great Leap did strain state-society and intraparty relations in the early 1960s, Mao's dominance in August 1958 is unquestionable. During the anti-Rightist campaign of 1957, Mao had crushed or at least silenced organized opposition to radical planning within the party and the society at large.[146] It was clear that, as in Korea, he had direct control over the early operations in the Taiwan Straits operation.[147] Mao's personal power was most convincingly demonstrated by his ability in 1959 to oust the top military leader, Peng Dehuai, for only mildly criticizing the already disastrous Great Leap.[148]

Was Mao Trying to Help Middle East Nationalists?

As mentioned above, in China one increasingly popular interpretation of Mao's motivations is that he was seeking to "grab America's head and pull it [from the Middle East] to China." (*ba Meiguo de tou la dao Zhongguo diqu*). In this account, Mao's primary goal was to help the anti-Western forces in Lebanon and Iraq by relieving the American military pressure on them. This interpretation agrees with my thesis in one important way: politics, not straightforward military goals, were "in command" in Mao's crisis strategy. Such an interpretation may seem incredible and might be dismissed out of hand, but there is some evidence that suggests its veracity.

Mao and Peng Dehuai first ordered air and artillery forces to Fujian on July 17 and 18, immediately following the onset of the Middle East

[145] For an analysis emphasizing these differences in 1957–58, see Bachman, *Bureaucracy, Economy and Leadership*. For an analysis that portrays Mao as above the factional fray and able to rally bandwagonning alliances behind the Great Leap, see Goldstein, *From Bandwagon to Balance-of-Power Politics*, pp. 103–109.

[146] Even powerful leaders, such as Zhou Enlai, were forced by Mao to make self-criticisms in early 1958. See Bachman, *Bureaucracy, Economy and Leadership*, p. 208.

[147] See Ye, *Ye Fei Huiyilu*, pp. 649–650. Ye, the local military commander during the 1958 straits crisis reports that Mao himself directed initial operations from Beidaihe.

[148] Bachman offers no explanation for why the liberal "financial coalition," if independently powerful, did not rally behind Peng Dehuai and put a stop to the Great Leap Forward. See Bachman, *Bureaucracy, Economy and Leadership*, p. 213. For a fascinating internal party document on this episode, see Peng, "Wei Shenme Yao Xie Xin Gei Mao Zhuxi."

crisis.[149] Chinese scholars and participants claim that, at this time, Mao made statements to party officials that the Chinese military must do more than back the Middle Eastern people with words; it must also take some visible action to demonstrate solidarity.[150] The initial attacks were planned for late July and early August so as to coincide with the Middle East crisis. However, Mao delayed implementation of the attacks in early August. Citing the long-term nature of the Middle East crisis, on July 27 Mao wrote to Peng Dehuai that China need not hurry to shell the islands.[151]

The problem with the Middle East assistance thesis is twofold. As Xu Yan points out, even if Mao's primary objective in preparing for the shelling of the offshore islands in July was to help ease tensions in the Middle East, this could not have been his motivation for attacking in late August. By that time the Middle East crisis was, for all intents and purposes, resolved.[152] It is, however, highly doubtful that anti-imperialist internationalism was ever Mao's primary motivation in the straits. After all, before the shelling began, Mao stated to the Beidaihe conference that continued American intervention in the Middle East was desirable. As discussed above, he cynically argued that CCP propaganda organs must demand American withdrawal, but that in fact continued American intervention was positive for China because it would help motivate Chinese workers and peasants to work harder for less.

Another Chinese historian with access to party archives argues that Mao monitored developments in the UN emergency session on the Middle East and waited to order the shelling of Quemoy until the passage of a resolution for U.S. withdrawal from the Middle East seemed secured. According to the author, Mao did this because: "After the resolution for America to withdraw from the Middle East was passed, the [tense] Middle East situation would become relaxed. [By ordering the shelling] the hot spot of international attention would be transferred to the Taiwan region. This would be useful to the struggle of the Chinese people."[153] Although the author is a bit cryptic about the "struggle" in which the Chinese people are engaged, the available evidence suggests that the scenario below seems plausible.

---

[149] Xu, *Jinmen Zhi Zhan*, p. 211.

[150] Interviews with the author, 1990–91. Also see Xiao, *Xiao Jinguang Huiyilu*, p. 153. Xiao reports that on July 18 Mao ordered troops to Fujian, stating: "We cannot just give moral support [to the Middle East peoples]; we must also support them with real actions."

[151] "A Letter to Peng Dehuai and Huang Kecheng concerning Ensuring the [Best] Opportunity for Attacking Quemoy," July 27, 1958, in *Jianguo Yilai Mao Zedong Wengao*, Vol. 7, p. 326.

[152] Xu, *Jinmen Zhi Zhan*, p. 220.

[153] Liao, "1958 Nian Mao Zedong Juece Paoji Jinmen de Lishi Kaocha," p. 32.

The Middle East crisis *was* apparently linked to Mao's thinking at the time, but not necessarily in the way posited by most PRC scholars. The July Middle East crisis provided a cheap way for Mao to rally domestic support for the Great Leap Forward around the theme of fighting American imperialism. Exploiting this opportunity, Mao publicly linked American imperialism in the Middle East with American designs in Asia and, particularly, the Taiwan Straits. Moreover, during the July steel drive the CCP propaganda machine linked production goals with the struggle against American imperialism while, in Henan, prototype communes and people's militias were created with propaganda referring to the Middle East, Taiwan, and the American threat.

In order to demonstrate the link between the Middle East and Taiwan and to prolong the domestic siege mentality he would require for nation-wide communization, Mao ordered Chinese forces to Fujian to prepare for an attack on the offshore islands. When, in late July and early August, the Middle East crisis seemed as if it might last, Mao may have decided that he could postpone attack on the islands because the Middle East tensions still provided a potent mobilizational tool. In late August, when the Middle East crisis drew to a close, Mao reversed his earlier wait-and-see posture and ordered the shelling in the straits. This facilitated the formation of a 300 million person national militia. The militia movement in turn provided the domestic legitimacy necessary for the nationwide commune program and massive state expropriation of capital from society.

Wu Lengxi states that Mao micromanaged press coverage of the straits crisis in a way consistent with the scenario described above. Mao avoided early, high-profile coverage of the shelling of Quemoy, instead awaiting America's response before allowing prominent coverage in the *People's Daily*. This strategy assisted Mao in comparing the straits crisis to other episodes of American imperialism and in blaming the crisis on American intervention in Chinese territorial waters.[154]

From the available evidence, it is difficult to determine with certainty whether mobilization politics were primary in Mao's mind as early as the middle of July. As Xu Yan argues, it is possible that Mao was initially sincere when he ordered the PLA to support Middle Eastern nationalists by preparing for military action in the straits. Then, in late August, as the conflict in the Middle East wound down, Mao's goals may have shifted, and mobilization politics may have only then become the most important factor in his decision making.[155] The media evidence from July demon-

---

[154] Wu, *Yi Mao Zhuxi*, pp. 76–77.

[155] Xu, *Jinmen Zhi Zhan*, p. 203. Xu also emphasizes Mao's desire to punish the KMT and the United States in July.

strates clearly that Mao was using the Middle East crisis and Taiwan policy for mobilizational purposes from the outset, but it cannot tell us how high mobilization was on Mao's list of priorities. Mao's cynical statements about the Middle East conflict on August 17 also cast doubt on the thesis that he ever really wanted to help anti-Western forces there, but we do not have similarly convincing documentary evidence from mid-July. But resolving this particular puzzle is not central to the thesis here. Regardless of whether mobilization was first and foremost in Mao's mind as early as mid-July, China's policy from August 23 until the end of the crisis fully accords with the theoretical approach offered in Chapter 2. International conflict was initiated and prolonged in the Taiwan Straits to mobilize support for a new grand strategy.

Any leader's behavior may have multiple causes, and a complicated person such as Mao is no exception. Many of the motivations listed above are mutually compatible. Still, the vast bulk of the evidence from the crisis suggests that if Mao had motives other than mobilization of the public around the Great Leap, they were secondary. Mao perhaps demonstrated his priorities most clearly by spending the second half of September touring the countryside to gain support for communization, rather than micromanaging military and diplomatic affairs, as he had done during the 1950 Korean crisis.

THE AFTERMATH OF THE STRAITS CRISIS

In addition to running a real risk of nuclear war on the Chinese mainland, the straits crisis of 1958 poisoned any chances of American or UN conciliation toward China for many years. Mao seemed to recognize the diplomatic costs involved in his railing against the West. At Beidaihe he seemed to anticipate that creating tensions with the West would further delay the establishment of favorable diplomatic and trade relations with Western countries. On August 17, Mao said: "As for the embargo, the tighter the better; the longer the UN refuses to recognize us the better. It would be best if they recognized us seven years from now. . . . By that time, we produce XX to XX million tons of steel."[156] Mao apparently did not reject the notion of better relations with the West in principle, but he felt that a further delay of rapprochement was justified if a current conflict could mobilize the Chinese people and allow for seven years of fast-paced economic growth. The resulting expansion of Chinese power would serve to improve Beijing's negotiating position when it ultimately established better relations with the West.

[156] MacFarquhar, Cheek, and Wu, *The Secret Speeches of Chairman Mao*, p. 403. The numbers for steel targets were deleted in the written text.

If Mao indeed surmised that the attack would have diplomatic costs, he was right. In addition to terrifying Moscow and further damaging Sino-Soviet relations, the 1958 crisis had real effects on American thinking at a time when there was at least some serious reconsideration of China policy.[157] The crisis reversed nascent trends in American public opinion that might have proved quite positive for China. In 1957, public opinion polls showed that a modest improvement of relations was quite possible. A majority of those polled would have approved of a meeting between Zhou Enlai and Dulles, and an increasing percentage of Americans approved of trade between the United States and the PRC.[158] Before the crisis there was also a steady increase in the minority of Americans who supported PRC admission to the UN.[159] This three-year trend in public opinion was halted and reversed by the Chinese attack. While the public did not want to go to war with China, let alone the Soviets, it clearly blamed Beijing for the tensions.[160] Before the crisis, there also was a warming trend among certain foreign policy elites in the United States. In the mid-1950s, a high-level Rockefeller Foundation study group on America's China policy was seriously evaluating the pros and cons of a broad range of conciliatory gestures toward Beijing, including diplomatic recognition. While not in office, members of this group, like its head, Dean Rusk, commanded respect both inside and outside the administration. But with the Taiwan Straits crisis came a change in the American domestic political climate, and these influential citizens became much less bold in their discussions and proposals.[161] In this sense, Mao's adventure carried real opportunity costs.

[157] In his 1959 review, cited above, Mao stated that the attack in the straits indeed frightened the Soviets.

[158] Fifty-four percent approved of such a meeting. "Recent Public Opinion Polls on U.S. Relations with Red China," Apr. 3, 1957, Foster Papers, Box 33, File: China, 1954–60, NA. For 1957 analyses of a long-term public warming trend toward trade, see "Popular Attitudes on Trade with Red China," Feb. 19, 1957, and "Recent Public Opinion Polls on U.S. Relations with Red China," Apr. 3, 1957, Foster Papers, Box 33, File: China, 1954–60, NA.

[159] Page and Shapiro, *The Rational Public*, p. 246.

[160] Ibid.

[161] Chang, *Friends and Enemies*, pp. 179–182.

CHAPTER 7

Conclusion

THIS CHAPTER reviews and compares the book's two major cases of grand strategy, domestic mobilization, and conflict manipulation: Truman's China policy during the early phases of the Cold War and Mao's policy toward the United States and the KMT during the most radical phases of the Great Leap Forward. After contrasting the causes and effects of the mobilization processes in the two cases, I argue that a relatively simple theoretical approach can still shed light on both. Advocating more collaboration between area studies and international relations theory, I discuss why the application of relatively parsimonious theories of foreign policy often requires a great deal of area-specific knowledge. With these caveats in mind, I then offer some suggestions for future research employing the approach developed in Chapter 2. Finally, I discuss how the findings of the book relate to various theoretical issues in the field of security studies and to analytical and normative questions about the role of elites and the public in the making of American national security policy.

AMERICAN CHINA POLICY: 1947–1950

In Chapters 3 and 4 we observed how Truman, Marshall, and Acheson reacted to the realization that the world was bipolar. British collapse forced the administration to break from the American peacetime tradition of isolationism and low spending on foreign policy. Truman not only needed to reverse the very popular trend of postwar demobilization but also required public support for expensive, controversial, and utterly novel policies such as the Marshall Plan, NATO, and the Military Assistance Program. These policies were designed primarily to keep industrial centers and resource-rich regions such as Western Europe, Japan, and the Middle East from falling under Soviet influence. After the Soviets developed nuclear weapons in 1949, the administration developed NSC 68. American grand strategists wanted to triple the defense budget and increase support for the NATO allies as soon as the American public would allow it.

In order to gain public backing for these programs, the administration and sympathetic Republican leaders decided to tap into pre-existing public hatreds and launch a rhetorical crusade against communism. From the outset, administration officials recognized the disjuncture between the conditionality of strongpoint defense and the sweeping responsibilities inherent in the rhetoric employed to sell it. But it was the rhetoric, combined with aggressive communist behavior in Berlin and Korea, that allowed Truman to bring the American public on board. The effort to translate short-term crises and specific examples of communist aggression into sustainable support for long-term policies did not come without costs. Each time the administration wanted to raise money for grand strategy, it had to compromise on its preferred strategy toward the Chinese Communists and the KMT.

Truman's inability to maintain public consensus behind grand strategy without first demonstrating an uncompromising position toward communism on the Asian mainland contributed to a great many foreign policy compromises: the failure to recognize the PRC, the consistent veto of PRC entrance into the UN, continued assistance to the KMT, the blocking of the Taiwan Straits in June 1950, the refusal to negotiate an East Asian peace plan after China entered the Korean War, and the placing of stricter embargoes on trade with China than with the USSR itself. All of these policies served to tighten the relationship between the PRC and the Soviet Union, one that the foreign policy makers in America saw as unhealthy to America's security interests.

As Chapter 5 made clear, American policies also contributed significantly to the escalation of the Korean War. By reversing Truman's pledge of nonintervention in the Chinese Civil War and blocking the Taiwan Straits in June 1950, America threatened China's southern and eastern flanks, complicating Mao's assessment of the threat posed by MacArthur's drive north of the 38th parallel. In the process, Truman also destroyed his own credibility in Mao's eyes, making it impossible to convince Mao that American forces in North Korea would not eventually invade China. Although the PRC was not always driven by defensive motivations, it was ultimately CCP leaders' perception of threat and mistrust of American intentions that caused China to enter the Korean War in force, driving American troops out of North Korea. A second critical policy contributing to Korean War escalation was the American decision not to recognize the new regime in Beijing. Because of this decision and Washington's refusal even to allow PRC entrance into the UN, in the fall of 1950 there were no U.S. officials in Beijing and no PRC officials in the United States. The failures of communication in that crucial period destroyed any hope of avoiding a wider war involving significant Chinese forces.

SPUTNIK, THE GREAT LEAP FORWARD, AND THE 1958 STRAITS CRISIS

Given the growth of Soviet power in the 1950s, symbolized by the launching of Sputnik in 1957, Mao worried that China was falling dangerously behind both the Western camp and its ally to the north. Chapter 6 described how Mao, fearing Soviet abandonment or domination, initiated the most radical phases of the Great Leap Forward. His goal was to launch China into the class of significant world powers within a period of several years by increasing industrial output and producing nuclear weapons.

In a backward and largely agricultural society such as China's in the 1950s, the massive capital necessary for heavy industrial and nuclear projects had to come from the countryside. To raise such capital Mao required the already poor Chinese citizenry to work harder for less remuneration. The problem for Mao was that similar efforts in 1955–56 had failed, leading to dissatisfaction among workers and peasants and a resulting slowdown in key sectors of the economy. In summer 1958, during the most radical phases of the Great Leap, Mao attempted to rectify this problem by creating and manipulating tensions with the United States, militarizing the society around the theme of people's militias, and in the process, communizing agriculture and mobilizing the labor force. Carefully controlling both propaganda and foreign policy, Mao first exploited American involvement in the Middle East, linking it to the question of American support for Chiang Kai-shek and the need for more steel output. Finally, just as he instituted national communization and a new push for steel production, and just as the Middle East Crisis began fizzling out, Mao manufactured a crisis in the Taiwan Straits to lend salience to his overall mobilization drive.

COMPARING THE TWO CASES

The Two Grand Strategies

Truman and Mao chose dramatically different grand strategies in response to their international environments. The American response to international changes was more directly oriented to foreign policy and arguably much more rational than Mao's disastrous Great Leap Forward. The Great Leap had some core aspects that were rational, but the intensity of the program, the near total rejection of individual economic incentives, and the pie-in-the-sky production targets demonstrated that Mao was not in touch with economic realities. Rather than trying to explain Mao's odd economic and political beliefs, I take as given Mao's ideological predispositions. Once we accept that Mao believed in the feasibility of the Great Leap, we can understand why he adopted the international and domestic tactics necessary to mobilize public enthusiasm for the program.

The obvious differences between the grand strategies of Truman and Mao need not be listed at length. It should be mentioned, however, that, despite the clear differences, there are important, theoretically relevant similarities in the two nations' approaches to long-term security. Both leaders felt that they needed to rely on their own citizens' efforts to improve their nations' long-term international position. In Waltz's terminology, both strategies were examples of "internal balancing." In the American case the need for home-based efforts arose from the recognition of the world as bipolar. Although America hoped to share burdens with its allies one day, it needed to raise resources in the short term to help rebuild those friendly countries. In the Chinese case, the push for self-reliance arose from growing wariness about the intentions and credibility of China's main supporter and ally, the Soviet Union, and from China's lengthy isolation from the West.

A second similarity between the two grand strategies is that they both focused on long-term economic development as an instrument of national security. In the American case, the Marshall Plan was designed to build up allies so they could later contribute to an American-led coalition against the Soviets. As discussed above, the Marshall Plan clearly cut into funds that could have provided a more short-term, military, and unilateral response to America's security problems. In 1958 Chinese grand strategy also emphasized long-term economic and technological development as opposed to short-term spending on military equipment.

Domestic Structure and the Impact on Mobilization and Foreign Policy

The processes by which domestic constraints affected state decision making are quite different in the two cases. This is not surprising, since Mao's China in 1958 was strongly authoritarian, if not totalitarian, while Truman's America was a liberal democracy. These structural differences help account for the differing levels of intensity in the two mobilization drives and the differing severity of their impact on foreign policy. In the 1958 Chinese case, Mao's domination of the government meant that the only significant hurdle to immediate, all-out mobilization was the morale and spirit of sacrifice in the population at large. Without legislative obstacles, Mao could launch a crash economic program on a scale totally alien to

Western politics. Mao's use of foreign policy as a mobilizing tool was also more dramatic than Truman's. Mao launched a direct military challenge to the forces of an American ally in order to stir up short-term tensions short of war.

In the case of Truman's grand strategy, the American legislative process required a longer, phased process of mobilization over a period of three years. With the important exception of the naval blockade of the Taiwan Straits, the need for consensus on grand strategy did not mean that Truman needed to adopt active military policies aimed against the Chinese Communists. Rather, the requisites of mobilization affected Truman's foreign policy by preventing him from distancing the United States from the Chinese Civil War. If he wanted to maintain long-term popular and congressional support for his core grand strategy, Truman could neither abandon Chiang nor improve relations with the Chinese Communists.

Fallout from Conflict Manipulation

Truman's use of China policy to maintain consensus around the strong-point containment strategy may have been more subtle than Mao's exploitation of the Taiwan Straits crisis, but oddly the international fallout from Truman's policies was more significant. Truman's failure to remove America from the Chinese Civil War and establish relations with Beijing contributed greatly to the outbreak of a Sino-American war in Korea. That war was an extremely bitter one for both sides and poisoned all aspects of bilateral relations for years. The American failure to withdraw from the Civil War also set the stage for the two later Taiwan Straits crises. Tensions over Taiwan remained the most important point of conflict between China and the United States after the 1971–72 rapprochement and continued to strain bilateral relations into the post–Cold War era.

In the long run, Mao's aggressive policy in the straits in 1958 made a deeper negative impression on the Soviets than on the Americans. Khrushchev was angered by the Chinese adventurism, and this contributed to the Sino-Soviet split of 1959–60.[1] The impact of the 1958 straits crisis on Sino-American relations was much less dramatic. Mao's attack in the straits did affect American public opinion and the willingness of

---

[1] Extremely contentious debates about the crisis took place among Chinese and Soviet elites during Khrushchev's 1959 visit to Beijing. For a record of the argument between Foreign Minister Chen Yi and Khrushchev, see Li, *Waijiao Wutaishang de Xin Zhongguo Lingxiu,* pp. 182–183. For a discussion of Sino-Soviet relations in 1958–59, see Zagoria, *Sino-Soviet Conflict.*

American elites to experiment with new China policies designed to hasten a split between Moscow and Beijing. But the public warming trend before the attack had not been dramatic, and the Eisenhower administration seemed set on maintaining a tough policy toward Beijing. Moreover, influential elites outside the administration were only just beginning to reconsider core policies, such as recognition, when the crisis started in the straits.

One might want to speculate about the possible outcomes if the slow warming trend toward Beijing had continued. One might focus on the fact that, despite his tough posturing toward the Chinese Communists during the debates with Nixon, President John F. Kennedy still wanted to improve relations with Beijing after assuming office.[2] But many factors contributed to the delay in reconciliation between Washington and Beijing. Most of these, including the Vietnam War and the Cultural Revolution, are unrelated to the straits crisis itself.

Political Culture, National Differences, and the Issue of Theoretical Parsimony

Obviously the United States and the People's Republic of China have very different political cultures. But this does not mean that the general mobilization model offered in Chapters 1 and 2 cannot shed light on the policies of both. In fact, the explanatory power of the general model is suggested precisely by the fact that it can apply to the policies of such different political systems. To some degree, national political culture is built into the measures of hurdles to mobilization. Because those hurdles are measured partially by the degree to which the new grand strategy breaks with prior national traditions, political tradition serves as a baseline of comparison, not as a variable in the model. Moreover, since the model focuses on cases in which leaders face major shifts in the international environment and decide to launch novel grand strategies, the role for traditional thinking in decision making is likely to be unusually small. This was certainly true in both 1947 America and 1958 China. Neither leader's grand strategy had firm roots in national culture.

The issue of differences in political culture relates to the tension between theoretical generalizability on the one hand and sensitivity to the unique aspects of particular cases on the other. For the most part, area specialists dislike general theories because they tend not to take into account the rich political, cultural, and historical context of each country. But the solution to this problem is not necessarily to abandon cross-

---

[2] Hilsman, *To Move a Nation*, pp. 302–317; interview with Roger Hilsman, Columbia University, December 12, 1989.

national comparisons and the search for widely applicable forms of analysis. Theories can be both generalizable and demanding of a great deal of area-specific knowledge in practical application.

By including domestic political variables that take national traditions into account, the approach here builds a bridge between international relations theory, comparative politics, and area studies. While the concepts employed in Chapter 2 are simple and generalizable across cultures and political systems, the application of the approach to any given country requires a great deal of knowledge about the nation in question. Because a key causal factor in the argument is the degree to which a proposed grand strategy diverges from the cultural and historical precedents of a given country, one needs to know quite a bit about that country to apply the model. First one needs to determine the historical baseline for grand strategies under comparable international conditions. Moreover, to develop measures of how much a citizenry is being asked to sacrifice for any given strategy, one needs to know something about the means of state resource accumulation in that country. Finally, to test the approach against competing explanations it is important to understand what leaders were actually thinking when they were creating new grand strategies, launching mobilization drives, and manipulating or prolonging conflict with foreign powers. To complete this task, one needs to do archival research, sometimes in a foreign language. All of these demands privilege the area expert over the generalist in applying the mobilization model to particular cases.

SUGGESTIONS FOR FURTHER RESEARCH

For all of the reasons cited above, one author cannot analyze multiple cases in depth in a single volume. Instead, here I briefly and cautiously consider some additional cases on which the model might shed some light. I mention these cases only for heuristic purposes. In order to demonstrate the true applicability of the model, one would need to undertake a detailed analysis of how leaders perceived international challenges, designed grand strategies, and tackled the domestic political problems involved in implementing those grand strategies.

Soviet Propaganda before Collectivization, 1927–1929

In the late 1920s, the Communist Party of the Soviet Union launched a series of radical collectivization policies that altered Soviet society and industrialized the Soviet economy. Stalin's strategy, completed in 1934, was designed to strengthen the world's only Communist state. The Soviets were surrounded by potentially powerful states to the east and west (Japan and Germany). Moreover, with some justification, Stalin believed that the Soviets had no friends or even potential allies in the international system. An external balancing strategy was therefore precluded.

The domestic hurdles to mobilization in this case were monumental. Soviet workers were asked to work harder for less. With extremely high capital accumulation rates, the Soviet economy quickly modernized. But high government taxation meant that average consumption simultaneously dropped. It is unclear just how much hardship was intentionally heaped on the Soviet people during collectivization, but there can be little doubt that Stalin knew that great sacrifices were being asked.[3]

In many ways the spiritual parent of Mao's Great Leap Forward, Stalin's grand strategy seemingly was to exploit an extended period of peace by industrializing the Soviet economy.[4] But before the collectivization program was implemented, the Soviet leadership launched a propaganda campaign in the press, warning of imminent war with the capitalist states.[5] Stalin and other party leaders apparently knew that such a short-term threat did not exist.[6] But, particularly in early 1929, war-scare propaganda was used to create the siege mentality that facilitated collectivization.[7] The Soviet Union took no concrete actions to create military tensions, but Soviet rhetoric severely alienated Western leaderships. In this way, Soviet verbal belligerence itself was an act of foreign policy. In London and Paris, Soviet statements created a legacy of hostility and suspicion that contributed to the delay in forming effective alliances against Hitler in World War II.

One key question for researchers is whether Stalin's collectivization program and the myth of the Soviet Union under siege were driven by Stalin's concern about his domestic adversaries or by a sincere desire to increase Soviet power in the international arena. If the former holds, then a standard diversionary conflict approach may better explain the war-

[3] Ulam, *Expansion and Coexistence*, p. 183.

[4] As Ulam writes: "Shouting about the imminence of war, inwardly convinced of a lengthy peaceful period ahead, the Soviet Union's leaders embarked in 1927–1928 on the execution of momentous policies, the total effect of which was to transform the Soviet Union and the world Communist movement." Ulam, *Expansion and Coexistence*, p. 183. Although after World War II Stalin portrayed the communization effort as a long-term balancing strategy, this may have been purely self-serving. One would need to research Soviet documents from the late 1920s to uncover Stalin's thinking at the time.

[5] Taubman, *Stalin's American Policy*, pp. 22–23.

[6] In June 1927 Georgy Chicherin explained to Stalin and the Politburo that the international setting was not dangerous, but the party continued to push the "war scare" line in its propaganda despite his efforts. See Reiman, *The Birth of Stalinism*, chap. 2.

[7] Ibid., p. 113.

scare effort than the approach offered in Chapter 2. In order to answer this question one would have to conduct a careful study of party documents from the period.

The CCP, the KMT, and the Anti-Japanese War

The KMT fought Japanese imperialist forces resolutely in the 1930s, particularly in the Shanghai and Nanjing regions. But after the government's forced retreat to the southwest, and particularly after the United States entered the Pacific war, KMT military strategists began saving some of their best material and human resources for the Civil War and regional power struggles to come. Such a strategy was favored by powerful generals, such as He Yingqin, who were obsessed with the long-term Communist threat.[8] Both because they were based nearer Japanese forces and because CCP leaders understood the mobilizational value of anti-Japanese resistance, the Chinese Communists remained more active in engaging Japanese forces in the early 1940s. This occurred despite the material weakness of Mao's forces and the lack of significant outside assistance to CCP base areas. While the CCP leaders were also wary of the risks of confronting the Japanese head-on, and therefore designed ways to minimize Chinese losses in the guerrilla campaigns, the CCP strategy led to relatively high levels of risk-acceptant belligerence under the banner of "the more we fight, the stronger we get."[9]

Analysis of only economic and military considerations would favor the KMT strategy over the CCP approach. But the CCP strategy was successful because Mao understood the pervasiveness of anti-Japanese sentiment and the importance of popular political support to his party's survival. In a particularly revealing statement, Madame Chiang Kai-shek exposed a key fault in the grand strategy of the KMT. In 1944, American reporters returned from a trip to Communist-held Yenan and informed her that the CCP enjoyed the support of the people over which they ruled. Madame

[8] For evidence of KMT reluctance to fight Japanese forces, see Boyle, *China and Japan at War*, pp. 310–330. For smoking-gun evidence of Chiang's contacts with Japanese leaders as early as March 1941, see *Documents on German Foreign Policy*, Vol. 12, p. 415, in which the Japanese foreign minister tells the German high command that he is "in personal contact with" and is "known and trusted" by Chiang.

[9] See Li, "Kang Da Kang Da Yue Kang Yue Da." The general trend of using the anti-Japanese struggle as a launching pad for building the Communist Party has been discussed by Johnson, *Peasant Nationalism and Communist Power;* and Morwood, *Duel for the Middle Kingdom*. While CCP military leaders were bold, they also were critical of overly aggressive strategies that stood little chance of success and put too many resources and soldiers at risk. Such tactics were criticized as "suicidal." See Boyle, *China and Japan at War*, p. 312.

Chiang scoffed; "Why those people have no idea what real power is!"[10] History would prove quite the opposite.

U.S. Strategy in World War II: Operation Torch

The model will generally apply best during peacetime, primarily because war itself tends to mobilize the public behind increased spending. Still, if the expense and sacrifice of a war outstrip those of previous wars, then, according to the measures advocated in Chapter 2, the hurdles to mobilization should still be high enough for the model to apply. American involvement in World War II provides a solid example of unprecedented wartime sacrifice. The model may then apply particularly well to the early stages of the war, when the United States was diverting most of its resources to the European theater for reasons of grand strategy, while the Japanese were providing the more immediate threat to American forces. Although Pearl Harbor mobilized the American public, it did not automatically mobilize it to do what it needed to do most, destroy Hitler's military before Germany defeated Britain and the Soviet Union.

After the United States entered World War II and began preparing to cross the English Channel with the British, disagreements arose between the British and the Americans as to the proper strategy to pursue.[11] The British favored a channel crossing in mid-1943 (the so-called Bolero-Roundup plan) or 1944 (the Overlord plan). They also found acceptable an alternative strategy of fighting in North Africa in 1942–43 (Torch). The American military supported Bolero-Roundup along with a back-up plan for a 1942 European invasion (Sledgehammer) to be used only in the event of an early collapse of the Soviet Red Army or a German implosion. The British were opposed to Sledgehammer because they believed it was too risky to launch a cross-channel invasion before the Americans could supply more than a handful of divisions for continental warfare. American military analysts opposed Torch because they viewed the North African campaign as an overly costly diversion of American resources in a secondary area of operations. American generals preferred saving American strength for either a 1943 or 1944 channel crossing.

In the final July 1942 decision in favor of Torch, mobilization politics were apparently important in Roosevelt's thinking. The British liked Torch because it ensured that the Americans would become actively involved in the struggle against Hitler and thus would not become overly distracted by the war in the Pacific. Roosevelt liked Torch for the same

---

[10] Morwood, *Duel for the Middle Kingdom*, p. 320.

[11] The analysis below is based on Greenfield, *American Strategy in World War II*, esp. pp. 56–66 and passim; and Funk, *The Politics of Torch*, chap. 4.

reason. He wanted American forces to become involved in active combat with the Germans before the close of 1942. Roosevelt believed that such a battle was necessary to stir the enthusiasm of the American public and justify both the high level of American wartime mobilization and the obvious bias toward the European over the Pacific theater in allocation of resources. While his military leaders argued for marshaling of limited resources for a later fight on the continent, Roosevelt argued that a current campaign was necessary to keep the American public behind the European effort. Without such public support, Roosevelt feared that the United States would not be able to supply the materiel and manpower necessary to carry out the eventual invasion of France.

THEORETICAL AND PRACTICAL POLICY LESSONS

Implications for Strategic Studies

The model offered in Chapter 2 combines both international and domestic variables. It does not simply state that domestic politics matter in foreign policy, but specifies the conditions under which they matter. If states act differently abroad during mobilization than they do at other times, then policies raised during mobilization may not reflect the state's long-term interests and intentions. Because interests and intentions are central to the study of international relations, the model here has broader implications for the field.

One long-running debate on which the mobilization model might shed some light is the question of the importance or lack of importance to the great powers of the strategic periphery.[12] In times of mobilization we should expect states to pay more attention to peripheral interests and conflicts than at other times. This is because peripheral conflicts provide visible but relatively inexpensive targets for crusading policies and demonstrations of ideological purity.

Another great debate in international relations theory revolves around the utility of deterrence theory models for explaining instances of war and peace. One school of critics attacks the assumptions of leadership rationality on which deterrence models are based. Irrational leaders certainly have existed and have undertaken policies unexplainable by deterrence theory.[13] Still, it is possible that certain critical cases of deterrence

---

[12] See Van Evera, "Why Europe Matters"; David, "Why the Third World Matters"; and Desch, "The Keys That Lock Up the World."

[13] For multicase psychological critiques of deterrence theory, see Jervis, *Perception and Misperception*, esp. Part 2; and Lebow, *Between Peace and War*.

failure were due not to psychological quirks but to the complex rationality of leaders who must play on a two-level gameboard. During mobilization, a nation may be much harder to deter from peripheral conflict than a nation whose leaders are engaged in business as usual. For example, in more normal political times in the United States, Chinese threats to enter the Korean War might have proven more effective. Not only did the needs of mobilization make Truman less likely to compromise in Korea, but they precluded sturdy lines of communication and thereby muted Chinese deterrent warnings.

On a more practical level, if foreign leaders understand that early-stage mobilization is often accompanied by short-lived but fiery antiforeign posturing, then they might avoid drawing inappropriate and dangerous conclusions from the behavior of mobilizing states. There may be no reason for the challenged nation to infer irredentism or the inevitability of long-term aggression from a mobilizer's hostile postures. If Mao had understood the politics of Cold War mobilization in the United States, he might not have concluded from American actions in Korea and Taiwan that the United States was planning to invade Manchuria. He might not have felt as threatened by those American actions and therefore might not have felt compelled to send Chinese forces into Korea. The same holds true for the 1958 Taiwan Straits crisis. The fact that China attacked in the straits in August 1958 does not mean that it was poised to seize Taiwan, let alone territory not considered to be part of China. American intelligence was quite effective in determining, early in the crisis, that Mao had very limited goals in the straits. But it seems these conclusions were drawn largely from a detailed analysis of China's military activities in Fujian, not from a political analysis of Mao's intentions in launching the initial limited attacks.[14]

Although one might conclude that it does not matter why American leaders drew the right conclusions in 1958, as long as they did draw them, the distinction between military and political intelligence is important for two reasons. First, military intelligence gathering and analysis may not always be as good as they were on the American side in 1958. Local military commanders on a challenger's side can also make operational mistakes, thus sending the wrong signal about a challenger's intentions. Given the terrifying contingency plans for American nuclear strikes against the mainland if the conflict had escalated, one should be nervous about relying solely on the study of military operations to determine a challenger's intentions. Second, if we do not know the reasons for an attack, as in the 1958 Taiwan Straits crisis, we may draw inappropriate

---

[14] Eliades, "Once More unto the Breech."

conclusions about the ability of American coercive diplomacy to limit aggression. If one believes, for example, that Chinese leaders strongly desired the recovery of the islands and backed down only because of an unexpected show of American force, then one might draw the conclusion that the threat of American force against China was more efficacious than it actually was. American analysts might then falsely and dangerously conclude that Washington could coerce China into abandoning other important goals, such as the prevention of Taiwanese independence.

CONTAINMENT: WHERE TO DRAW THE LINE AGAINST LEADERS LIKE MAO

Since Robert Jervis first compared the spiral and deterrence models, it has become common in political science to label leaders in crises as either aggressive and insatiable or fearful and protective of the status quo.[15] The distinction is often useful, but there is no reason to believe that leaders cannot be both aggressive and fearful. Mao was no lover of the status quo, as was proven by his material support to Kim Il-sung and the Vietnamese Communists even before the outbreak of the Korean War; but Mao was also almost paranoid in his feeling of insecurity about threats to his nation, as was demonstrated by his constant fear of foreign and domestic enemies. This type of leader is extremely difficult to deter. If one shows too little resolve, as the United States did by excluding South Korea from the defense perimeter in early 1950, the leader will promote aggression. If not for the adventurism of Kim Il-sung and the material and political support of that adventurism by Stalin and Mao, the Korean War would not have started in June 1950, and needless to say, it could not have escalated later if it had not started. But if one shows too hostile a posture, as the United States did by intervening in the Taiwan Straits, the leader will become panicky, difficult to reassure, and capable of rash action.

This is one reason why some American advisers in 1950 agreed with Rusk and Dulles that China should be contained but that the Taiwan Straits was a bad place to do so. By choosing a containment line outside of Taiwan they believed the United States could both contain and reassure the Chinese simultaneously. But perhaps the United States was correct to defend both Korea and Taiwan as part of a comprehensive and prudent containment strategy. A tough stand on Taiwan pinned down resources that, theoretically, could otherwise have gone to Ho Chi Minh, Kim Il-sung, or other regional revolutionaries.[16] Although this is undoubtedly true, a key question remains: would Mao have chosen to de-

[15] Jervis, *Perceptions and Misperceptions*, chap. 3.
[16] For this position, see Garver, "Polemics, Paradigms."

vote more or fewer resources to those causes had America abandoned Taiwan?

Mao had begun helping Ho with material and technical aid months before the Korean War broke out. According to Chen Jian, Mao had two early goals in Vietnam: on the one hand, Mao had agreed with Stalin that China should promote Asian revolution; on the other hand, for defensive reasons, Mao wanted buffers against American and KMT attack from Indochina, Taiwan, and Korea. In theory, American activity in Taiwan and Korea might have reduced Chinese support for Indochina; in fact, it had the opposite effect. According to Chen, on June 27, CCP leaders "accelerated their support" for Ho Chi Minh. A similar argument can be made for Beijing's assistance to Kim Il-sung. Rather than tying down PLA naval and ground forces in the Taiwan area, the presence of the American Seventh Fleet apparently freed some up by making the core goal of liberation impossible for the foreseeable future.[17]

Reducing the Danger of Mobilization: Public Opinion and Leadership

If the argument here is correct, Truman could have mobilized the American public for the global competition with the Soviet Union only if he adopted a consistently anticommunist grand strategy for Europe and Asia. Therefore, one cannot judge Truman's China policy in isolation from his broader Cold War grand strategy. If one believes that Truman's general policies—the Marshall Plan, nuclear research, NATO, MAP, and significant American peacetime defense spending—were justified by the power and political threat posed by the Soviet Union, then it becomes much more difficult to criticize Truman's policies in Asia.

Given the importance of these policies, one might ask whether the sacrifices made for American grand strategy in China and Korea were not ultimately worth their high price. The only apparent alternative was continued American lethargy after World War II. To return to the diagram in Chapter 2, given the bipolar structure of the international system and the nature of the Soviet Union before Mikhail Gorbachev, the overactive grand strategy adopted by Truman was arguably much wiser than the underactive strategy preferred by fiscal conservatives, liberal doves, and isolationists.

If one deems Truman's basic grand strategy to have been worthy of support, then in order to prescribe corrections for the mishaps in Asia one must focus on the impact of state-society relations on foreign policy

[17] Chen, "China and the First Indo-China War," pp. 90–92; and Chen, *China's Road*, p. 132. While some forces were committed to the northeast before the outbreak of war, many more were committed afterward.

in the United States. This involves the somewhat nebulous subject of public opinion toward foreign policy and the much more nebulous subject of leadership. Just how consistent is the public in its attitudes toward foreign policy? How much does the public accept the tenets of real-politik? What segments of the society are more likely to be dispassionate and farsighted about national strategy? What can leaders do to increase the size and power of those segments through public education and persuasion?

The degree of consistency and coherence in public opinion toward issues of foreign policy is a hotly debated topic in the field of American politics. While some have argued that public opinion is inconsistent and subject to wide, emotional swings, Benjamin Page and Robert Shapiro posit that the public is more rational than that. In discussing the early Cold War, they point out that the public was consistently internationalist, not isolationist, citing steady public support (75 percent) for an "active" American role in world affairs.[18]

The analysis of Page and Shapiro is correct and important. By demonstrating that the public is generally rational and consistent in its thinking, they defend the ideal of democratic input in foreign policy making. However, while useful for analyzing most periods, their approach does not help in analyzing the special problems leaders face when trying to mobilize the public for controversial, expensive, and novel grand strategies.[19] Those leaders need to get more than verbal support for policies; they need to get the public to pay for those policies. Words such as "active" are vague and laden with normative connotations. As we saw in Chapters 3 and 4, and as V. O. Key points out, the public's proclaimed commitment to a policy says little about public willingness to pay its costs.[20]

Although it has been widely criticized, on several counts Gabriel Almond's "mood theory" is still the most useful study of American public opinion toward foreign policy for the early postwar period. Almond argues that foreign policy programs did not maintain a position of primary salience in the minds of the American public and therefore were strongly supported only when an immediate and ideological threat was presented.[21] The mobilizational value of major world events such as the

[18] For the starkest portrayal of the public as irrational and inconsistent, see Converse, "The Nature of Belief Systems in Mass Publics." For contrary arguments, see Shapiro and Page, "Foreign Policy and the Rational Public"; and Page and Shapiro, *The Rational Public,* chap. 5.

[19] Bruce Russett, who agrees with the thrust of the Page and Shapiro thesis, also points out that public attitudes toward foreign policy did not stabilize until the early 1950s. See Russett, *Controlling the Sword,* p. 93.

[20] Key, *Public Opinion and American Democracy,* pp. 158–160.

[21] Almond, *The American People and Foreign Policy,* chap. 4. For an article supporting Almond's original interpretation, see Rockman, "Mobilizing Political Support for U.S. Na-

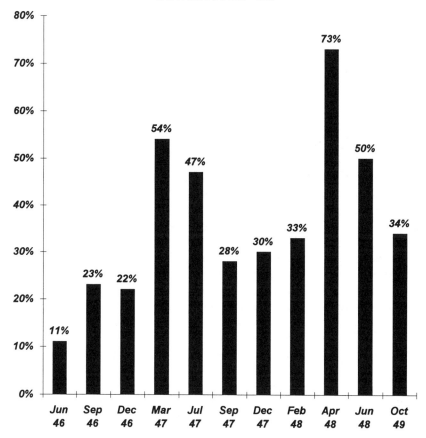

7.1. Almond's Salience Measure: Percentage Who Regarded Foreign Policy Issues as the Most Important Problems Facing the American People. Almond, *The American People and Foreign Policy*, p. 73.

Greece-Turkey crisis, the Czech coup, and the Berlin blockade was high but limited in duration. The same can be said for the mobilizational rhetoric that the administration used to drive home the importance of those crises. The evidence offered in Chapters 3 and 4 similarly demonstrates that shortly after the Truman Doctrine speech, the Marshall Plan appeals of early 1948, and the beginning of negotiations to lift the Berlin blockade in spring 1949, public support for European assistance dropped precipitously along with Almond's salience index, particularly when the costs of those programs were included in the questions. Kennan's analysis of security threats and his long-term prescriptive responses to them

tional Security." For critiques, see Caspary, "The Mood Theory"; and Shapiro and Page, "Foreign Policy and the Rational Public."

were far too subtle for Almond's "moody" American public. Changing levels of salience may not be crippling in other periods, but when leaders are attempting to sell an expensive, long-term security strategy, short public attention spans become critical national security problems.

An understanding of the problems of public attitudes toward foreign policy during mobilization allows one to see why some analysts have underestimated the importance of American public opinion on China policy. If Truman had been able to make the decision in isolation, he might have withdrawn from the Chinese Civil War with little political fallout, particularly if he appealed to fiscal conservatism and isolationism. But from the broader point of view of grand strategy, Truman and the supporters of a bipartisan foreign policy knew that he could not withdraw from China at the same time that he was mobilizing support for Europe. While raising funds for Europe, Truman needed a clear anticommunist message to mobilize the public. At each one of these crucial points (the raising of bills for interim aid, ERP, NATO, MAP), Asialationists would also demand continued commitments to Chiang. At these junctures any efforts to rationalize withdrawal from the China quagmire would have refuted Truman's own rhetorical arguments for policies toward Europe. The administration could not appeal to isolationism or downplay the spread of communism precisely when the passage of other programs required refuting isolationism and emphasizing the Communist threat.

It is this fundamental problem that also help explains the apparently disproportionate degree of power held by the small China Lobby in Congress. The real power behind Asialationism was not supplied by the Lobby itself but by the fiscal conservatives looking for points on which to criticize Truman's overseas spending programs. The China Lobby only steered the Asialationist ship by providing those fiscal conservatives with a salient demonstration of the contradictions between Truman's sweeping rhetoric and his more limited grand strategy.

Education and Support for Long-Term Grand Strategy

The American public was not uniformly reluctant to spend on long-term strategy or uniformly incapable of drawing distinctions between strongpoints and peripheries. The marketability of Truman's preferred grand strategy—help to Europe and simultaneous withdrawal from China—was positively and strongly correlated with education. As noted in Chapters 3 and 4, college-educated respondents were significantly more supportive of assistance to Europe, withdrawal from the Chinese Civil War, and direct dealings with the Chinese Communists than were those with less education. Those with the lowest levels of education were the least supportive of both the European Recovery Program and detente with the Chinese Communists.

In a large population, education levels are a fair proxy for economic status, as government opinion analysts consistently noted, so we may wonder whether reluctance to support containment strategies is a function of education or wealth, or both. While less-educated segments of the public should be less likely to understand long-term security policy, because they are also less wealthy they should be less willing to fund it. Among the least educated, the high degree of resistance to even frugal realist policies, like withdrawal of support from Chiang, suggests that something in addition to pure economic calculation was at work. It seems that, in addition to higher discount rates for the future, these groups also have a worldview that is far simpler than the requisites of strongpoint containment allow.

Because education matters a great deal to the marketability of abstract, long-term grand strategy, one can argue that a more educated population is a major security asset. This is true not simply because a more educated population produces more material resources, but also because it is more likely to allow those resources to be mobilized for long-term strategies without necessitating potentially costly forms of short-term conflict manipulation. In some cases, like those studied here, this is a power consideration as important as material production itself.

But social solutions, like improving education, are always long term. They do not help leaders who, in marketing current security policy, must better educate the population with which they have to work. Was Kennan realistic when in 1947–49 he repeatedly advocated that Marshall, Acheson, and Truman take the case of strongpoint containment to the people and explain why the circumstances in China were different from those in Greece or Turkey? It is difficult to prove definitively one way or the other. But judging from the polls and the advice that Truman received from a broad range of advisers, including Republicans such as Vandenberg, Herter, and Dulles, it seems that a purely rational sales pitch for grand strategy would not have been successful. While the administration might have done more to educate the public about foreign policy, any hope of clarifying and selling its strategy would have required a domestic ceasefire agreement from the Asialationists, who, given existing public trends, were acting in their own domestic interest by resisting mobilization and demanding ideological consistency in policy toward both Europe and Asia.

Since the public and its congressional representatives sometimes prevent the implementation of optimal grand strategies, one might conclude that rather than long-term education or short-term persuasion, full exclusion of the public and the legislative branch from foreign policy would best serve the national interest. This would be a gross misreading of the argument here. First, as the 1958 Taiwan Straits case demonstrates, even in countries in which the public is largely excluded from foreign policy debates, a degree of conflict manipulation may be necessary if the state is to extract resources for grand strategy. Second, in the model in Chapter 2, for the sake of argument and for the purpose of isolating the variables in which we are interested, we *assume* that leaders are acting with some degree of rationality and with the long-term security of the nation in mind. This is an assumption, not a statement of fact. In many cases, leaders are irrational or self-serving. In such cases a public brake on leadership activities may render the nation's foreign policy more, not less, consistent with the national interest. We should also keep in mind that mobilization drives of the type discussed here do not happen every day. In more normal times the public may have a much more positive, or at least benign, influence on foreign policy, as Page and Shapiro suggest.

Finally, however, we should avoid fully equating education levels with support of realpolitik. We should recognize that many in the public and in the elite are both aware of international events and self-consciously antirealist. They are unsatisfied with the coldhearted and often amoral underpinnings of balance-of-power politics. In judging American China policy under Truman, it is difficult to be critical of American intervention to protect Taiwan on anything but practical grounds. The only norm violated was that of nonintervention in another country's sovereign affairs. That norm bears little resemblance to what we would generally consider ethics or morals.[22] While it may not have been in America's broad security interest to protect Taiwan and thereby increase and prolong hostilities with Beijing, it almost certainly was in the interest of the people on Taiwan. It may be easy to criticize Chiang Kai-shek's regime on the mainland as brutal and unenlightened. But a comparison of life on Taiwan and the mainland from 1949 to the present would make it difficult to argue that, on moral grounds, the United States should have allowed the population of Taiwan to fall under Communist rule.[23]

The purpose of this book, however, is not to judge Truman's or Mao's policies on moral grounds, but rather to analyze why those leaders adopted important policies and how those policies intensified and prolonged conflict between the two sides. Such an analysis is a prerequisite,

[22] On this issue, see Hehir, "The Politics and Ethics of Intervention."

[23] One might also adopt a more sophisticated argument stating that the survival of Taiwan has also provided the mainland Chinese with an example of how a Chinese population can thrive in the world economy if market-based economics are adopted. More recently, Taiwan is providing an important refutation to the notion that Chinese culture is somehow at odds with democracy.

not a replacement, for careful normative judgments. International and domestic approaches in isolation cannot fully explain Sino-American relations from 1947 to 1958. International approaches miss important dynamics of the relationship by assuming away the political difficulties leaders face when mobilizing national resources. Purely domestic explanations also fail because they do not make the two-level connections between changes in the international environment, the creation of long-term grand strategies, problems of domestic mobilization, and the manipulation of short-term conflict. Truman in 1947–50 and Mao in 1958 exploited Sino-American conflict in order to gain consensus for controversial responses to a changing international environment. This holds true despite the differences in their grand strategies, their nations' strategic positions, and the domestic structures and ideologies within which they operated.

American Public Opinion Polls, 1947–1950

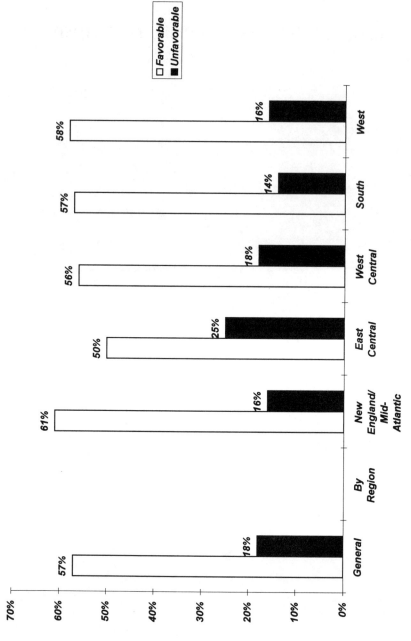

Poll 1. Respondents from different regions who had heard of the Marshall Plan were asked if they were favorable to the plan or not. *Source:* Gallup Poll, Mar. 3, 1948.

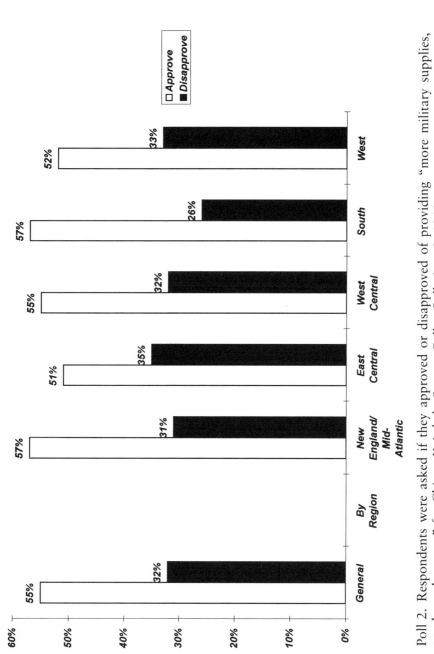

Poll 2. Respondents were asked if they approved or disapproved of providing "more military supplies, goods, and money," for Chiang Kai-shek. *Source:* Gallup Poll, Apr. 2, 1948.

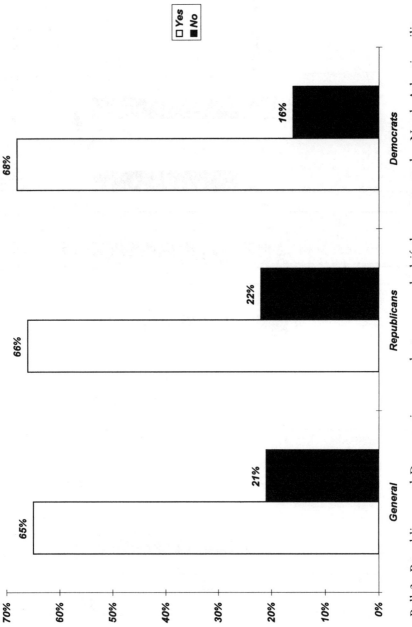

Poll 3. Republican and Democratic respondents were asked if they supported a North Atlantic military alliance. *Source:* Gallup Poll, May 21, 1948.

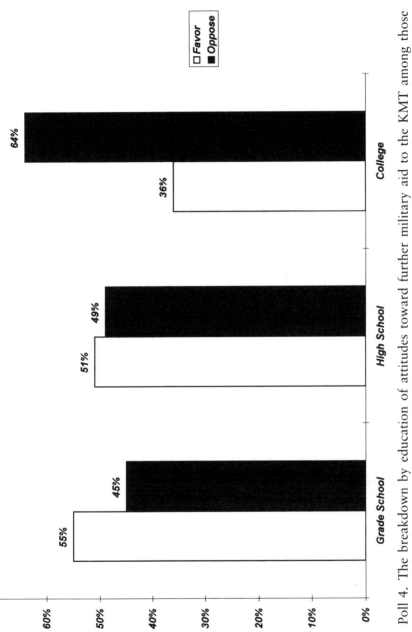

Poll 4. The breakdown by education of attitudes toward further military aid to the KMT among those aware of the Chinese Civil War and holding an opinion. *Source:* "Popular Attitudes toward U.S. Aid to Chiang," June 28, 1949, Foster Papers, Box 33, NA.

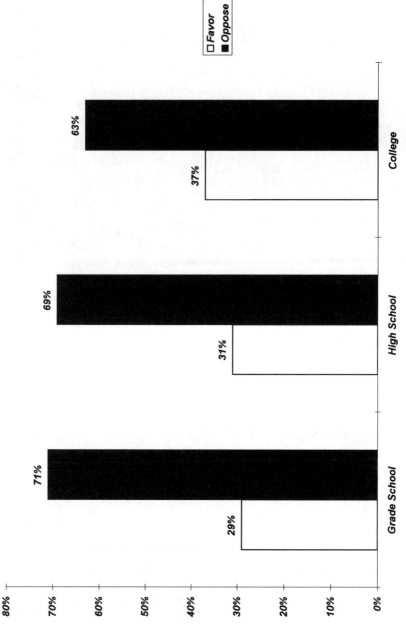

Poll 5. The breakdown by education of attitudes toward recognition of the CCP among those aware of the Chinese Civil War and holding an opinion. *Source:* "Gallup Poll Results on U.S. Relations with Chinese Communists," July 7, 1949, Foster Papers, Box 33, NA.

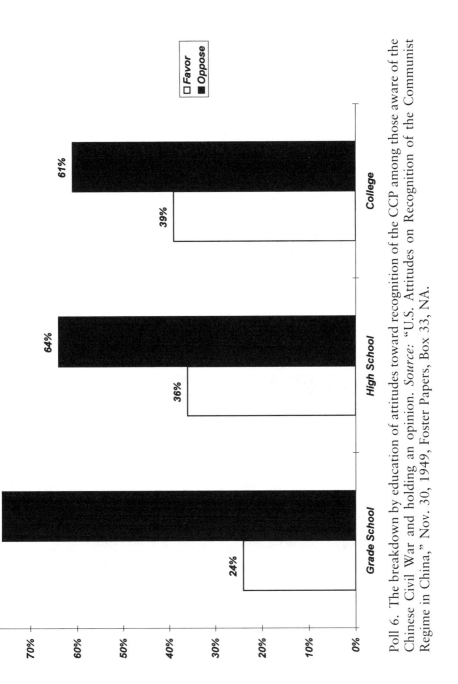

Poll 6. The breakdown by education of attitudes toward recognition of the CCP among those aware of the Chinese Civil War and holding an opinion. *Source:* "U.S. Attitudes on Recognition of the Communist Regime in China," Nov. 30, 1949, Foster Papers, Box 33, NA.

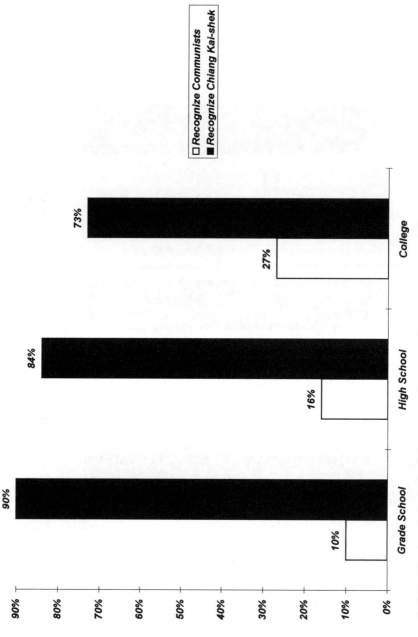

Poll 7. The breakdown by education of support for recognition of the CCP and Chiang among those with an opinion and a preference. *Source:* "Current Attitudes on U.S. Policy toward the Far East," Feb. 13, 1950, Foster Papers, Box 33, NA.

Mao's Korean War Telegrams

TELEGRAM TO STALIN CONCERNING THE DECISION TO SEND TROOPS INTO KOREA FOR COMBAT[1] (OCTOBER 2, 1950)

1) We have decided to send a part of the armed forces into Korea, under the title of Volunteer Army, to do combat with the forces of America and its running dog Syngman Rhee and to assist our Korean comrades. We recognize this course as necessary. If we allow the United States to occupy all of Korea, the revolutionary strength of Korea will suffer a fundamental defeat, and the American invaders will run more rampant, thus having negative effects for the entire Far East.

2) We recognize that since we have decided to dispatch Chinese troops to do combat in Korea, first, they must be able to solve the problem; they must be prepared to destroy and expel, within Korea itself, the armies of the United States and other countries; second, since Chinese troops will fight American troops in Korea (even though they will be using the title Volunteer Army), we must be prepared for the United States to declare and enter a state of war with China; we must be prepared [for the fact] that the United States may, at a minimum, use its air force to bomb many major cities and industrial centers in China, and use its navy to assault the coastal region.

3) Of these two problems, the primary problem is whether the Chinese Army can or cannot destroy the American forces within Korea itself and effectively resolve the Korean problem. As long as our forces can destroy the American forces within Korea itself, and most important, [as long as they can] destroy the American Eighth Army (an old army with combat

---

The three documents in this appendix are translated from *Manuscripts of Mao Zedong*, Vol. 1, *1949–50*, pp. 539–541, 556, and 560–561. All material within parentheses is in the original. Bracketed insertions were added by the translator.

[1] It is widely believed among China scholars that, while the document translated here is accurate, it is not complete. The original telegram apparently contains words that have been deleted from the internally circulated series cited here. Analyses of Russian archival sources call into question whether this telegram was ever sent. For discussion of this issue and why I believe this document represents Mao's own thinking on the Korean War, even if he never sent it, see chapter 5, pp. 159–166.

effectiveness), while the seriousness of the second problem (America's declaring war on China) will still exist, the situation will have already turned in favor of the revolutionary camp and China. This is to say, if the American forces are defeated, the Korean problem is, in fact, finished (it is possible that formally it may not be over, the United States may for a long time not recognize Korea's victory); so, even if the Americans have already openly declared war on China, the scope of this war will probably not be great, and the duration will not be long. We see the least advantageous situation as the Chinese army being unable to destroy the American forces in large number, the two armies becoming mutually deadlocked, and, in addition, the United States having already entered an open state of war with China, thus leading to the resulting destruction of the economic construction plan we have already begun, and moreover, arousing dissatisfaction toward us among the national bourgeoisie and other segments of the people (they are very afraid of war).

4) Under the present situation, we have decided that on October 15 we will begin dispatching the twelve divisions that have been transferred in advance to south Manchuria. They will locate themselves in appropriate districts of North Korea (not necessarily all the way to the 38th parallel). While they do combat with the enemy who dares to advance and attack north of the 38th parallel, in the first period fighting a defensive war to destroy small enemy detachments and gaining a clear understanding of the situation, they will await the arrival of Soviet weapons and the equipping of our army; and then [they will] coordinate a counterattack with the Korean comrades, destroying the invading American army.

5) According to our intelligence to date, an American army (two infantry divisions and one mechanized division) totals 1,500 pieces of artillery ranging from 7- to 24-centimeter caliber, including tank and antiaircraft artillery; and one of our armies (three divisions) only has 36 pieces of that type of artillery. The enemy has control of the air, and the air force we have begun training will not be able to put over 300 planes into the war until February 1951. Because of this, our forces are still unable to assure destruction of an American army in one blow. And, since we have decided to fight with Americans, we should be prepared so that, at the point in a campaign that the American command assembles its forces on the battlefield to fight with ours, our troop strength should be four times that of the enemy (using four of our armies to counter one of the enemy's) and our firepower should be one and a half to two times that of the enemy (using 2,200–3,000 of every type of artillery piece from seven centimeters and up to counter 1,500 enemy artillery pieces of the same caliber). Thus, they will assuredly, cleanly, and thoroughly destroy the one army of the enemy.

6) Besides the twelve divisions mentioned above, we are also in the process of transferring 24 divisions from south of the Yangtze River and from the ShaanGan [Shaanxi and Gansu] district to take up positions in the LongHai, JinPu, BeiNing Lines,[2] in order to form the second and third wave of military forces to assist Korea. We estimate that, in the spring and summer of next year, according to the circumstance at the time, they will progressively be employed.

TELEGRAM TO ZHOU ENLAI [IN MOSCOW][3] CONCERNING [WHY] OUR TROOPS SHOULD ENTER KOREA (OCTOBER 13, 1950)

1) The result of a discussion on the part of comrades of the Politburo is that we unanimously believe that our troops entering Korea is more advantageous [than the alternatives]. In the first period we can focus on attacking the puppet forces; our troops countering puppet forces is certain [of success]; we can open up a base in Korea in the large mountain region north of the Wonsan-Pyongyang line and can inspire the Korean people. In the first period, as long as we can destroy some divisions of the puppet army, the Korean situation can take a turn to our advantage.

2) The adoption of the active policy above will be extremely advantageous for China, Korea, the Far East, and the world; and on the other hand, if we do not send troops, allowing the enemy to press to the Yalu border, and the arrogance of reactionaries at home and abroad to grow, then this will be disadvantageous to all sides; above all it will be most disadvantageous to Manchuria; all of the northeastern border defense forces will be absorbed, and south Manchurian electrical power will be controlled [by the enemy].

In summation, we recognize that we should enter the war, we must enter the war, entering the war will have great benefits, the harm inflicted by not entering the war would be great.

[2] LongHai, JinPu, and BeiNing Lines are shorthand for three Chinese rail lines running between Xuzhou and Lanzhou, Tianjin and Pukou, and Beijing and Nanjing, respectively.

[3] The October 13 and 14 telegrams to Zhou were sent to Moscow, where Zhou was on a secret mission to negotiate Soviet aid for the war. For confirmation of this see Hao and Zhai, "China's Decision," p.111; Chen Jian, "The Sino-Soviet Alliance," p. 29; additional confirmation of Zhou's trip to Moscow is supplied by the recently published memoirs of Bo Yibo, a high ranking Chinese Communist Party official at the time. See Bo Yibo, *Ruogan Zhongda Juece yu Shijian de Huigu* [*Reflections on a Number of Important Decisions and Events*] (Beijing: Chinese Communist Party School Publishers, May, 1991), p. 44; also see Chai and Zhao, *Negotiations at Panmunjon*, p. 83.

TELEGRAM TO ZHOU ENLAI CONCERNING THE PRINCIPLES AND DEPLOYMENTS OF THE PEOPLE'S VOLUNTEER ARMY AS IT ENTERS KOREA FOR COMBAT (OCTOBER 14, 1950)

1) I have already instructed Peng Dehuai that after he arrives in Tokchon and analyzes the situation he is to build two or three defensive fronts in the region north of the Pyongyang-Wonsan Railroad and south of the Tokchon-Yongwon Road. If the enemy comes and attacks, then [he is to] cut them off and destroy them in front of the positions; if the Pyongyang American army and the Wonsan puppet army come from two fronts to attack, [he is to] attack the route which is relatively weak and isolated. Currently, we have resolved ourselves to attack the puppet armies; we may also attack some isolated American forces. If time allows, then we will continue to strengthen our defenses, and if, inside of [the next] six months, the enemy is firmly entrenched in Pyongyang, Wonsan and will not leave, then we will still not go and attack Pyongyang, Wonsan. When our forces are fully equipped and trained, and after in the air and on the land we enjoy a state of overwhelming superiority over enemy forces, then we will go back and attack Pyongyang, Wonsan, etc.; after six months we will then discuss the issue of attacking. This way of proceeding will be assured [to succeed] and will be very beneficial.

2) American forces are still stopped for a time at the 38th parallel; their offensive to Pyongyang will require time; the additional offensive from Pyongyang to Tokchon will require still more time. If the Pyongyang American forces do not advance toward Tokchon, the Wonsan puppet forces will probably have difficulty advancing alone; this will give our force time to move in and construct defenses.

3) Our forces have decided to move on October 19; the advance forces will need seven days to go on foot the 200 kilometers to Tokchon; they will rest for a day or two, and can, on October 28, begin building defenses in the region south of the Tokchon-Yongwon line. It will require ten days for the entire force of 260,000 troops to cross the Yalu River; we need until October 28 and then we can complete the river crossing.

4) In order to be prepared in November to strike a great victory when the enemy assaults the Tokchon region, we have decided that it is still for the best if we set out with 260,000 troops (12 infantry divisions and 3 artillery divisions) all moving in. Under conditions where we have already constructed defenses and the enemy also is entrenched in Pyongyang [and] Wonsan, not daring to come and attack, we will call back again about one half of the forces to within China for training exercises and provisions; when we fight our big battle they will go back again.

5) During the period in which our forces are moving in and half are building defenses, it will be advantageous [for us] if the Korean people's forces still continue resisting and delay to the utmost extent possible the advance of the American and puppet forces.

Bibliography

Chinese Documents

Communist China, 1955–59: Policy Documents with Analysis. Foreword by Robert Bowie and John King Fairbank. Cambridge, Mass.: Harvard University Press, 1962.

Dang De Wenxian (Party documents). Internally circulated.

Jianguo Yilai Mao Zedong Wengao (The manuscripts of Mao Zedong since the founding of the nation). Vols. 1–8. Beijing: Central Documents Publishing Company, 1987–90. Internally circulated.

MacFarquhar, Roderick, Timothy Cheek, and Eugene Wu. *The Secret Speeches of Chairman Mao.* Cambridge, Mass.: Harvard University Press, 1989.

Mao Zedong Junshi Wenji (Collected military manuscripts of Mao Zedong). Vols. 1–6. Beijing: Military Science and Central Documents Publishing Companies, 1993.

Mao Zedong Junshi Wenxuan (Selections of Mao Zedong's writings on military affairs). Beijing: Liberation Army Soldiers Press, 1981. Internally circulated.

Mao Zedong Sixiang Wansui! (Long live Mao Zedong thought!). Beijing, 1969.

Mao Zedong Waijiao Wenxuan (A selection of Mao's writings on diplomacy). Beijing: World Knowledge Press, 1994.

Nie Rongzhen Junshi Wenxuan (A selection of Nie Rongzhen's military writings). Beijing: Liberation Army Press, 1992.

Zhonggong Zhongyang Wenjian Xuanji (Selected documents of the Central Committee of the Chinese Communist Party). Vol. 18. Beijing: Central Party School of the Chinese Communist Party, 1992.

Zhonghua Renmin Gonghe Guo Waijiao Guanxi Wenjian (Documents on the foreign relations of the People's Republic of China). Beijing: World Knowledge Press.

Zhou Enlai Waijiao Wenxuan (A selection of Zhou Enlai's writings on foreign affairs). Beijing: Foreign Ministry of the PRC and Document Research Office of the Chinese Communist Party, 1990.

Chinese Communist Party Memoirs

Bo Yibo. *Ruogan Zhongda Juece yu Shijian de Huigu* (Reflections on a number of important decisions and events). Vols. 1 and 2. Beijing: Chinese Communist Party School Publishers, May 1991.

Chai Chengwen and Zhao Yongtian. *Banmendian Tanpan* (Panmunjon negotiations). Beijing: Liberation Army Press, August 1989.

Du Ping. *Zai Zhiyuan Jun Zongbu* (In the headquarters of the People's Volunteer Army). Beijing: Liberation Army Press, March 1991.

Hong Xuezhi. *Kangmei Yuanchao Zhanzheng Huiyi* (Recollections of the war to resist U.S. aggression and aid Korea). Beijing: Liberation Army Literary and Artistic Publishing House, November 1990.

Huang Hua. "My Contacts with John Leighton Stuart after Nanjing's Liberation." Trans. Li Xiaobing, in *Chinese Historians* V, no. 1 (Spring 1992): 47–56.

Lei Yingfu. "Kangmei Yuanchao Zhanzheng Ji Ge Zhongda Juece de Huiyi" (Recalling some major decisions of the war to resist America and aid Korea). Part 1, *Dang De Wenxian* (Party documents), no. 1 (1994): 24–30.

Li Yinqiao. *Zai Mao Zedong Shenbian Shiwu Nian* (Fifteen years at the side of Mao Zedong). Shijiazhuang: Hebei People's Publishers, June 1991.

Li Yueran. *Waijiao Wutaishang de Xin Zhongguo Lingxiu* (The leaders of New China on the diplomatic stage). Beijing: Liberation Army Press, 1989.

Liu Xiao. *Chushi Sulian Ba Nian* (Eight-year diplomatic mission to the Soviet Union). Beijing: Chinese Communist Party History Materials Press, 1986. Internally circulated.

Nie Rongzhen. *Inside the Red Star: The Memoirs of Marshall Nie Rongzhen.* Beijing: New World Press, 1988.

Peng Dehuai. *Memoirs of a Chinese Marshall.* Beijing: Foreign Languages Press, 1984.

———. "Wei Shenme Yao Xie Xin Gei Mao Zhuxi" (Why I wanted to write a letter to Chairman Mao). In *Zhonggong Dangshi Ziliao* (Chinese party history materials) 28 (1988): 1–7.

Shi Zhe. *Zai Lishi Juren Shenbian: Shi Zhe Huiyilu* (At the side of history's giants: The memoirs of Shi Zhe). Beijing: Chinese Central Documents Press, 1991.

Wang Bingnan. *Zhongmei Huitan Jiu Nian Huigu* (Review of the nine-year Sino-American ambassadorial talks). Beijing: World Knowledge Press, 1985.

Wu Lengxi. *Yi Mao Zhuxi: Wo Qinzi Jingli de Ruogan Zhongda Lishi Shijian de Pianduan* (Recalling Chairman Mao: Fragments of the important historical events that I personally experienced). Beijing: New China Publishers, 1995.

———. "Inside Story of the Decision Making during the Shelling of Jinmen." In Li Xiaobing, Chen Jian, and David L. Wilson, trans. and annotators, "Mao Zedong's Handling of the Taiwan Straits Crisis of 1958: Chinese Recollections and Documents." *Cold War International History Project Bulletin* 6–7 (Winter 1995–96): 208–215.

Wu Xiuquan. *Zai Waijiaobu Ba Nian de Jingli, 1950.1–1958* (Eight years' experience in the Foreign Ministry, January 1950–October 1958). Beijing: World Knowledge Press, 1988.

Xiao Jinguang. *Xiao Jinguang Huiyilu* (Memoirs of Xiao Jinguang). Vol. 2. Beijing: Liberation Army Press, 1988).

Ye Fei. *Ye Fei Huiyilu* (Memoirs of Ye Fei). Beijing: Liberation Army Press, 1988.

Chinese Language Books, Articles, and Interviews

Author interviews with scholars, People's Republic of China, 1990–1994 (not for attribution).

Chen Changzhi, ed. *Zhonghua Renmin Gonghe Guo Jingji Jianshi* (A concise economic history of the People's Republic of China). Chengdu: Sichuan University Press, 1989.

Chen Chonggui. "Paoji Jinmen Neimu" (The inside story of the shelling of

Quemoy). In Yu Qiping, ed., *Gonghe Guo San Jun Mi Lu* (The secret records of the republic's three armed forces). Beijing: Unity Press, 1993.

Chen Mingsheng, ed. *Xin Zhongguo Sishiwu Nian Yanjiu* (Research on 45 years of the New China). Beijing: Beijing Ligong University Press, 1994.

Cong Jin. *Quzhe Fazhan de Suiyue* (The years of tortuous development). Henan People's Publishers, 1989.

Dangdai Zhongguo Caizheng (Contemporary Chinese finance). Vol. 1. Beijing: China Social Sciences Press, 1988.

Dangdai Zhongguo de Jingji Guanli (Contemporary Chinese economic management). Beijing: China Social Sciences Press, 1986.

Dangdai Zhongguo Jundui de Junshi Gongzuo (shang) (The military work of the contemporary Chinese army). Vol. 1. Beijing: China Social Sciences Press, 1989.

Fan Shouxin. "Ba Da Guanyu Jingji Tizhi Gaige de Sixiang ji Qi Shixian" (The thought behind the economic structural reforms of the 8th Party Congress and its implementation). *Dangshi Yanjiu* (Research in party history), no. 5 (1985).

Fan Xizhou. "1958 Nian Taiwan Haixia Jinzhang Jushi Fenxi" (An analysis of the tense situation in the Taiwan Straits in 1958). *Taiwan Yanjiu Jikan* (Taiwan research quarterly), no. 4 (1990), pp. 33–42.

Han Gaorun and Song Zhongyue. *Dongya Heping yu Hezuo* (East Asian peace and cooperation). Beijing: National Defense University Press, 1994.

Han Nianlong and Xue Mouhong, chief eds. *Dangdai Zhongguo Waijiao* (Contemporary Chinese diplomatic relations). Beijing: China Social Sciences Press, 1987. Internally circulated.

He Di. "'Taihai Weiji' He Zhongguo Dui Jinmen Mazu Zhengce de Xingshi" (The Taiwan Straits crisis and the formation of Chinese policy toward Quemoy and Matsu). *Zhongguo Xiandai Shi* (Chinese contemporary history) (Oct. 1988): 31–48.

Hua Lin, ed. *Mao Zedong he Tade Zhanyoumen* (Mao Zedong and his comrades in arms). Beijing: Brilliant Age Publishers, 1990.

Jia Ennan. *Mao Zedong Renji Jiaowang Shilu: 1915–76* (The true record of Mao's personal contacts: 1915(n-1976). Jiangsu Literature and Arts Press, 1989).

Jin Chunming. "Dui Sannian 'Da Yuejin' de Zai Renshi" (A reconsideration of the three-year "Great Leap Forward"). *Dangshi Yanjiu* (Research in party history), no. 7 (1984).

Li Zhimin. "Kang Da Kang Da Yue Kang Yue Da" (The Chinese people's anti-Japanese military and political college: The more we fight the larger we get). In *Zhonggong Dangshi Ziliao* (Materials on Chinese Communist Party history) (Nov. 1983): 55–182. Internally circulated.

Liao Xinwen. "1958 Nian Mao Zedong Juece Paoji Jinmen de Lishi Kaocha" (Investigating the history of Mao's 1958 decision to shell Quemoy). *Dang De Wenxian*, no. 1 (1994): 31–36.

Lin Ch'engyi. *Yi Jiu Wu Ba Nian Taiwan Haixia Weiji Qijian Meiguo Dui Hua Zhengce* (America's China policy during the 1958 Taiwan Straits crisis). Taipei: Taiwan Commercial Press, 1985.

Liu Bocheng Zhuan (The biography of Liu Bocheng). Compiled by the editorial board of the Biography Series on Contemporary China's Leaders. Beijing: Contemporary China Press, 1992.

Liu Suinian and Wu Qungan, eds. *Dayuejin he Tiaozheng Shiqi de Guomin Jingji* (The national economy during the Great Leap Forward and adjustment period). Harbin: Heilongjiang People's Press, 1984. Internally circulated.

_____. *Di Yi Ge Wunian Jihua Shiqi de Guomin Jingji* (The national economy in the period of the first five-year plan) Harbin: Heilongjiang People's Press, 1984. Internally circulated.

Liu Zhihui. *Chashang Chibang de Long* (Dragon with wings). Beijing: Liberation Army Arts Press, 1992).

Lu Qiming. *Dahai de Jiaoao: Renmin Haijun Jishi Zhi Yi* (Pride of the seas: A record of the people's navy). Maritime Press, 1983.

Ma Qilin, ed. *Zhongguo Gongchandang Zhizheng Sishi Nian* (Forty years of Chinese Communist Party rule). Beijing: Chinese Communist Party History Materials Press, 1989.

Pei Di. "Yi Jiu Wu Ba Nian Ba Da Er Ci Huiyi" (The 1958 Second Plenum of the 8th Party Congress). In *Zhonggong Dangshi Ziliao* (Chinese Communist Party history materials). Vol. 29 (1989). Internally circulated.

Qiang Yuanjin and Chen Xuewei. "Chongping Yi Jiu Wu Liu Nian de 'Fan Maojin'" (Reconsidering the "anti-adventurism" movement of 1956. *Dangshi Yanjiu* (Research in party history), no. 6 (1980).

Quan Yanchi. *Mao Zedong yu Heluxiaofu: 1957–59 Zhong Su Guanxi Jishi* (Mao Zedong and Khruschchev: The true records of 1957–59 Sino-Soviet relations). Changchun: Jilin People's Press, 1989.

_____. *Zouxia Shentan de Mao Zedong* (The Mao Zedong who walked beneath the Temple of the Gods). Beijing: Chinese Cultural Press, 1984.

Shi Zhongquan. "Mao Zedong Dui Shehuizhuyi Fazhan Jieduan Lilun de Gongxian he Shiwu" (Mao Zedong's contributions and mistakes in the theory of socialist development stages). In *Zhonggong Dangshi Yanjiu* (Research in Chinese Communist Party history) 1 (1988): 46–54.

Wang Shaoguang. "Falling State Extractive Capacity in China and Its Results." In *21 Shiji* (The 21st century, Hong Kong), no. 21 (February 1994): 5–14.

Wang Suhong and Wang Yulin. *Kongzhan Zai Chaoxian* (The airwar in Korea). Beijing: Liberation Army Arts Press, 1992.

Wang Xiangen. *Zhongguo Mimi Da Fabing: Yuanyue Kangmei Shilu* (China's secret large-scale military expedition: The true story of assisting Vietnam and opposing America). Jinan: Jinan Press, 1992.

Wang Yaping. "Di Er Ge Wu Nian Jihua de Huigu" (Recollections of the second five-year plan) *Dangshi Yanjiu* (Research in party history), no. 4 (1987).

Wei Shiyan. "Geluomike Guanyu Taiwan Jushi Tong Mao Zhuxi Tanhua de Huiyi yu Shishi Bu Fu" (Gromyko's recollections of talks with Chairman Mao concerning the Taiwan situation are incompatible with reality). In *Xin Zhongguo Waijiao Fengyun* (The diplomatic crises of New China). Ed. Foreign Ministry Diplomatic History Editing Office. Beijing: World Knowledge Press, 1990).

Xie Chuntao. *Dayuejin Kuanglan* (The mad tide of the Great Leap Forward). Henan: Henan People's Press, 1990.

Xin Zhongguo Biannianshi (Annals of New China). Beijing: People's Publishers, 1989. Internally circulated.

Xin Zhongguo Waijiao Fengyun (The diplomatic storms of New China). Ed. Foreign Ministry Diplomatic History Editing Office. Beijing: World Knowledge Publishing House, 1990.

Xu Yan. *Jinmen Zhi Zhan* (The battle over Quemoy). Beijing: Chinese Broadcast Television Press, 1992.

————. *Di Yi Ci Jiaoliang* (The first trial of strength). Beijing: Chinese Broadcast Television Press, 1990.

Yan Shengyi, chief ed. *Shijie Zhengzhi Jingji yu Guoji Guanxi Cidian* (The dictionary of world politics, economics, and international affairs). Jilin: Jilin People's Press, 1988.

Yao Xu, *Cong Yalu Jiang Dao Banmendian* (From the Yalu River to Panmunjon). Beijing: People's Press, 1985. Internally circulated.

Ye Yumengg, *Chubing Chaoxian* (Dispatching troops to Korea). Beijing: October Literary and Artistic Press, 1990.

————. *Hei Xue: Chubing Chaoxian Jishi* (Black snow: The true record of the dispatch of troops into Korea). Beijing: Authors' Press, 1990.

Zhang Gong. "Guanghui de 'Ba Da'" (The brilliant Eighth Party Congress) *Dangshi Yanjiu* (Research in party history), no. 1 (1980).

Zhang Jian, ed. *Dangdai Zhongguo Jingji Gaishu* (A narrative of the contemporary Chinese economy). Canton: Guangdong People's Press, 1989.

Zhang Jian and Chen Shihui. "Lushan Huiyi ji Qi Lishi Jiaoxun" (The Lushan Conference and its lessons). *Dangshi Yanjiu* (Research in party history), no. 3 (1984).

Zhang Jing and Yao Yanjin. *Jiji Fangwei Zhanlüe Qianshuo* (A basic introduction to the active defense strategy). Beijing: Liberation Army Press, 1985. Internally circulated.

Zhao Desheng, ed. *Zhonghua Renmin Gonghe Guo Jingji Zhuanti Da Shiji: 1949–66* (A chronicle of special problems in the economy of the People's Republic of China: 1949–66). Henan: Henan People's Press, 1989.

Zheng Deying et al., eds. *Xin Zhonnguo Jishi: 1949–84* (Chronicles of New China). Dongbei Normal University Press, 1986).

Zhonggong Dangshi Dashi Nianbiao (Chronology of Chinese Communist Party history). Beijing: People's Press, 1981. Internally circulated.

Zhonggong Dangshi Liushi Nian (Sixty years of party history). Beijing: Liberation Army Press, 1984.

Zhongguo Jingji Fazhan Sishinian (Forty years of Chinese economic development). Beijing: People's Press, 1990.

Zhongguo Nongcun 40 Nian (Forty years of Chinese village life). Central Plains Peasant Press, 1989.

Zhongguo Nongye Dashiji: 1949–1980 (Chronicle of Chinese agriculture: 1949–1980). Beijing: Agricultural Publishers, 1982.

Zhongguo Tongji Nianjian: 1990 (China statistical yearbook: 1990). Beijing: Chinese Statistical Press, 1990.

Zhongguo Waijiao 40 Nian (Forty years of Chinese diplomacy). Shenyang: Shenyang Press, 1989.

Zhonghua Renmin Gonghe Guo Jingji Dashiji: 1949 Nian 10 Yue–1984 Nian 9 Yue (The record of great economic events in the People's Republic of China: October 1949–September 1984). Beijing: Beijing Press, 1985.

Zhou Chengen. "Renmin Gongshe he Shehuizhuyi Jianshe de Kongxiang Lun" (The utopian theory of the people's commune and socialist construction). In *Zhonggong Dangshi Yanjiu* (Research in Chinese Communist Party history), no. 5 (1988): 44–50.

———. "Ba Da Qianhou Dang Dui Shehuizhuyi Jianshe Daolu de Chubu Tansuo" (The preliminary analysis of the party toward the socialist path of national construction before and after the Eighth Party Congress) *Dangshi Yanjiu* (Research in party history), no. 2 (1986): 1–7.

Zhou Taihe, ed. *Dangdai Zhongguo de Jingji Tizhi Gaige* (Contemporary Chinese economic structural reform). Beijing: China Social Sciences Press, 1984.

Chinese Newspapers, Media, and Party Journals

Anhui Ribao (Anhui daily).
Caizheng (Finance).
Current Background (CB).
Dagong Bao.
Dangshi Tongxun (Party history report).
Dong Feng (East wind, Hebei Central Committee).
Extracts from Chinese Mainland Magazines (ECMM).
Fendou (Struggle, Gansu Central Committee).
Fenjin (Strive ahead, Jilin Central Committee).
Fujian Ribao (Fujian daily).
Gansu Ribao (Gansu daily).
Guangming Ribao (Guangming daily).
Guizhou Ribao (Guizhou daily).
Henan Ribao (Henan daily).
Hunan Ribao (Hunan daily).
Hong Qi (Red flag).
Hong Xing (Red star, Gansu Central Committee).
Jiang Hai Xuekan.
Joint Public Research Service (JPRS).
Laodong (Labor).
Ningxia Ribao (Ningxia daily).
Nongcun Gongzuo Tongxun (Rural village work report).
Qi Yi (July 1st, Hubei Central Committee).
Qianjin (Advance, Shanxi Central Committee).
Qinghai Ribao (Qinghai daily).
Qunzhong (The masses, Jiangsu Central Committee).
Renmin Ribao (People's daily).
Shangyou (Upstream, Guangdong Province Central Committee).
Shijie Zhishi (World knowledge).
Sichuan Ribao (Sichuan daily).
Survey of Chinese Mainland Press (SCMP).
Union Research Service.

Wenhui Bao (Wenhui daily).
Xinghuo (Spark, Ningxia Central Committee).
Xinhua Banyue Kan (New China bimonthly).
Xinhua Yuebao (New China monthly).
Xinjiang Hongqi (Xinjiang red flag, Xinjiang Central Committee).
Xin Lunyu (New analects, Shandong Central Committee).
Xu yu Shi (Theory and practice, Anhui Central Committee).
Yuejin (Leap forward, Jiangxi Central Committee).
Zhonggong Dangshi Yanjiu (Research in Chinese Communist Party history).
Zhonggong Dangshi Ziliao (Chinese Communist Party history materials).
Zhongguo Gongren (Chinese worker).
Zhongguo Gongren Banyue Kan (Chinese worker bimonthly).

American Documents

The China White Paper: August 1949. Stanford, Calif: Stanford University, 1967.
Congressional Record, 80th and 81st Congresses, 1946–48 and 1948–50. Washington, D.C.
Documents of the National Security Council. Ed. Paul Kesaris. Frederick, Md.: University Publishers of America. Microfilm Series plus Supplements 1–5.
"Draft Report of the National Security Council on the Position of the United States regarding Short-term Assistance to China, March 24, 1948."
Etzold, Thomas H., and John Lewis Gaddis. *Containment: Documents on American Foreign Policy and Strategy: 1945–50*. New York: Columbia University Press, 1978.
Executive Sessions of the Senate Foreign Relations Committee: 1947–49. Washington, D.C.: U.S. Government Printing Office, 1976.
Foreign Relations of the United States: 1946–54 and microfiche supplements. Washington, D.C.: U.S. Government Printing Office.
Gallup Poll: Public Opinion 1935–71, 2 vols. New York: Random House, 1972.
Military Assistance Program: 1949, Joint Hearings Held in Executive Session before the Committee on Foreign Relations and the Committee on Armed Services, 81st Congress, 1st sess.
"Military Situation in the Far East," *United States Congressional Hearings*, Vol. 31, no. 45, 1951.
"The United States and Communist China in 1949 and 1950: The Question of Rapprochement and Recognition." A Staff Study Prepared for Use of the Committee on Foreign Relations, United States Senate, January 1973.

The National Archives (NA)

United States State Department:
Record Group 59 (RG59)
    Confidential U.S. State Department Central Files, Library and Contract Microfilms (LM)
        China: Foreign Affairs
        China: Internal Affairs
    Decimal Files

H. Schuyler Foster Papers, Office of Public Opinion Studies
Records of the Executive Secretariat
Records of the Office of Chinese Affairs, 1945–1955 (microfilm C0012)
Records of the Policy Planning Staff
Record Group 84 (RG84)
    China Post Files

The National Security Archive, Gelman Library

The Harry S Truman Library

Papers and Files:
    The Files of Clark L. Clifford
    The Files of George Elsey
    Intelligence Files: Central Intelligence Reports
    The Files of Joseph M. Jones
    Meetings of the National Security Council: Memoranda for the President
    National Security Meetings: Memoranda for the President
    Papers of Dean Acheson, Secretary of State, 1949–1953
    Papers of Matthew J. Connelly: Minutes of Cabinet Meetings
    Papers of John D. Sumner
    President's Secretary's Files
    The Princeton Seminars
Oral Histories:
    W. Walton Butterworth
    John M. Cabot
    O. Edmund Clubb
    John F. Melby

English Language Books and Articles

Acheson, Dean. *Present at the Creation: My Years at the State Department*. New York: W. W. Norton, 1969.
———. *This Vast External Realm*. New York: W. W. Norton, 1973.
Allison, Graham T. *Essence of Decision: Explaining the Cuban Missile Crisis*. Boston.: Little, Brown, 1971.
Almond, Gabriel. *The American People and Foreign Policy*. New York: Praeger, 1960.
Appleman, Roy E. *South to the Naktong and North to the Yalu: June–November 1950*. Washington, D.C.: Department of the Army, 1961.
Apter, David A., ed. *Ideology and Discontent*. London: Free Press, 1964.
Art, Robert. "Bureaucratic Politics and American Foreign Policy: A Critique." *Policy Sciences* (Dec. 1973): 467–490.
Bachman, David. *Bureaucracy, Economy and Leadership in China: The Institutional Origins of the Great Leap Forward*. Cambridge, Eng.: Cambridge University Press, 1991.
Bajanov, Evgueni. "Assessing the Politics of the Korean War, 1949–51." *Cold War International History Project Bulletin* 6–7 (Winter 1995–96): 54, 87–91.
Baldwin, David. *Paradoxes of Power*. New York: Basil Blackwell, 1989.

Barnett, Michael. "High Politics Is Low Politics: The Domestic and Systemic Sources of Israeli Security Policy, 1967–77." *World Politics* (July 1990): 529–562.

Berghahn, Volker. "Naval Armaments and Social Crisis: Germany before 1914." In Geoffrey Best and Andrew Wheatcroft, eds., *War, Economy and the Military Mind,* pp. 61–88. London: Croom Helm, 1976.

Bertrand, C. L., ed. *Revolutionary Situations in Europe 1917–22.* Montreal: Interuniversity Centre for European Studies, 1977.

Best, Geoffrey, and Andrew Wheatcroft, eds. *War, Economy and the Military Mind.* London: Croom Helm, 1976.

Betts, Richard K. *Nuclear Blackmail and Nuclear Balance.* Washington, D.C.: Brookings Institution, 1987.

Blainey, Geoffrey. *The Causes of War.* New York: Free Press, 1973.

Blum, Robert. *Drawing the Line: The Origin of American Containment Policy in East Asia.* New York: W. W. Norton, 1982.

Bohlen, Charles E. *Witness to History: 1929–1969.* New York: W. W. Norton, 1973.

Borg, Dorothy, and Waldo Heinrichs, eds. *Uncertain Years: Chinese-American Relations, 1947–50.* New York: Columbia University Press, 1980.

Borisov, O. B., and B. T. Koloskov. *Soviet-Chinese Relations, 1945–1970,* ed. Vladimir Petrov. Bloomington: Indiana University Press, 1975.

Boyle, John Hunter. *China and Japan at War, 1937–45: The Politics of Collaboration.* Stanford, Calif.: Stanford University Press, 1972.

Brodie, Bernard. *War and Politics.* New York: Macmillan: 1973.

Brown, L. Carl, ed. *Centerstage: American Diplomacy since World War II.* New York: Holmes and Meier, 1990.

Bueno de Mesquita, Bruce. "Theories of International Conflict: An Analysis and an Appraisal." In T. R. Gurr, ed. *Handbook of Political Conflict.* New York: Free Press, 1980.

Bundy, McGeorge. *Danger and Survival: Choices About the Bomb in the First Fifty Years.* New York: Vintage Books, 1988.

Camilleri, Joseph. *Chinese Foreign Policy: The Maoist Era and Its Aftermath.* Oxford: Martin Robertson, 1980.

Carr, E. H. *The Twenty Years' Crisis: 1919–1939.* New York: Harper and Row, 1964.

Caspary, William R. "The Mood Theory: A Study of Public Opinion and Foreign Policy." *American Political Science Review* 64 (1970): 536–547.

Chang, Gordon H. *Friends and Enemies: The United States, China and the Soviet Union, 1948–72.* Stanford, Calif.: Stanford University Press, 1990.

Chang, Parris H. *Power and Policy in China.* 2d ed. University Park: Pennsylvania State University Press, 1978.

Chen Jian."China and the First Indo-China War, 1950–54" *China Quarterly* (Mar. 1993): 85–110

———. "China's Changing Aims during the Korean War, 1950–51." *Journal of American-East Asian Relations* (Spring 1992): 8–41.

———. "China's Involvement in the Vietnam War, 1964–69." *China Quarterly* (June 1995): 356–387.

———. *China's Road to the Korean War: The Making of Sino-American Confrontation*. New York: Columbia University Press, 1994.

———. "The Myth of America's Lost Chance in China: A Chinese Perspective in Light of New Evidence." Unpublished manuscript.

———. "The Sino-Soviet Alliance and China's Entry into the Korean War." A Working Paper of the Cold War History Project, Woodrow Wilson International Center for Scholars, Washington, D.C., 1991.

———. "The Ward Case and the Emergence of Sino-American Confrontation, 1948–50." *Australian Journal of Chinese Affairs* (July 1993): 149–170.

Cheng, Chu-Yuan. *China's Economic Development: Growth and Structural Change*. Boulder, Colo.: Westview Press, 1982.

Christensen, Thomas J. "A Lost Chance for What? Rethinking the Origins of U.S.-PRC Confrontation." *Journal of American–East Asian Relations* (Fall 1995): 249–278.

———. "Threats, Assurances and the Last Chance for Peace: The Lessons of Mao's Korean War Telegrams." *International Security* (Summer 1992): 122–154.

Christensen, Thomas J., and Jack Snyder. "Chain Gangs and Passed Bucks: Predicting Alliance Patterns in Multipolarity." *International Organization* (Spring 1990): 137–168.

Clemens, Walter C. *The Arms Race and Sino-Soviet Relations*. Stanford, Calif.: Hoover Institution, 1968.

Clifford, Clark, with Richard Holbrooke. *Counsel to the President: A Memoir*. New York: Random House, 1991.

Cline, Ray S. *World Power Assessment: A Calculus of Strategic Drift*. Boulder, Colo.: Westview Press, 1975.

Clodfelter, Mark. *The Limits of Air Power: The American Bombing of North Vietnam*. New York: Free Press, 1989.

Cohen, Eliot A., and John Gooch. *Military Misfortunes: The Anatomy of Failure in War*. New York: Free Press, 1990.

Cohen, Warren I. "Conversations with Chinese Friends: Zhou Enlai's Associates Reflect on Chinese-American Relations in the 1940s and the Korean War." *Diplomatic History* 11 (Summer 1987): 283–289.

Cohen, Warren I., and Akira Iriye, eds. *The Great Powers in East Asia: 1953–60*. New York: Columbia University Press: 1990.

Condit, Doris. *History of the Office of the Secretary of Defense*. Vol. 1. Washington, D.C.: Historical Office of Office of the Secretary of Defense, 1984.

Condit, Kenneth W. *The History of the Joint Chiefs of Staff*. Vol. 2, 1947–49. Wilmington, Del.: Glazier, 1979.

Congressional Quarterly, *Congress and the Nation, 1945–1964: A Review of Government and Politics in the Postwar Years*. Washington, D.C.: Congressional Quarterly, 1965.

Converse, Phillip E. "The Nature of Belief Systems in Mass Publics." In David A. Apter, ed., *Ideology and Discontent*. London: Free Press, 1964.

Coser, Lewis A. *The Functions of Social Conflict*. Glencoe, Ill.: Free Press, 1956.

Cotton, James, and Ian Neary, eds. *The Korean War in History*. Atlantic Highlands, N.J.: Humanities Press International, 1989.

Craig, Gordon A., and Alexander L. George. *Force and Statecraft: Diplomatic Problems of Our Time.* 2d ed. New York: Oxford University Press, 1990.

Cumings, Bruce. *Origins of the Korean War.* Vol. 2, *The Roaring of the Cataract, 1947–50.* Princeton, N.J.: Princeton University Press, 1992.

_____, ed., *Child of Conflict: The Korean-American Relationship, 1943–53.* Seattle: University of Washington Press, 1983.

Dalvi, J. P. *Himalayan Blunder: The Curtain-raiser to the Sino-Indian War of 1962.* Bombay: Thacker, 1969.

David, Steven R. "Why the Third World Matters." *International Security* (Summer 1989): 50–85.

Desch, Michael C. "The Keys That Lock Up the World: Identifying America's Interests in the Periphery." *International Security* (Summer 1989): 86–121.

Deutscher, Isaac. *Russia, China and the West: A Contemporary Chronicle, 1953–1966.* Ed. Fred Halliday. London: Oxford University Press, 1970.

Dingman, Roger. "Atomic Diplomacy during the Korean War." *International Security* (Winter 1988/89): pp. 50–91.

Divine, Robert A. *Foreign Policy and U.S. Presidential Elections.* New York: New Viewpoints, 1974.

Dmytryshyn, Basil. *The USSR: A Concise History.* 3d. ed. New York: Scribner's, 1978.

Documents on German Foreign Policy, 1918–1945, From the Archives of the German Foreign Ministry. Washington, D.C.: U.S. Government Printing Office, 1949–1960.

Doenecke, Justus D. Not to the Swift: The Old Isolationists in the Cold *War Era.* Lewisburg, Penn.: Bucknell University Press, 1979.

Donovan, Robert J. *Conflict and Crisis: The Presidency of Harry S Truman, 1945–48.* New York : W.W. Norton, 1977.

_____. "Truman's Perspective." In Francis H. Heller, ed. *Economics and the Truman Administration.* Lawrence, Ka.: Regents Press of Kansas, 1981.

_____. *Tumultuous Years: The Presidency of Harry S Truman, 1949–53.* New York: W. W. Norton, 1982.

Downs, Anthony. *An Economic Theory of Democracy.* New York: Harper, 1957.

Doyle, Michael. "Three Faces of Realism." Unpublished manuscript, 1989.

Dutt, Vidya Prakash. *China and the World: An Analysis of Communist China's Foreign Policy.* New York and Washington, D.C.: Frederick A. Praeger, 1966.

Edelstein, Michael. "What Price Cold War? Military Spending and Private Investment in the U.S., 1946–1979." *Cambridge Journal of Economics* (Dec. 1990): 421–437.

Eisenhower, Dwight D. *The White House Years: Mandate for Change 1953–56.* Garden City, N.Y.: Doubleday, 1963.

Eliades, George C. "Once More unto the Breach: Eisenhower, Dulles, and Public Opinion during the Offshore Islands Crisis of 1958." *Journal of American–East Asian Relations* (Winter 1993): 343–367.

Ellison, Herbert J., ed. *The Sino-Soviet Conflict: A Global Perspective.* Seattle: University of Washington Press, 1982.

Evans, Peter B., Dietrich Rueschemeyer, and Theda Skocpol, eds. *Bringing the State Back In.* Cambridge, Eng.: Cambridge University Press, 1985.

Evans, Peter B., Harold K. Jacobson, and Robert D. Putnam, eds. *Double-Edged Diplomacy: International Bargaining and Domestic Politics.* Berkeley, Calif.: University of California Press, 1993.

Farrar, Peter N. "A Pause for Negotiations: The British Buffer Plan of November, 1950." In James Cotton and Ian Neary, *The Korean War in History.* Atlantic Highlands, N.J.: Humanities Press International, 1989.

Feaver, John H. "The China Aid Bill of 1948: Limited Assistance as a Cold War Strategy." *Diplomatic History* (Spring 1981): 107–120.

Ferrell, Robert. *Harry S. Truman and the Modern American Presidency.* Boston: Little, Brown, 1983.

Ferris, John Robert. *Men, Money and Diplomacy: The Evolution of British Strategic Policy, 1919–1926.* Ithaca, N.Y.: Cornell University Press, 1989.

Finkelstein, David M. *Washington's Taiwan Dilemma, 1949–50: From Abandonment to Salvation.* Fairfax, Va: George Mason University Press, 1993.

Fischer, Fritz. *War of Illusions: German Policies from 1911 to 1914.* New York: W.W. Norton, 1975.

Foot, Rosemary. "Making Known the Unknown War: Policy Analysis of the Korean Conflict in the Last Decade." *Diplomatic History* (Summer 1991): 411–431.

———. "Nuclear Coercion and the Ending of the Korean Conflict." *International Security* (Winter 1988/89): 92–112.

———. *A Substitute for Victory: The Politics of Peacemaking at the Korean Armistice Talks.* Ithaca, N.Y.: Cornell University Press, 1990.

———. *The Wrong War: American Policy and the Dimensions of the Korean Conflict, 1950–1953.* Ithaca, N.Y.: Cornell University Press, 1985.

Fox, William T. R. "E. H. Carr and Political Realism: Vision and Revision." *Review of International Studies* (Jan. 1985): 1–3.

———. *The Super-Powers.* New York: Harcourt, Brace, 1944.

Freeland, Richard M. *The Truman Doctrine and the Origins of McCarthyism: Foreign Policy, Domestic Politics, and Internal Security, 1946–48.* New York: Shocken Books, 1974.

Frey, Frederick W. "The Problem of Actor Designation in Political Analysis." *Comparative Politics* (Jan. 1985): 127–152.

Funk, Arthur Layton. *The Politics of TORCH: The Allied Landings and the Algiers Putsch, 1942.* Lawrence: University of Kansas Press, 1974.

Gaddis, John Lewis. "The Emerging Post-Revisionist Synthesis on the Origins of the Cold War." *Diplomatic History* (Summer 1983): 171–190.

———. "Harry S Truman and the Origins of Containment." In Frank J. Merli and Theodore A. Wilson, eds., *Makers of American Diplomacy: From Benjamin Franklin to Henry Kissinger.* New York: Scribner's, 1974.

———. *The Long Peace: Inquiries into the History of the Cold War.* New York: Oxford University Press, 1987.

———. *Strategies of Containment: A Critical Appraisal of Postwar American National Security Policy.* New York: Oxford University Press, 1982.

———. *The United States and the Origins of the Cold War: 1941–1947.* New York: Columbia University Press, 1972.

_____. "Was the Truman Doctrine a Real Turning Point?" *Foreign Affairs* (Jan. 1974): 386–402

Gardner, Richard. *Sterling-Dollar Diplomacy in Current Perspective: The Origins and Prospects of Our International Economic Order.* New York: Columbia University Press, 1980.

Garrett, Banning. "The Strategic Basis of Learning in U.S. Policy toward China, 1949–88." In George W. Breslauer and Philip E. Tetlock, eds., *Learning in U.S. and Soviet Foreign Policy.* Boulder, Colo: Westview Press, 1991.

Garthoff, Raymond L. *Detente and Confrontation: American-Soviet Relations from Nixon to Reagan.* Washington, D.C.: Brookings Institution, 1985.

Garver, John. "Polemics, Paradigms, Responsibility, and the Origins of the U.S.-PRC Confrontation in the 1950s." *Journal of American–East Asian Relations* (Spring 1994): 1–34.

George, Alexander L., and Richard Smoke. "Domestic Constraints on Regime Change in U.S. Foreign Policy: The Need for Policy Legitimacy." In Ole R. Holsti, Randolph S. Siverson, and Alexander L. George, eds., *Change in the International System.* Boulder, Colo.: Westview Press, 1980.

_____. *Deterrence in American Foreign Policy: Theory and Practice.* New York: Columbia University Press, 1974.

Gershenkron, Alexander. *Economic Backwardness in Historical Perspective: A Book of Essays.* Cambridge, Mass: Belknap Press of Harvard University Press, 1962.

Giglio, James N., and Greg G. Thielen. *Truman in Cartoon and Caricature.* Ames: Iowa State University Press, 1984.

Gilpin, Robert. *War and Change in International Politics.* Cambridge, Eng.: Cambridge University Press, 1981.

Glunin, V. I., A. M. Grigoriev, et al. *The Recent History of China 1917–1970.* Moscow, 1972.

Goldstein, Avery. *From Bandwagon to Balance-of-Power Politics: Structural Constraints and Politics in China, 1949–1978.* Stanford, Calif.: Stanford University Press, 1991.

Goldstein, Steven M. "Chinese Communist Policy toward the United States: Opportunities and Constraints, 1944–50." In Dorothy Borg and Waldo Heinrichs, eds., *Uncertain Years: Chinese-American Relations, 1947–50.* New York: Columbia University Press, 1980.

_____. "Sino-American Relations, 1948–50: Lost Chance or No Chance?" In Yuan Ming and Harry Harding, eds., *Sino-American Relations 1945–55: A Joint Assessment of a Critical Decade.* Wilmington, Del.: Scholarly Resources, 1989.

Goncharov, Sergei N. "Stalin's Dialogue with Mao Zedong." *Journal of Northeast Asian Studies* (Winter 1991–92): 45–76.

Goncharov, Sergei N., John Wilson Lewis, and Xue Litai. *Uncertain Partners: Stalin, Mao and the Korean War.* Stanford, Calif.: Stanford University Press, 1993.

Gordon, Michael. "Domestic Conflict and the Origins of the First World War: The British and the German Cases." *Journal of Modern History* (June 1974): 191–226.

Gourevitch, Peter. *Politics in Hard Times: Comparative Responses to International Economic Crises.* Ithaca, N.Y.: Cornell University Press, 1986.

_____. "The Second Image Reversed: The International Sources of Domestic Politics." *International Organization* (Autumn 1978): 881–912.

Gowa, Joanne. "Bipolarity, Multipolarity and Free Trade." *American Political Science Review* (Dec. 1989): 1245–1256.

Graebner, Norman. *The New Isolationism: A Study in Politics and Foreign Policy since 1950.* New York: Ronald Press, 1956.

Green, Marshall, John H. Holdridge, and William N. Stokes. *War and Peace with China: First-hand Experiences in the Foreign Service of the United States.* Bethesda, Md.: DACOR Press, 1994.

Greenfield, Kent Roberts. *American Strategy in World War II: A Reconsideration.* Malabar, Fla.: Krieger, 1982.

Griffith, William E. *The Sino-Soviet Rift.* Cambridge, Mass.: MIT Press, 1964.

Griffiths, Franklin. "The Sources of American Conduct: Soviet Perspectives and Their Policy Implications." *International Security* (Fall 1984): 3–50.

Gurr, Ted R., ed. *Handbook of Political Conflict: Theory and Research.* New York: Free Press, 1980.

Gurr, Ted R., and Raymond Duvall. "Civil Conflict in the 1960's: A Reciprocal Theoretical System with Parameter Estimates." *Comparative Political Studies* (July 1973): 135–170.

Gurtov, Melvin. *The United States against the Third World: Antinationalism and Intervention.* New York: Praeger, 1974.

Gurtov, Melvin, and Byong-Moo Hwang. *China under Threat: The Politics of Strategy and Diplomacy.* Baltimore: Johns Hopkins University Press, 1980.

Haas, Ernest B., and Allen S. Whiting. *Dynamics of International Relations.* New York: McGraw-Hill, 1956.

Haggard, Stephen. "The Institutional Foundations of Hegemony: Explaining the Reciprocal Trade Agreement of 1934." In G. John Ikenberry, David A. Lake, and Michael Mastanduno, eds., *The State and American Economic Policy.* Ithaca, N.Y.: Cornell University Press, 1988.

Halliday, Jon. "Air Operations in Korea: The Soviet Side of the Story." In William J. Williams, *A Revolutionary War: Korea and the Transformation of the Postwar World.* Chicago: Imprint Publications, 1993.

_____. "A Secret War." *Far Eastern Economic Review* (Apr. 22, 1993): 32–36.

Halperin, Morton H. "The Decision to Deploy the ABM: Bureaucratic and Domestic Politics in the Johnson Administration." *World Politics* (Oct. 1972): 62–95.

_____. *Limited War in the Nuclear Age.* New York: Wiley, 1963.

_____. "The 1958 Taiwan Straits Crisis." Rand Research Memorandum. Santa Monica, Calif.: Rand Corporation, circa 1966.

_____, ed. *Sino-Soviet Relations and Arms Control.* Cambridge, Mass.: MIT Press, 1967.

Halperin, Morton H., and Tang Tsou. "The 1958 Quemoy Crisis." In Morton Halperin, ed., *Sino-Soviet Relations and Arms Control.* Cambridge, Mass.: MIT Press, 1967.

Hammond, Paul Y. "NSC 68: Prologue to Rearmament." In Warner S. Schilling, Paul Y. Hammond, and Glenn H. Snyder, *Strategy, Politics and Defense Budgets.* New York: Columbia University Press, 1962.

Hao Yufan and Zhai Zhihai. "China's Decision to Enter the Korean War: History Revisited." *China Quarterly* (Mar. 1990): 94–115.

Harding, Harry, ed., *China's Foreign Relations in the 1980s.* New Haven, Conn.: Yale University Press, 1984.

Hartmann, Susan M. *Truman and the 80th Congress.* Columbia: University of Missouri Press, 1971.

Hazlewood, Leo. "Diversion Mechanisms and Encapsulation Processes: The Domestic Conflict–Foreign Conflict Hypothesis Reconsidered." In Patrick G. McGowan, ed. *Sage International Yearbook of Foreign Policy Studies.* Beverly Hills, Calif.: Sage, 1975.

———. "Externalizing Systemic Stress: International Conflict as Adaptive Behavior." In Jonathan Wildenfield, ed. *Conflict Behavior and Linkage Politics.* New York: McKay, 1973.

He Di. "The Evolution of the People's Republic of China's Policy toward the Offshore Islands (Quemoy, Matsu)." In Warren I. Cohen and Akira Iriye, eds., *The Great Powers in East Asia: 1953–60.* New York: Columbia University Press: 1990.

———. "The Last Campaign to Unify China: The CCP's Unmaterialized Plan to Liberate Taiwan." *Chinese Historians* (Spring 1992): 1–16.

Hehir, Bryan J. "The Politics and Ethics of Intervention." In *Centerpiece: Newsletter of the Center for International Affairs, Harvard University* (Autumn 1994): 4–5.

Heller, Francis H., ed. *Economics and the Truman Administration.* Lawrence: Regents Press of Kansas, 1981.

Hero, Alfred O. *The Southerner in World Affairs.* Baton Rouge: Louisiana State University Press, 1965.

Higgs, Robert. "The Cold War Economy: Opportunity Costs, Ideology and the Politics of Crisis." Seattle University. Unpublished manuscript.

Hilsman, Roger. *The Politics of Policy-Making in Defense and Foreign Affairs: Conceptual Models and Bureaucratic Politics.* Englewood Cliffs, N.J.: Prentice-Hall, 1987.

———. *To Move a Nation: The Politics of Foreign Policy in the Administration of John F. Kennedy.* Garden City, N.Y.: Doubleday, 1967.

Hogan, Michael. *The Marshall Plan: America, Britain, and the Reconstruction of Western Europe, 1947–52.* New York: Cambridge University Press, 1987.

Holloway, David. *Stalin and the Bomb: The Soviet Union and Atomic Energy, 1939–56.* New Haven, Conn.: Yale University Press, 1994.

Hopf, Ted. "Polarity, the Offense-Defense Balance, and War." *American Political Science Review* (June 1991): 475–493.

Howard, Michael. *The Continental Commitment: The Dilemma of British Defense Policy in the Era of the Two World Wars.* London: Maurice Temple Smith, 1972.

Howe, Jonathan Trumbull. *Multicrises: Sea Power and Global Politics in the Missile Age.* Cambridge, Mass.: MIT Press, 1971.

Hsiao, Katherine Huang. *The Government Budget and Fiscal Policy in Mainland China.* Taipei, ROC: Chung-Hua Institution for Economic Research, 1987.

Hsieh, Alice Langley. *Communist China's Strategy in the Nuclear Era.* Englewood Cliffs, N.J.: Prentice-Hall, 1962.

Hunt, Michael H. "Beijing and the Korea Crisis." *Political Science Quarterly* (Fall 1992): 453–478.

———. "Mao Tse-tung and the Issue of Accommodation with the United States, 1948–1950." In Dorothy Borg and Waldo Heinrichs, eds., *Uncertain Years: Chinese American Relations, 1947–1950.* New York: Columbia University Press, 1980).

Huntington, Samuel P. *The Common Defense: Strategic Programs in National Politics.* New York: Columbia University Press, 1961.

———. *Political Order in Changing Societies.* New Haven, Conn.: Yale University Press, 1968.

Huth, Paul K. *Extended Deterrence and the Prevention of War.* New Haven, Conn.: Yale University Press, 1988.

Huth, Paul K., and Bruce Russett. "Testing Deterrence Theory: Rigor Makes a Difference." *World Politics* (July 1990): 466–501.

Ikenberry, G. John, David A. Lake, and Michael Mastanduno, eds. *The State and American Foreign Policy.* Ithaca, N.Y.: Cornell University Press, 1988.

Isaacson, Walter, and Evan Thomas. *The Wise Men: Six Friends and the World They Made.* New York: Simon and Schuster, 1986.

Jervis, Robert. "Cooperation under the Security Dilemma." *World Politics* (Jan. 1978): 167–214.

———. "Domino Beliefs and Strategic Behavior." In Robert Jervis and Jack Snyder, eds., *Dominoes and Bandwagons: Strategic Beliefs and Great Power Competition in the Eurasian Rimland.* Oxford, Eng.: Oxford University Press, 1991.

———. "The Impact of the Korean War on the Cold War." *Journal of Conflict Resolution* (Dec. 1980): 563–592.

———. *Perception and Misperception in International Politics.* Princeton, N.J.: Princeton University Press, 1976.

Johnson, Chalmers, ed. *Ideology and Politics in Contemporary China.* Seattle: University of Washington Press, 1973.

———. *Peasant Nationalism and Communist Power: The Emergence of Revolutionary China.* Stanford, Calif.: Stanford University Press, 1962.

Jones, Joseph Marion. *The Fifteen Weeks: February 21–June 5, 1947.* New York: Viking Press, 1955.

Kahn, Alfred A. "The Tyranny of Small Decisions: Market Failures, Imperfections, and the Limits of Econometrics." In Bruce Russett, ed., *Economic Theories of International Relations.* Chicago: Markham Publications, 1968.

Kalicki, Jan. *The Patterns of Sino-American Crises: Political-Military Interactions in the 1950s.* London: Cambridge University Press, 1975.

Kaplan, Lawrence S. *A Community of Interests: NATO and the Military Assistance Program: 1948–51.* Washington, D.C.: Office of the Secretary of Defense, Historical Office, 1980.

Kataoka, Tetsuya. *Resistance and Revolution in China: The Communists and the Second United Front.* Berkeley: University of California Press, 1974.

Katzenstein, Peter, ed. *Between Power and Plenty: Foreign Economic Politics of Advanced Industrial States.* Madison: University of Wisconsin Press, 1978.

Kaufman, Burton I. *The Korean War: Challenges in Crisis, Credibility and Command.* New York: Alfred A. Knopf, 1986.

Kendrick, M. Slade. *A Century and a Half of Federal Expenditures.* Occasional Paper 48. New York: National Bureau of Economic Research, 1955.

Kennan, George F. *Memoirs.* Vols. 1 and 2. Boston: Little, Brown, 1972.

Kennedy, Paul. *The Rise and Fall of the Great Powers.* New York: Random House, 1987.

Keohane, Robert. *After Hegemony: Cooperation and Discord in the World Political Economy.* Princeton, N.J.: Princeton University Press, 1984.

———. "The Theory of Hegemonic Stability and Changes in International Economic Regimes, 1967–77." In Ole Holsti, Randolph Siverson, and Alexander George, eds., *Change in the International System.* Boulder, Colo.: Westview Press, 1980.

———. "Theory of World Politics: Structural Realism and Beyond." In Keohane, ed., *Neorealism and Its Critics.* New York: Columbia University Press, 1986.

Kepley, David. *The Collapse of the Middle Way: Senate Republicans and Bipartisan Foreign Policy, 1948–52.* New York: Greenwood Press, 1988.

Key, V. O., Jr. *Public Opinion and American Democracy.* New York: Alfred A. Knopf, 1961.

Khong, Yuen Foong. *Analogies at War: Korea, Munich, Dien Bien Phu and the Vietnam Decisions of 1965.* Princeton, N.J.: Princeton University Press, 1992.

Kim, Samuel S., ed. *China and the World: Chinese Foreign Relations in the Post–Cold War Era,* 1st and 3d eds. Boulder, Colo.: Westview Press, 1984 and 1994.

Kindleberger, Charles. *The World in Depression, 1929–1939.* Berkeley: University of California Press, 1973.

King, Gary, Robert O. Keohane, and Sidney Verba. *Designing Social Inquiry: Scientific Inference in Qualitative Research.* Princeton, N.J.: Princeton University Press, 1994.

Kissinger, Henry. *The Troubled Partnership: A Reappraisal of the Atlantic Alliance.* New York: McGraw-Hill, 1965.

Knorr, Klauss. *The War Potential of Nations.* Princeton, N.J.: Princeton University Press, 1956.

Koen, Ross Y. *The China Lobby in American Politics.* New York: Harper and Row, 1974.

Kolko, Gabriel. *The Politics of War: The World and United States Foreign Policy, 1943–45.* New York: Random House, 1968.

Kolko, Joyce and Gabriel. *The Limits of Power: The World and United States Foreign Policy, 1945–54.* New York: Harper and Row, 1968.

Krasner, Stephen D. "Are Bureaucracies Important? (or Allison Wonderland)" *Foreign Policy* (Summer 1972): 159–179.

———. *Defending the National Interest: Raw Materials Investments and U.S. Foreign Policy.* Princeton, N.J.: Princeton University Press, 1978.

———. "State Power and the Structure of International Trade." *World Politics* (Apr. 1976): 317–347.

Krieger, Leonard, and Fritz Stern, eds. *The Responsibility of Power.* Garden City, N.Y.: Doubleday, 1967.

Kugler, Jacek, and William Domke. "Assessing Stable Deterrence." In Jacek

Kugler and Frank C. Zagare, *Exploring the Stability of Deterrence*. Boulder, Colo.: Lynne Rienner, 1987.

———. "Comparing the Strength of Nations." *Comparative Political Studies* (Apr. 1986): 39–69.

Kugler, Jacek, and Frank C. Zagare. *Exploring the Stability of Deterrence*. Boulder, Colo: Lynne Rienner, 1987.

Kusnitz, Leonard A. *Public Opinion and Foreign Policy: America's China Policy 1949–79*. Westport, Conn.: Greenwood Press, 1984.

LaFeber, Walter. "American Policy Makers, Public Opinion, and the Outbreak of the Cold War: 1945–50." In Yonosuke Nagai and Akira Iriye, eds., *The Origins of the Cold War in Asia*. New York: Columbia University Press, 1977.

———. *America, Russia and the Cold War, 1945–92*. 7th ed. New York: McGraw-Hill, 1993.

Lafore, Laurence. *The Long Fuse: An Interpretation of the Origins of World War I*. 2d ed. New York: J. B. Lippincott, 1971.

Lake, David. "International Economic Structures and American Foreign Economic Policy, 1887–1934." *World Politics* (July 1983): 517–543.

———. "The State and American Trade Strategy in the Pre-Hegemonic Era." In G. John Ikenberry, David A. Lake, and Michael Mastanduno, eds., *The State and American Foreign Economic Policy*. Ithaca, N.Y.: Cornell University Press, 1988.

Lamborn, Alan C. *The Price of Power: Risk and Foreign Policy in Britain, France, and Germany*. Boston: Unwin Hyman, 1991.

Laqueur, Walter. "Revolution." *International Encyclopedia of the Social Sciences*. Vol. 13. New York: Macmillan, 1968.

Lardy, Nicholas R. "Centralization and Decentralization in China's Fiscal Management." *China Quarterly* (Mar. 1975): 25–60.

Larson, Deborah Welch. *Origins of Containment: A Psychological Explanation*. Princeton, N.J.: Princeton University Press, 1985.

Lebow, Richard Ned. *Between Peace and War: The Nature of International Crises*. Baltimore, Md.: Johns Hopkins University Press, 1981.

Lebow, Richard Ned, and Janice Gross Stein. "Deterrence: The Elusive Dependent Variable," *World Politics* (Apr. 1990): 336–369.

Leffler, Melvyn. *A Preponderance of Power: National Security, the Truman Administration, and the Cold War*. Stanford, Calif.: Stanford University Press, 1992.

———. "Was 1947 a Turning Point in American Foreign Policy?" In L. Carl Brown, ed., *Centerstage: American Diplomacy since World War II*. New York: Holmes and Meier, 1990.

Lenin, V. I. *Imperialism*. New York: International Publishers, 1939.

Lerche, Charles O., Jr. *The Uncertain South: Its Changing Patterns of Politics in Foreign Policy*. Chicago: Quadrangle Books, 1964.

Levi, Margaret. *Of Rule and Revenue*. Berkeley: University of California Press, 1988.

Levy, Jack S. "The Diversionary Theory of War: A Critique." In Manus I. Midlarsky, ed., *The Handbook of War Studies*. Boston: Unwin Hyman, 1989.

Lewis, John Wilson, and Xue Litai. *China Builds the Bomb*. Stanford, Calif.: Stanford University Press, 1988.

———. *China's Strategic Seapower: The Politics of Force Modernization in the Nuclear Age*. Stanford, Calif.: Stanford University Press, 1994.

Lewis, John Wilson, and Hua Di. "China's Ballistic Missile Programs: Technologies, Strategies, Goals." *International Security* (Fall 1992): 5–40.

Liao, Kuang-sheng. *Antiforeignism and Modernization in China, 1860–1980*. Hong Kong: Chinese University of Hong Kong, 1990.

Lieberthal, Kenneth. "Domestic Politics and Foreign Policy." In Harry Harding, ed., *China's Foreign Relations in the 1980s*. New Haven, Conn.: Yale University Press, 1984.

Lindblom, Charles. "Science of Muddling Through." *Public Administration* (Spring 1959): 79–88.

Li Xiaobing, Chen Jian, and David L. Wilson, translators and annotators. "Mao Zedong's Handling of the Taiwan Straits Crisis of 1958: Chinese Recollections and Documents." *Cold War International History Project Bulletin* 6–7 (Winter 1995–96): 208–231.

Li Yuanchao. "The Politics of Artillery Shelling: A Study of the Taiwan Strait Crises." *Beijing Review* (Sept. 7, 1992): 36–38.

Lowi, Theodore J. *The End of Liberalism: Ideology, Policy and the Crisis of Public Authority*. New York: W. W. Norton, 1969.

———. *The End of Liberalism: The Second Republic of the United States*. 2d ed. New York: W. W. Norton, 1979.

MacArthur, Douglas. *Reminiscences*. New York: McGraw-Hill, 1964.

MacFarquhar, Roderick. *The Origins of the Cultural Revolution*. Vol. 2, *The Great Leap Forward, 1958–60*. New York: Columbia University Press, 1983.

McGovern, James. *To the Yalu: From the Chinese Invasion of Korea to MacArthur's Dismissal*. New York: Morrow, 1972.

McKeown, Timothy J. "The Foreign Policy of a Declining Power." *International Organization* (Spring 1991): 257–279.

McLellan, David. *Dean Acheson: State Department Years*. New York: Dodd, Mead, 1976.

Mansourov, Alexandre Y. "Stalin, Mao, Kim, and China's Decision to Enter the Korean War, September 16–October 15, 1950: New Evidence from the Russian Archives." *Cold War International History Project Bulletin* 6–7 (Winter 1995–96): 94–119.

March, James G. "The Power of Power." In David Easton, ed., *Varieties of Political Theory*. Englewood Cliffs, N.J.: Prentice-Hall, 1966.

Mastanduno, Michael. *Economic Containment: CoCom and the Politics of East-West Trade*. Ithaca, N.Y.: Cornell University Press, 1992.

Maxwell, Neville. *India's China War*. London: Jonathan Cape, 1970.

May, Ernest R. *"Lessons" of the Past: The Use and Misuse of History in American Foreign Policy*. New York: Oxford University Press, 1973.

———. *The Truman Administration and China: 1945–49*. Philadelphia: J. B. Lippincott, 1975.

Mayer, Arno J. "Domestic Causes of the First World War." In Leonard Krieger and Fritz Stern, eds., *The Responsibility of Power*. Garden City, N.Y.: Doubleday, 1967.

———. "Industrial Crises and War since 1870." In C. L. Bertrand, ed., *Revolutionary Situations in Europe 1917–22*. Montreal: Interuniversity Centre for European Studies, 1977.

———. "Internal Causes and Purposes of War in Europe, 1870–1956: A Research Assignment." *Journal of Modern History* (Sept. 1969): 291–303.

Mayers, David. *Cracking the Monolith: U.S. Policy toward the Sino-Soviet Alliance, 1949–55*. Baton Rouge: Louisianna State University Press, 1986.

———. *George Kennan and the Dilemmas of U.S. Foreign Policy*. New York: Oxford University Press, 1988.

Mee, Charles S. *The Marshall Plan: The Launching of the Pax Americana*. New York: Simon and Schuster, 1984.

Melby, John F. *The Mandate of Heaven: Record of a Civil War, China, 1945–49*. Toronto: University of Toronto Press, 1968.

Mercer, Jonathan. *Reputation in International Politics*. Ithaca, N.Y.: Cornell University Press, 1995.

Merli, Frank J., and Theodore A. Wilson, eds. *Makers of American Diplomacy: From Benjamin Franklin to Henry Kissinger*. New York: Scribner's, 1974.

Midlarsky, M. I. *The Onset of World War*. Boston: Unwin Hyman, 1988.

———, ed. *The Handbook of War Studies*. Boston: Unwin Hyman, 1989.

Millis, Walter, ed., with the collaboration of E. S. Duffield. *The Forrestal Diaries*. New York: Viking, 1951.

Milner, Helen. "Trading Places: Industries for Free Trade." *World Politics* (April 1988): 350–376.

Mineo, Nakajima. "The Sino-Soviet Confrontation in Historical Perspective." In Yonosuke Nagai and Akira Iriye, eds., *The Origins of the Cold War in Asia*. New York: Columbia University Press, 1977.

Miscamble, Wilson D. *George F. Kennan and the Making of American Foreign Policy, 1947–50*. Princeton, N.J.: Princeton University Press, 1992.

Morgenthau, Hans J. *Politics among Nations: The Struggle for Power and Peace*. 4th ed. New York: Alfred A. Knopf, 1967.

Morwood, William. *Duel for the Middle Kingdom: The Struggle between Chiang Kai-shek and Mao Tse-tung for Control of China*. New York: Everest House, 1980.

Nagai, Yonosuke, and Akira Iriye, eds. *The Origins of the Cold War in Asia*. New York: Columbia University Press, 1977.

Neustadt, Richard. *Presidential Power: The Politics of Leadership from FDR to Carter*. New York: Wiley, 1980.

Nitze, Paul H. *From Hiroshima to Glasnost: At the Center of Decision*. New York: Grove Weidenfeld, 1989.

North, Douglass C. *Structure and Change in Economic History*. New York: W. W. Norton, 1981.

Olson, Mancur. *The Logic of Collective Action: Public Goods and the Theory of Groups*. Cambridge, Mass.: Harvard University Press, 1965.

———. *The Rise and Decline of Nations: Economic Growth, Stagflation, and Social Rigidities*. New Haven, Conn.: Yale University Press, 1982.

Organski, A.F.K., and Jacek Kugler. *The War Ledger*. Chicago: University of Chicago Press, 1980.

Orme, John. "Deterrence Failures: A Second Look." *International Security* (Spring 1987): 96–124.

Osgood, Robert Endicott. *Limited War: The Challenge to American Strategy*. Chicago: University of Chicago Press, 1957.

Ostrom, C. W., and B. L. Job. "The President and the Political Use of Force." In *American Political Science Review* (June 1986): 541–566.

Page, Benjamin I., and Robert Y. Shapiro. *The Rational Public: Fifty Years of Trends in Americans' Policy Preferences*. Chicago: University of Chicago Press, 1992.

Paige, Glenn. *The Korean Decision, June 24–30, 1950*. New York: Free Press, 1968.

Paterson, Thomas. "If Europe, Why Not China?" *Prologue* (Spring 1981): 19–38.

Pollack, Jonathan D. "The Korean War and Sino-American Relations." In Yuan Ming and Harry Harding, eds., *Sino-American Relations 1945–55: A Joint Reassessment of a Decade*. Wilmington, Del.: Scholarly Resources, 1989.

———. "Perception and Action in Chinese Foreign Policy." Vol. 1, "The Quemoy Decision." Ph.D. diss., University of Michigan, 1976.

Pollard, Robert A. *Economic Security and the Origins of the Cold War: 1945–50*. New York: Columbia University Press, 1985.

Posen, Barry. *The Sources of Military Doctrine: France, Britain, and Germany between the World Wars*. Ithaca, N.Y.: Cornell University Press, 1984.

Purifoy, Lewis McCarroll. *Harry Truman's China Policy: McCarthyism and the Diplomacy of Hysteria, 1947–51*. N.Y.: New Viewpoints, 1976.

Putnam, Robert. "Diplomacy and Domestic Politics: The Logic of Two-Level Games." *International Organization* (Summer 1988): 427–460.

Quattrone, George, and Amos Tversky. "Contrasting Rational and Psychological Analyses of Political Choice." *American Political Science Review* (Sept. 1988): 719–736.

Rearden, Steven L. *History of the Office of the Secretary of Defense*. Vol. 1, *The Formative Years, 1947–50*. Washington, D.C.: History Office, Office of the Secretary of Defense, 1984.

Rees, David. *Korea: The Limited War*. London: Macmillan, 1964.

Reiman, Michael. *The Birth of Stalinism: The USSR on the Eve of the "Second Revolution."* Trans. George Saunders. Bloomington: Indiana University Press, 1987.

Richter, James. "Action and Reaction in Soviet Foreign policy." Ph.D. diss., University of California, Berkeley, 1989.

Riskin, Carl. *China's Political Economy: The Quest for Development since 1949*. Oxford, Eng.: Oxford University Press, 1987.

Rockman, Bert A. "Mobilizing Political Support for U.S. National Security." *Armed Forces and Society* (Fall 1987): 17–42.

Rose, Lisle. *Roots of Tragedy: The United States and the Struggle for Asia, 1945–53*. Westport, Conn.: Greenwood Press, 1976.

Rosecrance, Richard. *Action and Reaction in World Politics*. Westport, Conn.: Greenwood Press, 1977.

Rosecrance, Richard, and Arthur Stein, eds., *The Domestic Bases of Grand Strategy*. Ithaca, N.Y.: Cornell University Press, 1993.

Ross, Robert. "International Bargaining and Domestic Politics: U.S.-China Relations since 1972." *World Politics* (Jan. 1986): 256–287.

Rousso, Alan. "Tipping the Balance of Power: The Political Economy of Intra-Alliance Trade in the Nuclear Age." Ph.D. diss., Columbia University, 1994.

Rousseau, Jean Jacques. *The Social Contract and Discourses*. Trans. G.D.H. Cole. London: J. M. Dent, 1913.

Rozas, Danny, Chen Jian, and Kathryn Weathersby, trans. "Stalin's Conversations with Chinese Leaders: Talks with Mao Zedong, December 1949–1950, and with Zhou Enlai, August–September 1952." *Cold War International History Project Bulletin* 6–7 (Winter 1995–96): 4–20, 27–29.

Rummel, R. "Dimensions of Conflict Behavior within and between Nations." *General Systems* (1963): 1–50.

Russett, Bruce. *Controlling the Sword: The Democratic Governance of National Security*. Cambridge, Mass.: Harvard University Press, 1990.

———. "Economic Decline, Electoral Pressure and the Initiation of Interstate Conflict." In C. Gochman and A. N. Sabrosky, eds., *Prisoners of War? Nation States in the Modern Era*. Lexington Mass.: D. C. Heath, 1989.

Schaller, Michael. *The United States and China in the 20th Century*. New York: Oxford University Press, 1979.

Schelling, Thomas C. *Arms and Influence*. New Haven, Conn.: Yale University Press, 1966.

Schick, Jack. *The Berlin Crisis: 1958–62*. Philadephia: University of Pennsylvania Press, 1971.

Schilling, Warner R. "The Politics of National Defense: Fiscal 1950." In Warner S. Schilling, Paul Y. Hammond, and Glenn H. Snyder, *Strategy, Politics and Defense Budgets*. New York: Columbia University Press, 1962.

Schnabel, James F., and Robert J. Watson. *The History of the Joint Chiefs of Staff: The Joint Chiefs of Staff and National Policy*. Vol. 3, *The Korean War, Part 1*. Wilmington, Del.: Glazier, 1979.

Schoenhals, Michael. *Saltationist Socialism: Mao Zedong and the Great Leap Forward, 1958*. Stockholm: JINAB, 1987.

Schuker, Stephen A. "France and the Remilitarization of the Rhineland, 1936." *French Historical Studies* (Spring 1986): 299–338.

Schurmann, Franz. *Ideology and Organization in Communist China*. Berkeley: University of California Press, 1966.

———. *The Logic of World Power: An Inquiry into the Origins, Currents, and Contradictions of World Politics*. New York: Pantheon Books, 1974.

Schweller, Randall. "Domestic Structure and Preventive War: Are Democracies More Pacific?" *World Politics* (Jan. 1992): 235–269.

———. "Hitler's Tripolar Strategy for World Conquest." In Jack Snyder and Robert Jervis, eds., *Coping with Complexity in the International System*, chap. 10. Boulder, Colo., Westview Press, 1993.

———. "Tripolarity and the Second World War." *International Studies Quarterly* (Mar. 1993): 73–103.

Segal, Gerald. *Defending China*. Oxford, Eng.: Oxford University Press, 1985.

Shapiro, Robert Y., and Benjamin I. Page. "Foreign Policy and the Rational Public." *Journal of Conflict Resolution* (June 1988): 211–47.

Sharp, Samuel. *Poland: White Eagle on a Red Field*. Cambridge, Mass.: Harvard University Press, 1953.

Sheng, Michael M. "America's Lost Chance in China? A Reappraisal of Chinese Communist Policy toward the United States before 1945." *Australian Journal of Chinese Affairs* (Jan. 1993): 135–157.

Sigal, Leon V. "The 'Rational Policy' Model and the Formosa Straits Crisis." *International Studies Quarterly* (June 1970): 121–156.

Simmel, George. *Conflict*. Trans. K. H. Wolff. Glencoe, Ill.: Free Press, 1955.

Simon, Herbert A. *Models of Bounded Rationality*, 2 vols. Cambridge, Mass.: MIT Press, 1982.

Skocpol, Theda. "Bringing the State Back In: Strategies of Analysis in Current Research." In Peter B. Evans, Dietrich Rueschemeyer, and Theda Skocpol, eds., *Bringing the State Back In*. Cambridge, Eng.: Cambridge University Press, 1985.

———. *States and Social Revolutions: A Comparative Analysis of France, Russia, and China*. Cambridge, Eng.: Cambridge University Press, 1979.

Snidal, Duncan. "The Limits of Hegemonic Stability Theory." *International Organization* (Autumn 1985): 579–614.

Snyder, Jack L. *The Ideology of the Offensive: Military Decision Making and the Disasters of 1914*. Ithaca, N.Y.: Cornell University Press, 1984.

———. *Myths of Empire: Domestic Politics and International Ambition*. Ithaca, N.Y.: Cornell University Press, 1991.

Snyder, Jack L., and Robert Jervis, eds. *Coping with Complexity in the International System*. Boulder, Colo.: Westview Press, 1993.

Solomon, Richard. *Mao's Revolution and the Chinese Political Culture*. Berkeley: University of California Press, 1971.

Spanier, John. *The Truman-MacArthur Controversy and the Korean War*. New York: W. W. Norton, 1965.

Steel, Ronald. *Walter Lippmann and the American Century*. Boston: Little, Brown, 1980.

Stein, Arthur. "Conflict and Cohesion: A Review of the Literature." *Journal of Conflict Resolution* (Mar. 1976): 143–172.

———. *The Nation at War*. Baltimore, Md.: Johns Hopkins University Press, 1978.

Stephanson, Anders. *Kennan and the Art of Foreign Policy*. Cambridge, Mass.: Harvard University Press, 1989.

Stohl, Michael. "The Nexus of Civil and International Conflict." In T. R. Gurr, ed., *Handbook of Political Conflict*. New York: Free Press, 1980.

———. "War and Domestic Political Violence: The Case of the United States 1890–1970." *Journal of Conflict Resolution* (Summer 1975): 379–416.

Stokes, William N. "War and the Threat of War." In Marshall Green, John H. Holdridge, and William N. Stokes, *War and Peace with China*. Bethesda, Md.: DACOR Press, 1994.

Stolper, Thomas. *China, Taiwan, and the Offshore Islands: Together with an Implication for Outer Mongolia and Sino-Soviet Relations.* Armonk, N.Y.: M. E. Sharpe, 1985.

Stone, I. F. *The Hidden History of the Korean War.* New York: Monthly Review Press, 1952.

Stueck, William Whitney, Jr. "The Korean War, NATO, and Rearmament." In William J. Williams, ed., *A Revolutionary War: Korea and the Transformation of the Postwar World.* Chicago: Imprint Publications, 1993.

———. *The Road to Confrontation: American Policy toward China and Korea, 1947–1950.* Chapel Hill: University of North Carolina Press, 1981.

———. *The Wedemeyer Mission: American Politics and Foreign Policy During the Cold War.* Athens: University of Georgia Press, 1984.

Sumner, William Graham. *War and Other Essays.* New Haven, Conn.: Yale University Press, 1911.

Sundquist, James L. *The Decline and Resurgence of Congress.* Washington, D.C.: Brookings Institution, 1981.

Talbott, Strobe, trans. and ed. *Khrushchev Remembers: The Last Testament.* Boston: Little, Brown: 1974.

Tatsumi, Okabe. "The Cold War and China." In Yonosuke Nagai and Akira Iriye, eds., *The Origins of the Cold War in Asia.* New York: Columbia University Press, 1977.

Taubman, William. *Stalin's American Policy: From Entente to Detente to Cold War.* New York: W. W. Norton, 1982.

Teiwes, Frederick. *Leadership, Legitimacy and Conflict in China: From a Charismatic Mao to the Politics of Succession.* Armonk, N.Y.: M. E. Sharpe, 1984.

Thomas, John R. "Soviet Behavior in the Quemoy Crisis of 1958." *Orbis* (Spring 1962): 38–64.

Thornton, Richard. *China, A Political History: 1917–80.* Boulder, Colo.: Westview Press, 1982.

Tilly, Charles, "Western State-Making and Theories of Political Transformation." In Tilly, ed., *The Formation of National States in Western Europe.* Princeton, N.J.: Princeton University Press, 1975.

Trachtenberg, Marc. "A 'Wasting Asset': American Strategy and the Shifting Nuclear Balance, 1949–1954." *International Security* (Winter 1988/89): 5–49.

Treadgold, Donald W. "Alternative Western Views of the Sino-Soviet Conflict." In Herbert J. Ellison, ed., *The Sino-Soviet Conflict.* Seattle: University of Washington Press, 1982.

Trout, Thomas B. "Rhetoric Revisited: Political Legitimation and the Cold War." *International Studies Quarterly* (Sept. 1975): 251–284.

Truman, Harry S. *Memoirs.* Vol. 2, *Years of Trial and Hope.* Garden City, N.Y.: Doubleday, 1956.

Tsebelis, George. *Nested Games in Comparative Politics.* Berkeley: University of California Press, 1990.

Tsou, Tang. *America's Failure in China: 1941–50.* Chicago: University of Chicago Press, 1963.

Tuchman, Barbara. "If Mao Had Come to Washington: An Essay in Alternatives." *Foreign Affairs* (Oct. 1972): 44–64.

Tucker, Nancy Bernkopf. *Patterns in the Dust: Chinese-American Relations and the Recognition Controversy, 1949–50.* New York: Columbia University Press, 1983.

Twining, Nathan A. *Neither Liberty Nor Safety: A Hard Look at U.S. Military Policy and Strategy.* New York: Holt, Rinehart and Winston, 1966.

Ulam, Adam B. *Expansion and Coexistence: Soviet Foreign Policy, 1917–73.* 2d ed. New York: Praeger, 1974.

Ullman, Richard. "Redefining Security." *International Security* (Summer 1983): 129–153.

Vandenberg, Arthur H., Jr. *The Private Papers of Senator Vandenberg.* Boston: Houghton-Mifflin, 1952.

Van Evera, Stephen. "Causes of War." Ph.D. diss., University of California, Berkeley, 1984.

———. "The Cult of the Offensive and the Origins of the First World War." *International Security* (Summer 1984): 58–107.

———. "Why Europe Matters, Why the Third World Doesn't." *Journal of Strategic Studies* (June 1990): 1–51.

Viner, Jacob. "Power versus Plenty as Objectives of Foreign Policy in the Seventeenth and Eighteenth Centuries." *World Politics* (Oct. 1948): 1–29.

Vogel, Ezra. *Canton under Communism: Programs and Policies in a Provincial Capital, 1949–68.* Cambridge, Mass.: Harvard University Press, 1980.

Walder, Andrew G. *Communist Neo-traditionalism: Work and Authority in Chinese Industry.* Berkeley: University of California Press, 1986.

Walt, Stephen M. "The Case for Finite Containment: Analyzing U.S. Grand Strategy." *International Security* (Summer 1989): 5–49.

———. *The Origins of Alliances.* Ithaca, N.Y.: Cornell University Press, 1987.

Waltz, Kenneth N. *Man, the State and War: A Theoretical Analysis.* New York: Columbia University Press, 1959.

———. "The Politics of Peace." *International Studies Quarterly* (Sept. 1967): 199–211.

———. "A Response to My Critics." In Robert O. Keohane, ed., *Neorealism and Its Critics.* New York: Columbia University, 1986.

———. *Theory of International Politics.* Reading, Mass: Addison-Wesley, 1979.

Ward, Michael D., and Ulrich Widmaier. "The Domestic-International Conflict Nexus: New Evidence and Old Hypotheses." *International Interactions* 9:1 (1982): 75–101.

Weathersby, Kathryn. "New Findings on the Korean War." *Cold War International History Project Bulletin* (Fall 1993): 1, 14–18.

———. "New Russian Documents on the Korean War: Introduction and Translations." *Cold War International History Project Bulletin* 6–7 (Winter 1995–96): 30–84.

———. "Soviet Aims in Korea and the Origins of the Korean War, 1945–50: New Evidence from Russian Archives." Working Paper 8, Cold War International History Project, 1993.

Weede, E. "U.S. Support for Foreign Governments or Domestic Disorder and Imperial Intervention, 1958–65." *Comparative Political Studies* (1978): 497–527.

Wells, Samuel F., Jr. "Sounding the Tocsin: NSC 68 and the Soviet Threat." *International Security* (Fall 1979): 116–158.

Westad, Odd Arne. "Rivals and Allies: Stalin, Mao, and the Chinese Civil War, January 1949." *Cold War International History Project Bulletin* 6–7 (Winter 1995–96): 219, 226–227.

Westerfield, H. Bradford. *Foreign Policy and Party Politics: Pearl Harbor to Korea.* New Haven, Conn.: Yale University Press, 1955.

Wexler, Immanuel. *The Marshall Plan Revisited: The European Recovery Program in Economic Perspective.* Westport, Conn.: Greenwood Press, 1983.

Whiting, Allen S. *China Crosses the Yalu: The Decision to Enter the Korean War.* Stanford, Calif.: Stanford University Press, 1960.

_____. "Mao, China, and the Cold War." In Yonosuke Nagai and Akira Iriye, eds., *The Origins of the Cold War in Asia.* New York: Columbia University Press, 1977.

_____. "Quemoy 1958: Mao's Miscalculations." *China Quarterly* (June 1975): 263–270.

Williams, William Appleman. *The Tragedy of American Diplomacy.* Cleveland, Ohio: World Publishing, 1959.

Wolfers, Arnold. *Discord and Collaboration: Essays on International Politics.* Baltimore, Md.: Johns Hopkins University Press, 1962.

Xu Yan. "New Materials on the Origins of the Korean War." Unpublished manuscript.

Yang Kuisong. "The Soviet Factor and the CCP's Policy toward the United States in the 1940s." *Chinese Historians* (Spring 1992): 17–34.

Young, Kenneth T. *Negotiating with the Chinese Communists: The United States Experience, 1953–1967.* New York: McGraw-Hill, 1968.

Zagoria, Donald S. *The Sino-Soviet Conflict: 1956–61.* Princeton, N.J.: Princeton University Press, 1962.

Zelman, Walter. "Chinese Intervention in the Korean War: A Bilateral Failure of Deterrence." UCLA Security Studies Project 11, 1967.

Zhang Shu Guang. *Deterrence and Strategic Culture: Chinese-American Confrontations, 1949–58.* Ithaca, N.Y.: Cornell University Press, 1992.

_____. "'Preparedness Eliminates Mishaps': The CCP's Security Concerns in 1949–50 and the Origins of Sino-American Confrontation." *Journal of American–East Asian Relations* (Spring 1992): 42–72.

Zhang Shu Guang and Chen Jian, translators and annotators. "The Emerging Dispute between Beijing and Moscow: Ten Newly Available Chinese Documents." *Cold War International History Project Bulletin* 6–7 (Winter 1995–96): 148–169.

Zhao Quansheng. "Micro-Macro Linkages in the Study of Chinese Foreign Policy." Unpublished manuscript.

Zhu Jiasui. "Soviet Strategic Inferiority Damaged the Sino-Soviet Alliance." University of Hawaii at Manoa, 1992. Unpublished manuscript.

Zinnes, Dina. *Contemporary Research in International Relations: A Perspective and a Critical Appraisal.* New York: Free Press, 1976.

Zubok, Vladislav. "'To Hell with Yalta!'—Stalin Opts for a New Status Quo."

Cold War International History Project Bulletin 6–7 (Winter 1995–96): 24–27.

_____. "Khrushchev's Nuclear Promise to Beijing during the 1958 Crisis." *Cold War International History Project Bulletin* 6–7 (Winter 1995–96): 219, 226–227.

Acheson, Dean, 8, 24, 30, 62, 72, 72n, 77–137 passim, 175, 180, 189; and China policy, 62, 77–137, 138, 242; and Congress, 52, 82–83, 88–90, 93–96, 109–113; and Delta Conference speech (1947), 53; and ERP (*see* ERP); and grand strategy, 78, 82, 113; and Greece-Turkey Crisis (1947), 49–50; and Korea, 116, 152; and Korean War, 133–137, 154, 156, 166n, 169n, 180–192 (*see also* Korean War); and MAP (*see* MAP); and NSC-68, 124–126; and Press Club Speech (1950), 113; and proposed Stuart mission to Beiping (1949), 86–88; and recognition issue, 97–115, 117, 120–122 (*see also* recognition issue); and Sino-Soviet relations, 78; and Taiwan, 106–109, 117–122, 128–137, 179; and Truman-Attlee talks (Dec. 1950), 181–192; and Truman Doctrine, 52, 53; as "two-level player," 77. *See also* State Department; Truman administration; entries under U.S.
Air Force (U.S.), 44, 47, 48, 171
alignment. *See* alliances
alliances, 7, 14, 30, 37, 124, 139, 206, 216, 225, 245. *See also* Mutual Defense Treaty; NATO; SEATO; Sino-Soviet relations
Almond, Gabriel, 17n, 256–258
America first. *See* isolationism
Amoy. *See* Xiamen
anticommunism, 5, 8, 51, 52, 54, 57, 58, 62, 68–70, 72–73, 76, 78–80, 90, 95, 99, 106, 111–115, 121, 125, 127, 137, 179, 243. *See also* Congress; McCarthyism; media; public opinion (U.S.); Truman administration
anti-Japanese War, 9, 205, 216, 218, 221–222, 250
anti-Rightist campaign (1957), 237
arms control, 23n
Army (U.S.), 47, 271–272
"Asia-first," 70–71, 93

Asialationism, 69–76, 95, 107, 115, 123, 137, 258–259. *See also* isolationism
Attlee, Clement, 181–192
attritional war, 173
Austria, 57
autarky. *See* self-reliance
authoritarian states, 18n, 21, 22, 245

Bachman, David, 237n
balance-of-power: international, 23; shifts in, 6, 7, 27
balance-of-power politics. *See* realism
balance-of-power theory. *See* realism
Baldwin, Stanley, 24n, 28
Battle of Britain, 28
Beam, Jacob, 226
Beidaihe Conference (1958), 200, 213, 216, 219, 221n, 225–226, 238, 240
Berlin, 43; blockade of (1948–49), 43n, 58, 75, 84, 90, 101, 243, 257
Betts, Richard, 164n
bipartisanship. *See* Congress
bipolarity, 4, 7, 32, 35–37, 189, 242, 245
Blair House, 133, 135, 137n
Blum, Robert, 116
Bo Yibo, 144–145, 211–212
Bradley, Omar, 108, 134n, 135, 136n, 179n, 187
Brewster, Owen, 63
Bridges, Styles, 52n
bridging theories. *See* two-level theories
budget deficits, 26, 42
buck-passing. *See* free-riding
buffer zones, 149, 154, 162, 166–174
Bullitt, William, 65
Bundy, McGeorge, 115
bureaucratic politics, 21, 204, 237n
Burma, 110, 145–146
Butterworth, Walton, 65, 79, 85, 88, 107
Byrnes, James, 33, 72n

Cabot, John, 86, 89, 92, 93n
Cairo Declaration (1943), 105, 109–110, 132, 182, 191

Cannon, Clarence, 47n
capital accumulation. *See* state extraction
capitalism, 33
capital markets, 26
Carr, E. H., 20, 22
CCP (Chinese Communist Party), 8, 9, 18n, 21, 59, 66–67, 69n, 79, 85–88, 92, 96, 114–115, 117–118, 124, 131n, 138, 139–146, 157, 159, 176, 182, 190, 204, 211, 247, 250, 258; Central Committee of, 164–165; Central Military Commission of, 165; factions in, 87, 92, 118, 204, 237n; ideology of, 138, 242; Politburo of, 160, 164, 165; relations with U.S. (*see* U.S. and Chinese Communists); and Taiwan, 130; Titoism in, 77, 91–92, 103, 107, 108, 114, 117, 121. *See also* anti-Japanese War; Chinese Civil War; Great Leap Forward; Korean War; Mao Zedong; PRC; Sino-Soviet relations; Taiwan Straits Crisis (1954–55); Taiwan Straits Crisis (1958); U.S. and Chinese Communists
Central Intelligence Agency. *See* CIA
Central Committee. *See* CCP
Central Military Commission. *See* CCP
Chan, Anita, 215n
Chen Jian, 102, 157, 175, 255
Chen Mingshu, 85, 88, 91–92, 144. *See also* Chen-Stuart meeting
Chennault, Claire, 119
Chen-Stuart meeting (1949), 91–92
Chen Yi, 86, 246
Chiang Kai-shek, Generalissimo, 8, 9, 59, 62–76, 78n, 79, 117–122, 130, 136, 140, 141, 146, 160, 175, 183, 198, 221, 230–233, 246, 259–260. *See also* Chinese Civil War; KMT; Mutual Defense Treaty; Taiwan; Taiwan Straits Crisis (1954–55); Taiwan Straits Crisis (1958); U.S. and KMT
Chiang Kai-shek, Madame, 250
China, People's Republic of. *See* PRC
China, Republic of (ROC), post-1945. *See* KMT; Mutual Defense Treaty; Taiwan
China Aid Bill (1948), 58, 61–65, 69, 74, 82–83
China Bloc. *See* China Lobby
China Lobby, 63, 69, 71, 74, 78, 82, 93, 95, 116, 136, 258. *See also* Congress, and China policy

"China under threat" thesis, 201–202, 225–227
China White Paper (1949), 96–97
Chinese Civil War, 8, 9, 59–62, 66, 76–82, 107–114, 119, 122, 132, 135, 138, 140, 142, 144, 162, 191, 205, 216, 221, 246, 250–251, 258
Chinese Communist Party. *See* CCP
Chinese Nationalists. *See* Kuomintang
Chinese People's Volunteers, 157. *See also* Korean War
Churchill, Winston, 24n, 33, 125; "Iron Curtain" speech (March 1946), 33
CIA (Central Intelligence Agency), 212–213
Clay, General Lucius, 43n
Clifford, Clark, 34, 35, 48, 53n
Clifford-Elsey report (1946), 34, 34n, 124
Clubb, O. Edmund, 68, 85, 86, 100, 131, 143, 145
coalition politics, in U.S., 70, 71
coercion: strategy of, 167
cognitive explanations. *See* psychological explanations
collective action, 20
collective goods, 19, 21
collectivization. *See* Little Leap Forward
command economies, 21
communication channels. *See* deterrence
communism, 35, 36, 38, 52, 62, 183n; in Asia, 115; spread of, 78, 82, 117n. *See also* anticommunism
communist bloc, 37, 164, 177, 184, 205
communization. *See* Great Leap Forward
conflict manipulation, 6–9, 14, 17, 18, 22, 30, 190, 204–205, 217–227, 229, 231–234, 238–241, 244, 246–248, 253
Congress (U.S.), 15, 34, 36, 41n, 42, 54, 61, 78, 176–179, 190, 243, 259–260; and anticommunism, 57, 71–74, 89 (*see also* anticommunism); and Asialationism (*see* Asialationism); and bipartisanship, 41, 74, 82, 84, 89, 95, 101, 111, 129–130; and China policy, 61–65, 68–75, 79–83, 87–89, 95–101, 105, 110–115, 122, 129–130 (*see also* China Lobby); and defense spending, 44–48, 123–124, 180, 186, 190 (*see also* defense spending); and European aid, 49–50, 54, 56, 58, 71n, 73, 79–

80, 84, 93–96, 124, 186, 189–190; fiscal conservatives in (see fiscal conservatism); and Korea, 116; and NATO, 88, 186; and taxation, 47–48, 72, 190. See also China Lobby; Democratic Party; fiscal conservatives; isolationism; party politics; Republican Party; taxation
—Committees of: House Appropriations Committee, 73; House Armed Services Committee, 73, 109; House Foreign Affairs Committee, 59n, 65n, 71n, 73, 111; Senate Foreign Relations Committee, 50, 52, 53, 59n, 121, 122
—Houses of: House of Representatives, 59n, 65n, 71n, 73, 109, 111, 113, 116; Senate, 50, 52, 53, 59n, 83, 94–95, 100, 113, 121, 122, 126, 170, 178
Connally, Tom, 52n, 82, 95, 110
conscription, 19, 21, 26
Coser, Lewis, 15n, 16n
coup d'état: threat of, 15, 18n
crisis manipulation. See conflict manipulation
Cultural Revolution, 14, 171, 247
Czech Coup (1948), 54, 58, 75
Czechoslovakia, 133

Dairen, 66n
Davies, Joseph, 60, 88
decision making, 30
Defense Department (U.S.), 129, 152n. See also defense spending; Forrestal, James; Johnson, Louis
defense spending, 7, 21, 22, 27, 152, 190; of PRC, 217, 226, 243; of U.S., 38, 43, 44–49, 93, 106, 122–124, 152, 169–170, 179–180, 186, 189–190, 225
deficits. See budget deficits
Delta Conference (1947), 53
demobilization, 18, 189
democracy, 18n, 21–22, 33, 51, 245, 260; support for in U.S. foreign policy, 34
Democratic Party, 30, 40n, 41n, 72, 89, 180
Democratic People's Republic of Korea. See DPRK
Deng Xiaoping, 21, 144
deterrence, 149, 155, 164n, 194, 252–255; and communication channels, 146,

151, 174, 175, 176, 180–181, 192, 243, 253; and rationality assumption, 252–253; and reassurances, 149, 153–154, 166–174, 176; and threats, 149, 153–154, 163–166, 176, 228
discounting, 18, 19
diversionary conflict models, 15
domestic mobilization. See mobilization
domestic mobilization model, 12, 22
domestic political explanations, 6, 15, 204, 237
domestic political hurdles. See mobilization
domestic stability, 21, 23
domestic structures, 9, 20, 21
domino theory, 156, 183
DPRK (Democratic People's Republic of Korea), 149, 152, 156–158, 161–162, 168–169, 179–180. See also Korea; Korean War; Republic of Korea
draft. See conscription
Dulles, John Foster, 24, 30, 95, 123, 128–131, 136, 177–178, 195, 197, 222, 226, 228, 241, 255, 259. See also Eisenhower, Dwight D.; State Department; Truman administration; U.S.

"East wind prevails over west wind." See Mao Zedong
Eastern Europe. See Europe, Eastern
Eaton, Charles, 110–111
Economic Cooperation Administration (ECA). See ERP
education (U.S.), 90–91, 99–101; and American public opinion, 17, 82n, 84n, 114–115, 267–270; and support for foreign policies, 40, 57, 83n, 114; and wealth, 18, 91
Eisenhower, Dwight D., 8–9, 194–195, 197, 202, 247
Eisenhower administration. See Eisenhower, Dwight D.
Elsey, George, 34, 35, 53
encompassing coalitions, 21
ERP (European Recovery Program), 7, 28, 29, 35–36, 39–42, 45–49, 53, 56, 75–76, 86, 93, 101–102, 122, 185, 189, 245, 257–259; Acheson and, 54, 82, 181; and China policy, 60, 64, 65, 67–69, 72–73, 75, 78, 82, 97, 107, 110, 113, 122, 258; and Congress (see Con-

ERP (European Recovery Program) (*cont.*)
gress); and ECA, 79, 105, 122; and interim aid, 54, 55, 73 (*see also* interim
aid); and public opinion (*see* public
opinion [U.S.]); Marshall and, 54, 67;
the media (*see* media [U.S.]). *See also*
Acheson, Dean; Kennan, George F.;
Marshall, George C.; State Department;
strongpoint defense; Truman
administration
Europe, Eastern, 54, 198, 206, 231
Europe, Western, 56, 67, 243; as bulwark
against communism, 38; and Korean
War, 134–135, 181; and U.S. (*see* ERP;
interim aid; MAP; NATO)
"Europe-first," 70–71, 93
European Recovery Program. *See* ERP
"everyone a soldier." *See* Great Leap Forward: and militia drive
executive branch, 15
extraction. *See* state extraction

factional politics, 5, 30, 87, 92, 118, 204,
237n
fascism, 33
Feis, Herbert, 115
fiscal conservatism (U.S.), 8, 36, 40, 41,
47, 73, 78, 123, 255; and China policy,
113, 116; and foreign aid, 95; in U.S.
public opinion, 34, 40 (*see also* public
opinion [U.S.]); in U.S. Congress, 34,
40, 71, 72, 74, 113. *See also* Congress
foreign aid (U.S.). *See* listings for individual aid packages
former Soviet Union, 29. *See also* Soviet
Union
Formosa. *See* Taiwan
Forrestal, James, 46, 47, 48n, 50
"Fortress America." *See* isolationism
France, 24n, 43, 57, 93, 132, 135, 169, 252
Franks, Oliver, 183–184, 188
Freeland, Richard, 33n, 52
free-riding, 19, 20, 34
Fugh, Philip, 85, 88
Fujian, China, 195, 239, 253. *See also*
Xiamen, China (Amoy)

Gaddis, John L., 38, 52n, 125
Gardner, Richard, 35
GATT (General Agreement on Tariffs and
Trade), 41

General Agreement on Tariffs and Trade.
See GATT
Geneva, 198
Germany, 24, 43, 249, 251–252
Goldstein, Avery, 237n
Gomulka, Wladyslaw, 236
Goncharov, Sergei, 91n
Gorbachev, Mikhail, 5n, 255
GNP, 26, 44, 49
grand strategy, 7–9, 11–16, 21, 22–25,
29, 76, 82, 96, 112, 121, 138, 177–
178, 185, 244–245, 255, 258–260;
definition of, 7; overactive, 13, 14, 121,
255; of PRC (*see* Great Leap Forward);
preferred, 13, 24, 29, 82, 96, 112, 121;
and public opinion, 26, 57, 61, 91, 93;
and public sacrifices, 26, 84, 91; underactive, 13, 14, 30, 76, 255; of U.S., 6–
69, 78, 82–83, 90, 96, 99, 105–106,
109, 111–116, 118, 121, 124, 136 (*see
also* New Look; NSC 68; periphery;
strongpoint defense; and individual
countries and regions
Great Britain, 3n, 24, 28, 43, 52, 86, 132,
143, 211, 221, 224, 236; as balancer in
Europe, 35, 49; decline in power of, 7,
35–36, 56, 243; and Greece-Turkey
Crisis (1947), 34–40; interwar period
strategy of, 14; and Korean War, 172,
181–192 (*see also* Korean War); and
Middle East Crisis (*see* Middle East
Crisis); postwar economic difficulties of,
34–35; and PRC entry to UN, 131–
132; and recognition of PRC, 97–99,
102, 105, 117–118, 130, 146; and Taiwan, 130, 135; and U.S., 7, 32, 34–40,
49, 52, 97–99, 102, 105, 117–118,
130–132, 181–192, 251–252; and
World War II, 251–252
Great Leap Forward, 9, 200–201, 204,
211–220, 224–225, 231, 237–240,
242, 244–245, 249; and capital accumulation, 212, 213–217, 244; and
communization, 200, 213, 214, 216,
217–220, 224–225, 239–240, 244–
245; and conflict manipulation, 217–
227, 229, 231–234, 238–241, 244,
246; and defense spending, 217, 226;
and famine, 214; and hurdles to mobilization, 213–217, 245–246; and industrial production drive, 200, 211, 212,

214–215, 219, 244; and international factors, 205–213; and Mao's decision to launch, 205–217; and militia drive, 200–201, 217–225, 239, 244; and nuclear weapons, 211–214, 217, 244; and private plots, 213; and public sacrifice, 213–217; and steel production drive, 200–201, 212–213, 224, 236, 239–240; and wages, 200, 213, 215; and women, 214

Greece, 33, 36, 49, 51. *See also* Greece-Turkey Crisis

Greece-Turkey Crisis (1947), 34–40, 43, 49, 50, 52, 54, 61–63, 110, 257, 259; and China, 110; and Great Britain, 34, 35; and Soviet Union, 33, 35; and U.S. aid, 34–40, 74, 189. *See also* Greece; Turkey

Gromyko, Andrei, 197, 235. *See also* Sino-Soviet relations; Taiwan Straits Crisis (1958)

Gross National Product. *See* GNP

guerilla war, 167, 250

Gurtov, Melvin, 202

Hainan, 103, 161

Halperin, Morton, 228

Hammond, Paul, 46n

Han Xianchu, 230

Harriman, Averell, 186

Hebei, 218

He Long, 209

Henan, 200, 224–225, 239

Henderson, Loy, 165

Herter, Christian, 52, 259; and Herter Committee, 57

He Yingqin, 221–222, 250

Hickenlooper, Bourke, 70

historical precedents, 93; and foreign aid, 48; and grand strategies, 248; and international challenges, 27; and tax and nontax sacrifices, 26

Hitler, Adolph, 133, 249, 251

Ho Chi Minh, 129, 234–235, 254–255

Hoffman, Paul, 122

Hogan, Michael, 33n

House of Representatives (U.S.). *See* Congress

Huang Hua, 85, 87, 143–144, 145n

Hume, David, 19

Huntington, Samuel, 21

hurdles to mobilization. *See* mobilization

Hwang, Byong-moo, 202

hypothesis testing, 29

ICBMs (intercontinental ballistic missiles), 199, 207, 209. *See also* Sputnik

ideological conflict (East-West), 33, 38

ideological crusading, 7, 16, 17, 18, 20, 22, 30, 38, 53, 71, 125–126, 178–179, 182, 243

ideological explanations, 3, 6

ideology, 20, 139. *See also* ideological conflict; ideological crusading

Inchon Landing. *See* Korean War

India, 23, 98, 110, 112, 151, 165, 176–178, 191–192

industrialization, 27. *See also* Great Leap Forward

inflation, 26, 40n, 41–43

intelligence, 253. *See also* CIA

intercontinental ballistic missiles. *See* ICBMs

interim aid (1947), 54, 58, 73; and China policy, 64, 75, 258. *See also* ERP

international challenges, 13, 14, 20, 22, 205, 247; comparison of across historical periods, 27; directness of, 25, 27, 43, 44, 47, 49, 216–217, 256. *See also* balance-of-power: shifts in

international explanations, 201–203, 205–213, 225–236. *See also* realism

internationalism (U.S.), 95, 111, 256. *See also* isolationism

Iran, 33, 43

Iraq. *See* Middle East Crisis

"Iron Curtain" speech (1946). *See* Churchill, Winston

isolationism (U.S.), 7, 8, 37, 47, 62, 71, 74, 255–256, 258; and Congress, 82, 111, 113, 116; and U.S. public opinion, 39, 84

Italy, 57

Japan, 21, 36, 43, 85, 97–98, 106n, 109, 118, 130, 161, 192, 242, 249–250

JCS (Joint Chiefs-of-Staff [U.S.]), 45, 61, 63, 64, 93n, 106–108, 134, 152n, 196

Jervis, Robert, 254

Jessup, Philip, 96n, 99, 105

Johnson, Louis, 107, 112n, 123, 128–129, 131, 135, 136, 179n

Joint Chiefs-of-Staff [U.S.]. *See* JCS
joint fleet controversy. *See* Sino-Soviet relations
Jones, Joseph, 50, 51, 52n, 63
Jordan. *See* Middle East Crisis
Judd, Walter, 61n, 63, 110

Katzenstein, Peter, 21
Kee, John, 109
Kennan, George F., 7, 24, 25, 32, 33, 35, 37, 38, 60, 73n, 77, 257; and China policy, 60, 61, 66n, 67–68, 69, 88–89, 98, 100, 176–181, 192; and Korean War, 127, 176–181; and "Long Telegram" (1946), 33; and public opinion, 259; and Sino-Soviet relations, 60; and Taiwan, 107; and Truman Doctrine, 52, 53, 61. *See also* grand strategy; Policy Planning Staff; State Department; strongpoint defense; Truman administration; U.S.
Kennedy, John F., 247
Keohane, Robert, 4, 5
Key, V. O., 256
Keynesian economics, 44
Khrushchev, Nikita, 199, 206, 246n; and accommodation with U.S., 9; and Anti-Party Group, 199, 206–207; and de-Stalinization, 199; and Mao Zedong, 199, 206, 210, 232–236; and nuclear nonproliferation, 206; and peaceful co-existence strategy, 206. *See also* Sino-Soviet relations; Soviet Union; Sputnik; Taiwan Straits Crisis (1958)
Kim Il-sung, 148n, 157, 161, 162, 165. *See also* DPRK; Korean War; ROK
Kirk, Alan, 92, 97
Kissinger, Henry, 5
KMT (Kuomintang), 8, 9, 66, 68, 72, 74–75, 79, 130, 135–136, 141, 143, 145, 160–161, 192–193, 221, 223, 228, 250, 260; air force of, 119–120, 165, 194–195; and anti-Japanese war, 250–251; and bombing of Shanghai, 119–120; corruption of, 96; and expected "fall" of on Taiwan, 115–118; and loss of mainland, 78, 85, 96; and U.S. assistance (*see* U.S. and KMT). *See also* Chiang Kai-shek; China Aid Bills; China Lobby; Chinese Civil War; Mutual Defense Treaty; offshore islands;

Taiwan; Taiwan Straits Crisis (1954–55); Taiwan Straits Crisis (1958); U.S. and KMT
Knowland, William, 95, 110, 112, 116, 190
Korea (peninsula), 109, 130, 141, 151, 177, 192, 253–255; map of, 150. *See also* DPRK; Korean Aid Bills; Korean War; ROK
Korean Aid Bills (1949 and 1950), 115–117, 136, 160
Korean War, 8, 101, 138, 140, 148–193, 237, 240, 243; DPRK initiation of (June 25, 1950), 78, 124, 131, 132, 133–137, 151, 161, 162n, 169, 179; and early U.S.-PRC engagements (Oct. 1950), 153; escalation of, 140, 149, 154; and Great Britain, 172, 181–192; and Inchon landing, 151, 157, 174; Mao's strategy in, 155–175, 271–275; and Mao's telegrams to Moscow, 271–276; and peace proposals, 172, 176, 177, 182–192; and PRC counter-offensive (Nov. 26, 1950), 154, 172, 181, 182, 184, 191, 243; and PRC decision to enter, 134, 146, 149, 157, 158, 159, 160, 162, 163, 164, 165, 166, 169, 174, 243, 246, 253, 271–275; and PRC deterrent threats (*see* Zhou-Panikkar communique); and PRC disengagement (Nov. 7, 1950), 155, 170–174; and PRC goal of expelling UN forces, 165, 166, 167, 172–173, 174n, 243, 271–272; and Soviet air activities, 127, 163, 168, 169; and Soviet military aid, 158–159, 160, 162n, 163, 168, 169, 199, 208, 272; and Soviet personnel, 168; Stalin's strategy in, 134, 148, 159, 160, 163, 169; and Taiwan, 133–137; and U.S.-British relations, 181–192; and U.S. crossing of 38th parallel (Oct. 7, 1950), 127, 134, 149, 151, 152, 153, 157, 159, 162, 164, 168, 170, 172, 174, 176, 181, 193, 272; and U.S. decision to enter, 133–137, 161, 179; and U.S. drive to the Yalu River (Nov. 24, 1950), 154, 165, 168, 169, 171, 190, 243; and U.S. threat to PRC, 154, 156, 164, 165, 166, 271–272; and U.S. war aims, 175. *See also* buffer zones; deterrence;

DPRK; Korea; Korean Aid Bills; Manchuria; Panmunjon Armistice; ROK; Sino-Soviet relations; thirty-eighth parallel; Yalu River; Zhou-Panikkar communique; and various cities and locations in Korea
Krasner, Stephen, 14
Krock, Arthur, 97
Krug, Julius, 62
Kuomintang. *See* KMT
Kurile Islands, 109

LaFeber, Walter, 75
Lake, David, 14
Lamborn, Alan C., 15n
Larson, Deborah, 33n
leadership, 255–261
Lebanon. *See* Middle East Crisis
Leahy, William, 62
"lean to one side policy." *See* Sino-Soviet relations
Lebow, Richard Ned, 153
Levi, Margaret, 18n
Lewis, John, 91n, 207
Liao Xinwen, 238n
Lie, Trygve, 147
limited containment. *See* grand strategy; strongpoint defense
limited information, 18; public and, 17
limited rationality. *See* rationality: bounded
Little Leap Forward (1955–56), 205, 215, 217, 244
Liu Bocheng, 212
Liu Xiao, 206, 226n, 234
Li Yueran, 207
logrolling, 5, 70–71
"Long Telegram." *See* Kennan, George F.
lost-chance thesis, 139–142
Lovett, Robert, 79
Lowi, Theodore, 22, 53
Loyalty Program, 68n

MacArthur, Douglas, 107, 112, 118, 129, 135–136, 149–159, 165–171, 174, 179, 190. *See also* Korean War
Machiavelli, Niccolò, 20
Manchuria, 66, 119, 154, 156, 163, 168, 210n, 272, 273
Mansourov, Alexandre, 159, 160n, 163n, 164, 168n
Mao Zedong, 4, 6, 9, 114, 117–118, 142,

158–159, 161–162, 154–165, 177, 194–241 passim, 242–246, 253, 260–261; and "East Wind" thesis, 199, 206, 236; and grand strategy (*see* Great Leap Forward); and Great Leap Forward (*see* Great Leap Forward); and Khrushchev, 199, 206, 210, 232–236 (*see also* Sino-Soviet relations); and Korean War (*see* Korean War); and Little Leap Forward (*see* Little Leap Forward); and nonsocialist countries, 145–146; and "paper tiger" thesis, 199, 203, 204n, 236; and proposed Stuart mission to Beiping, 144; and recognition issue, 141, 143–145, 148 (*see also* recognition issue); and shelling of offshore islands (*see* offshore islands); and Stalin, 140n, 145, 146n, 148, 159, 161–162n, 164 (*see also* Sino-Soviet relations); and Taiwan, 162, 187, 195, 225; and Taiwan Straits crises (*see* Taiwan Straits Crisis [1954–55]; Taiwan Straits Crisis [1958]); and view of Soviet Union, 139, 146, 148–149, 159–160, 164–165, 199, 206, 210, 232–236 (*see also* Sino-Soviet relations); and view of U.S., 4, 77, 86–87, 92, 139, 142, 146–147, 160–161, 162, 198 (*see also* Truman, Harry S; U.S. and Chinese Communists). *See also* CCP; Chinese Civil War; Great Leap Forward; Korean War; offshore islands; PRC; Sino-Soviet Relations; Taiwan Straits Crisis (1954–55); Taiwan Straits Crisis (1958); U.S. and Chinese Communists; U.S. and KMT
MAP (Military Assistance Program), 39, 45, 46, 48, 84, 93–96, 101, 255; and China policy, 63, 83, 95, 110, 122, 242, 258
Marshall, George C., 8, 48n, 58, 74, 77; and China, 59, 62, 64–67, 78, 83, 89, 93n, 100–101, 186–189, 243, 259; and Greece-Turkey Crisis, 49–50; and Marshall mission, 59, 92; and Marshall Plan speech (Harvard), 53; and Truman doctrine, 52. *See also* ERP; State Department; Truman administration; and various headings under U.S.
Marshall Plan. *See* ERP
Masaryk, Jan, 58. *See also* Czech Coup
Matador missiles, 198, 201, 225

Matsu (Mazu). *See* offshore islands

Maverick, Maury, 103–104

Maxwell, Neville, 23, 24n

McCarran, Pat, 82

McCarthy, Joseph, 63, 122, 179. *See also* McCarthyism

McCarthyism, 123. *See also* anticommunism

McCormick, Anna, 110

media: (CCP), 211, 218n, 219–222, 223n, 225, 229, 236n, 238

—(U.S.), 62n; and anticommunism, 104; and China policy, 82, 88, 96–97, 101, 107, 110–116; and ERP, 54; and PRC, 72n, 80; and recognition (*see* recognition); and Taiwan, 109–116

—(USSR), 249

Melby, John, 66, 96–97, 105. *See also* China White Paper

mercantilism, 11n

Merchant, Livingston, 120

Middle East Crisis (1958), 196, 200–201, 203, 219–227, 237–240

Mikoyan, Anastas, 142, 149

Military Assistance Program. *See* MAP

military budgets. *See* defense spending

military modernization. *See* defense spending

militia drive (PRC, 1958). *See* Great Leap Forward

mobilization, 7, 12, 13, 14, 15, 16, 18, 20, 22, 27, 29, 31, 32, 36, 53, 71, 77, 95, 123, 175–176, 178–179, 185, 245, 248–249; domestic political hurdles to, 13, 14, 24–27, 29–31, 39–49, 121, 213–217, 245–246 (*see also* conflict manipulation; Great Leap Forward; ideological crusading; NSC 68; public opinion; Truman Doctrine; and entries for particular policies and strategies)

Mongolia, 106

moral crusading. *See* ideological crusading

Morgenthau, Hans, 5, 22, 23, 24, 25

Mukden, 65, 77, 86

multilateralism, 40

multipolarity, 30

Mutual Defense Treaty, US-ROC, 9, 60, 194, 196

Nanjing, 142–143

national debt. *See* U.S.: federal budget of

national interest, 16, 24, 129, 179

national morale. *See* national political power; public opinion

national political power, 12, 20, 23; definition of, 11; operationalization of, 22–24; in U.S., 124. *See also* national power

national power, 23, 236, 240; economic, 12, 125; measurement of, 12, 125; military, 12; political (*see* national political power)

National Security Council. *See* NSC

NATO (North Atlantic Treaty Organization), 8, 39, 49, 83–91, 93, 111, 123, 183, 187, 243, 255, 258. *See also* MAP

Navy (U.S.), 47, 129, 138, 142, 162, 196, 203, 255

Nehru, Jawaharlal, 176–178

New Look, 194

Newport Declaration (Sept. 4, 1958), 197, 228

Nie Rongzhen, 151, 164

Nitze, Paul, 71n, 125–127, 181n, 188

Nixon administration, 4. *See also* Nixon, Richard M.

Nixon, Richard M., 5, 18n, 247

North, Douglas, 19n

North Atlantic Treaty Organization. *See* NATO

North Korea. *See* DPRK

Norway, 134

novelty of policies, 25, 28, 248

NSC (National Security Council), 78, 128, 175, 184, 188; and aid to KMT, 68

—and Council directives: NSC 37 (1948–49), 106; NSC 41 (1949), 79, 86, 98; NSC 48 (1949), 104; NSC 68 (1950) (*see* NSC 68)

NSC 68: 70, 122–127, 139, 152, 176–177, 185, 242; and China policy, 139, 169–170; and defense of Taiwan, 128–133; and Korean War, 169–170, 177, 180–181

nuclear submarines. *See* Sino-Soviet relations

nuclear weapons, 38, 47, 125, 164n, 181, 194, 196, 204–214, 217, 242, 244; China and, 9, 211–214, 217, 244; Soviet Union and, 95–96, 122; U.S. and, 7, 39, 43, 47, 122

offshore islands, 9, 194–196, 228; and KMT crisis behavior, 230n, 231n; and KMT deployments, 195–198, 201–205; and KMT legitimacy, 198; and KMT operations against mainland, 198, 201, 203, 226; and PRC plans to seize, 223, 227–233; PRC shelling and blockade of (Aug.–Oct. 1958), 195–198, 201–205, 216, 219–220, 221–223, 227–232, 235, 238–240; and proposed KMT withdrawal, 197–198, 231–233; U.S. commitment to, 196–197, 201–202, 221, 228, 235. *See also* KMT; PRC; Soviet Union; Taiwan Straits Crisis (1958); U.S. and Chinese Communists; U.S. and KMT

O'Konski, Alvin E., 62–63

Olson, Mancur, 19n, 20n

Operation Torch, 251–252

Oppenheimer, Robert J., 47n, 71

overactive strategies. *See* grand strategy

overseas deployment, 26

party politics. *See* U.S.: party politics

Page, Benjamin, 256, 260

Panikkar, K. M., 151, 152n, 153, 174

Panmunjon Armistice, 192, 194

"paper tiger" thesis. *See* Mao Zedong

Pareto, Vilfredo, 15

Patel, Sardar V., 24n

peaceful coexistence. *See* Khrushchev, Nikita

peak-level organizations, 21

Pearl Harbor, 27

Peng Dehuai, 163–165, 167, 171–173, 191, 226, 233, 237–238, 274. *See also* Korean War; offshore islands; Taiwan Straits Crisis (1958)

People's communes. *See* Great Leap Forward

People's Liberation Army. *See* PLA

People's militia. *See* Great Leap Forward

People's Republic of China. *See* PRC

periphery, 37–38; China as, 58–67, 83, 106; conflicts in, 252–253; Korea as, 116; Taiwan as, 116, 118

Philippines, 106, 118, 130, 135

PLA (People's Liberation Army), 9, 85, 96, 118, 129, 142–144, 157, 161, 168, 195, 219, 227, 230–233. *See also* CCP; Chinese Civil War; Chinese People's

Volunteers; Korean War; offshore islands; Peng Dehuai; PRC; Taiwan Straits Crisis (1954–55); Taiwan Straits Crisis (1958)

policy novelty. *See* novelty of policies

Policy Planning Staff. *See* PPS

policy trade-offs, 11, 30

Politburo (CCP). *See* CCP

political culture, 9, 247–248

political hurdles. *See* mobilization; public opinion

political participation, 21

political power. *See* national political power

Pollack, Jonathan, 173n, 204n, 227, 228–230

power. *See* balance-of-power; national political power; national power; power resources

power resources: economic, 11; military, 11

presidency, 22

PPS (Policy Planning Staff), 60–61, 66–67, 69, 88–89, 91, 98, 104n, 125, 183n. *See also* Kennan, George F.; Nitze, Paul

PRC (People's Republic of China), 142, 145, 180, 192, 245, 247, 255; and anti-Americanism, 59, 78, 87, 108, 110; army of (*see* PLA); Dengist reforms in, 21; economy of, 21, 22; establishment of (1949), 23, 24n, 96, 100–102; and Great Britain, 86, 97–99, 102, 105, 117–119, 130, 146; and India, 23, 98, 110, 112, 151, 165, 176–178, 191–192; and Korean War (*see* Korean War); and Middle East Crisis (*see* Middle East Crisis); and nationalism, 78, 96, 98; and non-socialist countries, 145–146; and nuclear weapons, 205–214, 217, 244; and offshore islands (*see* offshore islands); and Soviet Union (*see* Sino-Soviet relations); and Taiwan, 105, 161, 195; and Taiwan Straits Crises (*see* Taiwan Straits Crisis [1954–55]; Taiwan Straits Crisis [1958]); and U.N., 147, 176–177, 182, 191–192; and U.S. (*see* U.S. and Chinese Communists); and Vietnam, 3, 129, 158n, 234–235, 254–255; and Yugoslavia, 200. *See also* CCP; Chinese Civil War; Great Leap

PRC (People's Republic of China) (*cont.*) Forward; Korean War; Mao Zedong; offshore islands; Sino-Soviet relations; Taiwan Straits Crisis [1954–55]; Taiwan Straits Crisis [1958]; U.S. and Chinese Communists; U.S. and KMT

private plots. *See* Great Leap Forward

prisoners of war, 171, 194

psychological explanations, 3, 6, 30, 33n, 153, 203–204, 236, 252–253

public opinion, 11, 12, 13, 16–27. *See also* education level; mobilization; public opinion (PRC); public opinion (U.S.); salience; taxation: public opinion toward

public opinion (PRC): and anti-Americanism (*see* China [PRC]); and Little Leap Forward, 215; and U.S. support for KMT, 78–79

public opinion (U.S.), 39–40, 57, 83n, 84, 114–115, 123–124, 137, 176–180, 185–187, 194, 255–259; and aid to Europe, 39–41, 55n, 57–58, 70–71, 75n, 82–83, 90, 94, 101, 122, 124, 264; and anticommunism (*see* anticommunism); and China policy, 64–74, 80–90, 96–99, 102, 105, 112–117, 127–129, 133, 137, 190, 196, 241, 246, 259, 265, 267–270; consistency of, 255–259; and defense spending, 48, 180, 185–186; and education levels (*see* education); and grand strategy, 57, 61, 91, 93; and inflation, 40–42; and isolationism, 39, 84; and Korean War, 178–179, 186, 188, 190; management of, 78, 117; and NATO, 83n, 84, 266; and party politics, 266; and regional politics, 71, 264, 265; State Department analyses of (*see* State Department); and taxation, 40–42, 48, 70, 73, 83; and wealth, 18, 91; and World War II demobilization, 34, 39

Pusan, Korea, 157, 167, 173

Pusan perimeter. *See* Pusan, Korea

Pyongyang, Korea, 155, 158n, 166–168, 172, 273–274

Quemoy (Jinmen). *See* offshore islands

Quirino, Elpidio, 118, 135

rationality, 15; assumption of, 12, 252–253, 260; bounded, 12, 15, 17. *See also* deterrence

Rau, Sir Benegal, 191

Reagan, Ronald, 46

realism, 3–8, 11–15, 17, 20, 22, 23, 37, 38, 124, 180, 236, 260

realpolitik. *See* realism

rebellion. *See* revolution

recognition issue (U.S.-China), 8, 97–118, 122, 132–133, 138–144, 146n, 148, 149, 151, 174–175, 191, 193, 241, 243, 247; and Great Britain, 97–99, 102, 105, 117–118, 130, 146; and JCS, 112; and Mao, 141, 144, 145, 146n, 147, 167; and media, 105, 110–116; and New Zealand, 110; and PPS, 102; and public opinion (U.S.), 102, 105, 112, 114, 127, 133, 268–270 (*see also* public opinion [U.S.]: and China policy); and State Department, 102, 105, 111–112, 132; and Soviet Union, 147. *See also* U.S. and Chinese Communists; U.S. and KMT

Republic of China (ROC). *See* Chiang Kai-shek; KMT; Mutual Defense Treaty; Taiwan

Republic of Korea. *See* ROK

Republican Party, 30, 40, 41, 42, 58, 65, 71n, 72, 88–89, 113, 116, 190, 243, 259

resolve. *See* national political power

Reston, James, 58, 111–113, 191

revolution, 15, 18. *See also* Chinese Civil War

Ridgway, Matthew M., 173

ROC (Republic of China). *See* Chiang Kai-shek; KMT; Mutual Defense Treaty; Taiwan

Rockefeller Foundation, 241

ROK, 148n, 152, 161, 172, 179, 187, 271–275. *See also* Korea; Korean War; thirty-eighth parallel; and individual cities

rollback, 125–127, 166

Roosevelt, Franklin D., 27, 97, 251–252

Ross, Robert, 5n

Rousseau, Jean Jacques, 16

Rusk, Dean, 85, 98, 120, 128–131, 134n, 136, 165, 166n, 241, 254

Russett, Bruce, 256n

Ryukyu Islands, 109

salience in U.S. public opinion, 27; of China policy, 82; of communism, 74; of

historical precedents, 28 (*see also* historical precedents); of international politics, 74, 256–259; of Ward case, 103
scapegoat theories. *See* diversionary conflict models
Schelling, Thomas, 153–154
Schilling, Warner, 44
Schweller, Randall, 20n
SEATO (Southeast Asia Treaty Organization), 195
second-strike capability, 207
self-reliance, 9, 205, 208, 211, 221, 245
Senate (U.S.). *See* Congress
Seoul, 167, 173
Seventh Fleet. *See* Navy (U.S.)
Shanghai, 142, 167, 196, 219
Shapiro, Robert, 256, 260
Shenyang. *See* Mukden
Simmel, George, 15n
Simon, Herbert, 15
Sinkiang. *See* Xinjiang
Sino-Soviet defense treaty. *See* Sino-Soviet relations
Sino-Soviet relations (USSR-CCP, pre-1949; USSR-PRC, post-1949), 8, 9, 59n, 60, 66–67, 77–93, 101, 108, 117–121, 128–131, 138–140, 146–149, 158, 164, 176–177, 180–184, 191–192, 198–199, 206–211, 243, 271–276; and Anti-Party Group, 199, 206–207; and Chinese Titoism, 146; and joint fleet controversy, 208n, 210–211; and Korean War (*see* Korean War); and Mao's "lean to one side" policy, 77–78, 91–92, 193; and nuclear submarine controversy, 208–209; and nuclear weapons, 199, 206–207, 217; and PRC admission to UN, 176–177; and radio transmitter controversy, 210–211; and Sino-Soviet Defense Treaty, 77–78, 114, 117–121, 128, 146n, 164–166, 197, 205–213, 244–245; and Soviet economic aid, 205–211; and Soviet military assistance, 199, 205–211, 234; split in, 79, 93n, 102–106, 118, 246; and Sputnik (*see* Sputnik); and Taiwan Straits Crisis (1958) (*see* Taiwan Straits Crisis [1958]); and trade, 119, 146; and U.S. recognition policy, 146–149. *See also* Great Leap Forward; Khrushchev, Nikita; Mao

Zedong; PRC; Soviet Union; Sputnik; Stalin, Joseph
Sixth Fleet. *See* Navy (U.S.)
Smith, H. Alexander, 110, 116
Snyder, Jack, 70–71
Snyder, John, 190
social spending, 44
South Korea. *See* ROK
Southeast Asia, 130–132
Southeast Asia Treaty Organization. *See* SEATO
Soviet Bloc. *See* communist bloc
Soviet Union, 3–5, 9, 23n, 26, 32–34, 36, 37, 38, 52, 53, 101, 124, 134, 137n, 140, 146–147, 158, 164n, 176–177, 180, 182–184, 188, 190–192, 223n, 242–243, 251; army of, 108; and CCP (*see* Sino-Soviet Relations); collectivization in, 248–250; and Eastern Europe, 198, 206; expansionism of, 8, 33, 39, 50, 100; and Greece-Turkey Crisis, 33, 35; and Korean War (*see* Korean War); and nuclear weapons, 95–96, 122, 199, 206–207, 217, 242; and PRC (*see* Sino-Soviet relations); and Taiwan Straits Crisis (1958) (*see* Taiwan Straits Crisis [1958]); and United States (*see* U.S.-Soviet relations). *See also* Khrushchev, Nikita; Sputnik; Stalin, Joseph
Sputnik, 9, 199, 202–203, 206–207, 213, 236, 244
Stalin, Joseph, 139, 142, 147, 156, 163–164, 167, 169, 172, 177, 184, 192, 209; and collectivization, 248–250; and Kim Il-sung, 158–159, 161; and Mao Zedong, 140n, 145, 147–149, 159, 161, 162n, 164; presidential speech of (Feb. 1946), 33. *See also* Korean War; Sino-Soviet relations; Soviet Union; U.S.-Soviet relations
State Department (U.S.), 40, 42, 54, 56, 58, 88, 121, 131, 165, 183, 196; analyses of U.S. public opinion by, 40, 42, 50, 58, 70, 75, 80, 84, 90, 114–115 (*see also* public opinion [U.S.]); and China policy, 58, 60, 63, 64, 67–68, 73, 79–80, 87, 93n, 97, 100–106, 117, 121, 126, 128, 131; and Sino-Soviet relations, 61; and Taiwan, 106–109, 116–120, 134. *See also* Policy Planning Staff

state, 15, 20; concept of, 14–15; democratic, 26; and foreign policy elites, 17;
nondemocratic, 26; strength of, 21. *See
also* state extraction; state-society nexus
state extraction, 9, 19, 25–26; comparisons of across regime types, 21, 22, 26;
in PRC, 212, 213–217, 244
state-society nexus, 16, 20, 21, 24, 25, 71,
255
steel production drive. *See* Great Leap
Forward
Stilwell, Joseph, 92
strategic probe thesis, 195, 202, 227–229
strongpoint defense, 7, 36, 37–38, 65,
67–69, 77, 84, 91, 99, 105–106, 112,
114–115, 125, 187, 243
Stuart, John Leighton, 78, 85, 87n, 88;
and meeting with Chen Mingshu, 91–
92; and proposed trip to Beiping, 86–
89, 91, 104, 143–144, 145n
subversion, 141–142
supply system, 213. *See also* Great Leap
Forward
Su Yu, 161n
Symington, Stuart, 189–190

Taber, John, 54n, 73
Taegu, Korea, 167, 173
Taft, Robert, 54, 111, 122
Taiwan (Formosa), 8, 9, 101, 103, 105–
120, 121, 124n, 125–126, 128–137,
146n, 161–163, 179, 182, 187, 191–
197, 202, 219, 226, 246, 253–254,
260; expected "fall" of, 115–118; and
fiscal conservatives, 105; independence
of, 132, 231, 254; and Korean Aid Bill,
115–117; strategic value of, 106, 114,
134 (*see also* grand strategy); and U.S.
decision to protect (1950), 128, 133–
137, 138, 160–162, 170, 174, 175,
183, 187, 193, 194 (*see also* Mutual
Defense Treaty). *See also* KMT; Mutual
Defense Treaty; Taiwan Straits Crisis
(1954–55); Taiwan Straits Crisis
(1958); U.S. and Chinese Communists
(CCP and PRC); U.S. and KMT
Taiwan Straits Crisis (1954–55), 9, 193–
195, 205, 246
Taiwan Straits Crisis (1958), 9, 193, 195–
206, 217–241, 244, 246, 253, 258; explanations for, 201–205; and Great

Leap Forward mobilization, 201–203,
205–206, 217–241, 244, 246; and
Middle East Crisis (*see* Middle East
Crisis); and nuclear escalation dangers,
196, 233–235, 253; and offshore islands (*see* offshore islands); and PLA
deployments, 200; PRC restraint during, 196–198, 227–230; and PRC surrender calls, 230; and Soviet Union,
197, 202–203, 231–236, 241, 246; and
U.S. ceasefire proposals, 231–232; U.S.
deployments during, 196, 226, 229. *See
also* Chiang Kai-shek; Dulles, John
Foster; Eisenhower, Dwight D.;
Khrushchev, Nikita; KMT; Mutual Defense Treaty; offshore islands; Mao
Zedong; PRC; Sino-Soviet relations;
Soviet Union; U.S. and Chinese
Communists
taxation, 21, 22, 26, 29, 40–42, 47–48,
70–73, 83, 190, 212–217, 248–249;
and Congress (*see* Congress); evasion
of, 19; and foreign policy, 40n, 41, 84;
graduated, 18n; legislation and, 26; and
nontax sacrifices, 25–26; and public
opinion (*see* public opinion [U.S.]). *See
also* state extraction
thirty-eighth parallel, 127, 134, 149, 150–
154, 157–160, 162, 164, 166–170,
172–176, 181, 193–194, 272
threats. *See* international challenges
Tianjin, 142
Tibet, 24n
Tito (Josip Broz), 60–61, 87, 148. *See
also* Titoism
Titoism, 60–61, 77–78, 86–87, 91–92,
103, 107, 108, 114, 117, 121, 127,
146, 148, 176, 183–184
Tokchon, 274
Torch. *See* Operation Torch
Truman, Harry S, 6, 7, 8, 18n, 24, 30,
32, 34, 40, 42, 47, 50, 53n, 62, 69n,
74–75, 123, 126, 131n, 133–138, 153,
160–162, 174–176, 179, 180–192,
194, 242–243, 246, 253, 255, 259–
261; and China, 77, 80, 101, 103, 109,
138, 190 (*see also* U.S. and Chinese
Communists; U.S. and KMT); on defense spending, 44–45, 180–181, 188–
190 (*see also* defense spending [U.S.]);
and defense of Taiwan, 133–137; inau-

gural address of (1949), 80; and Korean War (*see* Korean War). *See also* strong-point defense; Truman-Attlee talks; Truman administration; Truman Doctrine; Truman, Harry S; U.S.; U.S. and Chinese Communists; U.S. and KMT; and listings for leading administration officials, policies, strategies, and U.S. relations with other nations and regions

Truman administration, 7, 32–33, 42–43, 47, 50–56, 58, 62, 75, 77, 82, 84, 89–90, 96–97, 101–105, 107, 111–113, 116, 125–126, 138–139, 176–193, 242–243, 244–248, 252–261; and Congress (*see* Congress); defense spending of (*see* defense spending [U.S.]); and public opinion (*see* public opinion [U.S.]). *See also* Truman Doctrine; Truman, Harry S; U.S.; U.S. and Chinese Communists; U.S. and KMT; and listings for leading administration officials, policies, strategies, and U.S. relations with other nations and regions

Truman-Attlee talks, 181–192

Truman Doctrine, 32, 36, 49–52, 58, 111, 190, 257; and China policy, 61–64, 72, 74, 75, 110, 111–112

Tsou, Tang, 66n

Tucker, Nancy, 74n, 136

Turkey, 23, 36, 49. *See also* Greece-Turkey Crisis

"two-China policy," 198. *See also* Taiwan

two-level theories, 6, 13, 16, 24, 204–205, 252–254

Tydings, Millard, 178

typhoons, 227

UMT (Universal Military Training), 72

underactive. *See* grand strategy: underactive

unequal treaties, 146

United Nations, 40, 116, 129–133, 147, 153, 166, 172–173, 176–181, 192, 221, 232, 240; and Korean War (*see* Korean War); and PRC admission, 131–132, 176–181

United States. *See* U.S.

Universal Military Training. *See* UMT

U.S.: alliances of (*see* Mutual Defense Treaty; NATO; SEATO); and European aid (*see* Greece-Turkey Crisis; ERP;

MAP); and China (*see* U.S. and Chinese Communists; U.S. and KMT); Congress of (*see* Congress); defense budget of (*see* defense spending: of U.S.); federal budget of, 15, 25, 26, 40, 41n, 42–44, 46, 47, 49, 54, 71, 72, 93, 107; and foreign aid (*see* foreign aid; listings for particular policies); grand strategy of (*see* grand strategy: of U.S.); and Great Britain (*see* Great Britain); interwar strategy of, 14; and Korea (*see* Korea; Korean Aid Bill; Korean War); media of (*see* media: [U.S.]); and Middle East Crisis (*see* Middle East Crisis); and nuclear weapons (*see* nuclear weapons); party politics in, 30, 72, 80, 111 (*see also* Democratic Party; Republican Party); prestige of, 108, 120, 183–184; public opinion in (*see* public opinion [U.S.]); and Soviet Union (*see* U.S.-Soviet relations); and Vietnam, 4, 14; and World War II, 251–252. *See also* listings for particular administrations, crises and conflicts, grand strategies, leaders, policies, countries and regions

U.S. and Chinese Communists (CCP, pre-Oct. 1949; PRC, post-Oct. 1949), 8, 58, 63–64, 77–80, 83, 85–89, 91–92, 104, 107–109, 116, 140, 144, 146–147, 193, 243, 258; and ambassadorial-level talks, 197–198, 201, 226, 213–232; and blocking of Taiwan Straits by U.S. (1950), 128, 133–137, 138, 160–162, 170, 174, 175, 183, 187, 193, 243, 254–255, 260; and Congress (*see* Congress); and economic and trade relations, 79, 97–98, 100, 119–121; and ERP, 65, 67–68, 73, 82; and freezing of Chinese assets, 192; and Korean War (*see* Korean War); and Middle East Crisis (*see* Middle East Crisis); Open Door Policy, 99, 109, 116, 117, 121; and PRC seizure of U.S. consulates, 104, 117; and proposed aid to CCP-held areas, 79–80; and recognition issue (*see* recognition issue); and Soviet Union (*see* U.S.-Soviet relations; Sino-Soviet relations); and Taiwan Straits Crises (*see* offshore islands; Taiwan Straits Crisis [1954–55]; Taiwan Straits Crisis [1958]); and trade embargo,

U.S. and Chinese Communists (*cont.*)
192, 221, 240; and United Nations (*see*
United Nations); and U.S. Tito strategy
(*see* Titoism)
U.S. and KMT, 7–8, 58–77, 78–91, 93–
137, 272, 243, 246, 255; and arms embargo, 63–64; and offshore islands (*see*
offshore islands); and China Aid Bill
(*see* China Aid Bill); and proposed U.S.
abandonment of KMT, 9, 80–85, 92,
99–121, 137, 175, 187, 193, 227, 243,
246, 255; and recognition issue (*see* recognition issue); and Taiwan Straits
Crises (*see* offshore islands; Taiwan
Straits Crisis [1954–55 and 1958]); and
U.S. aid and support for KMT, 58, 59,
60–65, 68–70, 74–75, 78–79, 81–87,
90, 104–121, 138–144, 148, 162, 243;
and U.S. decision to protect Taiwan
(1950), 128–138, 160–162, 170, 174,
175, 183, 187, 193–195 (*see also* Mutual Defense Treaty). *See also* Chiang
Kai-shek; Chinese Civil War; Mutual
Defense Treaty; Taiwan; Taiwan Straits
Crisis (1954–55); Taiwan Straits Crisis
(1958)
U.S. and Korean War. *See* Korean War
U.S.-Soviet relations, 3–5, 7–8, 32–34,
36–39, 43n, 49–58, 101, 122–127,
133, 242–243, 255–256, 257
U.S. Congress. *See* Congress

Vandenberg, Arthur, 30, 41n, 46, 50,
54n, 58, 94–95, 111, 259; and China
policy, 62n, 65, 69, 70, 73, 81–83, 88,
122
Vietnam, 3–4, 158, 247, 254–255
Vincent, John Carter, 59–60
Vorys, John (Representative), 65, 110

wage incentives. *See* Great Leap Forward
Walter, George, 70
Waltz, Kenneth, 5, 11, 12, 22, 38, 145
Ward, Angus, 65n, 77, 86, 98–104
Ward case. *See* Ward, Angus
warlords, 141
Warsaw, 197, 226
Weathersby, Kathryn, 148, 163
Webb, James, 48n
Wedemeyer, Albert, 65–66, 92
Wedemeyer Mission, 65–66

Wells, Samuel, 43n
Western Europe. *See* Europe, Western
Wherry, Kenneth, 110
White Paper (1949). *See* China White
Paper
Whiting, Allen, 96n, 151, 155–156, 168n
Williams, William Appleman, 33n
Wonsan, Korea, 155, 158n, 166–168,
172, 273–274
World Court, 232
World War I, 23, 28
World War II, 33, 49, 61, 72, 82, 92, 97,
249, 251–252
Wu Lengxi, 221, 229, 230n, 239
Wu Xiuquan, 200

Xiamen, China (Amoy), 195–196, 200–
201, 226
Xiao Jinguang, 206
Xinhua News Service, 221. *See also* Wu
Lengxi
Xinjiang, 106
Xue Litai, 91n, 207, 208n
Xu Yan, 157, 203n, 219, 238–239

Yalta, 66, 66n, 67n
Yalu River, 138, 147, 149, 153–154, 156,
159, 168, 273, 274. *See also* Korean
War
Yangtze River. *See* Yangzi River
Yangzi River, 142
Yao Yilin, 85, 143
Ye Fei, 221n, 227, 230, 237n
Yenan, 250
Yongwon, Korea, 274
Young, Kenneth, 232
Yudin, P. F., 208
Yugoslavia, 77–78, 86, 200. *See also*
Tito; Titoism

Zhang Shuguang, 141n, 202n
Zhou Enlai, 143, 144n, 145n, 147, 156–
159, 163, 167, 174, 175n, 177, 191,
197, 223, 232–235, 237n, 241; and
Korean War, 143, 144n, 145n, 147,
151–153, 156–159, 163, 167, 174,
175n, 177, 191, 273–274 (*see also*
Zhou-Panikkar communique); and Marshall Mission, 59; and relations with
American representatives in China, 85–
87, 91–92, 100. *See also* CCP; Korean

War; offshore islands; PRC; Sino-Soviet relations; Taiwan Straits Crisis (1958); U.S. and Chinese Communists; U.S. and KMT

Zhou Mingxun, 118–119
Zhou-Panikkar Communique (Zhou Enlai-K. M. Panikkar), 151–153, 157, 175, 191–192, 253